A
JESUIT
EDUCATION
READER

A JESUIT EDUCATION READER

EDITED BY

GEORGE W. TRAUB, SJ

LOYOLA PRESS.
A JESUIT MINISTRY
Chicago

LOYOLA PRESS.
A JESUIT MINISTRY

3441 N. Ashland Avenue
Chicago, Illinois 60657
(800) 621-1008
www.loyolapress.com

Cover photograph: RF imagery
Cover design by Judine O'Shea
Interior design by Think Design Group and Joan Bledig

Library of Congress Cataloging-in-Publication Data
A Jesuit education reader / edited by George W. Traub.
     p. cm
  ISBN-13: 978-0-8294-2722-6
  ISBN-10: 0-8294-2722-8
  1. Jesuits--Education. 2. Jesuits--United States. 3. Catholic Church--Education--United States.
  I. Traub, George W.
  LC493.J388 2008
  371.071'2--dc22

                                                                              2008000642

Printed in the United States of America
17 18 19 20 21 22 23 24 TPS 10 9 8 7 6 5

For

Leo Klein, SJ
Eunice Staples (+1994)
Carol Kelley
Joe Wessling
Debra Mooney
Rebecca Schroer
and Laura Keitel

people I've had the privilege to work with
in Xavier University's Ignatian Programs
over the past twenty-one years

Contents

The Issue of Catholic Identity

Ignatian /Jesuit Pedagogy

Practical Applications: Walking the Ignatian/ Jesuit Walk

Preface

Some years ago, my friend and colleague Leo Klein, SJ, longtime vice president for mission and ministry at Xavier University in Cincinnati, came back from a Lilly Fellows Program annual meeting with a copy of *The Lutheran Reader*. He showed it to me and said, "Maybe someday you'll do a Jesuit reader." Well, "someday" has finally arrived. When Xavier University granted me a sabbatical from directing its Ignatian Programs in the academic year 2003–2004, I began this project, and my partners in Ignatian Programs—Debra Mooney, Rebecca Schroer, and briefly Laura Keitel—carried most of the usual programming burden during the summer and fall of 2005 and the spring, summer, fall, and winter of 2006–07, while I completed it.

A Jesuit Education Reader is designed first of all for those across the country engaged in the work of Jesuit education—faculty, administrators, staff, and trustees. But those involved in other Catholic and Christian colleges and universities as well as those in secondary schools and even those not engaged in formal education may also find valuable material here.

This anthology seeks to make available from a wide variety of sources—some not readily accessible—the finest recent short essays on Jesuit education (most of them fifteen pages or fewer, many only five to ten pages). The work of Jesuit education—as I conceive of it—grows out of the unique spirituality that informs all ministries begun by Jesuits. The Jesuit mission in education and Ignatian spirituality cannot be separated. Thus, a companion volume, *An Ignatian Spirituality Reader*, is available; it deals with Ignatius of Loyola and Ignatian spirituality and it informs this present book.

As with all anthologies, the selection process was not an easy one. Some of my favorite pieces ultimately had to be left out or just mentioned in the "Further Reading" essays. In both volumes, I was guided by writings that have been particularly fruitful when used in our Ignatian Programs at Xavier University: "Manresa," the initial process of orientation for new faculty, staff, and administrators; "AFMIX," or Assuring the Future Mission and Identity of Xavier, an elective two-year process of further development that helps people carry out their particular work in a more mission-focused way; and the "Ignatian Mentoring Program," funded initially by a grant from the Lilly Fellows Program, which pairs second-year tenure-track faculty with senior faculty members who have been involved in AFMIX.

This anthology is not the sort of book you're likely to sit down and read from cover to cover. Whether you're an individual seeking further knowledge about a subject or the planner of an orientation, seminar, or other group program, I hope that the section headings will help you quickly find what you're looking for at any given time. Sometimes the placement of an essay within a section is obvious; at other times, I must admit, an essay might just as well fit under one or two other categories. So if you don't find what you seek at first glance, I encourage you to search around, use the index. Further, you may notice ideas or themes from earlier essays repeated in later sections. Because the goal is not merely to acquire information but also to assimilate it, such "Ignatian repetition" can facilitate a fuller personal appropriation of the material.

From the beginning, I have thought of this reader as a companion to my short glossary of Ignatian terms, *Do You Speak Ignatian?* At times in the anthology, I recommend reading or rereading one or more of the brief entries in *Do You Speak Ignatian?* as a prelude to a section or an individual essay, to enrich your understanding of key terms and concepts. For your convenience, that glossary is reprinted as an appendix to this volume.

A final note: for all my twenty-one years of mission and identity work, my knowledge of resources has its limitations. And so I have been assisted in my selection for this reader by colleagues—mostly from Jesuit schools and other Jesuit ministries—who have drawn on their own expertise, experience, and practice. Needless to say, I am grateful to all the authors, editors, and publishers for making this reader possible. Publication has been aided by grants from presidents of U.S. Jesuit colleges and universities. Thanks to them and to Charles Currie, SJ, president of the Association of Jesuit Colleges and Universities, for their support.

Special thanks to George Lane, SJ, president of Loyola Press, for his support of this project from the beginning all the way through publication, and to my good editors at the press, Matthew Diener and Heidi Toboni.

May you find *A Jesuit Education Reader* useful, enlightening, even inspiring!

George Traub, SJ
Xavier University
December 3, 2007
Feast of St. Francis Xavier

The Principle Underlying Early Jesuit Mission— and the Schools

Jesuit Mission Today

Introduction

In the final chapter of *The First Jesuits*, an authoritative treatment of the first twenty-five years of Jesuit history and this section's opening selection, author John O'Malley, SJ, formerly distinguished professor of church history at Weston Jesuit School of Theology (in Cambridge, Massachusetts) and now university professor in the theology department at Georgetown University, asks an important question: is there some key doctrine, principle, or teaching that distinguishes the early Jesuits? No, not in the sense of Martin Luther's doctrine of justification by faith alone. In fact, the Jesuits focused on the gospel and the whole life of Jesus, not just on a single idea. Still, O'Malley concludes, there was "one 'doctrine' that was fundamental for them, one that gave orientation to all their ministries and to the way they wanted to lead their own lives. It was the basic premise of the Exercises . . . : the Creator deals directly with the creature, and the creature deals directly with the Creator. . . . Upon this teaching Jesuits based their more characteristic themes—indifference, discernment, and inner devotion, or consolation."

Ignatius Loyola—cofounder of the Jesuit order and its first superior general—was originally dead set against founding and running schools, for he thought that would restrict what he envisioned as a highly mobile and missionary-focused new order. But operating from this basic premise of the Spiritual Exercises—God deals directly with the person, and the person directly with God, to enable discernment and the following of God's will—Ignatius agreed to establishing a few schools and was quickly able to recognize the immense good that could come from this new ministry. Jesuits gave themselves to learning—including the "secular" disciplines—so they could teach and form the future leaders of civil society. Thus were they plunged, as O'Malley writes, "into secular culture and civic responsibility to a degree unknown to earlier [religious] orders." Within just a few years, Ignatius had effected a 180-degree turn in the direction and primary occupation of the fledgling order.

The second and third essays here deal with Jesuit mission today. We have, first of all, one of the key documents to come from the Thirty-fourth General Congregation of the Society of Jesus: "Our Mission and Culture." In the winter of 1995, 223 Jesuits from sixty-one countries met in Rome to chart a vision for Jesuit mission in the years to come. In this vision the Jesuits see themselves as "servants of Christ's mission." It is a justice-based mission mindful of the needs of the poor and marginal; it seeks to understand different cultures on their own terms; it is open to the religious experience of people from other traditions; it works with the laity; it learns from women; it serves and enables others.

Following a Jesuit missionary tradition dating back to Matteo Ricci in the sixteenth century, the congregation expounds, in this second essay, a missiology based on inculturation—a presentation of the gospel not in European or Western terms but in terms of the culture being approached. For Jesuits, God is already present in that culture and in that work: "God's action is antecedent to what we do." This is true even with people in our post-Christian culture of critical modernity and postmodernity. According to the congregation, "a genuine attempt to work from within the shared experience of Christians and unbelievers in a secular and critical culture, built upon respect and friendship, is the only successful starting point." It will either be "a meeting of equal partners in dialogue, addressing common questions, or it will be hollow." At the same time, the presence of the gospel in a given culture is not simply receptive. As the document expresses it, the gospel exercises a prophetic and critical witness "in the all-too-human city where there is poverty of body and spirit, domination and control, manipulation of mind and heart."

The third and last essay selected is "The Ignatian Mission." In it, Howard Gray, SJ, internationally known scholar of all things Ignatian, is concerned with formation for mission. "Three apostolic principles—(1) to help people (2) in a discerning and (3) adapting way to come to the life and truth of the Gospel—structured Jesuit ministry [and formation for ministry] from the outset." These same principles can guide the formation of lay women and men who serve in Jesuit apostolates today.

Gray is convinced that "the foundation of effective lay formation for apostolic ministries lies in the experience of the Spiritual Exercises." But at the same time, he realizes that the Exercises—whether made full-time for thirty days (the classic format) or part-time spread out over thirty-some weeks in the midst of the daily life of home and work responsibilities (known as the "nineteenth annotation" format)—is more than many people can realistically undertake. We need, therefore, to create adaptations of the Exercises to fit the schedules and resources of a greater number of laypeople who want to be more intimately involved in Ignatian ministry.

Understanding the Terminology: Suggested Readings from *Do You Speak Ignatian?*

- Ignatius of Loyola
- The Spiritual Exercises
- Religious Order/Religious Life
- The Society of Jesus
- The Service of Faith and the Promotion of Justice
- Apostle/Apostolate/Apostolic
- Inculturation

Conclusion to *The First Jesuits*

John W. O'Malley, SJ

From *The First Jesuits*, 1993

The Jesuits saw their style as constitutive of their identity and as distinctive of them as an organization. No doubt characteristics . . . that they cultivated in themselves helped distinguish them from others, to a greater or lesser degree. Some of these traits, however, were also cultivated by others in almost identical terms. They were, moreover, ideals. They were hopes and aims, which are never the same thing as the lived reality.

As the Jesuits tried to describe to themselves and to others just what made them what they were, they sometimes missed or failed to stress the obvious. They were too close to see it. With the hindsight of over four hundred years, we see more clearly than they did that the *Spiritual Exercises* and the schools were the two most important institutional factors that, when taken in their full implications, shaped the distinctive character of the Society of Jesus.

The first Jesuits recognized the importance of the *Exercises* and occasionally spoke of them as giving their life and ministries their fundamental orientation. Polanco [Ignatius's secretary and collaborator in the writing of the *Constitutions* and his letters] called them the compendium of all the means the Jesuits had for helping souls. Behind Nadal's exhorting Jesuits to regular repetition of them in abbreviated form had to lie an intuition of their conclusive importance for motivation and for corporate cohesion [Nadal had been commissioned by

Ignatius to travel around the Society and explain the *Constitutions*]. Often, however, Jesuits spoke of them as simply one among the many *consueta ministeria* [usual ministries], without pinpointing how the *Exercises* articulated principles and designs that tended to permeate everything they undertook. Jesuit commentators have sometimes said that the *Constitutions* were a translation of the *Exercises* into institutional form. That is an exaggeration, but it contains more than a grain of truth.

Luther claimed that the doctrine of justification by faith alone was the quintessence of the gospel, the core of the Christian message. It was certainly the central doctrine for him, the doctrine upon which his theology rested and according to which his practical and pastoral decisions were made. Did the Jesuits have a doctrine or teaching that they similarly singled out or exalted? If so, was it good works, papal primacy, seven sacraments, real presence?

The Jesuits never professed to have one. In fact, Luther's designation of a "doctrine"—an idea—as bearing the burden of the Christian message ran contrary to the traditional persuasion that the life of Christ was the best expression of what Christianity was all about. Luther shifted the focus from the synoptic Gospels to the epistle to the Romans. This represented and promoted a subtle but extraordinarily significant change in religious sensibilities. Although the Jesuits would not be unaffected by the change, they were, through the *Exercises* and many other factors, firmly rooted in the earlier tradition. In any case, they were reluctant to pronounce one doctrine more important than another, even though the controversies of the day brought them to speak about some more frequently and to give them a new emphasis—a phenomenon that made the Jesuits agents in the practical imbalance in confessional professions of orthodoxy in post-Reformation Christianity.

There was, however, one "doctrine" that was fundamental for them, one that gave orientation to all their ministries and to the way they wanted to lead their own lives. It was the basic premise of the *Exercises*, even though it was buried unobtrusively in the fifteenth "Preliminary Observation": the Creator deals directly with the creature, and the creature deals directly with the Creator—heart to heart, one might say. Upon this teaching Jesuits based their more characteristic themes—indifference, discernment, and inner devotion, or consolation.

It was this teaching that in one form or another brought Ignatius into question with ecclesiastical authorities at Alcalá, Salamanca, Paris, Venice, and Rome. It was this teaching that sounded to many like the teaching of the Alumbrados ["enlightened ones" in Spain], Erasmians [followers of the Dutch Christian humanist Desiderius Erasmus (1466?–1536)], and Lutherans. It was this teaching that set the Jesuits off from some of their fellow Catholics who sought a better church. . . . The rage of those who abhorred teaching like this as almost ipso facto heretical drove Catholicism in Italy and Spain into major crisis.

The Jesuits did not suffer as much in the wake of the crisis as did others. . . . Ignatius and the Jesuits, at least, understood the teaching within the safe boundaries of Catholic tradition, and they were anything but founders of a Church of the Free Spirit. The fact that the teaching could be questioned or, indeed, attacked so vigorously is a window into sixteenth-century Catholicism. That it received general acceptance is yet another. Later in the century, however, Everard Mercurian, the fourth [superior] general, adopted even inside the Society of Jesus a cautious policy that tended to reduce the devout life to moralizing calculation and safe asceticism.

Besides the *Exercises*, what particularly distinguished the Jesuits was their schools. Within a few years of [the founding of the first school for those who were not Jesuits at] Messina [in Sicily—1547] they assigned [the schools], in fact if not always in theory, a preeminent priority among their ministries. This meant some diminution in quantity and intensity of the other *consueta ministeria*, but not so much as we may at first imagine because the schools served as their bases. Not in that way, therefore, did the schools have their greatest impact on the Society.

Part of "our way," part of Jesuit style, was learning. Ignatius and his companions from the beginning advocated and exemplified a learned ministry. This did not, taken in the abstract, distinguish them from their contemporaries but conformed them to the consensus of their age. With the schools, however, came an intensification—as the Jesuits learned in order to teach. Along with intensification came a new modality—as the Jesuits became professionals in the teaching of the pagan classics, the natural sciences, and the performing arts, somehow or other in relationship to *pietas* [a sense of religious and civic duty], somehow or other in relationship to *Christianitas* ["Christianity," that is, the formation of the good Christian]. The Jesuits—as a group, systemically—became learned clergy their "way." The schools inserted them into secular culture and civic responsibility to a degree unknown to earlier orders. The *Formula* [of the Jesuit institute] had committed them to work for the "common good," but the schools gave that commitment an institutional grounding that was quite special.

The most important impact the schools had upon the Society was, therefore, cultural. More easily tracked, however, was their sociological impact—on the size of communities, on the practical demotion suffered by professed houses [communities that had no fixed income], on the implicit redefinition of aspects of Jesuit poverty when the vast majority of Jesuits began to live in endowed institutions, on a closer bonding with the socioeconomic elite. Last but far from least, the schools recast the ideal of itinerant ministry, the ideal symbolized by the special vow "concerning missions"—the "beginning and principal foundation" of the Society, as Ignatius said of it in 1545.

Ignatius—how did he fit in the ongoing transformation of the Society of Jesus, especially after 1540 or 1547? Remarkable in the nascent Society was the talent and especially the intense and unwavering dedication of so many who joined it. Nonetheless, there would be no Society of Jesus, even after *Regimini Militantis Ecclesiae* [Pope Paul III's document approving the Society of Jesus as a religious order], without Ignatius of Loyola. Rodrigues and Bobadilla [two of the original founders with Ignatius] were correct in a formal sense when they clamored that the founding was a corporate venture. But Ignatius was the leader.

He inspired confidence and won affection. When Xavier voted for him as general, he voted for "our old leader and true father, Don Ignacio, who, since he brought us together with no little effort, will also with similar effort know how to preserve, govern, and help us

advance from good to better." While Ignatius was general, his subjects respected him especially for listening to them with care until
they were sure they had been understood. Salmerón [another of the
founders] burst into tears when he heard of his death. Nadal confessed
in his journal that he never visited the room where he died without
"spontaneous and sweet tears."

Ignatius was, however, a complex man. He on occasion dealt
in harsh and seemingly arbitrary ways with those in Rome who
were closest to him. He did not always bear criticism gracefully.
Once when Laínez [another of the founders, who would be elected
Ignatius's successor] insisted too strongly, he exploded with, "Here,
you take the Society and govern it!"

His natural reticence about himself and his stilted and conventional style of writing drew a curtain across much that we would
like to know. Early on, moreover, his Jesuit contemporaries began to
speak and write of him with a reverence that rendered edifying his
every act, making it particularly difficult for later historians to find
the man behind the hagiographical veil.

In this atmosphere Bobadilla's taunts can feel like a breath of
fresh air. More important, they also raise again the difficult question
of where, in the practical governance of the Society, Ignatius's part
ended and Polanco's began. It is absolutely clear, however, that even
toward the very end of Ignatius's life, when he was chronically sick,
he made every major decision. He delegated a great deal, but he continued in charge to the end. His importance for the order looms of
course much larger, as by now must be clear. No one more than he
helped create its way of proceeding, and, in the eyes of his contemporaries, nobody better exemplified it.

But he did three things that were utterly crucial for the ethos of
the Society. First, he wrote the *Exercises* and made them the basic book
of the institution. Second, he was the force behind a most remarkable
instrument of governance, the *Constitutions*. Third, when the proper
moment arrived for making a decision about the schools, he opened
the throttle to full speed ahead.

Leadership is a gift difficult to analyze, but it consists to a large
extent in vision, in the ability to see how at a given juncture change is

more consistent with one's scope than staying the course. It consists as well in the courage and self-possession required to make the actual decision to change and to convince others of the validity and viability of the new direction. Such was Ignatius's vision and courage about the schools. . . .

Our Mission and Culture

Jesuit General Congregation 34

From *Documents of the Thirty-fourth General Congregation of the Society of Jesus*, 1995

Decree Four

1. General Congregation 34 has brought together Jesuits from the cultures of Asia, the former Communist countries of Eastern Europe, the European Community, Africa, North America, Australia, and Latin America; this composition has heightened our awareness of the diversity of cultures in both the world and the Society, and of the need to address the importance for our mission of the gospel and culture.[1]

2. In recent years, the church has made this theme one of its central points of reflection. Pope Paul VI wrote that "the split between the Gospel and culture is without a doubt the tragedy of our time." More recently, Pope John Paul II has presented inculturation as one of the fundamental aspects of the church's total evangelizing mission, and points to the mutuality between the gospel and the cultures it engages. The Christian message is to be open to all cultures, bound to no single culture, and made accessible to every human person through a process of inculturation, by which the gospel introduces something new

into the culture and the culture brings something new to the richness of the gospel:

> Through inculturation the church makes the gospel incarnate in different cultures and at the same time introduces people, together with their cultures, into her own community. She transmits to them her own values, at the same time taking the good elements that already exist in them and renewing them from within.

3. The process of inculturating the gospel of Jesus Christ within human culture is a form of incarnation of the Word of God in all the diversity of human experience, in which the Word of God comes to take up a dwelling place in the human family (see John 1:14). When the Word of God becomes embedded in the heart of a culture, it is like a buried seed that draws its nourishment from the earth around it and grows to maturity. Inculturation can also be related to the paschal mystery: cultures, under the impact of the liberating power of the gospel, rid themselves of their negative features and enter the freedom of God's kingdom. The gospel brings a prophetic challenge to every culture to remove all those things that inhibit the justice of the kingdom. Inculturating the gospel means allowing the Word of God to exercise a power within the lives of the people, without at the same time imposing alien cultural factors which would make it difficult for them truly to receive that Word. "Evangelization is not possible without inculturation. Inculturation is the existential dialogue between a living people and the living gospel."

4. This process has always been a part of the life of the church: in the early Christian centuries, the church, while proclaiming its faith in ways that a Hellenistic culture could receive, was at the same time shaped by that culture. Insights that first originated outside the Jewish and Christian context came to find a place within the very heart of Christianity. A similar process is going on today in many parts of the world, as representatives

of indigenous cultures, the great religious traditions, and critical modernity bring insights which the church must consider as part of the dialogue between Christian experience and the diversity of other experiences. In this way, the church is recovering, in our times, the creativity shown in the early centuries and in the best of its evangelizing work.

5.   Particular challenges must be faced today in order to enable an existential dialogue of this kind to take place amid the wide variety of cultures in which the church is present:

5.1.   Contemporary secular culture, which has developed partly in opposition to the church, often excludes religious faith from among its accepted values. Consequently, some cultures that were once shaped by Christian faith have, in differing degrees, turned away from Christianity toward a form of life in which the values of the gospel are marginal. Religious belief is often dismissed as a disruptive source of social divisions that the human family has outgrown; in the eyes of many of our contemporaries, the church has no credibility as a commentator on human affairs.

5.2.   The great cultures of Asia, in spite of centuries of missionary activity, still do not regard Christian faith as a living presence at the heart of the Asian experience. In general, it is inseparably linked with a Western culture that they distrust. Many committed Christians in Asia feel a split between their Asian cultural experience and the still-Western character of what they experience in the church.

5.3.   All over the world, the increasing pace of urbanization leads to impoverished millions in the great cities. These people are struggling with an agonizing cultural transition as they emigrate from rural areas and are forced to leave behind their traditional cultures. At the same time, this transition is producing a new cultural synthesis in which elements of traditional wisdom are woven into new forms of popular organization and celebration.

5.4. Among indigenous people there has been a resurgence of consciousness of their distinctive cultures, and they must be supported with the liberating power of the gospel.

5.5. In Africa, there is a great desire to create a truly African Christianity, in which the church and African cultures form an inseparable union. There is also a desire to free the gospel from a colonial legacy that undervalued the quality of indigenous African cultural values, and to bring it into a more profound contact with African life.

Jesuit Mission and Culture

6. As Jesuits we live a faith directed toward the kingdom, through which justice becomes a shaping reality in the world; we therefore bring the particular quality of that faith into dialogue with members of the religions and cultures of our contemporary world. We have said in the decree "Servants of Christ's Mission" that "our mission of the service of faith and the promotion of justice must be broadened to include, as integral dimensions, proclamation of the gospel, dialogue, and the evangelization of culture"; we have insisted on the inseparability of justice, dialogue, and the evangelization of culture.

7. This is not just a pragmatic apostolic strategy; it is rooted in the mysticism flowing from the experience of Ignatius, which directs us simultaneously toward the mystery of God and the activity of God in his creation. Both in our personal lives of faith and in our ministries, it is never a question of choosing either God or the world; rather, it is always God in the world, laboring to bring it to perfection so that the world comes, finally, to be fully in God.

Ignatius proclaims that for human beings there is no authentic search for God without an insertion into the life of the creation, and that, on the other hand, all solidarity with human beings and every engagement with the created world cannot be authentic without a discovery of God.

8. The mission of the Society, in service to the crucified and risen Christ, is directed to the ways in which he makes his presence felt in the diversity of human cultural experiences, in order that we may present the gospel as Christ's explicitly liberating presence. Ours must be a dialogue, born of respect for people, especially the poor, in which we share their cultural and spiritual values and offer our own cultural and spiritual treasures, in order to build up a communion of peoples instructed by God's Word and enlivened by the Spirit as at Pentecost. Our service of the Christian faith must never disrupt the best impulses of the culture in which we work, nor can it be an alien imposition from outside. It is directed toward working in such a way that the line of development springing from the heart of a culture leads it to the kingdom.

9. In the exercise of our mission, we bring a simple criterion from our Ignatian tradition: in our personal lives of faith, we learn that we are in consolation when we are fully in touch with what God is doing in our hearts, and we are in desolation when our lives are in conflict with his action. So, too, our ministry of evangelizing culture will be a ministry of consolation when it is guided by ways that bring to light the character of God's activity in those cultures and that strengthen our sense of the divine mystery. But our efforts will be misguided, and even destructive, when our activity runs contrary to the grain of his presence in the cultures which the church addresses, or when we claim to exercise sole proprietorial rights over the affairs of God.

10. This intuition is what has led Jesuits to adopt such a positive approach to the religions and cultures in which they work. The

early Jesuits, in their schools, linked Christian catechesis to an education in classical humanism, art, and theater, in order to make their students versed both in faith and in European culture. It is also what prompted Jesuits outside Europe to express a profound respect for indigenous cultures and to compose dictionaries and grammars of local languages, and pioneering studies of the people among whom they worked and whom they tried to understand.

11. Particularly at the present time, when the sensitive quality of so many indigenous cultures is threatened by powerful, but less benign, pressures, we want to recover a reverence for culture as exemplified by the best of our predecessors. Throughout the world, Jesuits are working with great numbers of ethnic groups, tribes, and countries with traditional cultures. Theirs is a wonderful patrimony of culture, religion, and ancient wisdom that has molded their people's identities. These peoples are now struggling to affirm their cultural identity by incorporating elements of modern and global culture. We must do what we can to keep this relation between traditional cultures and modernity from becoming an imposition and try to make it a genuine intercultural dialogue. This would be a sign of liberation for both sides. Our intuition is that the gospel resonates with what is good in each culture.

12. At the same time, we acknowledge that we have not always followed this intuition. We have not always recognized that aggression and coercion have no place in the preaching of the gospel of freedom, especially in cultures that are vulnerable to manipulation by more powerful forces. In particular, we recognize that

• we have often contributed to the alienation of the very people we wanted to serve;

- Jesuit evangelizers have often failed to insert themselves into the heart of a culture, but instead have remained a foreign presence;
- in our mission, we have failed to discover the treasures of humanity: the values, depth, and transcendence of other cultures, which manifest the action of the Spirit;
- we have sometimes sided with the "high culture" of the elite in a particular setting: disregarding the cultures of the poor and sometimes, by our passivity, allowing indigenous cultures or communities to be destroyed.

We acknowledge these mistakes and now seek to profit from the cultural diversity and complexity within the apostolic body of the Society today. We realize that the process of inculturation is difficult yet progressive.

13.   As the greater part of our men work within their own cultures, they will, in the service of faith, enter into dialogue with their own cultural world, witness to the creative and prophetic Spirit, and thus enable the gospel to enrich these various cultures—and, in turn, be enriched by its inculturated presence in different contexts. We try to understand the reality of people's experience, because only then can the proclamation of the gospel relate to their lives. We bring the gospel into an open dialogue with the positive and negative elements that these cultures present. In this way, the gospel comes to be seen in a new light: its meaning is enriched, renewed, even transformed by what these cultures bring to it. Father Pedro Arrupe drew attention to the importance of inculturation for the contemporary Jesuit mission:

Inculturation is the incarnation of Christian life and of the Christian message in a particular cultural context, in such a way that this experience not only finds expression through elements proper to the culture in question, but becomes a principle that animates, directs, and unifies the culture, transforming it and remaking it so as to bring about a "new creation."

God's Dialogue with the World

14. The gospel, God's prophetic word, continues the dialogue that God has begun with all men and women, who already share in the mystery of unity begun in creation. It brings them explicitly into contact with his mystery of salvation. God opens their hearts to the mystery of fullness, "through the invisible action of the Spirit of Christ," which awaits the human family as its destiny.

15. As disciples of the risen Lord, we believe that his paschal mystery radiates throughout the whole of human history, touching every religion, every culture, and every person, including those who do not know him and those who, in conscience, cannot bring themselves to have faith in him. The centrality of the paschal mystery, *Gaudium et Spes* [the final document of Vatican Council II—"The Church in the Modern World"] declares,

applies not only to Christians but to all people of good will in whose hearts grace is secretly at work. Since Christ died for everyone, and since the ultimate calling of each of us comes from God and is therefore a universal one, we are obliged to hold that the Holy Spirit offers everyone the possibility of sharing in this paschal mystery in a manner known to God.

16. How everyone shares in the paschal mystery is known to God; that they share in it is what the church is led by God to believe. It is the risen Christ who is constantly active in all dimensions of the world's growth, in its diversity of cultures and its varied spiritual experience. As there is a unified goodness in God's work of creation, so in Christ's redemptive work, the

fragmentation caused by sin is being healed by a single thread of grace throughout the restored creation.

17. One way of serving God's mystery of salvation is through dialogue, a spiritual conversation of equal partners, that opens human beings to the core of their identity. In such a dialogue, we come into contact with the activity of God in the lives of other men and women, and deepen our sense of this divine action: "By dialogue, we let God be present in our midst; for as we open ourselves in dialogue to one another, we also open ourselves to God." We try to enable people to become aware of God's presence in their culture and to help them evangelize others in their turn. The ministry of dialogue is conducted with a sense that God's action is antecedent to ours. We do not plant the seed of his presence, for he has already done that in the culture; he is already bringing it to fruitfulness, embracing all the diversity of creation, and our role is to cooperate with this divine activity.

18. The work of God in the diversity of human history is seen in the long process of enlightened human growth—still incomplete!—as expressed in religious, social, moral, and cultural forms that bear the mark of the silent work of the Spirit. In the conceptions of the mind, in the habits of the heart, in the root metaphors and values of all cultures—even, we might say, in the very process by which our physical bodies become capable of intense spiritual experience—God is preparing the conditions in his creatures for the loving acknowledgment of his truth, making them ready for the transformation promised in Christ. "All are called to a common destiny, the fullness of life in God."

Our Mission and Critical Postmodern Culture

19. This is true even of those cultures where there is a difficult dialogue with men and women who think they have gone beyond

Christianity or any religious commitment. We need to pay particular attention to them because of their influence throughout the world. Some cultures today are inclined so to restrict religious faith to the realm of the private and the personal, even regarding it as a strange eccentricity, that it is difficult for the gospel to "animate, direct, and unify" contemporary secular culture. We recognize that many of our contemporaries judge that neither Christian faith nor any religious belief is good for humanity.

20.   The problems of working in these contexts need no elaboration here, because the boundary line between the gospel and the modern and postmodern culture passes through the heart of each of us. Each Jesuit encounters the impulse to unbelief first of all in himself; it is only when we deal with that dimension in ourselves that we can speak to others of the reality of God. In addition, we cannot speak to others if the religious language we use is completely foreign to them: the theology we use in our ministry cannot ignore the vista of modern critical questions within which we too live. Only when we make sense of our own experience and understanding of God can we say things that make sense to contemporary agnosticism.

21.   This is a ministry that should not ignore the Christian mystical tradition that repeatedly treats of the wordless and imageless experience of God, which surpasses human concepts: "Si comprehendis, non est Deus" ["If you comprehend, that is not God"], said Augustine. The experience of a silence surrounding the nature of God may be the starting point for many of our contemporaries, but it is also found within the depths of Christian experience and faith. There is a fragmentation of Christian faith in God in postmodern culture, in which human spirituality becomes detached from an explicitly religious expression. People's spiritual lives have not died; they are simply taking place outside the church. "Post-Christian culture" witnesses, strangely and implicitly, to a reverence for the God who cannot

be imaged by human beings without destroying the divine mystery: this is related to what Christians mean by "the Father." It also tries to find meaning within the very structure of human, embodied experience: this is related to the Christian belief that the "meaning" of the world (the "Logos") is made known to us in the humanity of Jesus. And there is a deep desire, expressed through a concern for the environment, to revere the natural order as a place where there is an immanent but transcendent presence: this connects with what Christians call the "Spirit."

22.   The aim of an inculturated evangelization in post-Christian contexts is not to secularize or dilute the gospel by accommodating it to the horizon of modernity, but to introduce the possibility and reality of God through practical witness and dialogue. We have to recognize that today humanity can find many answers in science that earlier generations could derive only from religion. In a predominantly secular context, our faith and our understanding of faith are often freed from contingent cultural complications and, as a result, purified and deepened.

23.   A genuine attempt to work from within the shared experience of Christians and unbelievers in a secular and critical culture, built upon respect and friendship, is the only successful starting point. Our ministry towards atheists and agnostics will either be a meeting of equal partners in dialogue, addressing common questions, or it will be hollow. This dialogue will be based upon a sharing of life, a shared commitment to action for human development and liberation, a sharing of values and a sharing of human experience. Through dialogue, modern and postmodern cultures may be challenged to become more open to approaches and experiences that, though rooted in human history, are new to them. At the same time theology, when developed with an eye to contemporary critical culture, may help people discover the limits of immanence and the human necessity of transcendence.

24. We need to recognize that the gospel of Christ will always provoke resistance; it challenges men and women and requires of them a conversion of mind, heart, and behavior. It is not difficult to see that a modernist, scientific-technological culture, too often one-sidedly rationalistic and secular in tone, can be destructive of human and spiritual values. As Ignatius makes clear in the Meditation on Two Standards, the call of Christ is always radically opposed to values that refuse spiritual transcendence and promote a pattern of selfish life. Sin is social in its expression, as is the counterwitness offered by grace: unless a Christian life distinctly differs from the values of secular modernity, it will have nothing special to offer. One of the most important contributions we can make to critical contemporary culture is to show that the structural injustice in the world is rooted in value systems promoted by a powerful modern culture, which is becoming global in its impact.

Change and Hope

25. It is part of our Jesuit tradition to be involved in the transformation of every human culture, as human beings begin to reshape their patterns of social relations, their cultural inheritance, their intellectual projects, their critical perspectives on religion, truth, and morality, their whole scientific and technological understanding of themselves and the world in which they live. We commit ourselves to accompany people, in different contexts, as they and their culture make difficult transitions. We commit ourselves to develop the dimension of an inculturated evangelization within our mission of the service of faith and the promotion of justice.

26. "Ignatius loved the great cities"; they were where this transformation of the human community was taking place, and he wanted Jesuits to be involved in the process. The city can be for us the symbol of our current efforts to bring fulfillment to

human culture. That the project, in its present form, is seriously flawed no one doubts; that we are more skeptical now than we were even thirty years ago is true; that there have been massive dislocations and inequalities is clear to all; that the totalitarian experiments of this century have been brutal and almost demonic in intensity none will dispute; that it seems sometimes to resemble the Babel and Babylon of the Bible is all too evident. But our aim is the confused but inescapable attempt to cooperate in the creation of that community which, according to the Book of Revelation, God will bring about—and God *will* bring it about—in the form of the holy city, the radiant New Jerusalem: "By its light shall the nations walk; and the kings of the earth shall bring their glory into it, and its gates shall never be shut by day—and there shall be no night there. They shall bring into it the glory and the honor of the nations" (Rev. 21:24–26). Until that day arrives, our vocation is to work generously with the risen Christ in the all-too-human city where there is poverty of body and spirit, domination and control, manipulation of mind and heart; and to serve the Lord there until he returns to bring to perfection the world in which he died.

Perspectives

27.1. We must recognize the complexities of achieving a fully inculturated evangelization within the life of a people; while all our ministries have to be conducted with an awareness of their cultural dimension, the inculturation of the gospel may be slow simply because cultural changes are slow.

27.2. We must recognize that our world is increasingly aware of the rights as well as the diversity of cultures, and that each cultural group is properly asserting the qualities of its heritage. We need to respect these diverse cultures in their self-affirmation and to work along with them creatively.

27.3. In every ministry, we must recognize that the salvific work of God's revelation is already present in every culture and that God will bring it to completion.

27.4. We must remember that we do not directly "evangelize cultures"; we evangelize people in their culture. Whether we are working in our own culture or in another, as servants of the gospel we must not impose our own cultural structures, but witness to the creativity of the Spirit that is also at work in others. Ultimately, the people of a culture are the ones who root the church and the gospel in their lives.

27.5. All of us need to recognize that every large culture contains within it a range of ethnic cultures and new subcultures that are often ignored.

27.6. The call to inculturated evangelization is not simply for those working in a land other than their own. All of our works take place in a particular cultural setting with positive and negative features that the gospel must touch.

27.7. We need to listen carefully when people say that the gospel does not speak to them, and begin to understand the cultural experience behind this statement. Does what we say, and what we do, correspond to the real and urgent needs of the people around us in their relationship to God and to others? If the answer is negative, then perhaps we are not fully engaged in the lives of the people we serve.

Guidelines

28. To further the Society's ability to promote inculturation, we offer the following guidelines:

28.1. Our option for the poor should reach out also to their cultures and values, often based on a rich and fruitful tradition. This will permit a creative and mutual respect within societies, and the promotion of a more fertile cultural and religious atmosphere.

28.2. The lifestyle of Jesuit communities should bear credible witness to the countercultural values of the gospel, so that our service of faith can effectively transform the patterns of local culture.

28.3. Our commitment to social justice and ongoing human development must focus on transforming the cultural values that sustain an unjust and oppressive social order.

28.4. Each stage of our formation programs should root us in the cultures of the people we serve. They should focus on sharing the life and experience of those people and on trying to understand the culture from within.

28.5. There must be an integration of the dynamic of inculturation and the apostolic renewal both of Jesuits and of those who work with us. This is essential for our own conversion of heart and for a rediscovery of the freshness of the gospel through its dialogue with culture.

28.6. An experience of a culture other than our own will help us grow into a vision more open to what is universal and more objective about our own native cultures.

28.7. Our educational institutions, in particular, have a crucial role to play in linking Christian faith to the core elements in contemporary and traditional cultures.

28.8. We commit ourselves to the creation of genuinely "local churches" which can contribute to the richness of the universal communion of the Church of Christ. We will also look for ways of creating indigenous theology, liturgy, and spirituality, and of promoting the right and freedom of peoples to encounter the gospel without being alienated from their culture.

28.9. As an international apostolic body, the Society is uniquely able to draw upon a range of cultural experience in its ministries and to promote an intercultural dialogue, contributing in this way to the church's mission, at the service of God's plan to bring together all peoples into the communion of his kingdom (Eph. 1:10; 2 Cor. 5:19).

NOTES

1. *Culture* means the way in which a group of people live, think, feel, organize themselves, celebrate, and share life. In every culture, there are underlying systems of values, meanings, and views of the world, which are expressed, visibly, in language, gestures, symbols, rituals, and styles.

The Ignatian Mission: Lay and Jesuit Companions on the Journey

Howard Gray, SJ

From *In All Things: A Jesuit Journal of the Social Apostolate*, 2003

Jesuit ministry is about people who want to work in ways that help other people. That humble phrase, "to help people," was the axle of grace for Ignatius of Loyola, transforming his religious experience from an introspective examination of his own life before God to a mystic summons to see the world as God sees it. Ignatian mission evolved from a conversion within a conversion and set Ignatius on a pilgrimage of service. Much of his early apostolic life was a search for ways to help people. Because there are many ways to do this, Ignatius and his early companions catalogued a host of helping ministries. They did not privilege any one means, but gathered these apostolic possibilities under the general heading of "Ministries of the Word." What they meant at first was to make the gospel story of Jesus normative for how people live, work, and make those choices that form them as ethical and spiritual personalities.

Ignatius went on to codify the process of gospel decision making in *The Spiritual Exercises*. Later he codified Jesuit apostolic life and work in another key document, *The Constitutions of the Society of Jesus*.

This experience of responding to God's leadership and the principles that guide both the *Exercises* and the *Constitutions* undergirds all Jesuit apostolic formation. But, again, essential to its inspiration and operative in evaluating its apostolic effectiveness is that humble Ignatian question: does this help people?

The directness and simplicity of this question is far removed from a fundamentalism that offers easy answers to complex realities. In the Ignatian apostolic scheme of formation, there are two other principles that guide the response to that question. These principles are discernment and adaptation.

Discernment

Discernment is the process of choosing from among many possible goods the specific good that God wants me to choose here and now. For example, in a world that desperately needs all kinds of help, what now is the most effective, most enduring, most universal, most appropriate gospel service that we can offer? Is it to found a school? To renew parish life? To focus resources on meeting urban poverty, violence, and hopelessness by establishing a network of neighborhood centers? Apostolic discernment presumes the generosity and the capability of helping people and then asks the crucial question: how will you help these people here and now? Such discernment, precisely because it is focused on the gospel for inspiration, has to be prayerful, courageous, and truly integral—that is, a concern for the good of the other and not a political ploy or a delaying tactic to protect comfortable lifestyles.

Adaptation

Adaptation is the ability to fit the discerned good to the specific cultural, social, and psychological realities of a person, a group, or an institution. The Ignatian principle of adaptation answers a third question: what is the best way to fit this good to the concrete realities of this situation, to the particular history and personality of this man or woman, to the needs and opportunities of this institution?

For the early Jesuits, adaptation was essential in all their ministries. For example, in giving the Spiritual Exercises, one asks, which form of prayer will most help this person to find God? In working with little children, how can this gospel be made intelligible and attractive? In a non-Western country, rich in its own culture and profoundly committed to its own philosophy and religion, how do you translate the gospel so that it can enhance and not violate that culture? Adaptation was the style of these early Jesuits, what they called "our way of proceeding." It meant building bridges between the gospel and contemporary seekers.

These three apostolic principles—to help people in a discerning and adapting way to come to the life and truth of the gospel—structured Jesuit ministry from the outset. These three principles similarly structured Jesuit formation, the way young men became incorporated into the life and work of the Society of Jesus. Ignatian formation today asks these same questions of those lay men and women who want to be part of Jesuit apostolic work or who invite Jesuits to participate in their apostolic formation.

Evaluation

Clearly, antecedent to any program of formation, there must be some kind of scrutiny or evaluation of those who want to enter into an Ignatian apostolic mission. Does this man or woman have a desire to help people? From where does this desire come? Does this individual show the kind of sound judgment and flexibility of spirit that are a prerequisite for discernment and apostolic adaptation? In any serious apostolic formation program, screening and assessment are important. Here, the Ignatian criteria for making the Spiritual Exercises and the dispositions necessary for Ignatian apostolic mission coalesce. As in the Exercises so, too, in apostolic service, one looks for generosity, religious maturity, self-reflection and self-knowledge, a faithful heart, psychological balance, and a desire to serve the priorities embedded in the gospel. Clearly, simply being employed in a work sponsored by Jesuits is not enough. We are talking about those who want to become more directly involved in deepening the religious foundations of a Jesuit . . . ministry. These are the kinds of people who can profit from Ignatian formation, because they possess both the call and the grace to answer that call.

Apostolic Formation

Formation is not a term universally understood in the same way. Ignatian formation is closely associated with integration, or bringing together in a harmonious way. It is a process that takes time, patience, and mentoring. The Spiritual Exercises should be an integrating process, as men and women look at how they have incorporated God's hopes for them into their lives.

Throughout the four Gospel portraits of Jesus, we meet someone conscious of his call as a summons from his father. The father's call guides Jesus' choices: what to teach, how to heal, when to comfort and when to confront, with whom to share his mission as his disciples. In the Spiritual Exercises, Christ is central as the integrated, fully formed way to God. The work of the Exercises is to learn him, to love him, and to serve him. These Ignatian guidelines constitute the imitation of Christ: to accept his truth, to accept his friendship, and to accept his mission. Ignatius presents a developmental process, a formation that brings heart and head and soul together in relationship to Christian discipleship. He called the personal acceptance of this discipleship an election. It means integrating one's life with Christ. It does not replace other loves—for family, for friends, for life—but it does reorient them into a relationship of even deeper loyalty and care. Everything I genuinely love is more deeply loved by Christ.

Ignatian formation is radically spiritual. Consequently, it is a liberating formation. It is a formation that can take place only within my freedom, one that honors my personal experience and guides my talents and graces. This freely chosen and personally enriching process of following Christ creates a feeling of consolation, an affective realization that I am doing what God wants me to do. The call is God's, the inspiration is Christ's, but the acceptance is mine.

What should be clear is that someone who wants to become intimately involved in an Ignatian enterprise has to have a desire to link that work—be it a school, a retreat center, a social work, a parish—to the ongoing work of the kingdom preached by Jesus. Professional excellence, years of practical experience, quality training, specialized skills—all these can serve the kingdom, but only a genuine union with Christ can reveal what the kingdom means: to help people to love God and to love their neighbor.

There is vulnerability in such spiritual formation. Easy pieties, sentimental devotions, and do-it-yourself mysticism crowd today's bookstores under the headings of inspiration, meditation, and spirituality. What most of these present is self-fulfillment without self-sacrifice or a life conversion. What Ignatian formation demands is the radical humility to stand before God as a loved sinner who serves best when he or she acknowledges the weaknesses that have led to loving Christ as Redeemer. The First Week experience of the Spiritual Exercises has to be incorporated into any Ignatian formation process. Radically, one helps others best by a profound experience of the solidarity of helplessness. Because I know my need of Christ, I can work all the more humanely to make his forgiveness and compassion available to others.

Foundation of Formation

For these reasons, then, I am increasingly convinced that the foundation of effective lay formation for apostolic ministries lies in the experience of the Spiritual Exercises. But I am also aware that few lay colleagues have either the time or the financial resources to make the full thirty-day retreat. Likewise, while the adapted retreat in everyday life is more accessible, it, too, demands a consistent outlay of time that many will not be able to sustain. Therefore, we need to create adaptations of the Exercises to fit the schedules and resources of lay women and men who want to be more intimately involved in Jesuit apostolic work. For example, create a formation cycle in which laypeople can make a week of the Exercises over the course of a year. In a three-year cycle of formation, lay men and women could make the Exercises and also have the opportunity to discuss what this spirituality means in their . . . [particular] ministries. The possibilities of an accessible but in-depth program of lay formation are exciting and challenging.

Further Reading

I recommend John O'Malley's superb essay "Five Missions of the Jesuit Charism: Content and Method" (*Studies in the Spirituality of Jesuits*, Winter 2006). O'Malley draws not just on early official documents but also on the practice of the early Jesuits and the principles underlying that practice, all of which have relevance for the Jesuit mission today.

History

Introduction

The first selection, "Jesuits and Jesuit Education: A Primer," is part of a longer paper that the Boston College Jesuit community shared with its lay colleagues in 1994 (*Jesuits and Boston College: A Working Paper for Discussion*); it provides us with a brief history of Jesuit education.

The second selection is "How the First Jesuits Became Involved in Education," by John O'Malley, SJ. O'Malley is concerned here not just with how the Jesuit tradition in education began but also with "what it was trying to accomplish, and how it developed, especially in the foundational years." It inherited from the Middle Ages the scholastic learning of the schools (that is, the universities), with their graduated organization and speculative and professional pursuit of truth. It inherited from the Renaissance (especially in Italy) the humanist educational ideal of the reform of church and civil society. In addition, the Jesuit educational tradition was heir to the spirituality of St. Ignatius and his first Jesuit companions, with primacy given to personal spiritual experience, with the gradual development of a "world-friendly" Christianity, and with a call to be of help to others. Once the first schools were founded, the advantages of an institutional approach to education became evident. And as the network of Jesuit schools grew, so too did the communication among them and the sharing of teaching and organizational methods. Within each school, the attention given to the arts—including the fine arts and not just the sciences—was remarkable.

It is also possible to ask and answer the question of the influences on Jesuit education in a quite different way—from within the life experience of Ignatius—which is what Howard Gray does in the final essay of this section.

Understanding the Terminology: Suggested Readings from *Do You Speak Ignatian?*

- Education, Jesuit
- Finding God in All Things
- Ignatian/Jesuit Vision, Characteristics of the
- Ratio Studiorum

Jesuits and Jesuit Education: A Primer

The Boston College Jesuit Community

From *Jesuits and Boston College: A Working Paper for Discussion*, 1994

Ignatius Loyola and his nine companions had no intention of establishing colleges and universities when they founded the Society of Jesus in 1540. They saw themselves as itinerant preachers, lecturers on sacred subjects, hearers of confession and givers of spiritual counsel, teachers of catechism to the unlettered young, helpers of the poor and the sick. However, they were all masters of the University of Paris and they were formed by a spirituality that led them to prefer the ministry of the word. That preference disposed them to accept the care of schools when unexpectedly the opportunity was offered. In time this was to become their characteristic work. Ignatius's Spiritual Exercises are about prayerful reflection and decision. Those who make them are helped to be aware of how God is acting in their lives and to choose what to do in response. This is a pedagogy of the heart, a pedagogy of spiritual formation and of action. But it opens one to a reverence for all God's gifts, and Ignatius taught his friends and followers to have a special reverence for intelligence and for learning. The first Jesuits founded colleges to educate the young men flocking to join the new Society. When in 1547 Ignatius was asked to open a school in Sicily for young men who were not Jesuits, he seems to have seen the opportunity as a powerful means of forming the mind and the soul. To bring people to God, he sought to form those who in their turn would form or influence many others.

By the death of Ignatius in 1556 there were some thirty-five Jesuit colleges (we would call them secondary schools today) across Europe, and two hundred years later more than eight hundred in both the Old and New Worlds. Ignatius had stipulated that these schools should be "for everybody, poor and rich." Endowments from civic leaders and benefactors enabled them to charge no fees, so they made education accessible to large numbers of the less well off. They succeeded because they wedded the views of the humanists, grounded in the classical conception of rhetoric as training in clear thinking and expression, to a methodical pedagogy that the first Jesuits had learned at Paris. Like their Catholic and Protestant counterparts in the best schools of the time, Jesuits created a system of humanistic education that was international and intercontinental, one that brought together learned men from various languages, cultures, and nations in one common enterprise. Graduates of these schools played a central role in the evolution of seventeenth- and eighteenth-century thought in Europe and in the New World. Jesuit astronomers, dramatists, theologians, linguists, painters, architects, mathematicians, and scholars of every stamp were immersed in the intellectual movements of the day.

Widespread and influential as these schools were, they existed in the context of intellectual and political forces that greatly shaped their destinies. Enlightenment culture and institutional religion were increasingly hostile to one another and Jesuits made enemies on both sides. Individual Jesuits were involved in the court politics of eighteenth-century Europe and thus drew the criticism of powerful figures in both church and state. The influence of Jesuit schools and their successes were resented. In 1773 the Society was suppressed by order of the pope. Reborn in 1814, its schools in Europe regained only vestiges of the prominence they had had in the two hundred years following Ignatius's death, and they were heavily implicated in the agenda of restoration and of resistance to modern thought that was characteristic of so much intellectual life in nineteenth-century Catholicism.

In other parts of the world, in Asia and Latin America and especially in the United States, Jesuit education took on new life. Wherever
Catholics settled in America in any number, Jesuits founded schools.
These institutions mirrored the original movement of the population
westward as well as the later waves of European immigration to the
urban centers of the East and Midwest. Georgetown was the first
Jesuit institution in 1789, Boston College the eleventh when John
McElroy and his companions received a charter from the common-
wealth of Massachusetts in 1863 to found a college for the growing
Catholic population of Boston. Most of these institutions followed the
pattern of growth typical of American higher education, beginning as
six-year secondary schools or colleges conceived along European lines
and growing into universities as they added bachelor programs and
then graduate and professional degrees. Their development accelerated significantly in the boom years after World War II, under the
influence of the GI Bill, when most American colleges and universities raised their institutional ambitions and began to compete more
vigorously for funding and distinction. Some of these institutions,
like Boston College, became universities with national reputations
and distinguished programs and faculties.

Even this summary sketch suggests that the history of Jesuit education is a tapestry where religious motives, the intellectual climate,
local needs, entrepreneurial opportunities, and changing social and
political contexts are intertwined in a complex texture. There is
no Jesuit theory of a university, but there are principles in Ignatian
spirituality and Jesuit practice that suggest a characteristic point of
view toward education. One source is the plan of a university that
Ignatius sketched out in the last two years of his life, in Part IV of
the *Constitutions of the Society*, modeled on his vision of the preeminent educational institution of the Society in his day, the Collegio
Romano, now the Gregorian University.

Three features of this plan are especially interesting. One is the
motive for establishing a university under Jesuit auspices: to educate
those, especially teachers, who will have more influence in the world
of civil and religious affairs. This word *more* is central in Ignatius's
spirituality. He is zealous for what gives greater glory to God, what

is more conducive to the spiritual good of men and women, what demands more generosity from his followers, activities that are more likely to have an influence on the world.

A second feature is the concept of the humanities that formed the central disciplines studied in a Jesuit college. The word *humanitas* translated the Greek word *paideia*, which had come to mean both the process and the studies that developed moral goodness, devotion to truth, and a disposition to act for the civic good: languages, poetry, history, rhetoric, and logic, along with mathematics, the sciences, and philosophy of nature. For the humanists these were the subjects that opened the mind, sharpened wits, deepened human sympathy, developed clarity of thought and force in expressing it. They gave students an adroitness of mind in meeting new questions, and laid a foundation from which to explore the more important questions they would come to later in their studies.

The third distinctive feature was the integration and order that Ignatius envisioned among the subjects to be studied, leading from lesser to more important ones, culminating in the study of theology. At Paris he had learned that subjects should be studied in an orderly way, languages and humanities preceding the sciences and philosophy. And he was part of that tradition that had for centuries seen theology as the enquiry that was the culmination of the intellectual enterprise and that integrated all the parts of the intellectual life. This principle flowed out of the central theme of his spirituality, that the whole world discloses God at work. All the academic disciplines, therefore, contribute to the intelligibility of the world in their own proper ways and play a key role in making theology intelligible. Theology, focusing on the questions at the center of the mystery of God's self-disclosing activity, completes and integrates the knowledges developed by all the other disciplines of the university.

To these characteristics that Ignatius prescribed for the Roman College should be added a fourth one, evidenced in the history of Jesuit schools and one that is especially instructive for our own time. Jesuit education, in Rome and elsewhere, was a network that transcended boundaries of language, culture, and nationhood, one that was intercultural and global in perspective. This is arguably an essential but fragile element of Jesuit education, which could be lost as institutions are tempted to find their own way amid competing pressures to survive and achieve distinctive identities suited to their individual missions.

An idea of the university that proposes that students should study the best of human culture, relate this to their experience of God, use their knowledge for the common good, and imagine themselves as citizens of a global culture concerned about the well-being of all its people is certainly relevant to the needs of our own time.

How the First Jesuits Became Involved in Education

John W. O'Malley, SJ

From *The Jesuit Ratio Studiorum: 400th Anniversary Perspectives*, 2000

In 1548, just a little over 450 years ago, ten members of the recently founded Society of Jesus opened the first Jesuit school in Messina in Sicily. That event would have immense repercussions on the character of the Society of Jesus, giving it a new and quite special relationship to culture; but it was also a crucial event in the history of schooling within the Catholic Church and in Western civilization.[1] Within a few years the Jesuits had opened some thirty more primary/secondary schools, but also the so-called Roman College, which would soon develop into the first real Jesuit university (Gregorian University). In 1585, they opened in East Asia a school in Macao that also soon developed into a university, and about the same time they founded in Japan a remarkable art school and workshop in which local painters were introduced to Western techniques. In Rome they hired Palestrina as the music teacher and chapelmaster for their students, and later in Paris they did the same for Charpentier. They were the teachers of Descartes, Molière, and, yes, Voltaire. In Latin America they had constructed magnificent schools of stone and brick, with huge libraries, before any serious school of any kind had been founded in the British colonies.

By 1773, the year the Society of Jesus was suppressed by papal edict, the Jesuits were in charge of some eight hundred educational institutions around the globe. The system was almost wiped out by the stroke of a pen, but after the Society was restored in the early nineteenth century, the Jesuits with considerable success, especially in North America, revived their tradition.

Just as important as the work the Jesuits themselves accomplished in education has been their role, as the first teaching order within the Catholic Church, in inspiring other religious orders to do the same. The seventeenth century saw an outburst of such foundations, as did the nineteenth. Most spectacular within the panorama, perhaps, is the model the Jesuits provided for women's orders, beginning in seventeenth-century France. The Ursulines are only the best known among the many such institutions that had such an impressive impact upon Catholicism and upon women's roles in society—an impact about which we were almost without clue until the recent outpouring of writings on it from a feminist perspective. I refer you especially to Elizabeth Rapley's book on the subject.[2]

A word of explanation may be in order. What is meant by the expression "the first teaching order within the Catholic Church"? What about the monasteries of the Benedictines in the Middle Ages, and what about the great Dominican and Franciscan teachers at the medieval universities? The Jesuits differed from these and similar prototypes in three significant ways. First, after a certain point, they formally and professedly designated the staffing and management of schools a true ministry of the order, indeed its primary ministry, whereas in the prototypes it never achieved such a status. Second, they actually set about to create such institutions and assumed responsibility for their continuance. Third, these institutions were not primarily intended for the training of the clergy but for boys and young men who envisaged a worldly career. No group in the church, or in society at large, had ever undertaken an enterprise on such a grand scale in which these three factors coalesced.

But here I want to deal more directly with how the Jesuit involvement in formal schooling originated, not about its impact. I do so because I believe there is something stabilizing, even invigorating, about being part of a long-standing tradition, if of course one understands both its achievements and its limitations and is therefore free to take from it what is life-giving and helpful and leave the rest.

Like all traditions, the Jesuit tradition has, to be sure, its dark side. Its embodiment up to 1773 has been criticized for being elitist, paternalistic, backward looking, religiously bigoted. In its restored form from the nineteenth century forward, it has been criticized for being reactionary and repressive, ghetto-enclosed.[3] Such criticisms are too persistent not to deserve attention. I merely call attention to them here so that you know I am keenly aware of them. But this afternoon I do not stand before you to criticize the Jesuit tradition or to praise it. I am here to sketch with very broad strokes how it began, what it was trying to accomplish, and how it developed especially in the foundational years. There . . . is no way of talking about how the Jesuits got involved in education without dealing with the humanistic tradition. . . .

I begin by describing for you two contexts for the founding of the school at Messina in 1548—the state of formal schooling in Europe at that moment . . . and the state of the nascent Society of Jesus. First of all, the state of formal schooling. Two institutions were confronting and trying to accommodate each other—the university, a medieval foundation, and the humanistic primary and secondary schools, which began to take shape in fifteenth-century Italy with great Renaissance educators like Vittorino da Feltre and Guarino da Verona.[4] These two institutions were based on fundamentally different, almost opposed, philosophies of education.

The universities, as you know well, sprang up in the late twelfth and thirteen centuries largely in response to the recovery in the West of Aristotle's works on logic and what we today would call the sciences—biology, zoology, astronomy, physics, and so forth. The universities almost overnight became highly sophisticated institutions with structures, procedures, personnel, and offices that have persisted with strikingly little change down to the present. They professionalized learning, something the ancient world had never really known, and that professionalization was most evident in the creation of what we today call graduate or professional schools, like medicine and law.

Their goal, even in what we might call the "undergraduate college" (the arts faculty), was the pursuit of truth. Their problem was how to reconcile Christian truth, that is, the Bible, with pagan scientific (or "philosophical") truth, that is, Aristotle. Great theologians like Aquinas believed they had achieved a genuine reconciliation, which meant recognizing the limitations and errors of "philosophy" in relationship to revelation.

The second institution was the humanistic schools first created in Renaissance Italy in the fifteenth century, created to some extent as a counter-statement to the university system. The humanistic schools took not ancient scientific texts but ancient works of literature as the basis for their curriculum, the so-called *studia humanitatis*.[5] These works of poetry, drama, oratory, and history were assumed not only to produce eloquence in those studying them but were also assumed to inspire noble and uplifting ideals. They would, if properly taught, render the student a better human being, imbued especially with an ideal of service to the common good, in imitation of the great heroes of antiquity—an ideal certainly befitting the Christian. The purpose of this schooling was not so much the pursuit of abstract or speculative truth, which is what the universities pursued, as the character formation of the student, an ideal the humanists encapsulated in the word *pietas*—not to be translated as "piety," though it included it, but as "upright character."

This education, unlike that of the university that could be protracted until the student was in his thirties or forties, was concluded in one's late teens. At that point the student could enter the active life that was to be his future. By the early decades of the sixteenth century these secondary schools had begun to spread outside Italy to many other countries of Western Europe. When we think of the sixteenth century, we automatically think of the religious controversies unleashed by Luther and of the great voyages of discovery and conquest. What we also need to realize is that it was an age mad for education, when support for it and belief in its therapeutic powers for the good of society reached an almost unprecedented peak.

That is the first context that I need to set. Now let us turn to the second, the founding of the Society of Jesus. As you know well, this began with the association together of six, then ten, students at the University of Paris in the early 1530s. Ignatius Loyola, a layman, was the leader of the group, their spiritual guide, who brought them all, one by one, to deeper religious conversion through the *Spiritual Exercises* he had already composed. These ten eventually decided they wanted to be missionaries to the Holy Land; but when that plan fell through, they went to Rome to place themselves at the disposition of the pope, and then in 1539–40 decided on their own initiative to stay together to found a new religious order.

The basic impulse behind the new order was missionary. They formulated for themselves a special fourth vow that obliged them to travel anywhere in the world where there was hope of God's greater service and the good of souls—a vow often misunderstood as a kind of loyalty oath to the pope, whereas it is really a vow to be a missionary. Even as the order was receiving papal approval in 1540, St. Francis Xavier was on his way to India, thence to Japan, and almost to China before he died in 1552. The missionary impulse would continue to define the order down to the present.

From the *Spiritual Exercises*, however, the order had another important impulse, and that was to interiority, that is, to heartfelt acceptance of God's action in one's life through cultivation of prayer and reception of personalized forms of guidance in matters pertaining to one's progress in spiritual motivation and in purity of conscience. Derived from the *Exercises*, this impulse was a kind of recapitulation of the early religious experience of Ignatius. This call to interiority was one of many alternatives in the sixteenth century to the almost arithmetic and highly ritualized forms of religious practice that were in great vogue. It is important to note that the Jesuits did not begin because of some mandate from above or even because they wanted to deal with institutional issues besetting sixteenth-century Christianity, but because each of them sought peace of soul and a more deeply interiorized sense of purpose that they hoped to share with others.

The impulse to interiority manifested itself even in the way the Jesuits went about the teaching of catechism to adults and children, one of the first ministries they undertook. Catechism meant teaching the rudiments of Christian belief and practice with a view to living a devout life. The contents of the teaching was the Apostles' Creed, the Ten Commandments, and basic prayers, but also included the so-called spiritual and corporal works of mercy—feeding the hungry, clothing the naked, welcoming the stranger. These were ultimately derived from the twenty-fifth chapter of Matthew's gospel, where Jesus said that to do these things for the needy was to do them to Him. The motivation was powerful. In the sixteenth century the practice of these works, this art of Christian living, was called *Christianitas*—and in my opinion was what the Jesuits were fundamentally all about once they began to work together, that is, persuading and teaching others how to be Christians in the fullest sense, with a special awareness of social responsibility.[6]

Three aspects of the spiritual development that Ignatius Loyola himself underwent are pertinent here. The first I would call the primacy of personal spiritual experience. While Ignatius underwent his great conversion at the castle of Loyola in 1521 when recovering from his battle wounds and especially when immediately thereafter spending months in prayer and contemplation at the little town of Manresa outside Barcelona, he became convinced that he was being taught by God alone—taught through his experience of joy and sadness, of hope and despair, of desire and revulsion, of enlightenment and confusion. Through all this God was trying to communicate with him, in a personal and direct way, so as to guide him in his life and choices. It was on this conviction that the *Spiritual Exercises* were based, for this action of God was somehow operative or wanted to be operative in every human life.

An important conclusion follows from this premise that had—or at least ought to have had—some importance for the Jesuit tradition of education. That is, it is of the utmost importance for every human being to attain personal, inward freedom, so as to be able to follow the movements toward light and life that God puts within us, or, if you prefer a less religious formulation, to allow us to live our lives in ways that satisfy the deepest yearnings of our hearts.

The second aspect, also related to Ignatius's personal evolution into spiritual maturity, we can call his "reconciliation with the world." At the beginning of his conversion at Loyola in 1521 and the early months at Manresa, he gave himself over to severe fasting and other penances, let his hair and his fingernails grow, dressed himself in rags. But as his spiritual enlightenments continued, he began to modify this behavior and then give it up altogether, as he grew to love and see as a gift of God the things he earlier feared. He changed from being a disheveled and repulsive-looking hermit to a man determined to pursue his education in the most prestigious academic institution of his day, the University of Paris. He was on the way toward developing what might be called a world-friendly spirituality.

While at the university, he, at least in some limited way, studied the theology of Aquinas, in which he would have found justification for this change, for of all Christian theologians Thomas was the most positive in his appreciation of this world—intent, as I indicated, on reconciling nature and grace, reconciling Aristotle and the Bible, reconciling human culture and religion, so that they are appreciated not in competition with each other but in cooperation, both coming from God and leading to God. Ignatius must have found in Aquinas confirmation for the last and culminating meditation in the *Exercises*, the meditation on the love of God, for it contains insights along this line. The conclusion Ignatius drew from these insights was that God could be found in all things in this world, for they were created good, found in all circumstances (except of course in one's personal sin). The Jesuit *Constitutions* would later specify Aquinas as the special theologian to be cultivated in the order.[7]

As St. Ignatius evolved in his own life from being a hermit to being reconciled with the world, he simultaneously developed the third aspect of his spirituality that is pertinent for our topic. He ever more explicitly and fully saw the Christian life as a call to be of help to others. This desire appeared in the earliest days of his conversion at Loyola but became ever stronger and more pervasive. No expression appears more often in his correspondence—on practically every page—than "the help of souls." That is what he wanted the Society of Jesus to be all about.

As the years wore on, he also evolved into a believer in social institutions as especially powerful means for "the help of souls." This is exemplified most dramatically in his work in founding the Society of Jesus and in saying good-bye to what he called his "pilgrim years" to become the chief administrator in that institution from 1541 until his death in 1556. This change in Ignatius has been little emphasized by historians, but it is obvious and of paramount importance. From 1521, the year of his conversion, until practically 1540, he was either on the road or leading the rootless life of a student. That ended with the founding of the Society, and it can be taken as a symptom in him of a deeper psychological shift. This evolution prepared the way for the Jesuits undertaking formal schooling as their primary ministry.

The road to that decision, however, was not easy or straight. The original ten founding members of the Society were, cumulatively, an extraordinarily learned group, all graduates of the University of Paris, which was still the most prestigious academic institution in Europe. As they envisaged the Society in the foundational documents of the earliest years, they not only did not foresee Jesuits as schoolteachers, but they expressly excluded it as a possibility for themselves. In fact, they decided that they would not even teach the younger members of the order but send them to already-established universities.

Nonetheless, they gradually began to offer some instruction to younger Jesuits, and from this humble beginning the idea began to arise in the Society and to some extent outside the Society that members might do some formal teaching—on a restricted basis and in extraordinary circumstances. This gentle but momentous shift of perspective took place within a three- or four-year period, leading up to 1547.

By that year, the Society of Jesus had several hundred members, many of them with humanistic secondary education and many of them located in Italy. Those who had been trained outside Italy, especially in Paris, realized that they had learned some pedagogical principles practically unknown in Italy and that allowed students to make fast progress. This was the so-called "Parisian method," about which Father Codina, the international expert on the subject, has so well informed us. Most of the elements have persisted in schools up to this day to the point we cannot imagine education without students being divided into classes, with progress from one class to a higher one in a graduated system. We also at least pay lip service to the idea that the best way to acquire skill in writing and speaking is not simply to read good authors but to be an active learner by being forced to compose speeches and deliver them in the classroom and elsewhere. Particularly important for the Jesuit system was the specification that it was not enough to read great drama; students should act in them, and such "acting" often had to include singing and dancing. This Parisian style of pedagogy would give the Jesuits an edge in Italy that made their schools more attractive than the alternatives.

Thus the stage was set for the Jesuits to enter the world of formal education. In place was an educational theory compatible with their self-definition, that is, the *pietas* of the humanists correlated with the inculcation of *Christianitas* that was their mission. Moreover, schools were a ready-made institution in which to perform one of the works of mercy—instructing the ignorant. When St. Ignatius spoke of the schools, he in fact described them as a work of charity, a contribution to what he called the "common good" of society at large. The schools were a way of "helping." He and other Jesuits also saw that the schools gave them a special entrée into the life of the city and into the lives of parents of their students. Finally, the Jesuits had techniques and pedagogical principles that would make them especially successful teachers. In other words, it was something that by talent, background, and training they were highly qualified to do.

Yes, the stage was set, but there was no guarantee the play would be performed. The Jesuits could very easily have stuck to their original resolve and not become involved in offering instruction on any regular basis. There is no indication from these early years that Ignatius was guiding the Society in this direction or that he entertained any thoughts that formal schooling might be a venture the Society might explore. Why should he? No religious order had ever undertaken such an enterprise. The Jesuits, I think we have to admit, got into education almost by the back door.

In 1547, some citizens of the city of Messina, prompted by a Jesuit named Doménech, who had been working in Sicily for some time, asked Ignatius to send some Jesuits to open what we would call a secondary school in the humanist mode to educate their sons. Somehow, in the minds of Doménech and other influential Jesuits, this idea had been germinating. Negotiations opened, with the citizens of Messina offering to supply food, clothing, and lodging not only for the five Jesuit teachers but also for as many as five young Jesuits who might also study there. Ignatius accepted the invitation, surely in part because he saw it as an opportunity to get funding for the education of Jesuits themselves; but he must also have sensed something more profound, though we have no information as to what was passing through his mind at the time. In any case, he gathered for the venture ten of the most talented Jesuits in Rome. The school opened the next year, and, despite many tribulations, it was in the main a resounding success. A few months later, the senators of the city of Palermo petitioned for a similar institution in their city, and Ignatius acquiesced—with similarly happy results.

With that, enthusiasm for this new ministry—new to the Jesuits and new to the Catholic Church—seized Jesuit leadership, and school after school was opened, including the Roman College in 1552, which as I said would develop into the first real Jesuit university. It seems that once they made the decision to create schools of their own, they easily accepted the idea that some of these might be universities where the so-called higher disciplines like theology and philosophy would be taught.

By 1560, a letter from Jesuit headquarters in Rome acknowledged that the schools had become the primary ministry of the Society, the primary base for most of the other ministries.[8] The order had in effect redefined itself. From a group imaging itself as a corps of itinerant preachers and missioners, it—without ever renouncing that ideal—now reframed it with a commitment to permanent educational institutions. By 1773, the Jesuit network of some eight hundred educational institutions had become the most immense operating under a single aegis on an international basis that the world had ever seen.

What did the Jesuits hope to accomplish by these schools? Why did they do it? It is often said that in them the Jesuits wanted to oppose Protestantism and promote the reform of the Catholic Church. Certainly these reasons came to play a role, and in certain parts of Europe the defense of Catholics against Protestantism and then a counterattack played a large role in Jesuit self-understanding and mission, especially by the end of the sixteenth century and into the seventeenth. But these reasons were not at the core of their motivation, especially when they worked in territories where Protestantism was not seen as a threat, which are the territories in fact where most Jesuits lived and worked.

Their real goals for their secondary schools were those I have already suggested, borrowed more or less from the humanists themselves. Pedro Ribadeneira, one of the important early Jesuits, explained the purpose of Jesuit schools in a letter to King Philip II of Spain by saying *institutio puerorum, reformatio mundi*—I will tone him down a little bit by translating it as "the proper education of youth will mean improvement for the whole world."9 Ribadeneira was simply echoing the principal article in the humanists' creed—for their faith in their style of education was ardent and their expectations high. Exaggerated though those claims might sound today, even ridiculous, like any great faith they had a certain self-fulfilling dynamism. Don't you agree? An educator who has no faith in the high potential of the enterprise, no matter how defined, is hardly an educator at all.

Other early Jesuits were more modest and down-to-earth than Ribadeneira in what they expected, while still believing firmly in the value of the schools for society at large. In this regard they rode the enthusiasm of their times. Juan Alfonso de Polanco, executive secretary of the Society from 1547 until 1572, at one point drew up for his fellow Jesuits a quasi-official list of fifteen reasons for the schools, in which, it is interesting to note, opposing Protestantism and reforming the Catholic Church are not even hinted at. Among Polanco's reasons are that poor boys, who could not possibly pay for teachers, much less for private tutors, will make progress in learning and that their parents will be able to satisfy their obligation to educate their children. The final reason he gives is the most encompassing and reveals the social dimension of the whole undertaking: "Those who are now only students will grow up to be pastors, civic officials, administrators of justice, and will fill other important posts to everybody's profit and advantage."10

The schools, in other words, were, as I said earlier, undertaken as a contribution to the common good of society at large. This was true as well for the Jesuit universities, where the cultivation of the sciences would be especially noteworthy, for, we need to remind ourselves, "philosophy," that central plank in the "undergraduate" curriculum, meant for the most part "natural philosophy," that is, the sciences. Moreover, the basic design for the universities, in accordance with the tradition of the University of Paris, put theology as the preeminent "graduate school," the culmination of the system. In the religiously turbulent sixteenth century, the Jesuits realized the importance of well-trained theologians.

The Jesuits were a Roman Catholic religious order, and they of course retained their religious aims. But, especially with the schools, they began to have an altogether special relationship to culture and to have a more alert eye for what they called "the common good." In other words, the "help of souls" was not just help in getting people to heaven, but it included in a noteworthy way concern for the well-being of the earthly city. It was thus less exclusively churchy than we have sometimes been led to believe, partly because, I am convinced, of their spiritual vision of the world as "charged with the grandeur of God."

One of the special features of the Jesuit schools was that they were open to students from every social class. This was made possible by Ignatius's insistence that, in some fashion or other, the schools be endowed, so that tuition would not be necessary. In their ministries he wanted the Jesuits to minister to anybody in need, regardless of social status or socioeconomic class. Regarding the schools, he specifically enjoined that they be open "to rich and poor alike, without distinction."[11]

Jesuit schools even in the beginning are usually described as catering to the rich, and there is no doubt that over the course of the years and then of the centuries most of the schools tended to move in that direction. But this was far, far from the original intention, never actualized in the degree usually attributed to it, and insofar as it occurred was the result not so much of deliberate choices as of the special nature of the humanistic curriculum. That curriculum postulated the Latin and Greek classics as its principal subject matter, with appreciation for literature and eloquence as its primary focus. Such an education simply did not appeal to many parents and potential students, who preferred a more "practical" education in the trades or in commercial skills. The same could be said a fortiori for the kind of training the universities offered. In any case, while the Jesuits of course had no idea of what we today call "upward social mobility," the schools in fact acted in some instances as an opportunity for precisely that. The Jesuits were aware of this reality and in a few instances had to defend themselves against critics who thought the prospect corrosive of the stability of society.

Were the Jesuit schools, then, identical in every way with other schools? Did the Jesuits simply do what others were doing, but with the considerable advantage that students did not have to pay tuition? No, I think that is a simplistic reading of what happened. It is true that in their secondary schools, as well as in the few universities they ran, they in the main conformed to the consensus of their age about what constituted a good education. This is a fact often overlooked when people today ask what a "Jesuit education" is. But there were some features that were special, if not quite unique, to them that began to give a special character to what they did, so that we no longer speak of them as following the Parisian style in the education but as developing their own Jesuit style.

I will describe only one of those features. Unlike some of their contemporaries, they did not oppose humanistic education to scholastic (university or professional) education, as if these were two incompatible systems or cultures. They saw them, rather, as complementary. They esteemed the intellectual rigor of the scholastic system and the power of the detached analysis it provided, and they believed in its goal of training highly skilled graduates in the sciences and in the professions of law, medicine, and theology. They saw this graduate training as especially appropriate in theology for their own members and even for a few select students for the diocesan clergy. In this instance they saw it as a help to a more "professionally" reliable ministry, for they shared the goal of both Protestant and Catholic leaders to produce a literate, more learned clergy.

They at the same time esteemed in the humanist system (primary and secondary education) the potential of poetry, oratory, and drama to elicit and foster noble sentiments and ideals, especially in younger boys; they believed in its potential to foster *pietas*—that is, good character. Moreover, this system taught eloquence, for rhetoric was at the center of the curriculum; that is, it taught oratory, the power to move others to action—action in a *good* cause.

Furthermore, from both these systems of education they appropriated the conviction that human culture and religion were not competing but complementary values, each enriching and challenging the other. Both systems taught in fact that philosophical, ethical, and to some extent even religious truths were available outside Christianity, and that these truths had to be respected. They were both thus reconciliatory in their ultimate dynamism. In the philosopher Aristotle the scholastic Aquinas found truths about the universe and human morality. In Virgil and Cicero the humanists found truths about human nature and its destiny. I do not know of any Jesuit going so far as the humanist Erasmus did in his famous prayer, "O, St. Socrates, pray for us," but some of them came close.

I am not the only scholar to suggest that the benign attitude Jesuit missioners like Matteo Ricci took toward Confucianism in China and Roberto de Nobili toward Hinduism in India related in some way especially to the humanist education that the Jesuits cultivated for their own members to a degree no other order ever did—they had to, for practically every Jesuit was called upon at some point to teach "the humanities," that is, the Latin and Greek literary classics.

My impression is that the Jesuits, for all that, saw the boundaries between these two educational philosophies, unlike the blur that occurs in North America today where the undergraduate college both is the direct heir of the humanistic system and at the same time, by being part of the university, partakes of the technical or even vocational training reserved to "professionals." What is education for? It is for many things, according to one's philosophy, but it is difficult to be successful in it if it is seen to be for many things competing at the same time for the same person.

The Jesuits, I believe, wanted to preserve the best of two great educational ideals, the intellectual rigor and professionalism of the scholastic system and the more personalist, societal, and even practical goals of the humanists. I am not trying to say they were successful—or unsuccessful—in doing so. Indeed, I wonder if a final resolution of such disparate goals is possible within any educational vision and, unless we clearly opt for one of the two alternatives, if we are not perpetually condemned to some compromise rather than synthesis. Already in the sixteenth century, a certain ambivalence about the purpose even of university education was introduced by the Jesuits and others, and that ambivalence persists even today, though the terms in which it manifests itself are of course quite different.

By 1599, in any case, the Jesuits had had enough experience in education to try to codify their methods and ideals, and they did so by producing the famous *Ratio Studiorum*, or plan of studies. . . . They had tried to produce it earlier but were not able to bring it about. The *Ratio* would serve them as a guide throughout the world, really down to the nineteenth century. Basically a codification of curricular, administrative, and pedagogical principles, it had all the advantages and the many disadvantages of any such codification. It provided a firm structure and assured a certain level of quality control. It ran the danger of dampening initiative and inhibiting needed changes as the decades and then the centuries rolled on. At a certain point it desperately needed revision, but revision was resisted. Perhaps most important, it failed to highlight the larger vision and deeper assumptions that had originally animated the Jesuit educational undertak[ing]—partly because it took them for granted, partly because they were half-forgotten. Much scholarly commentary on Jesuit education has taken the *Ratio* as almost the only document studied, with the result that what I consider most important in Jesuit education has been slighted or even altogether missed.

There are two further aspects of the Jesuit enterprise that the *Ratio* and most scholarship has missed and that I think are crucially important. I have become increasing[ly] aware of these in recent years, and especially during the international conference that I helped organize two years ago at Boston College, entitled "The Jesuits: Cultures, Sciences, and the Arts, 1540–1773." Most of the papers from the conference—some thirty-five of them—have just been published in a volume from the University of Toronto Press.[12]

The first aspect of which the conference made me increasingly aware is the attention the Jesuits gave to the arts. Official Jesuit legislation and directives in this regard are generally quite deceptive, for they are few, and those few tend to be cautious and restrictive. The importance of Jesuit theater has long been recognized, but it has been little recognized in the American scholarship and generally treated as a subject in itself, not integrated into the educational enterprise as such.

In any case, the more I study the history of Jesuit education, the more integral to the program of the schools the arts seem to be, many of them consequences of the early Jesuit commitment to theater—which of course was itself part of the Parisian style, which the Jesuits interpreted to mean that the plays of Terence should not simply be read but be performed. The plays, besides inevitably entailing music and dance, sometimes required elaborate sets and other parapher-nalia of dramatic productions. The arts took the form of what we would today call extra-curriculars, but they were done in many of the schools in a way that fitted them into a clear program—and often carried out with great expense. The great collegiate churches attached to Jesuit schools often employed architects, painters, and sculptors of the highest local standing for their construction and decoration—but not only of local standing, for the Jesuits employed in the early seventeenth century the most celebrated artist of the day, Rubens, and after Rubens's death, the subsequently most celebrated Gian Lorenzo Bernini. Thus, education took place outside the often-narrow confines of the classroom.

Louise Rice wrote in the Toronto volume on the celebrations that took place at the Roman College in the seventeenth century on the occasion of academic disputations or degree defenses of the lay stu-dents.[13] These were great public affairs, with distinguished guests, who were entertained with instrumental and vocal music at various moments in the program, with the hall sometimes elaborately deco-rated according to the design of a local artist. An unexamined field in the history of architecture, it seems to me, is the development of formal school buildings as almost a new genre. The Jesuits sparked this development. At least in Italy before the Jesuits opened their schools, no such buildings existed for primary or secondary education, for "schools" were such informal institutions, usually meeting in the house of the schoolmaster. One of the great changes that the Jesuits helped promote was the development of teams of teachers—a real faculty—for such schools, which might range from five or six teachers up to thirty or forty. A faculty of such size required many classrooms, and hence required a building specially constructed for that scope.

A second aspect called to my attention by the Boston conference is the working of the very network itself, that is, the working of the communication of Jesuit schools with one another; or, even more impressive, communication with Jesuits working "in the field" in newly discovered lands. Steve Harris has published, again in the Toronto volume, an article on this subject, which he calls the Jesuit "geography of knowledge." Harris is a historian of science, and his specialty is Jesuit science in the seventeenth and eighteenth centuries, a subject now experiencing an upgraded evaluation among many such historians. Jesuits were committed to the university program in place at Paris and elsewhere, whose lower college was that of the arts, that is, of philosophy—that is, as I said, of natural philosophy or science. It is this curricular fact that accounts for the many Jesuit astronomical observatories and laboratories in their larger schools and for a certain Jesuit preeminence in this domain.

But one advantage the Jesuits had over others was the reports from the overseas fields of their brethren, who also had had good training "in philosophy" as astronomers, geographers, and naturalists. These reports often took the form of the "edifying letters" the Jesuits sent to broad audiences to win support for their work abroad. In Harris's opinion, it was not only the quantity and frequency of this correspondence that gave some Jesuit centers a privileged access to new information about the natural world. It was also the quality of the observation and the dependability of remote agents in executing requests from the Jesuit scientists back home for measurements, descriptions, and the sending back to Europe of natural objects, which could be examined and then put on display. The Jesuits shared this information with colleagues who did not share their own confessional allegiance. As Harris says, at least within the history of science, Jesuit letters can be found in the correspondence of every major figure from Tycho Brahe in the sixteenth century to Kepler, Galileo, Descartes, Newton, and Leibniz in the seventeenth, and to similarly distinguished figures in the eighteenth.

When the Jesuits opened their first school in Messina, Europe was not only in the throes of the great religious turmoil in the wake of the Reformation but also at one of the great turning points in the history of formal schooling. The fifteenth-century humanists in Italy had set in motion a movement that bit by bit was creating a brand-new institution—the primary/secondary school pretty much as we know it today. This new institution was of course derived from principles enunciated in ancient Greece and Rome, but it was being put into a systematic form that Cicero and Quintilian did not know. The Jesuits arrived on the scene at just the right moment to capitalize on what was happening, and they play an important role in the development of the new system. They were far from being alone in such development, but because of the way they were organized, because of the special backgrounds they came from and then devised for themselves, their role was special. I have tried to indicate a few ways in which this was true.

These schools must of course be placed in the context of what we can call the confessionalization of Europe, for they became confessional schools, intent on establishing for their students clear Roman Catholic identity. But they had other aspects to them that were broader in their scope, as I hope I have suggested, that helped lift them out of the special context of the sixteenth and seventeenth centuries.

The Jesuits also appropriated the older institution of learning— the university. This too gave them a special role in European culture, of which science was a particularly important and perhaps somewhat surprising manifestation. By the seventeenth century, the universities began to undergo important changes, as science moved away from the text of Aristotle to more experimental modes, in which individual Jesuits took part even as the Jesuit educational institutions tended to remain fixed in the more text-bound mode.

I exaggerate when I say that the Jesuits got into formal schooling almost by a series of historical accidents, but there is at least a grain of truth in it. I find that they were not always clear in explaining to themselves or others why they remained in it or what they hoped to accomplish—sometimes repeating what sound suspiciously like bromides. But let me put words in their mouths.

First, they were convinced that formal schooling was a good thing for society at large. They were content through their schools to contribute to the common good. Second, they believed that ethical and religious formation should not be confined to the pulpit, for it was a concern much too broad for such a boundary. Third, they were not fundamentalists, for, though not uncritical, they saw culture and education not as enemies but as friends. They derived this last conviction from the basically reconciliatory dynamics of the Thomistic [drawn ultimately from Thomas Aquinas] system of scholasticism and from the reconciliatory dynamics of the humanists' attitude toward good literature. They derived it as well from the founder of their order, who, a few years after his conversion, decided that he needed a university education in order, as he said, "better to help souls."

NOTES

1. For general background, see Paul F. Grendler, *Schooling in Renaissance Italy: Literacy and Learning, 1300–1600* (Baltimore: Johns Hopkins University Press, 1989). For specific background, see John W. O'Malley, *The First Jesuits* (Cambridge, MA: Harvard University Press, 1993), especially 200–42.

2. Elizabeth Rapley, *The Dévotées: Women and Church in Seventeenth-Century France* (Montreal: McGill-Queen's University Press, 1990).

3. See John W. O'Malley, "The Historiography of the Society of Jesus: Where Does It Stand Today?" in *The Jesuits: Cultures, Sciences, and the Arts, 1540–1733*, ed. John W. O'Malley et al. (Toronto: University of Toronto Press, 1999), 3–37.

4. Besides Grendler's *Schooling*, mentioned above, the best entrance into this world is still William Harrison Woodward, *Vittorino da Feltre and Other Humanist Educators* (1897; repr., New York: Teachers College, Columbia University, 1963).

5. See the insightful article by Craig R. Thompson, "Better Teachers than Scotus or Aquinas," in *Medieval and Renaissance Studies*, ed. John L. Lievsay (Durham: Duke University Press, 1968), 114–45.

6. For a description of *Christianitas* and its importance in the Middle Ages, see the brilliant article by John Van Engen, "The Christian Middle Ages as an Historiographical Problem," *The American Historical Review*, 91 (1996): 519–52.

7. See John W. O'Malley, "Early Jesuit Spirituality: Spain and Italy," in *Christian Spirituality: Post-Reformation and Modern*, ed. Louis Dupré and Don E. Saliers, vol. 18, *World Spirituality: An Encyclopedic History of the Religious Quest* (New York: Crossroad, 1989), 3–27.

8. See O'Malley, *First Jesuits*, 200.

9. Ibid., 209.

10. Ibid., 212–3.

11. Ibid., 211.

12. O'Malley, *The Jesuits* (see note 3 above). See also Gauvin Alexander Bailey, *Art on the Jesuit Missions in Asia and Latin American, 1542–1773* (Toronto: University of Toronto Press, 1999).

13. Louise Rice, "Jesuit Thesis Prints and the Festive Academic Defence at the Collegio Romano," in *The Jesuits*, ed. O'Malley et al., 148–69.

The Experience of Ignatius Loyola: Background to Jesuit Education

Howard Gray, SJ

From *The Jesuit Ratio Studiorum: 400th Anniversary Perspectives*, 2000

In 1933, Edward Fitzpatrick, dean of the Graduate School of Marquette University and President of Mount Mary College, aptly summarized the formal education of Ignatius Loyola.

> The most interesting and most striking incidents of St. Ignatius's life are included in the eleven years of his student days, commencing when he was thirty-three years old (March, 1524) and extending into his forty-fourth year (April, 1535). He began with the study of grammar for two years at Barcelona. He continued (1526) with the study of philosophy at Alcala.
>
> At Paris he repeated his studies in grammar and the humanities, and then philosophy for three and a half years, receiving the Master of Arts degree in Lent, 1533, at the age of forty-two. He then studied theology for about two years, discontinued it because of illness, and never completed it. His formal studies ended in Paris in 1535.[1]

Sixty-six years separate us from Dr. Fitzpatrick's perspective; however, I suspect that most professional educators would read the data similarly. It is this perspective that I want to engage as I establish some focus for the discussion of the experience of St. Ignatius as background to Jesuit education. In attempting to bring a particular focus to this discussion, I do not want to minimize the importance of the eleven years that Ignatius spent as a student. These were the years of personal maturation and integration for him. They also were years in which he forged enduring friendships with a group of remarkable fellow students who became his companions in founding the Society of Jesus. We would not have had the Jesuit order as we know it without the experience of Ignatius's student years.[2] But I want to emphasize that education for Ignatius antedated those eleven years and persisted until his death. It is the focus of lifelong education that I want to offer here as a constitutive perspective from which to interpret the influence of Ignatius on Jesuit education.

This presentation has three major sections: (1) for Ignatius education was an event that came "from above," from within, and from outside himself; (2) for Ignatius education was a code that socialized his experiences so that others could share these; and (3) for Ignatius education was an apostolic enterprise that would have an impact on both the church and civil society. I shall conclude with some exploratory reflections on what this might mean for Jesuit education today.

Education as an Event

In his dictated memoir, Ignatius summarizes an important aspect of his time at Manresa in these words:

> During this period God was dealing with him in the same way a schoolteacher deals with a child while instructing him. This was because either he was thick and dull of brain, or because of the firm will that God Himself had implanted in him to serve Him—but he

clearly recognized and has always recognized that it was in this way that God dealt with him. Furthermore, if he were to doubt this, he would think he was offending the Divine Majesty.[3]

Ignatius then cites five extraordinary instances of divine tutelage, climaxing in the pivotal illumination at the River Cardoner. Of this extraordinary divine intervention, Ignatius says: "He cannot expound in detail what he then understood, for they were many things, but he can say that he received such a lucidity in understanding that during the course of his entire life—now having passed his sixty-second year—if he were to gather all the help he received from God and everything he knew, and add them together, he does not think they would add up to all he had received on that occasion."[4]

Ignatius's account of his transformation strikes me as important not only because it represents a moral conversion but an intellectual reorientation, a way of viewing God as inspiration and the world as a source of knowledge. Moreover, the primitive exercise of discernment initiated at Loyola was becoming at Manresa a habit of heart. This graced intervention was a communication not merely about the things of God but of God Himself. Later, Ignatius struggled to articulate what this relationship meant, especially as he began to see that the process was one he could share with others. The God of revelation was a God who communicated in order to lead men and women to decisions about how they would live their lives, employ their talents, and direct their resources. Consequently, from this Manresa experience, Ignatius was to lay down an essential principle in the *Spiritual Exercises*:

[D]uring these Spiritual Exercises when a person is seeking God's will, it is more appropriate and far better that the Creator and Lord Himself should communicate himself to the devout soul, embracing it in love and praise, and disposing it for the way which enable the soul to serve him better in the future. Accordingly, the one giving the Exercises ought not to lean or incline in either direction but rather, while standing by like a pointer of a scale in equilibrium, to allow the Creator to

deal immediately with the creature and the creature with its Creator
and Lord.[5]

In other words, out of his own experience of divine intervention,
Ignatius came to understand the universality of God's desire to communicate personally with men and women, to engage their histories
with a new interpretation, to reorient their imaginations with new
possibilities, and to redirect their talents and opportunities toward
new enterprises. He was to term this divine intervention *de arriba*,
a gift not only of understanding God's descent into the human but
of the human ability to rise to God from created reality.[6] It is this
graced ability that became for Ignatius the habit of finding God in all
things. As Hugo Rahner explains: "From [Manresa] on, his theological thought became a descending movement from God to creatures,
in which created things and all earthly beauty, wisdom and righteous-
ness were merely reflected splendour of what he had already grasped
in the immediacy of his mystical contemplation of God Himself."[7]

But the privileged particularity of his illuminations did not inhibit
Ignatius from constructing a system of prayer and reflection that
would invite other men and women of good will to find how God
could also enter their lives, *de arriba*, "from above," and how this
grace would enable them, too, to find God in all things. Thus, inherent first in the Manresa experiences and then in the processes he
proposed to others through the *Exercises* was the reverence Ignatius
had for teaching and learning as metaphors for God's way in guiding
human decisions.[8]

There are important consequences for the way God instructs. If
the divine can enter into human consciousness and reorient a life, then
people can trust the effect this has within them. The gift from above
becomes a gift within the human reality of the person. Indeed, the
revelation of God to a man or woman demands personal appropriation. It is personal history that is reinterpreted, personal imagination
that accepts new possibilities, and personal talents and opportunities
that accept new enterprises. The Ignatian idea of an election—that
is, the choice that emerges out of the process of the Exercises—is not
that of imposition but of mutual acceptance, human and divine. It is

not just piety that prompts the Ignatian insistence that a colloquy conclude the prayer of the *Exercises*. This intimate conversation between a man or a woman and God is sacred because here is a privileged moment of mutual trust.[9]

Ignatius learned to trust his heart as a place of unique encounter with God. In that experience he also learned to trust the hearts of others as places for similar encounters. This movement represents a complex set of confidences: in one's own interiority, in the goodness of God, in the ability of others to find God too. From the opening of the *Exercises*—which encourages both the one who gives the Exercises and the one who makes them to trust one another throughout the process[10]—to the intense conclusion of the *Exercises*—in which the one who is making them holds the entire experience as an act of divine love, human acceptance, and mutual surrender—trust is the glue that holds this spiritual education together.[11] Trust is an essential component in Ignatian spirituality. Trust, in turn, will permeate the life and mission of the Society of Jesus. Trust will characterize the way Jesuits deal with people, cultures, and other religious experiences. For if Ignatius saw God as one who taught, he also saw God as one who taught out of trust for the unique reality of Ignatius's own temperament, history, and talents. God for Ignatius was an adapting God, a God who met created reality in trust. From God's trust Ignatius learned to trust—himself first and others later.[12]

This Ignatian trust of other created reality—other people, cultures, religious, experiences—founds why he can speak of finding God in all things and explains both the location and significance of the Contemplation to Attain Divine Love at the close of the *Exercises*. If one lives with God, then, one can find God's truth within life, God's direction within created energy, God's love dwelling deeply within creation. For Ignatius sin is the absence of God; it is uncovered in falsehood and deceit, in reckless ambition and oppression, in enmity, bias, and indifference to human anguish.[13] The Manresa experience did not exhaust Ignatius's education in divine wisdom. His subsequent years of study and then his governance over the young Society of Jesus contributed their own enrichments. But Manresa symbolizes the foundation of Ignatian education. It was an event that was experiential; it was based on trust; and it invited a discovery of God in a variety of created realities. Consequently, when we emphasize, as we should, the importance of adaptation in the *Spiritual Exercises*, we are reflecting what Ignatius discovered at Manresa about God. God adapts to the human to teach truth, to encourage our trust in our experiences, and to enrich the ways in which all creation can become a revelation about God's presence and action. Manresa was an event in divine tutelage for Ignatius, revealing how he was to help others to respond to that tutelage in their lives.[14] How was this help to be accomplished?

Codification of the Experience

Ignatius learned early the value of bringing inspiration into a system.[15] The *Spiritual Exercises* are an ordered set of instructions integrating the freedom necessary to any genuinely Christian religious experience with the guarantees that insure the experience is both authentically from God and respectful of human reason and dignity.[16] While these dual concerns are woven throughout the *Exercises*, Ignatius presents them most systematically in the twenty introductory reflections that he presents as aids to the one who gives the Exercises. These instructions fall under three general headings: about prayer, about discernment, and about choices. For example, when Ignatius gives suggestions about how prayer should be presented within the experience of the Exercises, he clearly expects the one who leads this experience to give instructions.[17] However, he also cautions that these instructions are to be brief in order to allow the one who makes the prayer the freedom to discover for himself or herself whatever God chooses to reveal.[18] To use another example, Ignatius lays out careful guidelines to help the one giving the Exercises to assess the movements of spirit that inevitably arise within the experience of the Exercises.[19] But he is equally solicitous that this instruction gradually empower the one making the Exercises to develop his or her own ability to distinguish what is from God and what is not from God, what is enduringly good from what is only an apparent good.[20] As a final example, while Ignatius relentlessly places before the one making the Exercises the ideals of the gospel, Ignatius is equally careful to insure that any personal choice that the one making the Exercises embraces be done with freedom from bias, prejudices, or outside influences.[21]

The *Spiritual Exercises* emerged out of Ignatius's stay at Manresa and then were refined over a number of years.[22] Ignatius viewed them as a way to help others find peace and direction in their lives out of the inspiration of the gospels. They were never intended to be coercive or insinuating. Rather, they were designed for people of maturity, freedom, and openness of heart who would be willing to consider how they could live lives of more profound dedication and generous service to others. To that end, Ignatius insisted on a certain solitude of soul, a separation from distractions, a willingness to take time to pray and to reflect, and a docility of heart to someone who would guide this experience. At the same time he cautioned the instructor of the *Exercises* to adapt them to the temperament, age, and experience of each person. As a document of Christian formation, the *Exercises* teach. As the initial codification of Ignatian principles of instruction, the *Exercises* establish important guidelines for Jesuit teaching.

While I have painted with a broad brush, the design of Ignatian instruction is clear. An ordered, humane approach to God's revelation presumes the freedom to find God for oneself, but within a communal revelation. Moreover, the *Exercises* insist on a person's willingness to test personal experience in order to choose what will be an enduring commitment to what will most direct one to God.[23]

Although the *Exercises* have sometimes been criticized as being too individualistic, they are, in fact, relentlessly oriented toward the life one lives outside of solitude—in the arena of public life, to the future. For example, the Ignatian view of Christ is that of Christ on mission—preaching, teaching, healing.[24] The decision to follow Christ is to follow him as humble, poor, and rejected within a culture that values wealth, power, influence, and prestige.[25] The virtues Ignatius emphasizes are those of freedom, magnanimity, and self-sacrifice, which lead to doing great deeds in the world but for the sake of the gospel. Consequently, as an educational tool, the *Exercises* were and remain a remarkable instrument of engagement with the world and culture of one's times.

The second significant area of codification I emphasize is the *Constitutions of the Society of Jesus*.[26] Pope Paul III approved the Society of Jesus in 1540; and on April 8, 1541, Ignatius was elected its first superior general. Ignatius was then fifty years of age and dedicated the remainder of his life to the direction of this new order. As superior general, one of his chief responsibilities was to give oversight to the writing of the *Constitutions*, which would express the aims and means that identify the life and work of the Society. It is this document I want to consider now, especially as an expression of educational aims and processes within the Jesuit community. In this examination I center first on the principles that governed the formation of Jesuits and then on that which governed Jesuits who had completed their formation and were involved in direct ministry.

There are three aspects of Jesuit formation that are crucial: the process of how to become a contemplative in action, the environment that promotes formation within the company, and the ways in which a man's ability to live Jesuit life and to do its ministry were assessed.

First, let me briefly explain this term "contemplative in action."[27] As we have seen, Ignatius valued the processes that led him to find God in the events of his life. He believed that the Exercises, if made well and in their integrity, could similarly help others to find God in their lives. He asked the same of the men who would be members of the Society of Jesus. In the *Constitutions* Ignatius spells out what the process might be that can dispose a man to become a contemplative in action.[28]

In Part III of the *Constitutions* Ignatius treats the spiritual formation of young Jesuits. In a remarkable section he counsels the importance of an asceticism that brings focus to a man's life, for example, silence, a certain self-composure, and effort to be at peace with oneself. Then he lays down the following wisdom directive:

> In everything they [the young Jesuits] should try and desire to give the advantage to the others, esteeming them all in their hearts as better than themselves [Phil. 2:3] and showing exteriorly, in an unassuming and simple religious manner, the respect and reverence befitting each

one's state, in such a manner that by observing one another they grow in devotion and praise God our Lord, whom each one should endeavor to recognize in his neighbor as in His image.[29]

This directive centers on three constitutive operations: *constitutive* of ways in which the young Jesuit can open himself to God's presence and action within human relationships; *operations* as distinct ways to achieve a certain openness to this experience. The first is what I would call attention, the ability to be present to a relationship in its particularity. It stands for that presence in which one person allows another reality, here another Jesuit, to enter his awareness on his own terms.[30] It is acceptance of the reality, not an intrusion—through fear or bias or lack of concentration—on that reality. The second operation is reverence, the ability to cherish the reality that reveals itself, here the other Jesuit, in all his integrity. It represents another level of acceptance, not only allowing the reality to be present to me but accepting that reality as different from, unique in his self-expression, worthy of his own integrity.[31] The third operation is actually the operation of grace. The word *devotion*, which denotes this third step, is precious to Ignatius.

> *Devocion*: a word which Ignatius uses with great frequency in all his works, especially his letters, *Spiritual Exercises*, *Spiritual Diary*, and *Constitutions*. It expressed his attitude of profound respect before God to whom he was totally dedicated in love and service, and he used it with multitudinous connotations, often mystical. In the *Constitutions*, . . . the word expresses the personal or communitarian pursuit of spiritual progress. [It was for Ignatius] "the actualization of the virtue of religion by means of an affection for God which is prompt, compliant, warmly loving, and impelled by charity. Its goal is the worship of God which is accomplished in all things and actions of oneself and one's fellow men, since it gives worship to Him by finding and serving him in all things."[32]

In other words, through attention and reverence one can hope to be led to devotion, the ability to discover how God exists in another, here in another Jesuit.

What Ignatius proposes as the touchstone of Jesuit formation is an asceticism that focuses a young Jesuit on the ability to be present to another reality, to hold in acceptance and a kind of awe the reality as he finds it, and out of this orientation to be sensitive to how God speaks to him through that other reality. Moreover, this kind of formation was not something to be done only within the novitiate [the first stage of a Jesuit's formation]. Rather it was to be inculcated as an abiding apostolic process that helped the Jesuit to become a man who could find God in all things, like studies, like other cultures, like people weighed down by sins, like art and music and science.[33] The ramifications of this formation directive are wide and rich, suggesting an important key not only to the personal religious event of finding God in all things but to the apostolic mind-set of expecting to find God in all people, places, and events. For what this education in attention, reverence, and devotion invites is an apostolic consciousness, a readiness to expect God to communicate his presence and intentionality within all created reality but especially within human relationships. For the Jesuit, then, the world became both a place of contemplation and a source for apostolic planning.[34]

In that same section of the *Constitutions*, Part III, Ignatius also describes the formation environment in which attention, reverence, and devotion can be best exemplified and taught. It is contained in his description of the director of novices:

> It will be beneficial to have a faithful and competent person whose function is to instruct and teach the novices in regard to their interior and exterior conduct, to encourage them toward this correct deportment, to remind them of it, and to give them kindly admonition; a person whom all those who are in probation may love and to whom they may have recourse in their temptations and open themselves with confidence, hoping to receive from him in our Lord counsel and aid in everything.[35]

I have referred to the importance of trust in Ignatian spirituality. This description of the Jesuit director of novices is but one more instance of this virtue. The director of novices models what he teaches in his relationship to his charges. Men learn attention, reverence, and devotion best when they see it exemplified in their own formation. This is as appropriate a place as any to call attention to how often Ignatius urges the power of good example to affect apostolic fruit.[36] People learn the gospel by seeing it lived out in their own regard. So, too, the Jesuit novices. By creating an environment of trust, the Jesuit director of novices makes the teaching about attention, reverence, and devotion credible and available.

The formation of men for the work of the apostolate, a work that frequently demanded that Jesuits work alone and in places with minimum ecclesial safeguards and support systems, had to include a component that would test the resiliency and fidelity of the novice. Can this man live this apostolic life with benefit both to himself and to the people he will serve? Can he practice attention, reverence, and devotion outside the security of the novitiate? To answer these kinds of questions Ignatius introduced a revolutionary form of novitiate training called experiments. What are these and how do they operate?[37]

There are six novitiate experiments that "constitute the Ignatian pattern of religious development into ministerial life."[38] Their aim was apostolic integration. What does this mean? The overall aim of the Society of Jesus was "to strive especially for the defense and propagation of the faith and for the progress of soul[s] in Christian life and doctrine"[39] and to accomplish this through a variety of ministries, chiefly centered on the word of God.[40] Moreover, Ignatius envisioned a group able to work on the frontiers of the church and even in lands and in enterprises that were not part of Christendom, much less Catholicism. In other words, the work of the Jesuits demanded capability and flexibility. The novitiate (and tertianship [the final stage of a Jesuit's early formation]) experiments, then, were ways to test the ability of young men to live this kind of life with benefit both to themselves and to others.[41]

By "apostolic integration" we mean that there is "a peculiar structure internal to the experiments, that they possess their own organic and evolving pattern, and that at their completion the novice or tertian has moved from an event of the deepest interiority and solitude into the ministerial life of the Society."[42] In other words, there is a harmony—psychological and religious—between the way a man prays and orients his life and the kind of ministerial presence he brings to his work with other people.

The six experiments ranged from the thirty days of Spiritual Exercises made under the guidance of an experienced Jesuit to work in a hospital, to a pilgrimage, to service within the Jesuit community, to teaching catechetics, to the ministries of preaching and hearing confessions. These latter two experiments were reserved for priest candidates or tertians. While a detailed analysis of the religious significance of these experiments is somewhat afar from the focus of this paper, their importance as an educational tool is not.

> [T]here is a more profound pedagogy at work here. These experiments move from devotion, the ability to find God in all things, through experiences which call upon humility, abnegation, and poverty, and to engagement in the ministerial life of the Society. . . . They are patterned on the life and ministry of Jesus. There must first be a profound contact with Christ our Lord, one that has been developing within the exercitant since the first events of the Exercises. Within that contact there is the experience of choice, of being sent, of being schooled with the "way Christ calls and wishes for all persons under his standard. . . ." The call of Christ into discipleship possesses a pattern that his life embodies. Ignatius sees this pattern in the earliest contemplations of his life. The movement of Jesus into his most profound ministry is through poverty and humiliations. The six experiments retrieve the structure of his life as the development of ministerial consciousness.[43]

These experiments, then, were part of the overall education of candidates into the Society of Jesus. They were part of a schooling for service. When these experiments were introduced, they contained "a great deal of daring and a considerable amount of novelty."[44] But Ignatius assumed that risk because he believed that only through concrete experiences of working for God and with God could a man learn how God works in life situations. As a result of this insistence of learning by doing, the Jesuit novice or tertian came to appreciate that his vocation was genuinely founded on what he himself possessed before God. On the other hand, the superiors of the Society of Jesus came to appreciate the kinds of men who had presented themselves for the life and the ministry of the Society. This kind of formation established a climate in which Jesuits expected to learn from one another. Consequently, a pattern of mutuality in learning characterizes not only the life of candidates to the Society but the life of those who had taken final vows. To be a Jesuit is to learn from one another.

In discussing the educational pattern within the life and work of formed Jesuits, I emphasize the idea of union in the Society of Jesus.[45] For the early Jesuits *union*, not *community*, was the operative word. And while Ignatius centers his *Constitutions* on the apostolic end of the Society of Jesus—that is, what it was meant to accomplish for the church and other people—what sustains this ministry is union, the union between God and the members of the Society and the union between the head of the Society and his fellow Jesuits:

> The chief bond to cement the union of the members among themselves and with their head is, on both sides, the love of God our Lord. For when the superior and subjects are closely united to His Divine and Supreme Goodness, they will easily be united among themselves, through that same love which will descend from the Divine Goodness and spread to all other men, and particularly into the body of the Society. Thus from both sides charity will come to further this union between superiors and subjects, and in general all goodness and virtues through which one proceeds in conformity with the spirit.[46]

As Ignatius indicates, this bonding of its very nature effects a mutuality of exchange both with the divine and with the human. The question emerges, then, how was the Society to keep this bonding alive; what means does it have to dispose itself both to the love of God and the love between the members? Clearly the fundamental means is the acknowledgment of the utter gratuity of such union, a grace given by God for a man to live this kind of life. Establishing that absolute priority, Ignatius then indicates a collection of human means to sustain an openness to this gift: selectivity of members; obedience; the exclusion of members who consistently undermine the unity of the Society; the moral, religious, and apostolic leadership of the superior general of the Society; a healthy uniformity; communication through letters.[47] But the chief means is the General Congregation, a juridical assembly of worldwide Jesuit representatives, called either to elect a superior general or "for matters of greater moment."[48] It is from this assembly that the Society of Jesus culls its directions for the future: its values, lifestyle, and apostolic priorities. The rhythm of a General Congregation arises out of the willingness of the delegates to assess the data, to listen to one another, to articulate emerging common concerns and opportunities, and then to forge these into appropriate legislation or directives for future development by the superior general. Consequently, the congregation is primarily a learning session before it becomes a legislating session.

In its spirituality and its government the Society of Jesus depends on the ability of its membership to discern, that is, to make religiously motivated decisions about the most appropriate way to live gospel values and to put these into practical operation. Discernment is a learning process that involves the cooperation of human beings who try to relate their lives, talents, and resources to God's priorities.[49] Throughout the Ignatian *Constitutions* there is a respect for learning that emerges both out of the Ignatian reverence for a God who teaches through life experiences and out of a similar reverence for the ability of the human mind and heart to be taught. In tracking the experiences of Ignatius that influence Jesuit education, this radical reverence for learning as a divine-human partnership cannot be exaggerated. These religious principles founded his legislation on formal education, which constitutes the important fourth part of the Jesuit *Constitutions*.

Education as an Apostolic Enterprise

What I have attempted to isolate are those elements that influenced the educational outlook of Ignatius Loyola and, in turn, structured the educational experience of the Society of Jesus. Those elements were:

- a reverence for the enduringly pedagogical character of God's revelation
- a trust that this process invited not only participation but imitation
- an assumption that this process was mutually beneficial both to the one who taught as well as to the one who learned
- in any learning experience the confirmation of God's presence was the way that it led a Jesuit to recognize his ability to help people as Christ had helped people and the way that it united him to the other members of the Society of Jesus

Part IV of the *Constitutions* presents how Jesuits themselves were to learn within school systems and then how they were to conduct their own schools.[50] This is ground that has been magisterially analyzed by Father George Ganss,[51] and more recently expertly revisited by John O'Malley[52] and Michael Buckley.[53] I do not wish to re-present their work here. What I do want to underscore here is that there is a continuity between the divine pedagogy Ignatius experienced throughout his life and the emphases he offered in Part IV of the *Constitutions*. He adapted divine wisdom to the secular reality of education and the schools.

There are seventeen chapters in Part IV of the *Constitutions*. Chapters one through ten are concerned with the formal education of Jesuits; chapters eleven to seventeen are concerned with the ministry of education that Jesuits carried on for others.

For Jesuits the overriding aim of formal education was to help them to learn how to help other people. Ignatius is straightforward in describing how people were to be helped: "To achieve this purpose, in addition to the example of one's life, learning and a method of expounding it are also necessary."[54] This is a rich program. Education should produce character, "the example of one's life."[55] The way that Jesuits learned was part of their mission. Their esteem for truth, their commitment to study for its own sake, their ability to succeed academically without alienating themselves from the humility and availability of the Master they followed—these were part of the educational program for Jesuits.[56] This implies a great deal. The

Jesuit scholastic was expected to integrate his formal education into the pattern of his apostolic life, to incorporate the empowerment of learning and professional competence into the availability of service to all people, the rich and the poor, the sophisticated and the simple, the young and the old. The good example that Ignatius presumes is not simply private virtue but rather a public persona that indicated a Jesuit was part of the human family he served. A Jesuit's education was supposed to enhance his apostolic labor, not his social status.

Presuming this sustained commitment to psychological and apostolic availability, Ignatius underscores two educational aims, learning and a method of expounding it. His own experience in education had taught Ignatius the value of sound learning—linguistic, literary, philosophical, theological. His experience of trying to explain the ways of God to men and women taught him the crucial importance of communication. He honored the need for adaptation, but demanded a structured program that insured educated ministers capable of touching the minds and hearts of people.[57] Formal education within the Society of Jesus was treated with deep reverence as an emblem of God's providence, part of God's plan to help people: "Therefore the human or acquired means ought to be sought with diligence, especially well-grounded and solid learning, and a method of proposing it to the people by means of sermons, lectures, and the art of dealing and conversing with men and women."[58] University education undertaken for non-Jesuits "will aid toward the same end, as long as the method of procedure described in Part IV [440–509] is preserved."[59]

Concerning these universities, there are three points I want to stress. First, the apostolate of education for "those outside the Society" is a sharing in the gifts of Jesuit education.[60] Second, Part IV clearly emphasizes that through the universities these gifts will "spread more universally through the branches taught, the number of persons attending, and the degrees that are conferred."[61] Third, the hope is that such an apostolate would produce graduates "able to teach with authority elsewhere what they have learned well in these universities of the Society for the glory of God our Lord."[62] In other words, the apostolate of Jesuit education is the expression of a mission that digs deeply into the traditions that identify Jesuit life and ministry. Like the giving of the Spiritual Exercises, this reliance on a tradition does not mean replicating the experience of Jesuits for non-Jesuits. However, it does mean honoring the presence of God's spirit in human life and liberating the dynamism of God's healing and consecrating power in human enterprises. The authenticity of Jesuit education, then, does not rely primarily on the details of Ignatius's life but on the vision he offered of the dignity of teaching, of the authority inherent in sound learning, and of the power of communicating well what one has learned. Finally, this vision proves its validity when, as it did for Ignatius, it empowers us to use what we are and what we have to help others.

Conclusion

In describing the impact of Ignatius Loyola on his life, one writer, not a Jesuit, expresses it in these words:

> I have read every major biography and book about Ignatius, I have held his shoes in my hands, I have walked through his freshly restored rooms in the house next to what is now the Church of the Gesù, and I have next to me as I write this a nail that was in one of the walls. Supernatural prodigies have nothing to do with my rapt and consuming interest in him. I have simply been trying to figure out how to live my life magnificently, as Ignatius did, who sought in all his works and activities the greater glory of God.[63]

I like the description for two immediate reasons. The appreciation testifies to accomplishment and to challenge. Ignatius truly did great deeds, and education was at the heart of these. Ignatius invites us to similar deeds, and education ought to be at the heart of these. Let me unpack these reflections, using the unpacking as a way to orient what I have summarized to the present condition of Jesuit and Catholic education today.

An increasing number of educators laments the lessening of the religious and the spiritual and the Catholic in higher education today.[64] But alongside these uneasy reflections there is also a lively resurrection of interest and activity about mission and identity and values.[65] People care deeply about those traditions that have bound faith and culture together in an integrated view of education. Many want to reclaim an authenticity not only of goals but of means. I suspect that throughout these days we shall hear much more about both goals and means. But the ultimate question, I suggest, is how do we relate to traditions? If we believe that we possess them, then we want to sustain their vigor. If we believe that we have lost them, then we want to recover their vigor. These are two different processes, but they are enlivened by a common inspiration: experience.

By experience I do not mean raw sense data nor a fleeting emotion but a sustained process that engages the humanity of a person.[66] In describing the processes of conversion, dedication, and accomplishment that characterize the life of Ignatius Loyola, I wanted to lay out such an experience. I wanted to describe something that was available to others in his day and remains available to us today. Do we/can we have access to this kind of religious sensibility today? Those of us involved in the work of mission and identity in our colleges and universities ask ourselves these questions daily. Those involved in development and fund-raising have to ask themselves these questions frequently. The discussions surrounding *Ex Corde Ecclesiae* ["From the heart of the church," Pope John Paul's treatise on Catholic education] and its application to the United States have involved administrators and faculty in significant discussions about the identity and mission of Jesuit, Catholic higher education.[67] In a pluralistic culture, how do we ask Ignatian questions and how do we present Ignatian ideals and values?

In the May 22, 1999, issue of *America*, John Donohue reflected on the significance of this four-hundredth birthday of the *Ratio*. His conclusion suggests a way, a means, whereby all of us in today's pluralistic culture can sustain or revive the Ignatian experience of education. "The secret of the success of those Jesuit schools cannot be found in the letter of the *Ratio*. It has been said that all the Renaissance school plans looked pretty much alike on paper. What made the seventeenth-century Jesuit schools effective could only have been the element that is indispensable for every school that works well—good teaching."[68] I agree. In the climate of university and college culture today teaching frequently competes with research; and research wins, at least when it comes to tenure. But my experience has been that the publishing faculty and research scholars among us are also dedicated to teaching, to a mentoring of excellence that they hope will be passed to others. It is this care for the generation at the cusp of scholarship and/or adulthood that we face in all our discussions. We want what we do to help people. It is this experience that I sometimes desperately assert to Boston College when I speak with faculty, staff, and administrators about the Ignatian tradition. It is here where I place my primary trust in my negotiations with faculty and staff about the mission. It is here where I find the Ignatian strategy of attention, reverence, and devotion capable of bridging gaps and translating competing values into generous, shared concerns about creating a new kind of academic community in which we can speak to one another in order to learn from one another. It is here where we have to start in the relationships that bind a school together.

If we fear that this may not be enough, I am heartened by another observation in John Donohue's *America* piece: "*Magistri sint insignes*— 'The teachers should be outstanding,' said a Spanish Jesuit writing some years before the *Ratio* appeared. Surely not all fully measured up. No doubt some were flat failures. It is a fair guess, though, that there were a fair number of competent teachers who did seriously care that their students should really learn and should also become good Christians."[69] Our aim today would be more ecumenical; but the concern is still there and the odds are that there are a large number who have remained in education because they believe in this care of the young, because they have an investment in the next generation of scholars and professionals. Would Ignatius believe that this basic experience of caring was foundation enough? Would he see in this kind of bond a union of minds and hearts? Would he believe that this common denominator can lead us to God? I believe that he would. I also believe that to ascribe to this vision and to foster the kind of conversation that invites a hunger and thirst for something more is to live in some ways as he did—magnificently.

NOTES

1. Edward A. Fitzpatrick, *St. Ignatius and the* Ratio Studiorum (New York: McGraw-Hill, 1933), 7–8.

2. Let me give just two examples. First, Ignatius saw the importance of order, personal appropriation, and balanced judgment because he experienced both their lack and their availability; see George E. Ganss, SJ, *Saint Ignatius' Idea of a Jesuit University: A Study in the History of Catholic Education* (Milwaukee: Marquette University Press, 1954), especially chap. 9, "Principles in the Spirit of St. Ignatius' *Constitutions* on Education," 185–93. Second, Ignatius found in the life of the university friends and the power of conversation; see Jose Ignacio Tellechea Idigoras, *Ignatius of Loyola: The Pilgrim Saint*, trans. and ed. Cornelius Michael Buckley, SJ (Chicago: Loyola University Press, 1994), chaps. 23–27.

3. Ignatius Loyola, *A Pilgrim's Journey, The Autobiography of Ignatius Loyola*, trans. Joseph N. Tylenda, SJ (Wilmington, DE: Michael Glazier, 1985), 35–36, no. 27.

4. Ibid., 39, no. 30.

5. Ignatius Loyola, *Spiritual Exercises of Saint Ignatius Loyola*, translation and commentary by George E. Ganss, SJ (St. Louis: Institute of Jesuit Sources, 1992), 25–26, no. 15.

6. See George E. Ganss, SJ, ed., *Ignatius of Loyola, The Spiritual Exercises and Selected Works* (New York: Paulist Press, 1991), 474, no. 86. The classic treatment is found in Hugo Rahner, SJ, *Ignatius the Theologian*, trans. Michael Barry (New York: Herder and Herder, 1968), 1–31.

7. Ibid., 4.

8. On the tradition, see Ben Witherington III, *Jesus the Sage. The Pilgrimage of Wisdom* (Minneapolis: Fortress Press, 1994).

9. Alexandre Brou, *Ignatian Method of Prayer*, trans. W. J. Young, SJ (Milwaukee: Bruce, 1949), 119–21.

10. *Spiritual Exercises*, no. 22.

11. Ibid., no. 234.

12. On the significance of adaptation and trust, see Waiter Brueggemann, "Nouns: Yahweh as Constant," in *Theology of the Old Testament* (Minneapolis: Fortress Press, 1997), 229–66; Michael Ivens, "The First Week: Some Notes on the Text," *The Way*, suppl. no. 48 (Autumn 1983): 6–8.

13. The imagery of the Satan in the Two Standards Meditation is the imagery of one who is "the mortal enemy of our human nature" (*Spiritual Exercises*, no. 136).

14. The key section in Ignatius's *Autobiography* is no. 29, p. 37, in the Tylenda edition: "It was likewise in Manresa—where he stayed for almost a year, after experiencing divine consolations and seeing the fruit that he was bringing forth in the souls he was helping—that he abandoned those extremes he had previously practiced and began to cut his nails and hair."

15. *Constitutions of the Society of Jesus*, trans. George E. Ganss, SJ (St. Louis: Institute of Jesuit Sources, 1970), "Preamble to the Constitutions," 119–20, [134]–[135].

16. A classic statement on "their proper place in the history of Christian piety" is Hugo Rahner's in *The Spirituality of St. Ignatius Loyola: An Account of Its Historical Development*, trans. Francis John Smith, SJ (Chicago: Loyola University Press, 1980), 88–96.

17. See, e.g., *Spiritual Exercises*, nos. 2, 6–10, 14, 17.

18. Ibid., no. 2.

19. Ibid., nos. 6–10, 14, 16–17.

20. Ibid., nos. 2, 5, 15, 20.

21. Ibid., no. 15, and especially the advice on the Election, nos. 169–87.

22. Joseph de Guibert, SJ, *The Jesuits: Their Spiritual Doctrine and Practice, A Historical Study*, trans. William J. Young, SJ (Chicago: Institute of Jesuit Sources, 1964), 113–22.

23. *Spiritual Exercises*, no. 169, "Introduction to the Election."

24. Note the first prelude of the Call of Christ, no. 191, which establishes both a tone and a perspective for Week II of the *Exercises*.

25. Ibid., "II Standards," nos. 136–47.

26. See the Ganss edition for a succinct overview of the genesis and spirit of the *Constitutions*, 3–59.

27. Joseph F. Conwell, SJ, *Contemplation in Action: A Study in Ignatian Prayer* (Spokane, WA: Gonzaga University Press, 1957).

28. *Constitutions*, [250].

29. Ibid.

30. An important discussion of "attention" can be found in Pierre Haclot, *Philosophy as a Way of Life*, trans. Michael Chase, ed. Arnold I. Davidson (Oxford: Blackwell, 1995), 126–44.

31. Charles O'Neill, SJ, "Acatamiento: Ignatian Reverence," *Studies in the Spirituality of the Jesuits* 8 (January 1976).

32. Ganss edition of *Constitutions*, 155–56 n. 5.

33. A specific example of this is Timothy B. Toohig, SJ, "Physics Research: A Search for God," *Studies in the Spirituality of the Jesuits* 31 (March 1999).

34. John W. O'Malley, SJ, "To Travel to Any Part of the World: Jeronimo Nadal and the Jesuit Vocation," *Studies in the Spirituality of the Jesuits* 16 (March 1984); Brian B. Daley, SJ, "'In Ten Thousand Places': Christian Universality and the Jesuit Mission," *Studies in the Spirituality of Jesuits* 17 (March, 1985).

35. *Constitutions*, [263].

36. See the extensive citation of "Edification" in Index 1 of the Ganss edition of *Constitutions*, 380.

37. The best treatment in English of the experiments is that of Michael J. Buckley, SJ, "Freedom, Election, and Self-Transcendence: Some Reflections upon the Ignatian Development of a Life of Ministry," in *Ignatian Spirituality in a Secular Age*, ed. George P. Schner, SJ (Waterloo, ON: Wilfrid Laurier University Press, 1984), 65–90.

38. Ibid., 81.

39. "Formula of the Institute," in *Constitutions*, [3].

40. Ibid.

41. The apostolic centrality of the Jesuits demanded a long training begun in the novitiate and climaxed by a final formation period now called tertianship. After tertianship, the young Jesuit was eligible for final profession into the Society of Jesus. See *Constitutions*, 233 n. 4, 234–35 n. 1.

42. Buckley, "Freedom, Election, and Self-Transcendence," 81.

43. Ibid., 84–85.

44. De Guibert, *The Jesuits*, 103.

45. Central to the *Constitutions* are Part VII, on the apostolic work of the Society, and Part VIII, on the union of the members. That an entire section of the *Constitutions* should be centered on union emphasizes the essential movement outside the community toward the labor of the Society. For an

informative discussion of this, see Jean-Yves Calvez, SJ, "Union: Community for Mission," in *Constitutions of the Society of Jesus, Incorporation of a Spirit* (Rome: Secretariatus Spiritualitatis Ignatianae, 1993), 311–26.

46. *Constitutions*, [671].

47. Ibid., [657]–[667], [673]–[676].

48. Ibid., chaps. 2–7 treat the General Congregation.

49. Ibid., especially chap. 7.

50. A most helpful treatment of the genesis of Jesuit education as intramural and then apostolic can be found in Pedro Leturia, SJ, "Why the Society of Jesus Became a Teaching Order," *Jesuit Educational Quarterly* 4, no. 1 (1941): 31–54.

51. Ganss, *Saint Ignatius' Idea of a Jesuit University*.

52. John W. O'Malley, SJ, "The Schools," in *The First Jesuits* (Cambridge, MA: Harvard University Press, 1993), 200–242.

53. Michael J. Buckley, SJ, *The Catholic University as Promise and Project: Reflections in a Jesuit Idiom*, part 2, "The Universities of the Society" (Washington, DC: Georgetown University Press, 1998), 53–147.

54. *Constitutions*, [307].

55. Ibid.

56. See the extraordinary letter of Ignatius to the community at the Jesuit college in Coimbra. The young Jesuits there had embarked on a set of extreme penances and public testimonies that witnessed to great enthusiasm but not much prudence. Ignatius's letter is at once understanding of their good will but firm in reorienting their energies to the humbler abnegation of solid study for the more enduring good of the kingdom. *Letters of St. Ignatius of Loyola*, trans. William J. Young, SJ (Chicago: Loyola University Press, 1959), 120–30.

57. See Ganss, *Saint Ignatius' Idea of a Jesuit University*, chaps. 4–6.

58. *Constitutions*, [814].

59. Ibid., [815].

60. Ibid., [440].

61. Ibid. See Buckley, "Ignatius Understanding of the Jesuit University," in *The Catholic University*, 57–63.

62. Ibid.

63. Ron Hansen, "Saint Ignatius of Loyola, The Pilgrim," in *A Tremor of Bliss: Contemporary Writers on the Saints*, ed. Paul Elie (New York: Riverhead Books, 1995), 112. [This essay is included in the companion volume, *An Ignatian Spirituality Reader*—Ed.]

64. For example: James Tunstead Burtchaell, CSC, *The Dying of the Light: The Disengagement of Colleges and Universities from Their Christian Churches* (Grand Rapids, MI: Eerdmans, 1998). In his preface, Burtchaell cites the "magisterial work already done by George Mardsen, Philip Gleason, and Douglas Sloan," ix–xiii. To this list I would add: Buckley, "A Conversation with a Friend," in *The Catholic University*, 40–51; David W. Gill, ed., *Should God Get Tenure?* (Grand Rapids, MI: Eerdmans, 1997); Alvin Kernan, ed., *What's Happened to the Humanities?* (Princeton, NJ: Princeton University Press, 1997); Warren F. Nord, *Religion and American Education: Rethinking a National Dilemma* (Chapel Hill: University of North Carolina Press, 1995).

65. For example, the annual meeting of the Committee on Identity and Mission of the Association of Jesuit Colleges and Universities brings together a number of representatives, male and female, Jesuits and others, whose universities have delegated them to give specific oversight to the promotion of Jesuit and Catholic values in higher education.

66. Tad Dunne has provided a succinct overview of this in his contribution "Experience," in *The New Dictionary of Catholic Spirituality*, ed. Michael Downey (Collegeville, MN: The Liturgical Press, 1993), 365–77. A more recent study, while focused on spirituality, develops much of what I suggest in this presentation: Ronald Rolheiser, *The Holy Longing: The Search for a Christian Spirituality* (New York: Doubleday, 1999).

67. A recent issue of *Origins* provides both a copy of the National Catholic Conference of Bishops committee's most recent draft and a margin history of the discussion: "An Application to the United States of *Ex Corde Ecclesiae*," *Origins*, September 30, 1999, 245, 247–54. James Burtchaell has provided a slanted, albeit entertaining, resume of the proceedings in *Crisis* for July/August, 1999; I received my copy through the Internet: http://www.catholic.net/rcc/penodicals/crisis/July–Aug99/everything.html.

68. John W. Donahue, "A School Plans 400th Birthday," *America*, May 22, 1999, 26.

69. Ibid.

Further Reading

A fuller treatment of the antecedents of Jesuit education in medieval scholastic learning and in sixteenth-century humanism can be found in an earlier O'Malley essay entitled "The Jesuit Educational Enterprise in Historical Perspective" (*Jesuit Higher Education: Essays on an American Tradition of Excellence*, ed. Rolando F. Bonachea. Pittsburgh: Duquesne University Press, 1989, 10–25).

Chapter 6 of O'Malley's *The First Jesuits* (Cambridge, MA: Harvard University Press, 1993, 200–242) deals with "The Schools" in a comprehensive way.

A sense of the breadth and depth of Jesuit involvement in the sciences and the arts emerges from three volumes of specialized studies (mostly by non-Jesuit scholars) edited by John O'Malley and others:

The Jesuits: Cultures, Sciences, and the Arts, 1540–1773 (Toronto: University of Toronto Press, 1999).

The Jesuits and the Arts, 1540–1773 (Philadelphia: St. Joseph's University Press, 2005).

Jesuits II: Cultures, Sciences, and the Arts, 1540–1773 (Toronto: University of Toronto Press, 2006).

The Current Problematic

Introduction

In the first of the two selections in this part, Patrick A. Heelan, SJ, Irish Jesuit philosopher at Georgetown, presents us with a challenge. What he says in "Ignatian Discernment, Aesthetic Play, and Scientific Inquiry" is relevant to our understanding the current problematic. Heelan deals with today's understanding of knowledge and its perceived antagonism with personal experience and our own sacred stories. In view of "the postmodern condition of knowledge," argues Heelan—where reaching the truth about anything is out of the question and the specialized languages of science only cut us off from our own lived experience—we need an art for enriching "the language of strategic living" and thus an art for enabling ourselves to renew contact with the biblical stories and recover the power of spiritual discernment.

Will we be able? It's a tall order and the jury is still out. But a good many of the essays in this reader are helping us on the way. Because Heelan's essay makes for difficult reading, I have chosen to provide a selective summary—often using his own words, indicated in quotation marks—rather than the full essay.

After such a heady trip with Heelan, we turn to something more concrete: Fordham philosopher Dominic Balestra's essay "Where Loyalties Lie?" on the apparently conflicting loyalties in today's Jesuit university.

Understanding the Terminology: Suggested Readings from *Do You Speak Ignatian?*

- Education, Jesuit
- Vatican Council II (Vatican II for short)
- *Cura Personalis*
- *Magis*

Ignatian Discernment, Aesthetic Play, and Scientific Inquiry

Patrick A. Heelan, SJ

A selective summary, from *Minding the Time, 1492–1992: Jesuit Education and Issues in American Culture*, 1992

Over the course of his life, Ignatius grew ever sharper in his ability to use his "spiritual senses," to dwell imaginatively in the gospel stories and to let the experience of them become touchstones for good decision making. For more than two hundred years, he and the Jesuits who came after him lived and worked and made good decisions that had a profound impact on the world. With the suppression of the Jesuit order in 1773, however, this living tradition was lost. For us today, then, the question is, can Ignatian spiritual discernment—"with its seemingly naive, premodern assumptions based on the power of story telling and belief in the invisible hand of God's providence"—come alive again in Catholic and Jesuit higher education?

For many centuries, Catholic and secular higher education shared the same assumption: "that universal, perennial, and objective truth . . . is available to human reason unhampered by bias." And both have now, "in the postmodern condition of knowledge," "come to share the crisis of disillusion" with that assumption. Rather than "the truth," in academe we have a cacophonous multitude of voices with no criteria for assessing the value of any of them. Does science provide a foothold? Only within its own specialized environment; once it leaves there, it becomes "pop science," which "uses the language of science to displace and make unreal the verities [truths, wisdom] that we know—or are now persuaded that we falsely thought we knew." In other words, the specialized languages of academe have invaded our language of strategic living and set up a barrier between "what we think we know and what we need to know, making it impossible for us to do what Ignatius did, to relive the mythic narrative of biblical faith."

Despite such a formidable obstacle, can we in the university "enrich the language of strategic living rather than . . . build glass walls that separate us from life? I trust that there is an art for enriching the language of strategic living. If so, we, faculty and students, will be able once more to renew our contact with the seemingly antiquated biblical myths and recover the spiritual senses and the power of spiritual discernment that made Ignatius [such] a master."[1]

_____

NOTES

1. Perhaps what Heelan is looking for here is akin to the "secondary immediacy" or "second naïveté" developed by the distinguished French philosopher Paul Ricoeur (1913–2005) (*The Symbolism of Evil*, trans. Emerson Buchanan [Boston: Beacon Press, 1967], 352)—Editor

Where Loyalties Lie?

Dominic J. Balestra

From *Conversations on Jesuit Higher Education,*
Fall 2003

At the end of my first run as chair of the philosophy department, 1989–1995, my experience—in the curriculum wars, with an external review of the department's Ph.D. program, with reappointments and tenure decisions, and especially with our hiring—left me with a haunting impression that a significant shift had taken place, or at least was in the making. A shift in what might be called faculty loyalties. After I returned as chair, 1999–2002, this impression has developed into a strong conviction. Further reading of applications for our graduate program, more hiring experience, working with our own graduate students as they enter into the search for that first faculty appointment, and conversations with new chairs and new colleagues at Fordham and other Jesuit institutions have only confirmed my sense about this shift.

Just when this impression struck me I cannot say; it emerged gradually during the department's hiring process, which included interviewing many strong candidates who far outnumbered the positions for which they were competing. So many excellent candidates seeking to fill far fewer positions recalled my own, sometimes lonely, job search in the mid seventies, when I was filled with apprehension about first impressions in the initial interviews at the American Philosophical Association meeting between Christmas and the New

94

Year. I distinctly recall the orienting questions entering those interviews: How might I fit in with this department and this school? How
might I become a part of this community, this university? Within
that horizon of expectation there was no question that my primary
allegiance would be to the university I would join as a member of its
faculty, that my graduate education was a preparation for this end.
To be sure, continued study, research, publication, and participation in the wider profession were essential parts of that horizon, but
clearly as subsidiary to the end of serving the university I might join
as my primary academic community. In this way the disciplinary
community of philosophers beyond my university, the "profession,"
was secondary and instrumental to the vocational community of my
university.

At that time, excited, grateful, and apprehensive, I entered my
first faculty appointment, here at Fordham University, believing, as
I still do, that without question a college or university professor's
primary allegiance is to his or her school. I also believed, and still do,
that this is all the more so for faculty at Jesuit institutions who accept
its educational ideal of *cura personalis* and the *magis* that is its telos, its
end or goal. A *magis*—a striving for something more—that includes
scholarship but not as an end in itself. I also had a sense that the other
baby boomers of my generation shared this horizon.

In contrast to our comportment back then, today's generation
of faculty candidates exhibits a much stronger concern about their
career development in their disciplinary profession. In my role as
chair of the philosophy department, I came to see and hear more
and more candidates, and new faculty, spending less time asking
about the school—its core curriculum, its faculty or students, its
mission and identity. Their questions shifted to matters of support
for research, travel to conferences, teaching loads (not in the interest
of teaching courses), release time for writing, and similar kinds of
concerns that manifest a preoccupation for how the university might
support their work! In spite of the fact that there were always many
more candidates for [the] faculty positions available, the "best" and
most competitive candidates with multiple job offers from competitive institutions more often acted like free agents in the draft.

I am not saying that I believe that my generation of young academic Pips with their great expectations was morally superior to today's, or that we had a superior sense of our primary allegiance. We simply were students of the sixties who did not see beyond a horizon of the single loyalty of the "organization man." When seen in the new context of what I should like to call today's "postmodern professionalism" in academia, the new generation emerges as no less responsible to the multiple communities and constellations of their professional engagement. But the ordering of the allegiances seems rearranged. Reverberations from the shadowy subtext underlying the particular questions asked by those smart candidates, newly exiled from the graduate program that was their Eden, disclose a drive to know how the university they might join would support them in their work, that is to say, their research, writing, and professional activities beyond the walls of their classrooms in face-to-face meeting with their students!

When I finished six years as chair in 1995, I wondered whether there was any truth to my impression about professionalism and its centrifugal impact at the local level where we teach and work while, at the same time, we constitute the various professions and disciplines that exert those pressures that can pull us apart. It also struck me, and still does, that the further irony is the fact that for virtually all faculty it is the university that continues to provide our primary financial means of support as we shift our primary allegiance to our respective professions. After completing a return as chair (1999–2002), I have little doubt that a significant shift has taken place in the primary allegiance among the newer generations of PhD's—a shift in where their first loyalties lie, from the university community where they teach, toward the wider disciplinary community that lies beyond the walls and halls of their home institutions, beyond the students and colleagues they engage weekly, if not daily, in the concrete lifeworld of their university. Four episodes offer a window onto this conviction.

The first was my reading of Mark Schwehn's insightful *Exiles from Eden*, which opens [by] recalling a seminar meeting of faculty

colleagues at the University of Chicago.[1] The group gathered that year
to examine aspects of the professionalization of the social sciences.
It was just after tax-filing time, so while waiting for all to arrive and
in line with the seminar's theme, one of those present asked each to
state what he or she had listed under the heading "occupation" on the
tax form. One after another reported writing "sociologist," "anthro-
pologist," "historian," and the like. Schwehn recounts his feeling of
alienation at the "combination of mild alarm and studied astonish-
ment" exhibited by his colleagues at his disclosure that he had listed
as his occupation "college teacher." Schwehn's opening pages immediately resonated with me, and the rest of this insightful exploration
of the distinctive tensions within an academic vocation for individuals
of religious faith assured me that my thinking about professionalism's
pull on our allegiances, especially for those at Jesuit schools, was not
misguided.

As the second episode occurred, I found myself understanding it
in light of Schwehn's work. It was in 1997 when I asked, one might
even say "pushed," my chair to consider the idea of what I called
a postdoctoral teaching fellowship. The idea was to address the
needs of the undergraduate core curriculum in a way that solved a
number of problems due to an increasing use of adjuncts to cover
core courses: availability of teachers to the students, exploitation
of adjuncts, and increasing professional demands on non-tenured
faculty. The department faculty decided to treat this as a "prestige"
postdoctoral appointment. They also decided to conduct the search
and hiring for the "best" candidate out there on the normal job market. That is, we announced the position and called for applications
in order to interview at the American Philosophical Association
meeting in December, just as we did for tenure-track, ranked faculty
positions. What was to serve the teaching needs in our core philosophy courses had been named a prestigious-sounding postdoctoral
fellowship, raising candidates' expectations of something more than
teaching core courses. The top three or four candidates, one after the
other, asked about prospects for teaching advanced courses, and even
a graduate course in their specialty, as well as the queries about travel

and research support. Thus, it was no surprise to me that among the top candidates, one after the other declined our offer. In fact, we failed to appoint any of our top five candidates. It was an interesting lesson in the new professionalism. Guided by Schwehn and my previous experience as chair, I learned that it was not simply a question of loyalty to Fordham or the profession. Rather, it was a question of how to bring together the interests of each in a mutually beneficial way. Today, adjusting to the new context, our postdoctoral teaching fellows program is in its third year, to the mutual benefit of Fordham's undergraduate students, our own graduate students, and other recent Ph.D.'s, as well as the philosophy profession at large.

The third episode illustrates how the profession transforms our home institutions. Rather than the "old" sabbatical leave, Fordham has a Faculty Fellowship system for which one must submit a plan of proposed research and writing for a semester or year released from teaching. It is not automatic, but the advantage is that one can apply every four years. Until recently only tenured faculty were eligible to apply. That "old" eligibility requirement reflected a sense that non-tenured faculty—as probationary—were not full members of the community, nor were they expected to publish like those who had release time from teaching. As the faculty, as well as deans, have come to require more research and publication for tenure, two years ago our faculty senate recommended that the board of trustees extend eligibility for a faculty fellowship to non-tenured faculty. Recognizing the state of the academic profession, the board approved this change. Finally, there has emerged in the past ten years or so a proliferation of graduate student conferences and journals with an ever-growing expectation that a graduate student will have presented papers at professional conferences, will have published at least one or two articles and some book reviews. All this before the dissertation is completed and defended. The question is not whether such widespread activity should be judged as premature, or even arrogant, as it might have been in the past. Rather, the question is how this new environment to which graduate students must adapt orients their loyalties. And what does this portend for the Jesuit university?

Professionalization within a Postmodern Horizon

In the mid-1960s, under financial constraints from their universities and challenges from a new generation of Jesuits more focused on a faith and justice ministry, Jesuit communities transferred fiduciary responsibility and legal authority to independent boards of trustees. No doubt Vatican II's call for a vigorous role for the laity and a new generation of successful, well-educated American Catholics made such a change conceivable. Though there were many Jesuits on those boards, the new configuration changed, albeit slowly, the culture of the boards from clerical to professional. For the lay members were lawyers and doctors, leaders in education and business, authors, and even actors. They were professionals who introduced a new perspective, professionalism, in directing the Catholic university to enter the mainstream of American higher education. By the mid seventies a more research-oriented, professional model[2] that was "religion blind" often guided the hiring and tenure of faculty. Its objectivist dimension—that of knowledge as value-neutral theory tested by independent facts—seemed especially appropriate to the professional conduct of academics in the business of disciplined, disinterested inquiry into truth.

The Jesuit university's appropriation of the professional model may now be seen as ironic. As Vatican II was opening the church to a modern world, releasing the Catholic university from its defensive posture toward modernity, in the twilight new thinkers led an intellectual movement mounting an epochal critique of modernity. The American Catholic university was catching up with the Enlightenment as it was waning. The irony here is double. For I believe a distinctively intellectual factor, postmodern thought, has worked unwittingly in consort with a growing professionalism to produce what I called a postmodern professionalism in academia. There seems to be a dynamic, reciprocal relationship between publication and specialization that mutually calls forth more of the one from the other. The profession's pressure to contribute, usually through research or scholarship that results in publications, demands more differentiation in respect to the subject investigated and thereby further specialization. This in turn generates differentiation of disciplines into new sub-disciplines and on occasion new disciplines, spawning new organizations or professional associations that may often result in new journals, association proceedings, and other venues that offer the fledgling academic professional many opportunities to publish the products of the work they have really been trained to do—research. It is not surprising that universities and colleges have pursued this Weberian direction, for it is the model of the graduate school under which most new academics have been formed. It is, in Schwehn's metaphor, the Eden from which the young, newly trained professional—just as she has proven herself—is exiled. Accordingly, they seek to return by seeking participation in the professional communities as extensions of their respective Edens.

Another outcome, perhaps better called "fallout," of this process of professionalized specialization and specialized professions is the fragmentation of a commonly shared discourse that, in its turn, weakens the university as an academic community eventually to the stage where no center holds.[3] This is most manifest by the virtual disappearance of a common core curriculum at too many universities and colleges, and a correlate weakening in many Jesuit schools. Of course, a decrease in the core curriculum permits more space for an increase of the requirements for the major. It effectively invites "outside" disciplinary and professional organizations to enact more demands on the major for accreditation.

A corresponding growth in the professionalization of administration across the university—in academic matters (from admission to graduation), in athletics, in student life, in alumni/ae affairs and other extracurricular areas—has only reinforced the transformation through its own legitimation of what might be described as an ideology of professionalization. In its way, C. P. Snow's prescient concern about the threat that the "two cultures"[4] posed for our thinking and willing anticipated in a vague way the fragmentation in our thinking and willing that is manifest in current postmodern critiques of modernity's reason. More recently, George Grant has articulated this fragmentation as the modern multiversity wherein thinking has devolved into scholarship, which has further devolved into research production.[5] The correlate loss of shared discourse inhibits conversation about what is thought and by whom (consider the disappearance of the author, the self, etc.). Dialogue that engages across the departments, sometimes even within departments, and within the colleges declines. When research output within strictly defined disciplinary boundaries becomes an end it itself, the university as a place for thinking through a common discourse cannot hold together. At best it is a multiversity!

One possible response is to resort to the ideal of the pursuit of truth and counter that each discipline's research results are for the purpose of getting closer to the truth of its respective subject matter in its distinctive way. The serious problem with this is that recent philosophy and sociology of science has made persuasive arguments that this is not the case in either the theory or the practice of science. Moreover, the postmodern discourse occurring in the academy has unveiled the "truth" that there may be a critical mass of the faculty who do not believe in a reasonable, sharable truth, even as a pursuable ideal. In its discourse, power replaces truth, and Thrasymachus's challenge to Socrates at the beginning of the *Republic*, that "might makes right," is transformed into a new challenge of "might makes truth." Sometimes it appears that it, the modern multiversity, is what we are; and it is about power—sometimes competing, sometimes conflicting, and sometimes cooperating power of the administration, the schools, the departments, and the various faculties. It also seems that this power is transferred through faculty and administrators to their respective, various professional organizations—the American Bar Association, the Association to Advance Collegiate Schools of Business, the American Philosophical Association, Middle States, the Association of Jesuit Colleges and Universities, and so on—which then direct it back upon us only to pull the university apart. If thinking has devolved in the modern multiversity as Grant has described it, can teaching's devolution from *educare* [literally, "to lead or draw out"] to professional preparation, to technical training be far behind? Most recently, the former president of Harvard, Derek Bok, has argued that the widespread commercialization of higher education in a market economy seriously threatens its integrity.[6] If he is right, the university devolves further into a marketplace where interpersonal relationships last no longer than the relationship between seller and buyer. In such a market, faculty act more and more like professional athletes, with the strongest professional academics acting like "free agents" selling their expertise to the highest bidder. For both professionals it is business, all business.

The Road Ahead

Since the mid nineties more and more universities have turned to address their identity and mission in seeming recognition of the challenges of the multiversity, of the divergent, sometimes competing interests of professional disciplines whose ends lie outside the center of one's university. Today, as more and more universities turn to considerations of identity and mission, Fathers Joseph Appleyard and Howard Gray . . . argue that the Jesuit university has also moved beyond the "professional model" to that of a "mission model." It has restored talk of Jesuit and Catholic identity, but in an environment of academic and administrative professionals with differentiated roles and distinct tasks, including an office of identity and mission. Appleyard and Gray further assert that in the current stage "loyalty is not to an organization or to a professional guild but is self directed."[7] They suggest that such direction is toward "what it means to be a 'whole person.'" But the very question of a whole—whether the whole of knowledge, or the whole of a community, or the whole of self—is what has been rendered problematic by postmodern critiques for many academics and intellectuals outside the university.

This problematic—whether the pursuit of any whole is tenable even as an ideal—coupled with the centrifugal forces of professionalism threatens the ideal of the whole as embodied in a community of scholars teaching students. As such, it places the Ignatian ideal of *cura personalis* at risk. Might we turn to another Ignatian ideal, that of the *magis* or "the more," to find the road from here? I suggest this is so only if we seek it in colleagues and students who manifest it in a living engagement of the academic community. Can such colleagues be found? In my own department two colleagues immediately come to mind, James Marsh and Merold Westphal. They are outstanding scholars, professionally active, excellent teachers, and true citizens of Fordham University. As such they give the lie to what I have said above, unless you understand that it is not a question of citizenship in either one's university or one's profession or one's religion. Rather, it is a question of how to navigate the new terrain of multiple allegiances in exemplary ways. By their example they teach many how to be more through multiple loyalties.

The upshot is that in the current intellectual milieu, professional allegiances and complex organizational structures make it all the more difficult to cultivate a sense of intellectually meaningful citizenship within a university. A time when Jesuit institutions are renewing mission and identity and navigating the new terrain of multiple loyalties distinctively challenges the Ignatian charism of *cura personalis*, finding God in all things, and the *magis*. When understood in the larger context of the Catholic mind, as one of faith seeking understanding, the Jesuit university as Jesuit can only continue as a community where faith and reason seek mutual growth in dialogue punctuated by moments of relative integration. This means if the Jesuit ideal of *cura personalis* is not to be an empty abstraction that diminishes into a marketing slogan, we as professional teachers and scholars must always remain in real presence to our colleagues and students within and outside our universities.

NOTES

1. Mark R. Schwehn, *Exiles from Eden: Religion and the Academic Vocation in America* (New York: Oxford University Press, 1993).

2. My characterization of an apologetic followed by a professional model parallels the developmental stages of a control model followed by the professional model of the Catholic university, in J. A. Appleyard, SJ, and Howard Gray, SJ, "Tracking the Mission and Identity Question," *Conversations* 18 (Fall 2000).

3. Recall Dr. [Frank] Rhodes' keynote address at [Assembly '89], Georgetown University ("The Mission and Ministry of Jesuits in Higher Education," *America* July 29–August 5, 1989), delivered to what was the largest gathering of faculty and administrators, Jesuit and lay, in Jesuit higher education in the United States. As he lauded the Jesuit institutions for retaining a center while most of higher education in America had abdicated any center, he exhorted us in Jesuit higher education to sustain a center and thereby show others a way to revive one.

4. C. P. Snow, *The Two Cultures and the Scientific Revolution* (Cambridge: Cambridge University Press, 1959).

5. "Faith and the Multiversity," in George P. Grant, *Technology and Justice*, (Notre Dame, IN: University of Notre Dame Press, 1986).

6. See Anthony Marx's remarks on Derek Bok, *Universities in the Marketplace: The Commercialization of Higher Education* (Princeton, NJ: Princeton University Press, 2003) in the *New York Times*, Saturday, May 17, 2003.

7. Appleyard and Gray, 13.

Further Reading

In June 1999, ten years after the historic "Assembly '89" at Georgetown, St. Joseph's University in Philadelphia hosted "Jesuit Education 21." With three hundred participants, this national conference "on the future of Jesuit Higher education" was much smaller than "Assembly '89" but more representative; lay women and men outnumbered Jesuits. Two addresses in particular from that conference are relevant to "the current problematic":

> Peter Steinfels, "A Mission for Jesuit Higher Education in the Twenty-first Century," in *Jesuit Education 21: Conference Proceedings on the Future of Jesuit Higher Education*, ed. Martin Tripole, SJ (Philadelphia: St. Joseph's University Press, 2000), 12–23.

> Brennan O'Donnell, "From Omaha to Philadelphia and Beyond: Jesuit-Lay Cooperation in Twenty-first Century Higher Education," in *Jesuit Education 21: Conference Proceedings on the Future of Jesuit Higher Education*, ed. Martin Tripole, SJ (Philadelphia: St. Joseph's University Press, 2000), 79–90.

Both of these speakers in 1999 saw the situation as somewhat encouraging, while emphasizing the long and difficult road ahead. Steinfels, university professor and co-director of the Fordham University Center on Religion and Culture, *New York Times* religion columnist, and author of *A People Adrift*, spoke of the progress made but also of the "feeling that these [mission] efforts remain like beachheads, still isolated conquests that threaten to remain just that and never coalesce into a breakout that would establish secure territory for the colleges and universities to flourish," both as academic institutions and as institutions that operate with a clear religious mission. O'Donnell, at the time professor of English at Loyola College in Maryland and editor of the semi-annual *Conversations on Jesuit Higher Education* and now dean of Fordham College at Rose Hill, likewise recognized gains since 1988, when the first "Conference on Collaboration" (in the ministry of Jesuit higher education) took place at Creighton University in Omaha. But he saw the most important challenge to further development as "getting the faculty—or at least a critical mass of it—involved fully *as* faculty":

> Conversations about Jesuit identity can go on a long time without any-one mentioning issues such as the Jesuit university's opportunity—or responsibility—to be a center for scholarly inquiry into (and in) the Catholic intellectual tradition, or its ability to offer intellectual guid-ance and scholarly support in the dialogue of faith and culture, or to function as a beacon in the American intellectual scene for powerful new *thinking* on issues of justice, or to be a place where some of the more relativistic, anti-religious, and even nihilistic recent trends in the humanities are challenged and the ideals of educating for human freedom unapologetically upheld. . . . The greatest shortcoming . . . [is the] relative failure thus far to challenge a majority of the faculty to think of their day-to-day teaching and scholarly life as shaped by their being at a Jesuit institution.

A wider perspective on faculty—not just on those from religious-affiliated schools—can be found in *Meaning and Spirituality in the Lives of College Faculty: A Study of Values, Authenticity, and Stress*, by Alexander W. Astin and Helen S. Astin (Los Angeles: Higher Education Research Institute [UCLA], 1999).

Principles

Introduction

In this, the longest section of the reader, there are nine selections of various lengths that try to show what makes Jesuit education "tick." What are its characteristics, its philosophy, its goals, its "way of proceeding"?

For openers, the late Robert A. Mitchell, SJ, who was president of the U.S. Jesuits and of two Jesuit schools, presents "Five Traits of Jesuit Education." And John Bennett of Quinnipiac University and Elizabeth Dreyer of Fairfield University, in "Spiritualities of—Not at—the University," paint a portrait of university spirituality in its negative element as marked by "insistent individualism" and offer an antidote in hospitality complemented by self-knowledge and asceticism.

As mentioned in the introduction to section 1, Jesuit General Congregation 34 (1995) stressed justice, inculturation, and inter-religious dialogue as key characteristics of Jesuit ministry for the twenty-first century. But the congregation also addressed itself to the particular circumstances of university life, and in the piece "Jesuits and University Life," it urges "that both the noun *university* and the adjective *Jesuit* always remain fully honored." Philosopher-theologian Michael J. Buckley, SJ, formerly of Boston College and now of Santa Clara University, explores two hallmarks of Jesuit education in "Education Marked by the Sign of the Cross," an address given at the inauguration of a new president at Spring Hill College in Mobile in 1990. First is concern with faith, that is, with the alienation from God of most American intellectual and professional culture. Second is concern with justice, that is, with the isolation of middle- and upper-class students from the vast suffering of humanity.

Three documents from the Society of Jesus follow. The first is "The Service of Faith and the Promotion of Justice in Jesuit Higher

Education," a major address given to a national audience at Santa Clara University by Jesuit general superior Peter-Hans Kolvenbach in October 2000 (for a detailed summary, see "Whole Persons of Solidarity" in *Do You Speak Ignatian?*). The second, Kolvenbach's "The Service of Faith in a Religiously Pluralistic World: The Challenge for Jesuit Higher Education," was delivered at the annual Xavier University Academic Day in October 2006 as part of the university's 175th anniversary celebration, but was intended for a wider public, as the subtitle indicates. The third, "Communal Reflection on the Jesuit Mission in Higher Education: A Way of Proceeding," published by the American Jesuits as an invitation to dialogue, is purposely more open ended. "The following characteristics and the process they invite are meant to enable each institution to locate its own sense of mission: Dedication to Human Dignity from a Catholic/Jesuit Perspective; Reverence for and Ongoing Reflection on Human Experience; Creative Companionship with Colleagues; Focused Care for Students; and Well-Educated Justice and Solidarity." Compare these five characteristics with Mitchell's five traits.

In a recent *America* magazine essay, New York Jesuit Dean Brackley, with his third-world perspective from El Salvador, goes right to the point and proclaims seven higher standards that ought to mark the Catholic (and therefore the Jesuit) university:

1. Strive "to *understand the real world*. . . . Many students graduate from college with little understanding of homelessness, abortion, or their own country's military adventures."
2. "*Focus on the big questions* . . . questions about the drama of life and death, about injustice and liberation, good and evil, grace and sin."
3. "*Free us from bias*. . . . Seeking truth includes uncovering hidden interests inside us and outside us. . . . It is naïve to suppose that reason alone will take us to it. . . . The pure reason paradigm [model] overlooks the need for moral conversion. Cognitive liberation requires personal change."
4. "*Help students discover their vocation in life—above all, their vocation to love and serve*. . . .*"

5. Diversity "must *include economic diversity*. Promote a culture of simplicity on campus; maximize scholarships based on need; include $50 million for scholarships in the next capital campaign."
6. "*Truth in* advertising. . . . We should fear the future if students are graduating with first-class training in, say, economics and only a First Communion or a *Newsweek* understanding of faith."
7. "*Speak to the wider world* . . . [and] demonstrate the courage to express uncomfortable truths, truths that may clash with public opinion but that are also necessary to safeguard the authentic good of society" (John Paul II, *Ex Corde Ecclesiae*, No. 32).

An apt conclusion to this part is the synthetic paper by Howard Gray, SJ, "Soul Education: An Ignatian Priority." Gray explains that Ignatian "soul education" involves appropriation, or "a reading of the textual tradition that presumes you want to enter into its experience"; is about the "social [justice] ramifications of learning"; and "reconciles a plurality of experiences within a Catholic commitment."

Understanding the Terminology: Suggested Readings from *Do You Speak Ignatian?*

- Ignatian/Jesuit Vision
- The Service of Faith and the Promotion of Justice
- Men and Women for Others/Whole Persons of Solidarity for the Real World
- *Cura Personalis*
- Arrupe, Pedro
- Kolvenbach, Peter-Hans

Five Traits of Jesuit Education

Robert A. Mitchell, SJ

From *Boston College Magazine*, 1988

The first characteristic of Jesuit institutions is a passion for quality. Excellence is important. This does not mean that Jesuit colleges have never had inferior programs, but it does mean that the institution—be it agricultural school, engineering, business or liberal arts college— has, in every age, sought good education, respected by those who know the field. Jesuit institutions respond well to a remark of Father General Peter-Hans Kolvenbach: only excellence is apostolic. Because of this, the schools set demanding standards for both students and faculty.

A second characteristic of Jesuit colleges and universities is the study of the humanities and the sciences no matter what specializations may be offered. These institutions want their students to be able to think and speak and write; to know something about history, literature, and art; to have their minds expanded by philosophy and theology; and to have some understanding of math and sciences. They want students prepared for living as well as for working—to have a liberal education, if you will. The kind of education I suggest is even more important today than it has ever been, despite the demand for increased technological training in today's world. We need engineers who have read Shakespeare and computer scientists who understand the history and roots of our civilization.

A third characteristic of Jesuit education has been a preoccupation with questions of ethics and values for both the personal and professional lives of graduates. Family values, personal integrity, and business ethics have always been important. In recent years, moreover, this characteristic has taken on added dimensions. Spurred by papal encyclicals and the strong social teaching of recent popes and our own American bishops, Jesuit institutions have tried to focus attention on the great questions of justice and fairness that confront our age: economic problems, racism, and unemployment in our own country; peace and war and the proliferation of arms; and poverty and oppression in the third world—to cite some examples. These are not easy questions, nor do they have any certain and universally accepted answers. But Jesuit institutions today feel compelled by their tradition to raise these questions for their students, not through sloganeering and political maneuvering, but in a way that is proper for higher education: through learning, research, reflection, and imagination.

A fourth characteristic of Jesuit education is the importance it gives to religious experience. It does this best, I suspect, for its Catholic students. However, especially in this ecumenical age, it tries to open this horizon for all its students, whatever their religious persuasion. Religious experience is important and it needs to be integrated into the education process so that a student has the opportunity to grow in both knowledge and faith, in both belief and learning; indeed belief can often sharpen and focus a mind. Prayer and liturgy are no threat to knowledge; they help form an education community in the fullest sense of the word.

Finally, related to this last is another characteristic of Jesuit education. It is person-centered. No matter how large or complex the institution, the individual is important and given as much personal attention as humanly possible, both in and out of the classroom. I believe that the reason for this specific attention to the individual is that for many in these institutions, teaching or administration is much more than a job—indeed, more than a profession. It is a vocation. This is true not only for members of religious orders but for so many lay men and women of different religious backgrounds who look on their work of teaching or administration as sharing in God's work, as ministry to others.

Spiritualities of—Not at—the University

John B. Bennett and Elizabeth A. Dreyer

From *Theoforum*, 2002

I. Introduction

Academics love to study everything, except ourselves. We study the ethics of business, politics, journalism, medicine, and more, but rarely do we reflect critically on our own personal and institutional behaviors. Likewise, though we are now appropriately beginning to study the spiritualities of various communities and movements, most of us have yet to attend to the spiritualities of our own academic callings and communities. As a contribution to this needed discussion, we propose elements of a spirituality for university life. After reviewing some problems of the reigning, all-too-dominant university spirituality, we offer an analysis of hospitality as a foundational virtue for the academy, followed by discussion of two related virtues: self-knowledge and asceticism.

Three presuppositions need to be elucidated. The first is the self-implicating nature of the intellectual life. The vocation of the academic—a commitment to the pursuit of truth—should, unless blocked, have an effect on the scholar as person. We ought to raise questions about the biologist who uses her leisure time to pollute the environment or abuse animals, the ethicist who cheats on his income tax, or the marketing professor who is consistently deceptive in her presentation of self. Contemporary philosophical, methodological, and pedagogical insights question whether the object of study can be neatly separated from social location, gender, or ethnic background. Not only are teaching and research influenced by one's identity and one's questions, but they also have an effect on who we become.

Second, we acknowledge the primacy of community. The identity of the individual is derivative, emerging out of implication in a variety of communities. The originating human experience is that of a deeply symbiotic relationship in the womb of the mother—a relationship of incredible intimacy in which the fetus shares the very physical, alimentary, and vascular structures of another human being. This initial community broadens to family, home, neighborhood, and world, all of which shape and enliven individual identity. The idea that someone can literally "pull oneself up by the boot straps" is simply false. Our accomplishments are never totally our own, and our behaviors can never finally be separated from effects on others and on the world.

Third, we suggest that in any environment, but especially in an educational one, teachers function as models for their students. Surveys of past and present students consistently confirm that in evaluating their academic careers, they mention the person of the teacher, not the subject matter, as the most important factor. Thus, in the academy, we must attend to who we are as well as to what we know and how we communicate that knowledge.

Each of these points provides a context for exploring a spirituality of the academy. Our vocation is an integral part of our identity and cannot be artificially cordoned off. The work at which we spend significant parts of our lives has an impact on our growth and development as human beings in intellectual, affective, spiritual, and social ways. In turn, this development of altruistic or selfish attitudes and behaviors influences what we study and teach, how we study and teach, and the kinds of outcomes that result from this studying and teaching. The academic calling at its best has a transformative effect on the practitioner. Engaged, authentic inquiry brings insight and sensitivity to what it means to be a human being, to the quest to be virtuous, and to the desire to make the world a better place for all its inhabitants.

We turn now to some dispositions, values, and practices that block the development of a life-giving university spirituality.

2. Negative Elements of University Spirituality

Insightful critics recognize the negative elements of what might be called a dominant spirituality of academics and their institutions today—a spirituality characterized by excessive individualism, what we call "insistent individualism." These critics decry the energies expended by individuals and institutions alike upon self-advancement and self-protection. At the individual level these behaviors contribute to the fierce battles over small stakes for which the academy is often known.[1] This spirituality also emphasizes teaching at the expense of learning, and both faculty and institutional authority are connected with controlling or unilateral rather than relational power. Fragmentation and isolation, as well as an agonistic culture, are typical consequences.[2]

Among faculty and administrators, two types of insistent individualists are common. The one is the aggressive, even abrasive individual bent upon self-promotion through any means necessary. Often the means are selected to co-opt parts of the regnant ethos. Thus, these individuals may appear loyal to institutional projects, but their real loyalty is to themselves, and others are used to serve this end. Aggressive individualists are skilled in intellectual combat and tenaciously pursue its fruits—credits, credentials, fame. Insistent individualists of the second type are less blatant or conspicuous in their self-promotion. They are more civil, but their pursuit of the common good is still in distant second place. Rarely will they challenge the excesses of the more aggressive individualist. For them, self-protection is the best avenue to self-promotion.

Of whatever stripe, insistent individualists often distinguish sharply between the personal and the professional. Personal identity is kept sequestered from work as a professional, usually with unfortunate consequences, particularly in teaching. Parker Palmer makes the point nicely in reporting about a student's inability to describe her good teachers because of their many differences, whereas she could easily describe her bad teachers: "their words float somewhere in front of their faces like the balloon speech in cartoons." Reflecting on this image, Palmer and the student agreed that

> with bad teaching, there is a disconnect between the stuff being taught and the self who is teaching it. . . . There is a distance, a coldness, a lack of community because in a secularized academy, we don't have the connective tissue of the sacred to hold this apparent fragmentation and chaos together.[3]

At the organizational level, institutions are often bent upon comparative success in ways that rival even the most aggressive and determined insistent individualist. Thoughtful and deeply knowledgeable critics like Alexander Astin have drawn our attention to the penchant of many institutions to pursue reputation and resources as the most effective way to achieve academic "excellence." Being at the top of comparative rankings and attracting the best and most academically meritorious students are judged more important than enhancing individual student talents and learning. That is, being perceived as smart is deemed a more important institutional value than actually developing student talent.[4]

Another way of describing the spirituality of much of today's academy is that "it is a culture of fear." Indeed, it seems to be fear of change and of loss of control that is largely behind insistent individualism and propels it. The "other" is seen as a competitor, challenging our identity and our values, rather than as a colleague presenting opportunities to grow and to pursue a common good. We cultivate fear rather than respect. Palmer writes: "In academic culture, I am carefully buffered, carefully walled off, through systematic disrespect, from all of those things that might challenge me, break me, open me, and change me. It is a fearful culture."[5]

In the next section of this essay, we offer an alternative to these unattractive hallmarks of too many academic settings by focusing on several key virtues. The topic of virtue has enjoyed renewed prominence in recent years, due, in part, to a perception that our society seems singularly lacking in this arena. The academy is no exception.[6]

3. Hospitality: The Foundational Virtue

Hospitality is central to healthy academic spiritualities at both the individual and the organizational levels. Indeed, hospitality is a cardinal academic value and virtue, central to the moral, intellectual, and spiritual dimensions of our work as academics. We know this is a bold statement in light of academy's penchant to neglect or abuse this virtue. By hospitality we mean radical openness in sharing with and receiving from the other. At the individual level, practicing hospitality means inviting and practicing reciprocity. At the organizational level, hospitality means creating internal structures that promote cooperation rather than destructive competition. And it means seeking collaboration with neighboring and peer institutions.

Hospitality is often taken to mean a superficial congeniality. Theologian Henri Nouwen notes that for most of us, hospitality suggests "tea parties, bland conversations, and a general atmosphere of coziness."[7] For academics it may also suggest that part of the curriculum concerned with hotel management. Because of this lamentable reduction of a term that points to so much more than this, hospitality is overlooked as an academic virtue. But this truncated view needs to be broadened. We need to take up Nouwen's challenge that "if there is any concept worth restoring to its original depth and evocative potential, it is the concept of hospitality."[8]

Hospitality as openness—welcoming, receiving from, and sharing with the other—ought to be conspicuous as an educational virtue, both of individuals and of institutions. As a root metaphor, it ought to trump such alternatives as education as production. Hospitality is deeply rooted in the Western tradition, both in Greek Homeric influences and in our rich Judeo-Christian inheritance. Homer's *Odyssey* reminds us of the importance of extending and receiving compassion and caring in the journey of life. Both Telemakhos and Odysseus were sustained by hospitality—extended by others because they too had been in need, or knew themselves likely to be. In Homer's view, hospitality stems from our common human condition.[9] Likewise, the Scriptures of both Old and New Testaments, as well as later tradition (especially the monastic communities, the Rule of St. Benedict being particularly paradigmatic), reinforce the importance of practicing hospitality toward the other—independent of personal status or appearance—because we have all first been extended hospitality ourselves by God.

Practicing openness to the other, the new and the unfamiliar—as well as the critical review of the familiar and the taken for granted—underlies and makes possible the liberation that pursuit of knowledge promises. It requires openness toward, not suspicion and distrust of, the other. Genuine hospitality has little to do with the exercise of power as control or manipulation. As Nouwen notes, the point of practicing hospitality "is not to change people, but to offer them space where change can take place . . . hospitality is not a subtle invitation to adopt the life style of the host, but the gift of a chance for the guest to find his own."[10]

One dimension of hospitable education to which Nouwen directs us is recognizing that education is for individuals, not for generic persons. In Nouwen's words, a hospitable educator works toward "the creation of space where students and teachers can enter into a fearless communication with each other and allow their respective life experiences to be their primary and most valuable source of growth and maturation."[11] To practice hospitality is to allow the other to grow without imposing our own personal requirements or expectations. It is to invite others into our community while also opening ourselves to their distinctive perspectives. To be genuinely hospitable and open to others is to attend to them.

Simone Weil reminds us of what it means to "attend" to the other. It involves holding in abeyance our own positions in order truly to hear the other.

> Attention consists of suspending our thought, leaving it detached, empty, and ready to be penetrated by the object; it means holding in

our minds, within reach of this thought, but on a lower level and not in contact with it, the diverse knowledge we have acquired.[12]

No matter how different the other is, he or she offers the possibility of enriching us—if we make the effort to attend to the other and to put ourselves in the other's place. The point is to understand the other not on our terms, but on his or her terms. Like Simone Weil, Parker Palmer suggests that this requires what he calls "the discipline of displacement," that is, holding one's own position in abeyance.[13]

In ancient times, practicing hospitality meant offering food and shelter to the other in need. In today's academy, it means offering intellectual resources to the other, regardless of the likelihood of reciprocity. Intellectual hospitality is marked by the fundamental value attached to inquiry: all are welcomed and social differences are transcended. It is also often marked by a sense of one's vulnerability as an educator. Professors share the experience of offering personally precious ideas to audiences that run the gamut from being receptive, to "I dare you to interest me," to being downright hostile. Hospitality suggests that knowing is a kind of stewardship rather than an act of possession.

Granted, to practice hospitality requires work and is by definition always partial. However, hospitality is life-giving in that it takes us beyond the routine, the narrow, and the dull. It takes us past and out of the fear of failure—of repeating past disappointments, remaining dull, or being hopelessly ensnarled in discrimination—respecting gender, race, class, ideology, or academic status. It takes us beyond the conflict and the indifference that saps the vitality of the academy. We are describing the ideal—our aspirations. By definition, the ideal can never be fully met. But unless we embrace, and allow ourselves to be guided by, these ideals, we condemn ourselves to the spirituality of insistent individualism.

It is important to note that spiritualities of higher education will vary dramatically from large public research universities, to small, religiously sponsored liberal arts colleges, to seminaries. However, these differences cannot deter us from the universal responsibility to establish and practice an ethics that encompasses all of higher education—an ethics that includes creating an hospitable ethos and attending to the common good.[14] In the following section of this essay, we discuss two additional virtues that complement and fill out the practice of hospitality in the academy: self-knowledge and asceticism. While we consider these virtues to be constitutive elements of any academic spirituality, we discuss them here in the context of a Christian college, university, or seminary.

4. Hospitality Extended: Self-knowledge and Asceticism

Self-knowledge

Recent discussions on virtue have turned from preoccupation with rules and acts toward analysis of character, attending to the *person* who acts and his or her context. We too argue that virtues develop within the unitive story of a person's entire life and intend a common good. Specific expressions of virtues and values are particular to a given age, culture, or religion; but, in some sense, all virtue reflects and points to the ideal of human fulfillment and well-being. Virtues are a constituent element of the spiritual journey and are thus always developing, never completed. Academics need to guard against the sentiment that vigilance and growth are no longer required. Indeed, it is salutary to reflect both on one's desire to live in the truth and on the vehicles one has to gain access to the truth about oneself.

For instance, in the Christian spiritual tradition, self-knowledge is central. This virtue has special relevance for academics whose vocation is to pursue the truth. At the beginning of her spiritual masterpiece *The Interior Castle*, Teresa of Ávila writes, "It is a shame and unfortunate that through our own fault we don't understand ourselves or know who we are."[15] Teresa wants her readers to be clear about some very basic elements of Christian identity before they enter too deeply into their spiritual journeys. She is not suggesting that one's identity has to be all worked out before one begins, but she does see the need for a certain kind of self-knowledge—what might be called the "first base" of the spiritual life. Without this basic awareness of self, the journey and the destination are likely to be skewed.

This sense of self is theologically grounded in the concepts of creation and sin. Three key elements to this Christian identity are awareness that one is a creature not the Creator; that one is a sinner, not perfect; and that one is made in the image and likeness of God, created with an unimaginable capacity to participate in the divine life. To acknowledge and embrace these attributes is simply to live in the truth. To deny them is to live in a world of falsehood and illusion (1 John 1:8). The belief that humanity is fashioned in the image and likeness of God (Gen. 1:26) links knowledge of self and knowledge of God in a reciprocal fashion. Among others, Catherine of Siena almost never speaks of one without the other.[16]

The fruits of this threefold knowledge of self are several. To begin, this knowledge of self is important simply because it is true. But that is not all. To acknowledge oneself as creature leads to gratitude. To accept that one is like God is to admit that it is possible to love much, to forgive much, to practice both ordinary and heroic virtue—*in the academy.* Indeed, one is invited to imitate God, to develop and nurture dispositions and behaviors that we attribute to deity.

On the other hand, awareness of failure to be godly leads to humility, an important aspect of the virtue of self-knowledge, albeit one not much in vogue these days. For an academic, whose calling involves being an "expert" in one's field, humility can be a particularly challenging virtue. Parker Palmer reminds us that "there is a great gulf between the way my ego wants to identify me, with its protective masks and self-serving fictions, and my true self."[17] With charity, humility has been a cornerstone of the Christian spiritual tradition and thus has been the subject of scores of spiritual treatises. It is defined in many ways, but some of the most accessible include "being down to earth about oneself," "being honest about oneself," and "a willingness to be who we truly are."[18] Humility also checks one's penchant for control.

In a post-Freudian world, this Christian anthropology has become linked with psychological concepts of the self. Psychoanalysis, for example, leads one through a process of introspection whose goal is self-knowledge, self-acceptance, self-control, and self-determination. Many in the wider population are now aware of the need to reflect on, and become engaged in, the process of self-appropriation: to name, celebrate, and use talents and gifts; to refrain from self-denigration or self-hate; to confront illusion and befriend our dark side; to examine motivations and negotiate inherited dispositions and behaviors. From different vantage points, Christian spirituality and psychology have a vested interest in distinguishing the false from the true self.

In the context of the university, these general norms for self-knowledge take on the flesh and blood of particular, historical settings. The sources of accurate self-knowledge are many. To begin, one can point to the relationship or disconnection between knowing something and living it. Society charges academics to explore, accumulate, understand, and disseminate knowledge. But knowing about something is not the same as appropriating or living out of that knowledge. It is an occupational hazard of the academy to think that it does. As noted above, to know a lot about morality is not the same thing as to live a moral life. To study the law is not equivalent to being just, although one may be deceived to think that it is. Thus, knowledge can provide an illusory sense of engagement in the good of the world. It can shield one from living, from getting one's hands dirty, from actually being engaged in a spiritual journey.

A second liability for the professoriat in the area of self-knowledge stems from a lack of checks and balances within the structures of university life. Mechanisms of the free market, while not perfect, can serve to prevent one segment of a community from engaging in autocratic behaviors or closing itself off from criticism. Professors can choose to open themselves to criticism from various parts of their environment, but usually after tenure they do not need to. Good administrators can invite or cajole, but they often have little structural leverage to insure that faculty members correct troublesome behaviors. Students are rarely in a position to offer genuine criticism. In terms of subject matter, they often do not know enough to be helpfully critical, and in terms of commenting on professors' attitudes and behaviors in and out of the classroom, students are part of a power arrangement that almost always precludes forthright communication about the instructor's dark side. In too many cases this setting nurtures the production of pseudo-accolades, offered by students who know how to play the game in order to protect their academic interests.

Another complication involves the often striking differences in perspective between faculty and other groups within the university. It is often the better part of wisdom to take some student complaints with a grain of salt. And board members with no background or experience in education can miss the mark on academic issues. But does this give us permission to dismiss all feedback? What are the mechanisms through which I can keep track of who I really am as a person and as a professional? Do I want to nurture dispositions that will allow me to "hear" and discern what I need to know about my attitudes and behaviors? These questions apply not only to individuals but to departments, divisions, schools, and the university as a whole.

Self-knowledge is closely linked to hospitality. The point of taking time to reflect honestly on one's inner life, values, and behaviors is not to enhance one's egoism and self-preoccupation. It is just the opposite. True knowledge of self bears fruit in relationship. This virtue reins in the need to be center stage, to exaggerate one's importance, to keep up defenses, to minimize the gifts of others so we can feel more valuable. Ironically, owning the truth about oneself can lead to the kind of self-forgetfulness that is able, in Simone Weil's terms, to truly "attend" to the other. Indeed, being honest about oneself is a way to honor and reverence the other. To engage honestly in the ongoing journey of self-knowledge is to prepare to receive and be received by the other in truth and love.

Love Starts Here

Asceticism

The term "asceticism" has its origins in the Greek idea of "exercise" or "training." This understanding gradually expanded to include not only physical training, but mental, spiritual, and ethical development as well. Through systematic, rigorous discipline, one could work toward excellence in virtue and holiness. Some form of spiritual asceticism—a voluntary, systematic program of self-discipline and self-denial—can be found in almost all religions. Practices include fasting, sexual abstinence, inflicting bodily pain, and solitude. Motivations for engaging in such practices might be purification, atonement for sin, avoidance of evil, or gaining access to spiritual realms through visions or extrasensory experiences.

The understanding of asceticism as the harsh denial of all sensual pleasure for the sake of higher spiritual states, motivated by anti-matter, anti-body dispositions, is undergoing reevaluation and transformation. In its place, asceticism may be seen as a way to deconstruct harmful, socially conditioned stereotypes of self in the interest of creating new, life-giving self-definition, marked by love, equality, and mutuality.[19] Ascetic practices can also serve to dismantle compulsive, addictive behaviors in favor of liberation and fullness of life—both sensual and intellectual—that have been buried beneath dulling, routinized patterns of living. Third, asceticism can be understood in relational, sociopolitical terms. Self-denial can result in enhanced sensitivity, compassion, and solidarity with the oppressed, leading to action on their behalf. In a more general vein, asceticism can be seen as a way to respond creatively to the suffering and stripping that is integral to daily life. Finally, asceticism can lead one to embrace living simply and acting energetically on behalf of our endangered ecosystem.

Most people also still think of asceticism in terms of things that we choose to do. But this is not the only, nor even the primary, way to understand this foundational aspect of the spiritual life. One does not need to live too long to discover that you do not have to go to Lent, because eventually Lent always comes to you. How can we think about this Lent that life brings, often unannounced and unanticipated? We suggest that the primary locus for asceticism is our normal (and not so normal!), everyday lives. What are some concrete examples of this kind of asceticism in the context of university life?

To begin, we return to our previous discussion about self-knowledge. The journey from illusion to truth is not an easy one—

whether this truth concerns ourselves, our professional activities, or our institutional affiliations. A commitment to discover the truth about oneself can be a rather rigorous form of asceticism. The tendency to see ourselves as better, more intelligent, more generous than others is a hallmark of the human condition. We create and maintain illusions as defense mechanisms against the gnawing fear that our feet may indeed be made of clay. In general, we like our illusions. They are familiar and comfortable and so we cling to them.

Academic asceticism involves soliciting honest feedback from colleagues and students. It means submitting research to the scrutiny of others who hold conflicting opinions. It involves working to create an atmosphere of trust and honesty in the classroom and engaging students in informal discussion about how things are going. These forms of asceticism involve relinquishing control as well as false images of ourselves. Desire for the truth leads one to engage in the painful stripping as layers of illusion are peeled away. We become willing to die to the old, egocentric self so that a new creation may emerge.

Another form of asceticism focuses on language, another key aspect of hospitality. Academics are skilled at the use of language. It is our job to be so. But this skill is often used to wound rather than to communicate or build up the other.[20] How often do we witness the "theatre" of faculty senate meetings, replete with inflated claims, empty rhetoric and posturing, the slash-and-burn techniques at professional gatherings, the know-it-all postures in the classroom? It is a form of asceticism both to refrain from violent and abusive language and to risk calling attention to it in order to stop it. Do we use tenure to empower us to risk telling the truth when this is difficult, or does it promote instead moral lethargy and narrow self-interest? An asceticism of language can lead us to offer the kind word instead of the cynical quip, to remain silent when this is appropriate, and to welcome and greet new as well as old faculty members and staff—find out who they are, marvel at their gifts, and express gratitude for their presence.

A third form of asceticism takes place in the classroom. We have already called attention to the stark vulnerability of standing year after year before thirty "I-dare-you-to-interest-me" twenty-year-olds. Academic spirituality involves prayerful reflection on this most central of university activities. Every conscientious teacher can recall experiences of "stripping" in the classroom: the favorite poem or novel that was received in stony silence; the appearance of the term "useless" on evaluations for a course into which one has put Herculean effort; low enrollments in a course that would lure and excite adult learners.

How does one evaluate, interpret, and respond to such diminishment? Acceptance, rather than anger, can be a way to begin. Encountering occasional affronts to one's dignity is an inescapable part of teaching young people, and keeping score or taking revenge is not a productive way to respond. Rather, the practice of asceticism calls for humility, forgiveness, compassion for the offenders, courage to go in and try again, humor, and even joy, to help us gain perspective in light of the larger canvases of life and world.

A final kind of academic asceticism can reshape one's attitudes toward the drudgery associated with university life: committee meetings, hundreds of papers to correct, teaching the same material year in and year out in fresh and creative ways, facing the ever-present blank page in one's research and writing efforts. It takes a great amount of care and discipline to develop a spirituality of the present moment, to focus on whatever is in front of me at the moment and give it as much attention as I can muster. This might mean contributing to make the meeting a better one, remembering that running a university requires meetings and students, acknowledging that there are people behind documents and institutional grids, and acknowledging the effort that colleagues put forward, even when you deem it less than successful. Heroic ascetic practices take the form of turning cynicism and complaining into acceptance, gratitude, and even joy in all aspects of one's work.

This way of embracing life's trials as integral to spiritual growth does not support the idea that suffering is "good for us." On the contrary, suffering is to be alleviated at every turn. Rather, the way of asceticism can lead us to experience the pain and suffering of human life in a new way and to discover ourselves in solidarity with those who suffer grievously across the globe. Ascetic practices invite us to see stripping experiences as sacred pieces of the mosaic of our journey to holiness. This vision of asceticism is overtly communal in its orientation and therefore has everything to do with being hospitable. Authentic, private ascetic practices are embraced with the welfare of the broader community in mind, but a true asceticism of everyday life, by its very nature, directly enhances our life together.

For Christians, solidarity in suffering is centered on the cross. A theology of incarnation demands that we understand the role of asceticism in the spiritual life in terms of life's everyday demands and struggles. We are invited to reflect on our suffering and sacrifice in light of the cross, the symbol of God's love for humanity, and to participate in that love. We have little control over the suffering that life brings, but we do have something to say about how we will respond. One response leads to the fullness of life; another leads to a life of anger, resentment, cynicism, and despair. True asceticism is nurtured by a loving, attentive, contemplative stance toward the persons in our lives, a willingness to "cross over" and walk in another's shoes, a desire to be patient and to commit to the long haul.

What a shame if we would miss these daily invitations to heroic asceticism, to self-denial, to the free and loving surrender of life for another, and instead limit ourselves to practices like occasional fasting, important as they might be. With a fresh view of asceticism we will be able to appreciate the holiness that surrounds us; to celebrate the presence of God in these forms of asceticism; to affirm, encourage, and console one another; and to look to models in our own search for a life-filled existence.[21]

5. Conclusion

Certainly basic to a healthy academic spirituality is periodic, honest review of the institutional mission and identity—a searching discussion of common purpose. However, this review involves more than preparation for periodic accreditation visits, helpful as these are. As we have seen, an authentic academic spirituality cuts more deeply on both the individual and the institutional levels, honestly probing issues of identity, purpose, commitment, behaviors, and outcomes. A spiritually healthy institution always seems to be more than an intellectual and morally upright institution—although it is certainly never less than that.

Michael Buckley and others have argued that oppositional contrasts between faith and reason in religiously sponsored universities are almost always unproductive and misleading. Instead, the more energetic the faith dimension, the better the university—understanding the energy of faith to point toward comprehensive understanding of the creation (both the natural world and human culture).[22] These ideas, broadly conceived, can be useful—*mutatis mutandis*—in all universities.

As Buckley observes, "the fundamental proposition that grounds the Catholic university is that the academic and the religious are intrinsically related, that they form an inherent unity, that one is incomplete without the other." As he elaborates this relationship, Buckley notes that "the intellectual dynamism inherent in all inquiry initiates processes or habits of questioning that—if not inhibited—inevitably bear upon the ultimate questions that engage religion." This energy flows both ways. Thus, "the dynamism inherent in the experience of faith . . . is toward the understanding both of itself and of its relationship to every other dimension of human life."[23] In short, in full development—the kinds of inhibitions we all too often create and display being absent—both inquiry and faith intrinsically lead into and engage the other.

Likewise, we suggest, in the spiritually healthy institution, divisions between discovery and advance of knowledge on the one hand and the development of character on the other are downplayed. Faith and reason, knowledge and character, are not extrinsically related. They are not distinct and sufficient unto themselves. Each involves the other. It is all the more important, therefore, that institutions regularly review the nature and quality of both faith and reason to determine that they are in fact representative of institutional mission and identity.

A spirituality of the university also demands that we reflect on how the specific charisms of our institutions—be they Franciscan,

Dominican, Augustinian, Josephite, or Ignatian—can be brought to bear on our corporate life. Do faculty and students have adequate knowledge of the tradition particular to their institution? It seems odd that we so often restrict use of these traditions to individuals, or a given course, or campus ministry. Are there not creative ways to adapt these traditions in order to call on their spiritual riches in a self-conscious, intentional way during times of crisis or when important decisions need to be made? Some may argue that the pluralistic nature of most universities precludes such engagement—but it seems a tragic loss for religiously sponsored institutions when, in conducting business day-to-day and year-to-year, they neglect these spiritual resources. Would it not be a shame if Quaker schools never turned to George Fox or John Woolman, or Jesuit schools never turned to the Ignatian rules for discernment?

The challenge and the lure of mapping and engaging a spirituality of university life emerges out of a desire for wholeness, for integrity, for holiness in our lives and in the workplace.[24] Parker Palmer invites us to ask if the life we are living is the same as the life that wants to live in us.[25] He understands vocation not so much as a goal to be achieved and then grasped, but rather as a gift to be received and nurtured.[26] This gift will be experienced in different ways depending on whether we find ourselves in graduate school, out of graduate school and unable to find employment in the academy, or schlocking from school to school in the hell of adjuncthood. We will experience it in the scramble for tenure or promotion, in the prime of our careers, or in the doldrums of disappointment and cynicism. The gift remains even when we are simply hanging on well beyond the moment at which we should have gracefully departed to make room for the next generation of scholars.

The aim of a university spirituality is to keep us honest, searching, alive, and in love. To teach and learn in a spiritual, or what might be called a "contemplative," mode is to look upon our students, our colleagues, our disciplines, and ourselves with a long, loving gaze. Lived with love and integrity, the academic life can be continually renewed, a growing experience of joy in which "our deep gladness meets the world's deep need."[27]

NOTES

1. See Deborah Tannen, "Agonism in the Academy: Surviving Higher Learning's Argument Culture," in The Chronicle of Higher Education (CHE), March 31, 2000, B7.

2. John B. Bennett develops a portrait of "insistent individualism" and offers an alternative paradigm in Collegial Professionalism: The Academy, Individualism, and the Common Good (Phoenix: Oryx Press, 1998).

3. Parker J. Palmer, "The Grace of Great Things: Reclaiming the Sacred in Knowing, Teaching, and Learning," in The Holistic Education Review (HER) 10, no. 3 (September 1997): 14.

4. See Alexander Astin, "Our Obsession with Being 'Smart' Is Distorting Intellectual Life," in CHE, September 26, 1997, A60. Astin observes that "my many years as a scholar of higher education and as an employee of a large university convince me that some of higher education's most serious problems can be traced to our uncritical acceptance of this value [being seen as smart at all costs], and to the fact that most of us are not even aware of the power and scope of its influence on our lives and institutions." See also the New York Times editorial, "A Reality Check for College Rankings," August 27, 2001, A14.

5. Palmer, "The Grace of Great Things," in HER 10, no. 3 (1997): 11.

6. In addition to the often-cited Alasdair MacIntyre, After Virtue (Notre Dame, IN: University of Notre Dame Press, 1981) and Robert N. Bellah et al., Habits of the Heart: Individualism and Commitment in American Life (Berkeley: University of California Press, 1985) and Richard Madsen et al., The Good Society (New York: Vintage Books, 1992), see also Lee H. Yearly, "Recent Work on Virtue," in Religious Studies Review 16, no. 1 (1990): 1–9; Donald Capps, Deadly Sins and Saving Virtues (Philadelphia: Fortress, 1987); John W. Crossin, What Are They Saying about Virtue? (Mahwah, NJ: Paulist Press, 1985); Judith Schklar, Ordinary Vices (Cambridge, MA: Harvard University Press, 1984); Henry Fairlie, The Seven Deadly Sins Today (South Bend, IN: University of Notre Dame, 1978).

7. Henri J. M. Nouwen, Reaching Out: Three Movements of the Spiritual Life (Garden City, NY: Doubleday, 1975), 66.

8. Nouwen, Reaching Out, 66.

9. For a thoughtful statement of some educational implications of hospitality, see William F. Losito, "Education as Hospitality: The Reclamation of Cultural Metaphor and Narrative," in In Other Voices: Expanding the Educational Conversation, ed. Warren Strandberg. (Richmond, VA: SAPES, 1992), 62–69.

10. Nouwen, *Reaching Out*, 51.

11. Nouwen, *Reaching Out*, 67.

12. Simone Weil, *Waiting for God*, trans. Emma Craufurd (New York: Harper and Row, 1951), 111.

13. Palmer, *To Know As We Are Known: A Spirituality of Higher Education* (San Francisco: Harper and Row, 1983), 115–16.

14. Bennett, *Collegial Professionalism*, lays out in some detail such a universal ethic.

15. Teresa of Ávila, *The Interior Castle* (Mahwah, NJ: Paulist Press, 1979), 36.

16. Catherine of Siena imagines the link between knowledge of self and knowledge of God as a circle. Her message from God is phrased thus: "this knowledge of yourself, and of me within yourself, is grounded in the soil of true humility, which is as great as the expanse of the circle (which is the knowledge of yourself united with me, as I have said). But if your knowledge of yourself were isolated from me there would be no full circle at all. Instead, there would be a beginning in self-knowledge, but apart from me it would end in confusion" (*The Dialogue* [Mahwah, NJ: Paulist Press, 1980], 42).

17. Palmer, *Let Your Life Speak: Listening for the Voice of Vocation* (San Francisco: Jossey-Bass, 2000), 5.

18. Richard Gula, *The Good Life: Where Morality and Spirituality Converge* (Mahwah, NJ: Paulist Press, 1999), 26–27.

19. See Margaret Miles, *Fullness of Life: Historical Foundations for a New Asceticism* (Philadelphia: Westminster Press, 1981), and "The Recovery of Asceticism," in *Commonweal*, January 28, 1983, 39–43; Karl Rahner, "New Asceticism," in *The Practice of Faith* (New York: Crossroad, 1983); *Weaving* 6 (November–December 1988) entire issue; Diarmuid O'Murchu, "Early Christian Asceticism and Its Relevance Today," in *Irish Theological Quarterly* 50 (1983–84), 86.

20. See John B. Bennett and Elizabeth A. Dreyer, "On Complaining about Students," in *American Association for Higher Education Bulletin* 46, no. 8 (April 1994): 7–8.

21. See E. A. Dreyer, *Earth Crammed with Heaven: A Spirituality of Everyday Life* (Mahwah, NJ: Paulist Press, 1994).

22. Michael J. Buckley, *The Catholic University as Promise and Project: Reflections in a Jesuit Idiom* (Washington, DC: Georgetown University Press, 1998).

23. Buckley, The Catholic University, 15–16.

24. Among the vast literature on this subject, see Gilbert C. Meilaender, ed., *Working: Its Meaning and Its Limits* (Notre Dame, IN: University of Notre Dame Press, 2000); Joseph G. Allegretti, *Loving Your Job, Finding Your Passion: Work and the Spiritual Life* (Mahwah, NJ: Paulist Press, 2000); Bernard A. Nagle and Perry Pascarella, *Leveraging People and Profit: The Hard Work of Soft Management* (Boston: Butterworth-Heinemann, 1998); Lee G. Bolman and Terrence E. Deal, *Leading with Soul: An Uncommon Journey of Spirit* (San Francisco: Jossey-Bass, 1995); John C. Haughey, *Converting 9 to 5: Bringing Spirituality to Your Daily Work* (New York: Crossroad, 1994); Matthew Fox, *The Reinvention of Work: A New Vision of Livelihood for Our Time* (San Francisco: HarperSanFrancisco, 1994); William Diehl, *The Monday Connection: On Being an Authentic Christian in a Weekday World* (San Francisco: HarperSanFrancisco, 1991); and P. J. Palmer, *The Active Life: Wisdom for Work, Creativity, and Caring* (San Francisco: HarperSanFrancisco, 1990).

25. Palmer, *Let Your Life Speak*, 2.

26. Palmer, *Let Your Life Speak*, 10.

27. Palmer, *Let Your Life Speak*, 36.

Jesuits and University Life

Jesuit General Congregation 34

From *Documents of the Thirty-Fourth General Congregation of the Society of Jesus*, 1995

1. Jesuits have been engaged in university teaching, research, and scholarly publication almost since the foundation of the Society. From astronomy to classical ballet, from the humanities to theology, Jesuits try to enter into the languages and discourses of their inherited or emerging cultures. They attempt to discover, shape, renew, or promote human wisdom, while at the same time respecting the integrity of disciplined scholarship. They also seek to accompany in faith the men and women molded by the potent cultural forces inherent in the university as an institution. St. Ignatius was aware of the wide cultural impact of universities and chose to send Jesuits there, as places where a more universal good might be achieved. Throughout our history we have continued to affirm this basic Ignatian intuition.

2. Today, approximately three thousand Jesuits work in nearly two hundred of our own institutions of higher learning, touching the lives of more than half a million students; other Jesuits exercise this mission in other universities. This apostolic activity not only has an influence on the lives of students; it goes beyond the immediate university milieu. We recognize that universities remain crucial institutional settings in society.

For the poor they serve as major channels for social advancement. In and through universities, important debates take place about ethics, future directions for economics and politics, and the very meaning of human existence, debates that shape our culture. Neither the university as an institution and as a value for humanity nor the still urgent imperative for an unflagging Jesuit commitment to our tradition of fostering university life stands in need of any fresh defense.

3. Moreover, many excellent documents already exist that treat the role and future of Jesuit universities. General Congregation 34 wishes only to encourage Jesuits engaged in this important and traditional Jesuit work and to consider two relatively fresh challenges to Jesuit universities.

A Challenge from the Structure of Universities

4. During the past thirty years, Jesuit higher education has undergone very rapid development in size, complexity, and more participative structures of government. During this same period, the number of Jesuits engaged in a university, or at least the proportion of Jesuits within the entire university community, has greatly diminished: lay and religious colleagues join with us in a common enterprise. In some places Jesuits no longer "own" our universities in any real sense. In others, government regulations create a situation in which we no longer fully "control" them. In places, some ecclesiastical superiors may be distrustful of the freedom necessary for a university truly to function in accord with its specific aims.

5. In response to this challenge, Jesuits must continue to work hard, with imagination and faith and often under very difficult circumstances, to maintain and even to strengthen the specific

character of each of our institutions both as Jesuit and as a university. As we look to the future, we need consciously to be on guard that both the noun "university" and the adjective "Jesuit" always remain fully honored.

6. The noun guarantees a commitment to the fundamental autonomy, integrity, and honesty of a university precisely as a university: a place of serene and open search for and discussion of the truth. It also points to the mission proper to every university—its dedication to research, teaching, and the various forms of service that correspond to its cultural mission—as the indispensable horizon and context for a genuine preservation, renewal, and communication of knowledge and human values. As Jesuits, we seek knowledge for its own sake and at the same time must regularly ask, "Knowledge for what?"

A Challenge from Faith and Justice

7. We affirm the adjective "Jesuit" no less strongly. This presupposes the authentic participation in our basic Jesuit identity and mission of any university calling itself Jesuit, or any university that operates ultimately under our responsibility. While we want to avoid any distortion of the nature of a university or any reduction of its mission to only one legitimate goal, the adjective "Jesuit" nevertheless requires that the university act in harmony with the demands of the service of faith and promotion of justice found in Decree 4 of General Congregation 32. A Jesuit university can and must discover in its own proper institutional forms and authentic purposes a specific and appropriate arena for the encounter with the faith that does justice.

8. We applaud the many ways in which Jesuit universities have tried to apply this decree, both in the lives of students through

outreach programs of mutual contact and service with the poor, and in the central teaching, research, and publication aims of the university. If it remains true that most Jesuit universities must, in various ways, strive to do even more in order to embody this mission of service to the faith and its concomitant promotion of justice, this only reflects the challenge all Jesuits face to find concrete and effective ways in which large and complex institutions can be guided by and to that justice that God himself so insistently calls for and enables. The task is possible; it has produced martyrs who have testified that "an institution of higher learning and research can become an instrument of justice in the name of the Gospel."

9. The complexity of a Jesuit university can call for new structures of government and control on the part of the Society in order to preserve its identity and at the same time allow it to relate effectively to the academic world and the society of which it is part, including the church and the Society of Jesus. More specifically, in order for an institution to call itself Jesuit, periodic evaluation and accountability to the Society are necessary in order to judge whether or not its dynamics are being developed in line with the Jesuit mission. The Jesuits who work in these universities, both as a community and as individuals, must actively commit themselves to the institution, assisting in its orientation, so that it can achieve the objectives desired for it by the Society.

10. Jesuit universities will promote interdisciplinary work; this implies a spirit of cooperation and dialogue among specialists within the university itself and with those of other universities. As a means toward serving the faith and promoting justice in accord with their proper nature as universities, they can discover new perspectives and new areas for research, teaching, and university extension services, by means of which they can contribute to the transformation of society toward more profound levels of justice and freedom. Thus, our universities

have a clear opportunity to promote interuniversity collaboration and, in particular, to undertake common projects between Jesuit universities of developed and developing countries.

11. A Jesuit university must be outstanding in its human, social, spiritual, and moral formation, as well as for its pastoral attention to its students and to the different groups of people who work in it or are related to it.

12. Finally, we recall how crucial it is for the whole church to continue to have dedicated Jesuits engaged in university work. They are committed, in the most profound sense, to the search for the fullness of truth. We are assured that, despite occasional appearances to the contrary, the truth we seek will ultimately be one. That truth, rooted as it is in God, will make us free. General Congregation 34 sends a warm word of greeting and encouragement to all those Jesuits dedicated to make authentic and currently fresh this longstanding but sometimes challenged Jesuit commitment to the university apostolate.

Education Marked with the Sign of the Cross

Michael J. Buckley, SJ

America, 1990

When a college inaugurates a new president, it celebrates both what it was and is—but most of all, what it can become. Then does it not strike us as strange—as almost abrasively inappropriate—to inaugurate the president of Spring Hill at such a time, in so stark a period of the church year, on this Saturday that opens into the week of the passion and death of Jesus? This is the day whose Gospel speaks of the final decision about Jesus, that he is to "die for the sake of the people and to gather into one the children of God who are scattered abroad" (John 11:51–52).

Does it jar to talk of educational vision and demands as the church enters into the time of its greatest and definitional remembrance— "the dense and the driven Passion" (as Gerard Manley Hopkins calls it)—when we came into our peace, in the terrible words of Colossians, "through the blood of the cross" (1:20)?

The choice of these readings and of this day in Lent have inescapably taken away from this moment the formal, ceremonial elegance that usually measures such an occasion. They give a very different tone to what we are about—because they have made the passion of Christ the context for understanding this college and the ministry of this president. They mark them today in this Eucharist with the Sign of the Cross.

It is true that for Ignatius of Loyola—in whose religious heritage this school stands—all Christian ministry is a continuation of this great work of Jesus for others. His passion and death. His struggles become ours. But one should not assume the costly Sign of the Cross too easily. Indeed, how can such a religious vision make any honest sense here? Spring Hill, Jesuit higher education—this obvious matter of students and faculty, of instruction and writing and examination, of books and discussions, of developing friendships or rivalries, and colleagues—we all know what this is. What sense can it possibly make to say that the religious call and meaning of this college is to be found in the cross, is to enter into and to continue the great struggles of Christ?

Pause, then, for a moment within the context of this liturgy and these readings, and ask a prior question: What, for Christ, was the actual experience of the passion? What were his struggles? What did he continually contend with, and agonize through, to become "a body broken for us and a blood poured out for us"?

Ignatius was very specific in the Spiritual Exercises. For Jesus, the passion was a twofold experience: It was the experience of the absence of God—"the divinity hides itself," even to the sense of the abandonment by God; and it was an experience of an enormity of human suffering—as His "humanity is left to suffer most cruelly." The hiddenness of God. Profound human suffering. It is against and within these experiences that Christ struggles as He moves faithfully toward His death in obedience and love.

Now, take these experiences and write them very large, and you will find the two major challenges of Jesuit education within the United States today: the massive absence of God from so much of the contemporary world—with all the final emptiness, religious cynicism, or meaninglessness of that experience; the suffering of humanity—with all of the wretchedness of the four million homeless in our major cities and the refugees at our border, impoverished families, boat people and the starving in Africa, the exploited and the tortured. The church, as a universal communion of people, must struggle with the contemporary experience of the absence of God and the cruel suffering of humanity. The church must take up its own cross.

Educate our students "comfortably," without the sensibility, the awareness, the reflective skills, and the desire to confront these two dimensions of human existence as our century draws to its close and you have not given them a Catholic education adequate for our time. You have never mediated between the Gospel, at its greatest intensity, and contemporary culture.

Spring Hill must reflect upon, must measure up to, each of these, if it is to be true to the vision out of which it came. Let us frame each within an appropriate vignette, what Ignatius would call a "composition of place."

Fifty-six years ago, at another institution of higher learning, the greatest American philosopher of the century, John Dewey, delivered the Terry Lectures on the relationship between religious belief and American culture. In these lectures, Dewey read an intractable conflict between the religious commitments that had characterized Western civilization for almost two thousand years and the rising sense of new scientific methods and what he called a "revolution in the seat of authority." For increasingly within American culture, "there is but one sure road of access to truth—the road of patient, cooperative inquiry operating by means of observation, experience, record, and controlled reflection"—the scientific method, in the most generous sense of that term.

It was a revolution because religious belief could not sustain itself before this advance. "The growth of Knowledge and of its methods and tests has been such as to make acceptance of these [religious] beliefs increasingly onerous and even impossible for large numbers of cultivated men and women." Dewey read American intellectual culture as increasingly alienated from belief in God.

Dewey is usually cited on such an occasion as ours to serve as a foil, an adversary whom the speaker or the preacher will demonstrate to be wrong. But it seems to me that Dewey was right in much of what he said—and that his diagnosis touches on something of the religious paradox of our nation.

If you inquire which of the major nations of the world are religious—where religious practice, attendance, speech, and symbols are most in evidence and most supported—you will find that there are two: India and the United States. But if you ask where in our country religious alienation, disinterest, aversion, or even contempt is most pervasive, you will find it not among the poor or among the immigrants, not among the workers or among the middle class. You will find this alienation principally among the highly educated and the professional elites. For much of American intellectual culture and distinguished academic circles, "the divinity is hidden." Further, what Cardinal John Henry Newman wrote sadly about the nineteenth-century Catholic Church in England can find its parallels with this estrangement: "Most probably I shall be able to do little more. It is so ordered on high that in our day Holy Church should present just that aspect to my countrymen which is most consonant with their ingrained prejudices against her."

What parallels the loss of the workers in nineteenth-century Europe is the religious alienation and disinterest that exist among many of the educated and the intellectuals in the United States. Studies reaching back to 1913 show that this has been the case. Those done in the 1980s show an inverse relation between exposure to higher education and adherence to such core religious beliefs as the existence of God, the divinity of Christ, life after death, religious conversion, etc. And the greatest degree of religious alienation is registered not among the scientists, such as those in physics and chemistry, but among those in the social sciences and humanities.

This pervasive religious alienation, the absence of God from so much of the intellectual and professional culture of the United States, must be addressed by the American church. But the average Catholic, the average priest or bishop or theologian, has so little contact with contemporary poetry, with deconstruction in literary criticism or determinism in biology, with causality in subatomic physics or complex economic theory, with advancements in the sociology of knowledge and artificial intelligence.

There must be a place where all this knowledge and the questions vital to American intellectual culture intersect with the reflection and wisdom of the church, a place of steady, open, and considered reflection and inner change, where the Gospel of Christ becomes incarnate in American intellectual culture.

Only the Catholic college or university can offer today this continual and unswerving service to the church and to the academic community in the United States. Only such an institution can forward a steady, reflective mediation between the church and the academy. Only through such an institution can the church habitually and regularly find entrance into the contemporary world of learning, where God is most hidden, and have the spirit of its inquiry, the weight of its questions, and the values of its ranging discussions treasured.

Do you remember last November 16? There was another lawn and another day for pictures, and there were other Jesuit teachers, and there was another bishop. Only those Jesuits were lying on the ground, with their heads blown open. And two women had been slaughtered to silence any possible witnesses to the murder. And the bishop was blessing their bodies as he had blessed their work for years at the University of Central America.

These men were university professors, like members of the faculty and administration here: sociologists, theologians, administrators, social psychologists, religious educators, and philosophers. They had been killed because of the questions to which they gave priority, the knowledge they thought most worth having, and the urgency they gave to the spirit and social commitments of the church. They were killed because the education they gave touched the enormity of human suffering all around them—where, in their world, "humanity is left to suffer most cruelly" among the homeless, the exploited, the seventy thousand dead.

What happened in El Salvador to these men is not so much a barbarous and bizarre anomaly as, somehow or other, a sacramental sign lifted up of what our higher education must always be about. Higher education is neither propaganda nor indoctrination. But Catholic and Jesuit higher education must also educate its students into the disciplined sensitivity toward the suffering in the world. It is part of their religious and humanistic education called for by the Gospel.

In this context, Jesuit educators at this college, but throughout the United States, must ask themselves: How many of our students in the United States and from Latin America over the past fifty years have returned to their homes so insensitive and so ignorant of this dimension of human existence that they have become part of the problem, not part of the solution? For without a specific and concentrated effort to bring about such a religious and humane education, such institutions graduate human beings unaware of the extent of human pain—underdeveloped religiously and humanistically because ignorantly indifferent to what is the lot of the great majority of human beings.

The Terry Lectures of John Dewey. Eight dead bodies in the house and on the lawn in El Salvador. They are marked in such different ways for us with the Sign of the Cross, the Sign of the Cross writ very large indeed: the hiddenness of God and the suffering of humanity.

This is the challenge of the Christian cross to the education given at this college—to become increasingly part of these enormous struggles, patterned on those of the passion of Christ, so that through the manifold and complicated struggles of administration and teaching, the energies expended and frustrated, the intentions directed or distorted or painfully misunderstood, the joy given and taken in the development of students and the advance of knowledge, the years of dedication and the daily, humble, unremitting and unspectacular work that is education, Christ and culture, Christ and the human condition, might come together and achieve a unity in awareness even within our world. in that way, even out of religious despair and great human suffering, the Kingdom of God might emerge.

There is no need to apologize, then, for the coice of this day and of its stark Gospel to inaugurate the new president of Spring Hill.

The Service of Faith and the Promotion of Justice in American Jesuit Higher Education

Peter-Hans Kolvenbach, SJ

From *Faith, Justice, and American Higher Education,*
2001

Introduction

This conference on the commitment to justice in American Jesuit higher education comes at an important moment in the rich history of the twenty-eight colleges and universities represented here this evening. We also join Santa Clara University in celebrating the 150th anniversary of its founding.

Just as significant as this moment in history is our location. Santa Clara Valley, named after the mission at the heart of this campus, is known worldwide as Silicon Valley, the home of the microchip. Surely when Father Nobili, the founder of this university, saw the dilapidated church and compound of the former Franciscan mission, he could never have imagined this valley as the center of a global technological revolution.

This juxtaposition of mission and microchip is emblematic of all the Jesuit schools. Originally founded to serve the educational and religious needs of poor immigrant populations, they have become highly sophisticated institutions of learning in the midst of global wealth, power, and culture. The turn of the millennium finds them in all their diversity: they are larger, better equipped, more complex and professional than ever before, and also more concerned about their Catholic, Jesuit identity.

In the history of American Jesuit higher education, there is much to be grateful for, first to God and the church, and surely to the many faculty, students, administrators, and benefactors who have made it what it is today. But this conference brings you together from across the United States with guests from Jesuit universities elsewhere, not for mutual congratulations, but for a strategic purpose. On behalf of the complex, professional, and pluralistic institutions you represent, you are here to face a question as difficult as it is central: how can the Jesuit colleges and universities in the United States express faith-filled concern for justice in what they are as Christian academies of higher learning, in what their faculty do, and in what their students become?

As a contribution to your response, I would like to (1) reflect with you on what faith and justice has meant for Jesuits since 1975, and then (2) consider some concrete circumstances of today, (3) suggest what justice rooted in faith could mean in American Jesuit higher education, and (4) conclude with an agenda for the first decade of the years 2000.

I. The Jesuit Commitment to Faith and Justice, New in 1975

I begin by recalling another anniversary that this conference commemorates. Twenty-five years ago, ten years after the closing of the Second Vatican Council, Jesuit delegates from around the world gathered at the Thirty-second General Congregation (GC 32), to consider how the Society of Jesus was responding to the deep transformation of all church life that was called for and launched by Vatican II.

After much prayer and deliberation, the congregation slowly realized that the entire Society of Jesus in all its many works was being invited by the Spirit of God to set out on a new direction. The over-riding purpose of the Society of Jesus, namely, "the service of faith," must also include "the promotion of justice." This new direction was not confined to those already working with the poor and marginalized in what was called "the social apostolate." Rather, this commitment was to be "a concern of our whole life and a dimension of all our apostolic endeavors."[1] So central to the mission of the entire Society was this union of faith and justice that it was to become the "integrating factor" of all the Society's works;[2] and in this light, "great attention" was to be paid to evaluating every work, including educational institutions.[3]

I myself attended GC 32, representing the Province of the Near East, where for centuries the apostolic activity of the Jesuits has concentrated on education in a famous university and some outstanding high schools. Of course, some Jesuits worked in very poor villages, refugee camps, or prisons, and some fought for the rights of workers, immigrants, and foreigners; but this was not always considered authentic, mainstream Jesuit work. In Beirut we were well aware that our medical school, staffed by very holy Jesuits, was producing, at least at that time, some of the most corrupt citizens in the city; but this was taken for granted. The social mood of the explosive Near East did not favor a struggle against sinful, unjust structures. The liberation of Palestine was the most important social issue. The Christian churches had committed themselves to many works of charity, but involvement in the promotion of justice would have tainted them by association with leftist movements and political turmoil.

The situation I describe in the Near East was not exceptional in the worldwide Society at that time. I was not the only delegate who was ignorant of matters pertaining to justice and injustice. The 1971 Synod of Bishops had prophetically declared, "Action on behalf of justice and participation in the transformation of the world fully appear to us as a constitutive dimension of the preaching of the gospel, or, in other words, of the church's mission for the redemption of the human race and its liberation from every oppressive situation," but few of us knew what this meant in our concrete circumstances.[4]

Earlier, in 1966, Father Arrupe had pointed out to the Latin American provincials how the socioeconomic situation throughout the continent contradicted the Gospel, and "from this situation rises the moral obligation of the Society to rethink all its ministries and every form of its apostolates to see if they really offer a response to the urgent priorities which justice and social equity call for."[5] Many of us failed to see the relevance of his message to our situation. But please note that Father Arrupe did not ask for the suppression of the apostolate of education in favor of social activity. On the contrary, he affirmed that "even an apostolate like education—at all levels—which is so sincerely wanted by the Society and whose importance is clear to the entire world, in its concrete forms today must be the object of reflection in the light of the demands of the social problem."[6]

Perhaps the incomprehension or reluctance of some of us delegates was one reason why GC 32 finally took a radical stand. With a passion both inspiring and disconcerting, the general congregation coined the formula "the service of faith and the promotion of justice," and used it adroitly to push every Jesuit work and every individual Jesuit to make a choice, providing little leeway for the fainthearted. Many inside and outside the Society were outraged by the "promotion of justice." As Father Arrupe rightly perceived, his Jesuits were collectively entering upon a more severe way of the cross, which would surely entail misunderstandings and even opposition on the part of civil and ecclesiastical authorities, many good friends, and some of our own members. Today, twenty-five years later, this option has become integral to our Jesuit identity, to the awareness of our mission, and to our public image in both church and society.[7]

The summary expression "the service of faith and the promotion of justice" has all the characteristics of a world-conquering slogan, using a minimum of words to inspire a maximum of dynamic vision; but it runs the risk of ambiguity. Let us examine, first the service of faith, then the promotion of justice.

The Service of Faith

From our origins in 1540, the Society has been officially and solemnly charged with "the defense and the propagation of the faith." In 1995, the congregation reaffirmed that, for us Jesuits, the defense and propagation of the faith is a matter of to be or not to be, even if the words themselves can change. Faithful to the Vatican Council, the congregation wanted our preaching and teaching not to proselytize, not to impose our religion on others, but rather to propose Jesus and his message of God's kingdom to everyone in a spirit of love.

Just as the Vatican had abandoned the name "Propaganda fidei," GC 32 passed from propagation to service of faith. In decree 4, the congregation did use the expression "the proclamation of faith," which I prefer.[8] In the context of centuries of Jesuit spirituality, however, "the service of faith" cannot mean anything other than to bring the countercultural gift of Christ to our world.[9]

But why "the service of faith"? The congregation itself answers this question by using the Greek expression "diakonia fidei" [the "ministry or service of faith"].[10] It refers to Christ the suffering Servant carrying out his "diakonia" in total service of his Father by laying down his life for the salvation of all. Thus, for a Jesuit, "not just any response to the needs of the men and women of today will do. The initiative must come from the Lord laboring in events and people here and now. God invites us to follow Christ in his labors, on his terms and in his way."[11]

I do not think we delegates at the Thirty-second Congregation were aware of the theological and ethical dimensions of Christ's mission of service. Greater attention to the "diakonia fidei" may have prevented some of the misunderstandings provoked by the phrase "the promotion of justice."

The Promotion of Justice

In many languages this expression is difficult to translate. We delegates were familiar with sales promotions in a department store or the promotion of friends or enemies to a higher rank or position; we were not familiar with the promotion of justice. To be fair, let us remember that a general congregation is not a scientific academy equipped to distinguish and to define, to clarify and to classify. In the face of radically new apostolic needs, it chose to inspire, to teach, and even to prophesy. In its desire to be more incisive in the promotion of justice, the congregation avoided traditional words like "charity," "mercy," or "love," unfashionable words in 1975. Neither philanthropy nor even development would do. The congregation instead used the word "promotion" with its connotation of a well-planned strategy to make the world just.

Since Saint Ignatius wanted love to be expressed not only in words but also in deeds, the congregation committed the Society to the promotion of justice as a concrete, radical, but proportionate response to an unjustly suffering world. Fostering the virtue of justice in people was not enough. Only a substantive justice can bring about the kinds of structural and attitudinal changes that are needed to uproot those sinful, oppressive injustices that are a scandal against humanity and God.

This sort of justice requires an action-oriented commitment to the poor, with a courageous personal option. In some ears the relatively mild expression "promotion of justice" echoed revolutionary, subversive, and even violent language. For example, the American State Department recently accused some Colombian Jesuits of being Marxist-inspired founders of a guerilla organization. When challenged, the U.S. government apologized for this mistake, which shows that some message did get through.

Just as in "diakonia fidei," the term "faith" is not specified, so in the "promotion of justice" the term "justice" also remains ambiguous. The Thirty-second Congregation would not have voted for decree 4 if, on the one hand, socioeconomic justice had been excluded or if, on the other hand, the justice of the Gospel had not been included. A stand in favor of social justice that was almost ideological, and simultaneously a strong option for "that justice of the Gospel which embodies God's love and saving mercy"[12] were both indispensable. Refusing to clarify the relationship between the two, GC 32 maintained its radicality by simply juxtaposing "diakonia fidei" and "promotion of justice."

In other decrees of the same congregation, when the two dimensions of the one mission of the Society were placed together, some delegates sought to achieve a more integrated expression by proposing amendments, such as the service of faith *through* or *in* the promotion of justice. Such expressions might better render the 1971 synod's identification of "action on behalf of justice and participation in the transformation of the world [as] a constitutive dimension of the preaching of the gospel."[13] But one can understand the congregation's fear that too neat or integrated an approach might weaken the prophetic appeal and water down the radical change in our mission.

In retrospect, this simple juxtaposition sometimes led to an "incomplete, slanted and unbalanced reading" of decree 4,[14] unilaterally emphasizing "one aspect of this mission to the detriment of the other,"[15] treating faith and justice as alternative or even rival tracks of ministry. "Dogmatism or ideology sometimes led us to treat each other more as adversaries than as companions. The promotion of justice has sometimes been separated from its wellspring of faith."[16]

On the one side, the faith dimension was too often presumed and left implicit, as if our identity as Jesuits were enough. Some rushed headlong towards the promotion of justice without much analysis or reflection and with only occasional reference to the justice of the Gospel. They seemed to consign the service of faith to a dying past.

Those on the other side clung to a certain style of faith and church. They gave the impression that God's grace had to do only with the next life and that divine reconciliation entailed no practical obligation to set things right here on earth.

In this frank assessment, I have used, not so much my own words, but rather those of subsequent congregations, so as to share with you the whole Society's remorse for whatever distortions or excesses occurred, and to demonstrate how, over the last twenty-five years, the Lord has patiently been teaching us to serve the faith that does justice in a more integral way.

The Ministry of Education

In the midst of radical statements and unilateral interpretations associated with decree 4, many raised doubts about our maintaining large educational institutions. They insinuated, if they did not insist, that direct social work among the poor and involvement with their movements should take priority. Today, however, the value of the educational apostolate is generally recognized—indeed, it is the sector occupying the greatest Jesuit manpower and resources—but only on condition that it transforms its goals, contents, and methods.

Even before GC 32, Father Arrupe had already fleshed out the meaning of "diakonia fidei" for educational ministries when he addressed the 1973 International Congress of Jesuit Alumni of Europe.

> Today our prime educational objective must be to form men for others; men who will live not for themselves but for God and his Christ—for the God-man who lived and died for all the world; men who cannot even conceive of love of God which does not include love for the least of their neighbors; men completely convinced that love of God which does not issue in justice for men is a farce.[17]

My predecessor's address was not well received by many alumni at the Valencia meeting, but the expression "men and women for others" really helped the educational institutions of the Society to ask serious questions that led to their transformation.[18]

Father Ignacio Ellacuría, in his 1982 convocation address here at Santa Clara University, eloquently expressed his conviction in favor of the promotion of justice in the educational apostolate:

> A Christian university must take into account the Gospel preference for the poor. This does not mean that only the poor study at the university; it does not mean that the university should abdicate its mission of academic excellence—excellence needed in order to solve complex social problems. It does mean that the university should be present intellectually where it is needed: to provide science for those who have no science; to provide skills for the unskilled; to be a voice for those who do not possess the academic qualifications to promote and legitimate their rights."[19]

In these two statements, we discover the same concern to go beyond a disincarnate spiritualism or a secular social activism, so as to renew the educational apostolate in word and in action at the service of the church in a world of unbelief and of injustice. We should be very grateful for all that has been achieved in this apostolate, both faithful to the characteristics of four hundred years of Ignatian education and open to the changing signs of the times. Today, one or two genera-tions after decree 4, we face a world that has an even greater need for the faith that does justice.

II. A "Composition" of Our Time and Place

Let us turn now to a mention of some of the changing signs of the times.

Meeting in Silicon Valley brings to mind not only the intersection of the mission and the microchip but also the dynamism and even dominance that are characteristics of the United States at this time. Enormous talent and unprecedented prosperity are concentrated in this country, which spawns sixty-four new millionaires every day. This is the headquarters of the new economy that reaches around the globe and is transforming the basic fabric of business, work, and communications. Thousands of immigrants arrive from everywhere: entrepreneurs from Europe, high-tech professionals from South Asia who staff the service industries, as well as workers from Latin America and Southeast Asia who do the physical labor—thus, a remarkable ethnic, cultural, and class diversity.

At the same time, the United States struggles with new social divisions aggravated by the "digital divide" between those with access to the world of technology and those left out. This rift, with its causes in class, racial, and economic differences, has its root cause in chronic discrepancies in the quality of education. Here in Silicon Valley, for example, some of the world's premier research universities flourish alongside struggling public schools where Afro-American and immi-grant students drop out in droves. Nationwide, one child in every six is condemned to ignorance and poverty.

This valley, this nation, and the whole world look very differ-ent from the way they looked twenty-five years ago. With the col-lapse of Communism and the end of the cold war, national and even international politics have been eclipsed by a resurgent capitalism that faces no ideological rival. The European Union slowly pulls the continent's age-old rivals together into a community but also a fortress. The former "Second World" struggles to repair the human and environmental damage left behind by so-called socialist regimes. Industries are relocating to poorer nations, not to distribute wealth and opportunity, but to exploit the relative advantage of low wages and lax environmental regulations. Many countries become yet poorer, especially where corruption and exploitation prevail over civil society and where violent conflict keeps erupting.

This composition of our time and place embraces six billion people with their faces young and old, some being born and others dying, some white and many brown and yellow and black.[20] Each one a unique individual, they all aspire to live life, to use their talents, to support their families and care for their children and elders, to enjoy peace and security, and to make tomorrow better.

Thanks to science and technology, human society is able to solve problems such as feeding the hungry, sheltering the homeless, or developing more just conditions of life, but stubbornly fails to accomplish this. How can a booming economy, the most prosperous and global ever, still leave over half of humanity in poverty?

GC 32 makes its own sober analysis and moral assessment:

> We can no longer pretend that the inequalities and injustices of our world must be borne as part of the inevitable order of things. It is now quite apparent that they are the result of what man himself, man in his selfishness, has done.
>
> [D]espite the opportunities offered by an ever more serviceable technology, we are simply not willing to pay the price of a more just and more humane society.[21]

Injustice is rooted in a spiritual problem, and its solution requires a spiritual conversion of each one's heart and a cultural conversion of our global society so that humankind, with all the powerful means at its disposal, might exercise the will to change the sinful structures afflicting our world. The yearly *Human Development Report* of the United Nations is a haunting challenge to look critically at basic conditions of life in the United States and the 175 other nations that share our one planet.[22]

Such is the world in all its complexity, with great global promises and countless tragic betrayals. Such is the world in which Jesuit institutions of higher education are called to serve faith and promote justice.

III. American Jesuit Higher Education for Faith and Justice

Within the complex time and place that are ours and in the light of the recent general congregations, I want to spell out several ideal characteristics, as manifest in three complementary dimensions of Jesuit higher education: in who our students become, in what our faculty do, and in how our universities proceed. Some of these ideals are easy to meet, others remain persistently challenging; but together they serve to orient our schools and, in the long run, to identify them. At the same time, the U.S. provincials have recently established the important Higher Education Committee to propose criteria on the staffing, leadership, and Jesuit sponsorship of our colleges and universities.[23] May these criteria help to implement the ideal characteristics we now meditate on together.

Formation and Learning

Today's predominant ideology reduces the human world to a global jungle whose primordial law is the survival of the fittest. Students who subscribe to this view want to be equipped with well-honed professional and technical skills in order to compete in the market and secure one of the relatively scarce fulfilling and lucrative jobs available. This is the success that many students (and parents!) expect.

All American universities, ours included, are under tremendous pressure to opt entirely for success in this sense. But what our students want—and deserve—includes but transcends this "worldly success" based on marketable skills. The real measure of our Jesuit universities lies in who our students become.

For 450 years, Jesuit education has sought to educate "the whole person" intellectually and professionally, psychologically, morally, and spiritually. But in the emerging global reality, with its great possibilities and deep contradictions, the whole person is different from the whole person of the Counter-Reformation, the Industrial Revolution, or the twentieth century. Tomorrow's "whole person" cannot be whole without an educated awareness of society and culture with which to contribute socially, generously, in the real world. Tomorrow's whole person must have, in brief, a well-educated solidarity.

We must therefore raise our Jesuit educational standard to "educate the whole person of solidarity for the real world." Solidarity is learned through "contact" rather than through "concepts," as the Holy Father said recently at an Italian university conference.[24] When the heart is touched by direct experience, the mind may be challenged to change. Personal involvement with innocent suffering, with the injustice others suffer, is the catalyst for solidarity, which then gives rise to intellectual inquiry and moral reflection.

Students, in the course of their formation, must let the gritty reality of this world into their lives, so they can learn to feel it, think about it critically, respond to its suffering, and engage it constructively. They should learn to perceive, think, judge, choose, and act for the rights of others, especially the disadvantaged and the oppressed. Campus ministry does much to foment such intelligent, responsible, and active compassion, compassion that deserves the name solidarity.

Our universities also boast a splendid variety of in-service programs, outreach programs, insertion programs, off-campus contacts, and hands-on courses. These should not be too optional or peripheral, but at the core of every Jesuit university's program of studies.

Our students are involved in every sort of social action—tutoring dropouts, demonstrating in Seattle, serving in soup kitchens, promoting pro-life, protesting against the School of the Americas—

and we are proud of them for it. But the measure of Jesuit universities is not what our students do but who they become and the adult Christian responsibility they will exercise in the future toward their neighbor and their world. For now, the activities they engage in, even with such good effect, are for their formation. This does not make the university a training camp for social activists. Rather, the students need close involvement with the poor and the marginal now, in order to learn about reality and become adults of solidarity in the future.

Research and Teaching

If the measure and purpose of our universities lie in what the students become, then the faculty are at the heart of universities. Their mission is tirelessly to seek the truth and to form each student into a whole person of solidarity who will take responsibility for the real world. What do they need in order to fulfill this essential vocation?

The faculty's "research, which must be rationally rigorous, firmly rooted in faith and open to dialogue with all people of good will,"[25] not only obeys the canons of each discipline, but ultimately embraces human reality in order to help make the world a more fitting place for six billion of us to inhabit. I want to affirm that university knowledge is valuable for its own sake and at the same time is knowledge that must ask itself, "For whom? For what?"[26]

Usually we speak of professors in the plural, but what is at stake is more than the sum of so many individual commitments and efforts. It is a sustained interdisciplinary dialogue of research and reflection, a continuous pooling of expertise. The purpose is to assimilate experiences and insights according to their different disciplines in "a vision of knowledge which, well aware of its limitations, is not satisfied with fragments but tries to integrate them into a true and wise synthesis" about the real world.[27] Unfortunately, many faculty still feel academically, humanly, and, I would say, spiritually unprepared for such an exchange.

In some disciplines, such as the life sciences, the social sciences, law, business, or medicine, the connections with "our time and place" may seem more obvious. These professors apply their disciplinary specialties to issues of justice and injustice in their research and teaching about health care, legal aid, public policy, and international relations. But every field or branch of knowledge has values to defend, with repercussions on the ethical level. Every discipline, beyond its necessary specialization, must engage with human society, human life, and the environment in appropriate ways, cultivating moral concern about how people ought to live together.

All professors, in spite of the cliché of the ivory tower, are in contact with the world. But no point of view is ever neutral or value free. By preference, by option, our Jesuit point of view is that of the poor. So our professors' commitment to faith and justice entails a most significant shift in viewpoint and choice of values. Adopting the point of view of those who suffer injustice, our professors seek the truth and share their search and its results with our students. A legitimate question, even if it does not sound academic, is for each professor to ask, "When researching and teaching, where and with whom is my heart?" To expect our professors to make such an explicit option and speak about it is obviously not easy; it entails risks. But I do believe that this is what Jesuit educators have publicly stated, in church and in society, to be our defining commitment.

To make sure that the real concerns of the poor find their place in research, faculty members need an organic collaboration with those in the church and in society who work among and for the poor and actively seek justice. They should be involved together in all aspects: presence among the poor, designing the research, gathering the data, thinking through problems, planning and action, doing evaluation and theological reflection. In each Jesuit province where our universities are found, the faculty's privileged working relationships should be with projects of the Jesuit social apostolate—on issues such as poverty and exclusion, housing, AIDS, ecology, and Third World debt—and with the Jesuit Refugee Service, helping refugees and forcibly displaced people.

Just as the students need the poor in order to learn, so the professors need partnerships with the social apostolate in order to research and teach and form. Such partnerships do not turn Jesuit universities into branch plants of social ministries or agencies of social change, as certain rhetoric of the past may have led some to fear, but are a verifiable pledge of the faculty's option and really help, as the colloquial expression goes, "to keep your feet to the fire!"

If the professors choose viewpoints incompatible with the justice of the Gospel and consider researching, teaching, and learning to be separable from moral responsibility for their social repercussions, they are sending a message to their students. They are telling them that they can pursue their careers and self-interest without reference to anyone "other" than themselves.

By contrast, when faculty do take up interdisciplinary dialogue and socially engaged research in partnership with social ministries, they are exemplifying and modeling knowledge that is service, and the students learn by imitating them as "masters of life and of moral commitment," as the Holy Father said.[28]

Our Way of Proceeding

If the measure of our universities is who the students become, and if the faculty are the heart of it all, then what is there left to say? It is perhaps the third topic, the character of our universities—how they proceed internally and how they impact on society—that is the most difficult.

We have already dwelt on the importance of formation and learning, of research and teaching. The social action that the students undertake and the socially relevant work that the professors do are vitally important and necessary, but these do not add up to the full character of a Jesuit university; they neither exhaust its faith-justice commitment nor really fulfill its responsibilities to society.

What, then, constitutes this ideal character? and what contributes to the public's perception of it? In the case of a Jesuit university, this character must surely be the mission, which is defined by GC 32 and reaffirmed by GC 34: the "diakonia fidei" and the promotion of justice, as the characteristic Jesuit-university way of proceeding and of serving socially.

In the words of GC 34, a Jesuit university must be faithful to both the noun "university" and to the adjective "Jesuit." To be a university requires dedication "to research, teaching, and the various forms of service that correspond to its cultural mission." To be Jesuit "requires that the university act in harmony with the demands of the service of faith and promotion of justice found in Decree 4 of GC 32."[29]

The first way, historically, that our universities began living out their faith-justice commitment was through their admissions policies, affirmative action for minorities, and scholarships for disadvantaged students;[30] and these continue to be effective means. An even more telling expression of the Jesuit university's nature is found in policies concerning hiring and tenure. As a university it must respect the established academic, professional, and labor norms, but as Jesuit it is essential to go beyond them and find ways of attracting, hiring, and promoting those who actively share the mission.

I believe that we have made considerable and laudable Jesuit efforts to go deeper and further: we have brought our Ignatian spirituality, our reflective capacities, some of our international resources, to bear. Good results are evident, for example, in the decree "Jesuits and University Life" of the last general congregation and in this very conference on "Commitment to Justice in Jesuit Higher Education"; and good results are hoped for from the Higher Education Committee working on Jesuit criteria.

Paraphrasing Ignacio Ellacuría, it is the nature of every university to be a social force, and it is the calling of a Jesuit university to take conscious responsibility for being such a force for faith and justice. Every Jesuit academy of higher learning is called to live in a social reality (as we saw in the "composition" of our time and place) and to live for that social reality, to shed university intelligence upon it, and to use university influence to transform it.[31] Thus Jesuit universities have stronger and different reasons than do many other academic and research institutions for addressing the actual world as it unjustly exists and for helping to reshape it in the light of the Gospel.

IV. In Conclusion, an Agenda

The twenty-fifth anniversary of GC 32 is a motive for great thanksgiving.

We give thanks for our Jesuit-university awareness of the world in its entirety and in its ultimate depth, created yet abused, sinful yet redeemed, and we take up our Jesuit-university responsibility for human society that is so scandalously unjust, so complex to understand, and so hard to change With the help of others and especially the poor, we want to play our role as students, as teachers and researchers, and as Jesuit university in society.

As Jesuit higher education, we embrace new ways of learning and being formed in the pursuit of adult solidarity, new methods of researching and teaching in an academic community of dialogue, and a new university way of practicing faith-justice in society.

As we assume our Jesuit-university characteristics in the new century, we do so with seriousness and hope. For this very mission has produced martyrs who prove that "an institution of higher learning and research can become an instrument of justice in the name of the Gospel."[32] But implementing decree 4 is not something a Jesuit university accomplishes once and for all. It is rather an ideal to keep taking up and working at, a cluster of characteristics to keep exploring and implementing, a conversion to keep praying for.

In *Ex Corde Ecclesiae*, Pope John Paul II charges Catholic universities with a challenging agenda for teaching, research, and service:

> The dignity of human life, the promotion of justice for all, the quality of personal and family life, the protection of nature, the search for peace and political stability, a more just sharing in the world's resources, and a new economic and political order that will better serve the human community at a national and international level.[33]

These are both high ideals and concrete tasks. I encourage our Jesuit colleges and universities to take them up with critical understanding and deep conviction, with buoyant faith and much hope in the early years of the new century.

The beautiful words of GC 32 show us a long path to follow:

[T]he way to faith and the way to justice are inseparable ways. It is up this undivided road, this steep road, that the pilgrim Church [the Society of Jesus, the Jesuit college and university] must travel and toil. Faith and justice are undivided in the Gospel, which teaches that "faith makes its power felt through love."[34] They cannot therefore be divided in our purpose, our action, our life.[35]

For the greater glory of God.

Thank you very much.

NOTES

1. GC 32, d. 4, no. 47.
2. GC 32, d. 2, no. 9.
3. See GC 32, d. 2, no. 9, and d. 4, no. 76.
4. 1971 Synod of Bishops, "Justice in the World."
5. Pedro Arrupe, SJ, "On the Social Apostolate in Latin America" (December 12, 1966), *Acta Romana* 14, no. 6 (1966): 791.
6. Ibid.
7. See Peter-Hans Kolvenbach, SJ, "On the Social Apostolate" (January 2000), no. 3.
8. "Since evangelization is proclamation of that faith which is made operative in love of others [see Gal. 5:6; Eph. 4:15], the promotion of justice is indispensable to it" (GC 32, d. 4, no. 28).
9. See GC 34, d. 26, no. 5.
10. For example, GC 32, d. 11, no. 13.
11. GC 34, d. 26, no. 8.
12. GC 33, d. 1, no. 32.
13. 1971 Synod of Bishops, "Justice in the World."
14. Pedro Arrupe, SJ, "Rooted and Grounded in Love," *Acta Romana* 18, no. 2 (1982): 500, no. 67.
15. GC 33, d. 1, no. 33.
16. GC 34, d. 3, no. 2.

17. Pedro Arrupe, SJ, Address to the European Jesuit Alumni Congress, Valencia, July 31, 1973: "Men for Others," *Justice with Faith Today: Selected Letters and Addresses* (St. Louis: Institute of Jesuit Sources, 1980), II, 124.

18. See *The Characteristics of Jesuit Education* (Washington, DC: Jesuit Secondary Education Association, 1987).

19. Ignacio Ellacuría, SJ, "The Task of a Christian University," Convocation address at the University of Santa Clara, June 12, 1982; "Una universidad para el pueblo," *Diakonia* 6, no. 23 (1982): 41–57.

20. See Ignatius of Loyola, "Contemplation on the Incarnation," in *Spiritual Exercises*, nos. 101–9.

21. GC 32, d. 4, nos. 27, 20.

22. United Nations Development Program, *Human Development Report*, 1990 to the present.

23. In February 2000 the Jesuit Conference established the five-man Committee on Higher Education to prepare recommendations regarding (1) sponsorship by the Society of U.S. Jesuit colleges and universities, (2) assignment of personnel to these institutions, and (3) selection of presidents (particularly non-Jesuit presidents) for these institutions.

24. John Paul II, in an address to Catholic University of the Sacred Heart, Milan, May 5, 2000, no. 9.

25. Ibid., no. 7.

26. See GC 34, d. 17, no. 6.

27. John Paul II, Catholic University address (see note 24 above), no. 5.

28. John Paul II, Address to the Faculty of Medicine at the Catholic University of the Sacred Heart, Milan, June 26, 1984.

29. GC 34, d. 17, nos. 6, 7.

30. "For the poor [the universities] serve as major channels for social advancement" (GC 34, d. 17, no. 2).

31. Ellacuría, "Task of a Christian University."

32. Peter-Hans Kolvenbach, SJ, Address to the Congregation of Provincials, September 20, 1990, *Acta Romana* 20, no. 3 (1990): 452.

33. John Paul II, *Ex Corde Ecclesiae* (August 1990), no. 32.

34. Gal. 5:6.

35. GC 32, d. 2, no. 8.

The Service of Faith in a Religiously Pluralistic World: The Challenge for Jesuit Higher Education[1]

Peter-Hans Kolvenbach, SJ

From *Conversations on Jesuit Higher Education*, 2007

Introduction

It gives me great pleasure to be with you today during this year of 2006 as we celebrate the five-hundredth anniversary of the birth of St. Francis Xavier, the great missionary of the sixteenth century. I thank you for all you have done and continue to do in this important—even crucial—apostolate of Jesuit higher education.

My words today will concentrate on our universities' commitment to the religious dimension of the whole person. I do this in order to stress the importance of conversation about religious subjects in all the areas of human existence. In a world in which specialization is increasingly more important, a world in which people learn more and more about less and less until they know everything there is about nothing at all, it is important to remember that religion and religious topics are not just the responsibility of specialized areas like the theology department or campus ministry. Rather, they are the responsibility of everyone at a university. Indeed, everyone involved in this enterprise has unique contributions and responsibilities regarding this central facet of human existence. In recent addresses on Jesuit higher education in the United States (at Santa Clara University and Spring Hill College), I have spoken about the service of faith with special attention to the promotion of justice. Today I will speak about the service of faith with particular attention to other religious traditions as it takes place in a particular culture.

I. Church Teaching, the Jesuit Mission, and the University's Mission

Our universities' fidelity to and participation in the ongoing development of the church and the Society of Jesus is quite obvious even in the most cursory examination of the past thirty-five years. In 1971, the Synod of Bishops boldly proclaimed that

> education demands a renewal of heart, a renewal based on the recognition of sin in its individual and social manifestations. It will also inculcate a truly and entirely human way of life in justice, love and simplicity. It will likewise awaken a critical sense, which will lead us to reflect on the society in which we live and on its values; it will make people ready to renounce these values when they cease to promote justice for all people.[2]

In responding to the church's vision articulated by the bishops, the Society of Jesus developed a similar emphasis in the documents of its Thirty-second General Congregation in 1975. In particular, Decree Four, "Our Mission Today: The Service of Faith and the Promotion of Justice," captured both imaginations and attention. In the years since 1975, this conviction about the relationship between faith and justice has been developed and nuanced, debated and challenged.

Justice, like *charity,* is a word that can easily be misunderstood. Some might say that justice is only about social action or legislation and that charity refers only to almsgiving. However, Pope John Paul II pointed out that the justice of the kingdom is the concrete, committed way to live out the new commandment of the gospel, and Pope Benedict XVI restored to charity the full divine and human meaning of love. Both popes have stressed that there will be no justice without Christ's love lived out by all of us; at the same time love will remain only a lovely word if it does not become concrete in deeds of charity and social assistance, of solidarity, and of justice.

In 1995, the Jesuits' most recent General Congregation addressed the relationship between justice and faith, both to emphasize its significance once again and to clarify its meaning. The congregation stated that the mission of the Society of Jesus and of its ministries, is "the service of faith of which the promotion of justice is an absolute requirement."[3] The integrating principle of this mission is the link between faith and the promotion of the justice of God's reign. Developing this line of thinking even more, the congregation stressed that an effective presentation of the gospel must include dialogue with members of other religious traditions and engagement with culture.[4]

Taking into consideration these documents of the church and the Society of Jesus, a few years ago the faculty of one university stated the university's purpose this way: "Our mission is to educate, to help develop a deeply human person, one of integrity, wholeness, and dedication, one equipped with values, knowledge, and skills related to the whole experience of living."[5]

Before going on, it might be helpful to note why an explicitly religious institution like the Society of Jesus is so interested in education. St. Ignatius and his companions expressed very simply the mission of the religious community they founded: "to help souls." The first Jesuits expanded this simple concept as they expressed their basic purpose in this way: "the propagation of the faith and the progress of souls in Christian life and doctrine." In his book *The First Jesuits*, Father John O'Malley helps us understand the meaning and significance of this purpose and of Ignatius's simple expression "to help souls." Ignatius and his followers used the phrase "as the best and most succinct description of what they were trying to do. . . . By 'soul' Jesuits meant the whole person. . . . [T]he Jesuits primarily wanted to help the person achieve an even better relationship with God."[6] Today, of course, we would use other words; however, the reality is the same: to help develop a deeply human person, one of integrity, wholeness, and dedication.

Although education was not part of Ignatius's original vision, it soon became a central facet of Jesuit life. Jesuits recognized that the best way to help people achieve a better relationship with God was by helping them understand their place in the world that God created. Through education, Jesuits sought to introduce students to the ever greater glory of God that is revealed as one came to know more and more about the universe and grasp the concepts and ideas that help us organize our understanding of, our place in, and our responsibility to all facets of creation. In 1586, the early educational theorist Father Diego Ledesma referred to the purpose of Jesuit schools this way:

> Whether they endeavor to teach the laws and form of government conducive to the public good; to contribute to the development, brilliance and perfection of the human mind; and, what is more important, to teach, defend and spread faith in God and religious practice, they should always and everywhere help people toward the easier and fuller attainment of their ultimate end.[7]

Jesuit higher education shares in this long and rich heritage.

As one might expect, then, there is an obvious connection between the teaching of the church, the mission of the Society of Jesus, and Jesuit universities' self-understanding. Your mission statements express well the truth that effective education is about formation of the whole person. True education, education really worthy of the name, is an organized effort to help people use their hearts, heads, and hands to contribute to the well-being of all of human society. Genuine education helps individuals develop their talents so they may become agents who act with others to make God's liberating and transforming love operative in the world.

Your statements on general education are contemporary expressions of the early Jesuits' commitment to a humanist education. Your continuing commitment to an extensive core curriculum is clearly one way to achieve the goal of understanding the world and one's place in that world. Your emphasis on academic service learning and the recurring attempts to renew programs within the core make important contributions to that process. However, it is important for us to recognize that your faculties' words apply to the activity of the entire university—faculty, staff, students, trustees. For all the functions of the university contribute to its mission of educating the whole person.

There are no neutral sciences, no pure academic disciplines that develop isolated from human problems in an ivory tower. Every branch of human knowledge raises questions today about meaning, ethical behavior, and moral responsibilities. As its very name—*university*—confirms, the whole university is involved in the process of educating the whole human being.

II. What Can Be Done to Serve Faith

Many of your students are at an age when they may be seriously searching for insight into faith and religion, perhaps questioning, doubting, rejecting. In educating the whole person, many different disciplines and facets of university life assist students as they search for meaning, offering light for the process of more deeply understanding what one believes about life's most profound questions such as who am I? and why am I here? In fact, many students come to a Jesuit, Catholic university because they expect to be helped to grapple with questions of faith in explicitly Jesuit and Catholic ways because of the university's tradition and because of the public image it presents.

Some of your students may identify themselves as members of a religious tradition without actually understanding or appreciating that tradition. How can you help them in a situation like that, especially if religious faith is sometimes seen as a uniquely private affair that has no place in public discourse or is seen at other times as something too important to be left unregulated by a culture's controls? How can you responsibly serve the faith in order to help them?

Doing the Work You Have Come Here to Do

First of all, most clearly and obviously you do this by doing the work you have come here to do, by being the best you can be at what you were hired to do, by accomplishing the vocation you have received through the unique combination of talents, training, and experience that qualify you to work at a Jesuit university. You help students the most by being dedicated teachers, by contributing to the growing deposit of knowledge about the universe and its operations, by serving the broader community in which the university exists. Whether through direct contact with students as professors or through all the supporting services that make education possible, each person at a Jesuit school can pass on what we know about human existence, contribute to understanding more about the universe in which we live, and serve the local community. You help students learn about their faith by faithfully expressing your own faith through the deeds of your lives.

Helping People Understand and Appropriate Their Own Religious Tradition—and Appreciate Others' Traditions

On another level, you can help students learn about their faith by helping them understand as clearly and as profoundly as possible their own religious tradition and by assisting them to find ways to nurture their commitment to this tradition. As a Catholic institution, a Jesuit university has particular responsibility to focus on Christianity, with special attention to Roman Catholicism. However, as a Jesuit institution attracts students of other religious traditions, it must explore ways to help them too, not only in academic courses but also in support from student services and campus ministry. As even the most cursory examination of a newspaper reminds us, this topic is essential for the health and safety of our world.

The profound vision of human solidarity articulated at the Second Vatican Council is a good place for understanding both this instinct for helping others and for seeing how it can be done:

One is the community of all peoples, one their origin, for God made the whole human race to live over the face of the earth. One also is their final goal, God. God's providence, manifestations of goodness, and saving design extend to all people, until that time when the elect will be united in the Holy City, the city ablaze with the glory of God, where the nations will walk in God's light.

The council continues:

[T]he Church therefore exhorts her sons and daughters, that through dialogue and collaboration with the followers of other religions, carried out with prudence and love and in witness to the Christian faith and life, they recognize, preserve and promote the good things, spiritual and moral, as well as the socio-cultural values found among these people.[8]

The Challenge of Interreligious Dialogue

We have come to understand, however, that dialogue has its own challenges, not immediately apparent to us at first. We can begin our journey of true dialogue by listening to one another in our various religious traditions. We can learn about one another's traditions. But true dialogue must move beyond mere "learning about" other religions to the level of conversation among those who profess these differing religious traditions.

Grounded in our own faith tradition, rooted in our personal faith commitment, we are called to encounter other religious traditions. In this we imitate the example of the Lord that is presented in the Gospels: he shared his faith with the Samaritan woman while respecting her convictions; he praised the way the Samaritan cared for the dying man on the road; he responded to the Romans looking for answers to their needs.

True openness to the faith of others can lead us to questions that can cause considerable discomfort. At times, we may be tempted to retreat to the comfort of our own personal, private faith as we have always known it, permitting no further challenges; at other times, we may be tempted to embrace a broad yet shallow tolerance that claims that truth is relative. Yet if we engage in serious conversation with people of other faith commitments, and engage in projects of social concern with them, we can often begin to experience our own faith more profoundly and more satisfyingly. What seemed to us as threatening challenges to our personal faith can become new windows of enlightenment to the possibilities of our faith and the faith of others in our world today.

The Society of Jesus, convened in 1995 as our Thirty-fourth General Congregation, summed up this challenge of dialogue in this way:

> In the context of the divisive, exploitative, and conflictual roles that religions, including Christianity, have played in history, dialogue seeks to develop the unifying and liberating potential of all religions, thus showing the relevance of religion for human well-being, justice, and world peace. Above all we need to relate positively to believers of other religions because they are our neighbors; the common elements of our religious heritages and our human concern force us to establish ever closer ties based on universally accepted ethical values. . . . To be religious today is to be interreligious in the sense that a positive relationship with believers of other faiths is a requirement in a world of religious pluralism.[9]

The "Four Dialogues"

In encouraging you to seek some concrete modes for helping your students, your colleagues, and your community, as well as yourselves, grapple with differences in faith traditions, let me suggest that the categories developed by the Pontifical Council for Interreligious Dialogue and Congregation for the Evangelization of People help organize your approach to the mission of any Jesuit university. The four dialogues recommended by the church were incorporated into the Society of Jesus' way of proceeding in 1995 in these words:

a. The *dialogue of life*, where people strive to live in an open and neighborly spirit, sharing their joys and sorrows, their human problems and preoccupations

b. The *dialogue of action*, in which Christians and others collaborate for the integral development and liberation of people

c. The *dialogue of religious experience*, where persons, rooted in their own religious traditions, share their spiritual riches, for instance, with regard to prayer and contemplation, faith and ways of searching for God or the Absolute

d. The *dialogue of theological exchange*, where specialists seek to deepen their understanding of their respective religious heritages, and to appreciate each other's spiritual values[10]

These four dialogues are already part of your way of being Jesuit universities. I mention them as a way to help you reflect on what you are already doing so that you can consider how to organize and channel your energies in ever more effectively accomplishing your mission to educate the whole person. You, of course, are the best situated to organize and accomplish these dialogues, but clearly they are at the heart of what a university tries to do in its teaching, research, and service. These dialogues take place in a particular place and time, within a unique culture. As you engage in these important dialogues of life, action, religious experience, and theological exchange, it is important to keep in mind the profound impact that comes from the various cultures that situate a university.

Engaging Culture

From the days of Francis Xavier (1506–1552) and Matteo Ricci (1552–1610) to the time of Pierre Teilhard de Chardin (1881–1955) and the present, Jesuits have recognized the necessity of engaging culture in their service of faith. Both appreciation and critique have characterized this engagement, gratefully acknowledging the goodness of human culture while rejecting whatever human customs are contrary to the revelation of the gospel. Both remain essential today;

and our universities, as Jesuit and Catholic, are well situated to contribute to this dimension of the service of faith.

The Second Vatican Council encourages this combination of appreciation and critique in its document "The Church in the Modern World":

> In every age, the church carries the responsibility of reading the signs of the times and of interpreting them in the light of the Gospel, if it is to carry out its task. . . .
>
> Ours is a new age of history with profound and rapid changes spreading gradually to all corners of the earth. They are the products of people's intelligence and creative activity. . . . A transformation of this kind brings with it the serious problems associated with any crisis of growth. Increase in power is not always accompanied by control of that power for the benefit of humanity. . . .
>
> Never before has the human race enjoyed such an abundance of wealth, resources, and economic power; and yet a huge proportion of the world's citizens are still tormented by hunger and poverty, while countless numbers suffer from total illiteracy. Never before have people had so keen an understanding of freedom, yet at the same time new forms of social and psychological slavery make their appearance. Although the world of today has a very vivid awareness of its unity and of how one person depends on another in needful solidarity, it is most grievously turned into opposing camps by conflicting forces. For political, social, economic, racial, and ideological disputes still continue bitterly, and with them the peril of a war which would reduce everything to ashes.[11]

The forty years that have passed since these insightful words were written have only intensified their depth, relevance, and challenge.

At the Thirty-fourth General Congregation in 1995, the Society of Jesus emphasized both what is good in the world's cultures and the need for proper enculturation in the proclamation of the gospel: "Our service of the Christian faith must never disrupt the best impulses of the culture in which we work, nor can it be an alien imposition from outside. . . . Our intuition is that the gospel resonates with what is good in each culture." The congregation acknowledged past mistakes by describing how Jesuits contributed to the alienation of the very people they wanted to serve and how Jesuits failed to discover "the values, depth and transcendence of other cultures, which manifest the action of the Spirit." However, it refused to let past mistakes forestall future efforts. Rather, its document on culture addressed the problems just mentioned in the long quotation from "The Church in the Modern World." The congregation stated, "The Gospel brings a prophetic challenge to every culture to remove all those things which inhibit the justice of the Kingdom."[12]

Thus, it is important for all members of the university community to dialogue with one another about the cultural dimensions of your educational efforts in order to determine your response to the dominant culture of the United States. What are the best impulses of the American culture in which you work, "the values, depth, and transcendence" in your own culture that manifest the action of the Lord's Spirit? What are those things that inhibit the justice of the kingdom of God from being manifested to all God's beloved daughters and sons? The same questions can be asked about various other cultural entities that contribute to the university's life.

How Can Diversity Help?

The cultural contexts and the importance of dialogue become obvious in discussing a topic like diversity. Many of our unexamined assumptions and biases become evident when we begin to consider the differences that exist among us. In recent years, I understand that much has been said about the need for gender diversity in some Jesuit schools' faculty, administration, and student body. We should never forget that the first pages of the Bible show the Lord bringing diversity to his creation by distinguishing day and night, land and sea; as expression of God's richness, no one tree is the same as any other tree, no one animal a mere clone of another. In a very special way, each human person is called by its name.

Unfortunately, instead of considering diversity as an expression of the infinite bounty of the Creator, we too easily use difference as a reason to hate one another. Color, gender, culture, and nationality as religion can be used to fight against one another. In the last pages of the

Bible, all the differences contribute to building up the new City of God among us. Our task will be to integrate the diversities in the unifying vision of the Creator for his new heaven and new earth. However, not all diversity, not all the differences, come from the Creator, and these need to be overcome or eliminated. Gender and racial diversity should enrich humanity; but diversity in health condition is to be overcome; the diversity between good will and ill will should not be tolerated. The existence of great diversity in religion is a fact that is not always God-given, unlike gender and racial diversity.

As you evaluate your university's diversity, you might ask your-selves what you accomplish with your diversity, what end you expect to attain. You strive for diversity and celebrate it with your publicity when you achieve it. However, this is only the beginning of appreciat-ing your diversity. What structures of dialogue would help promote serious conversations that might affect the very kind of women and men you are as teachers and as students? How can dialogues of life, action, religious experience, and theological exchange assist and deepen your experience as educators so that you might admit and take advantage of ethnic, racial, gender, and religious differences among you?

How can you take greater advantage of the rich religious resources that form part of the cultural heritage of your city? As a university which rightly sees itself as the meeting place for groups in the area concerned with racial and civic justice, how can a particular Jesuit and Catholic university see itself as the meeting place for the religions of the area? What greater claim could Xavier have for the service of faith than to have tapped religious diversity to engage in conversation intellectually, morally, and spiritually!

Conclusion: Using Your Dearly Purchased Freedom to Carry On the Conversation

The service of faith in Jesuit higher education, then, helps members of the university community develop a profound understanding of and commitment to their own religious tradition. This process necessarily includes openness to and learning from other religious traditions and appreciation and critique of culture. Religious diversity and cultural values are interdependent and overlapping—not independent—dimensions of our lives. Indeed, interreligious dialogue is one of the most powerful responses to the global cultural malaise. It will take the cooperation of the world's religions to address adequately dehumanizing cultural forces.

Your system of Jesuit and Catholic higher education in the United States is, as you well know, a very expensive one, involving hundreds of millions of dollars, which you must constantly struggle to maintain. That high cost, however, can be seen as the price of your freedom to raise questions about God and faith and religion in a way no government-supported university in your country has the right to do. You have paid the price for a number of years. You continue and will continue to pay the price. Yet you must also ask yourselves how thoroughly and well you are using the freedom for dialogue and conversation you have purchased at such a great cost.

Your responsibility as educators is certainly to help your students to live and achieve success in an ever more globally oriented society. However, a Jesuit and Catholic university has the responsibility for even more: to prepare students to be leaders in this globally oriented society. We have seen in recent years that much of world politics and economy is rooted in religion but also how political and economic values can become pseudo-religions. Your students must be able to understand how faith in God lies at the heart of our motivation, our compassion, and our dedication. With dearly purchased freedom to carry on the conversation among men and women of faith, the Jesuit universities in your country can be leaders in showing the relationship between faith and justice that leads humanity to "the Holy City, the city ablaze with the glory of God, where the nations will walk in God's light."[13]

NOTES

1. The text presented here is the one edited for inclusion in the Fall 2007 issue of *Conversations on Jesuit Higher Education*, with a few corrections.

Paragraphing, however, follows the original address delivered at Xavier University on October 3, 2006. The headings have been supplied by the present editor.

2. *Justice in the World*, World Synod of Catholic Bishops, 1971, no. 51.

3. Decree Four in *Documents of the Thirty-Second General Congregation[s] of the Society of Jesus* (St. Louis: Institute of Jesuit Sources, 1977), no. 2.

4. "Servants of Christ's Mission," Decree Two in *Documents of the Thirty-fourth General Congregation of the Society of Jesus* (St. Louis: Institute of Jesuit Sources, 1995), 40–42, nos. 15–17.

5. "General Education at Xavier University," 1.

6. John W. O'Malley, SJ, *The First Jesuits* (Cambridge, MA: Harvard University Press, 1993), 5, 18–19.

7. Diego Ledesma, SJ, *Monumenta Paedigogica*, ed. Ladislaus Lukas, SJ (Rome: Institutum Historicum Societatis Iesu, 1974), II, 528–29.

8. *Nostra Aetate*, "Declaration on the Relation of the Church to Non-Christian Religions," nos. 1–2.

9. "Our Mission and Interreligious Dialogue," Decree Five in *Documents of the Thirty-fourth General Congregation of the Society of Jesus*, no. 3.

10. "Our Mission and Interreligious Dialogue," no. 4.

11. *Gaudium et Spes*, "Pastoral Constitution on the Church in the Modern World," no. 4.

12. "Our Mission and Culture," Decree Four in *Documents of the Thirty-fourth General Congregation of the Society of Jesus*, no. 8, no. 11, no. 12, no. 3. [The decree is reprinted in its entirety earlier in this volume.—Editor]

13. *Nostra Aetate*, no. 1.

Communal Reflection on the Jesuit Mission in Higher Education: A Way of Proceeding

The Society of Jesus in the United States

From the Jesuit Conference, 2002

Preface from the Jesuit Conference Board

Dear Colleagues in Jesuit Higher Education:

In composing this document on the Jesuit, Catholic character of Jesuit higher education, we felt that some explanation of our intention would be helpful.

First, this document presumes that there has been local discussion on the essential characteristics of a Catholic university as these have been enunciated in *Ex Corde Ecclesiae*:[1]

- A Christian inspiration not only of individuals but of the university community as such;
- A continuing reflection in the light of the Catholic faith upon the growing treasury of human knowledge, to which it seeks to contribute by its own research;

- Fidelity to the Christian message as it comes to us through the church;
- An institutional commitment to the service of the people of God and of the human family in their pilgrimage to the transcendent goal, which gives meaning to life.

Second, we have prepared a document that invites inclusive local discussion, debate, and adaptation. By inclusive we mean that our universities *de facto* are ecumenical in their ethos. The higher education institutions that we call Jesuit are communities that represent a variety of beliefs and convictions. We are attempting here to present a document that is faithful to our distinctive Catholic and Jesuit tradition and yet open to the values and convictions of other members of our communities who join us in our mission. Further, we believe that the faculty, staff, and boards of our institutions will be engaged only if they themselves can contribute to their self-definition and self-assessment. For those reasons, we called this document "a way of proceeding" and invite the participants to "communal reflection." The document is *an* approach, not the only approach. It does indicate parameters of authenticity, but it does not dictate how these should be understood or implemented within each institution. It is meant to be a way to get people into conversation about the mission of their institutions.

Third, our aim was to help those institutions whose members have been working hard to create a Jesuit culture and Catholic ethos within their institutions. While we have tried to be sensitive to the rich variety of religious and ethical traditions that constitute our faculties, staffs, administrations, boards, and student bodies, we have turned our major focus on the mission of being a distinctive voice in North American higher education.

Fourth, we hope that these characteristics and their suggested focus questions will provide Jesuit higher education institutions with guidelines for their professional self-evaluations, their recruitment, and their fund-raising.

Fifth, it is up to the leadership within each Jesuit university to use this statement as a tool for discerning the emphases and directions

that their schools will take in sustaining and promoting their distinctive character as Jesuit and Catholic. Without local leadership we will
have one more document for storage, not an incentive for reflection,
discussion, and action.

The Board of the Jesuit Conference
May 2002

Introduction

The Thirty-fourth General Congregation and the recent addresses
of Peter-Hans Kolvenbach, superior general of the Society of Jesus,
attest to the importance of the work of higher education today and to
the need for all who are involved in this enterprise to be committed
to its distinctive character as Jesuit and Catholic. What governs the
enterprise of Jesuit higher education is its sense of mission. There are
three aspects to this mission.

First, it is a mission in continuity with the historical evolution of
the Ignatian charism. "In 1551, the Roman College opened its doors,
an emblematic figure of what would become the Society's venture in
the university field. Four and a half centuries later, the Society remains
intensely dedicated to the work of higher education with numberless
universities and other institutions throughout the world."[2]

Second, the contemporary mission respects the reality of being
both a university and a Jesuit apostolic work. In all its endeavors, Jesuit
education is distinguished by intellectual excellence and academic
rigor. "To be a university requires dedication to research, teaching, and
the various forms of service that correspond to its cultural mission."[3]
At the same time, a Jesuit university must reflect its specifically Jesuit
character. "To be Jesuit requires that the university act in harmony with
the demands of the service of faith and the promotion of justice found
in Decree 4 of the 32nd General Congregation."[4]

Third, the contemporary mission of Jesuit higher education relies,
perhaps as never before, on the collaborative talents and energies of

Jesuits and their colleagues. Today, Jesuits represent only a small numerical presence within those universities called Jesuit. The historical continuity of the mission and its crucial importance in engaging the needs of modern men and women require that a critical mass of the faculty and staff of Jesuit universities commit to and then work to advance that mission.

To engage the world in its own integrity is also to work within the cultural, social, ethical, and religious complexities of that world. To affirm the centrality of the wisdom, justice, and peace preached by Christ as characteristic of God's kingdom is to commit the resources of the Jesuit university to a work of sensitive mediation between the world and the gospel. Therefore, the world and the gospel must be in dialogue. Such dialogue needs discernment, the ability to judge when, where, and how the world and the gospel interact.

Characteristics of Jesuit Higher Education

The following characteristics of Jesuit higher education represent one way of proceeding in that discerning dialogue. These characteristics and the process that they invite are meant to enable each institution to locate its own sense of mission. Within each Jesuit university, groups of faculty, staff, administrators, students, and boards must engage in that dialogue out of their unique institutional histories, professional development, and local missions.

I. Dedication to Human Dignity from a Catholic/Jesuit Faith Perspective

Ignatian spirituality, the foundation of all Jesuit apostolic endeavors, views men and women as created in love and created to reflect the wisdom and goodness of God. The advent of Christ and the continued presence of Christ's Spirit enhance that created dignity.

Men and women are enfolded in God's care and compassion, offered companionship as the brothers and sisters of Christ, and empowered by the Spirit to complete the work of Christ on earth. Jesuits believe that their colleagues from other religious and ethical traditions share this dedication to human dignity and work for its implementation.

Sample Focus Questions

- How do the hiring and promotion practices in your institution reflect a belief in the human dignity of all faculty and staff?
- How do your students learn in an environment of respect? Do they learn respect for themselves, for others, for the global community, and for the universe itself? Do they learn to value care and compassion because they are being treated with care and compassion?
- How well are diverse groups incorporated into the life of your institution? Do you rejoice in your pluralism?
- Have your graduates integrated this regard for human dignity into their habitual attitudes and life choices? How have you been able to gauge this integration?
- How does your institution engage its Catholic identity? How does your institution serve the local Catholic diocese?
- How does your institution express its Catholic identity in its sacramental, liturgical, and prayer life?
- How does your institution encourage and support the spiritual development of its students, faculty, staff, and alumni?
- How are the Spiritual Exercises adapted and made available to all the members of your educational community?
- How does your institution support members of the community from differing religious and philosophical traditions?
- How well does your institution support the priorities of the Society of Jesus and the local Jesuit province that sponsors your institution?

2. Reverence for and an Ongoing Reflection on Human Experience

The Jesuit university or college must be a place of intellectual honesty, pluralism, and mutual respect where inquiry and open discussion characterize the environment of teaching, research, and professional development. The idea of reverence was a pivotal one for St. Ignatius Loyola. For him, reverence was first an attitude of regard before the majesty of God, but it was also a regard for all that God had created as both a gift from God and a way into God's presence. Inspired by this sense of reverence, the Jesuit ideal of seeking and finding God in all things presupposes this genuine regard for the mystery within the universe. It is an ideal that gives serious attention to those great and abiding questions about the meaning of life and the conduct of human affairs. It is an ideal that encourages an openness of mind and heart to the varieties of ways in which the human spirit has named God and defined the moral life. It is an ideal that promotes a rigorous yet sensitive attention to the demands of the professions and of technology. It is an ideal that exults in the world of creative energy in literature and music, in art and theater, in business and in the sciences. It is an ideal that engages the world both locally and globally.

Sample Focus Questions

- How is the Catholic and Jesuit character of your institution reflected in your undergraduate curriculum, graduate programs, and professional schools (e.g., in calling attention to the ethical and religious dimensions of every study, in hiring only faculty open to the full mission of the school, and in making known the specifically Catholic position on issues)?
- How does your institution acknowledge and reward excellence in research, in teaching, and in service? How does this contribute to the flourishing of Catholic intellectual life?
- Do you provide opportunities for interdisciplinary seminars, workshops, or institutes so that faculty and staff can come to know one another, share their perspectives, and enrich the community of reflection at your university or college?

In your undergraduate education, how do you help students to integrate their studies into a lifelong ability to learn, to reflect, to critique, and to celebrate the life of the mind, heart, imagination, and religious experience?

- What are the research projects that characterize your institution? Do they reflect the distinctive mission of your institution?
- How are interreligious dialogue and intercultural activity present in your campus?
- How are environmental and ecological concerns developed in and out of the classroom?
- How is a seamless respect for life taught and practiced on campus?

3. Creative Companionship with Colleagues

The contemporary Jesuit university is committed to creating a community of dialogue and service. Dialogue is the mutual investment in learning through listening, through honest exchange, and through a desire to come to a new level of understanding and appreciation. As such, dialogue enjoys a privileged place in the Ignatian tradition. Service signifies a mutual willingness among faculty, staff, and administration to enhance the entire environment of learning and service that should exist within the Jesuit university community and between it and the world outside its boundaries. There is a healthy professionalism that respects the differences in goals and methodologies among the various branches of knowledge and competencies. But the Jesuit educational ideal is also one that tries to find ways to transcend these boundaries in order to forge a community of scholarship and service.

Sample Focus Questions
- What mechanisms are in place within your institution to incorporate new faculty and staff into the overarching Jesuit, Catholic mission of your institution?
- How have faculty, staff, administrators, and board members—whether Catholic or from differing religious and

philosophical traditions—been helped to incorporate their faith into the school's mission? How has your institution encouraged and supported ecumenical and interfaith dialogue with the larger community in which it resides?

• How are students—graduate and undergraduate—taught to work together, to share their research, and to learn with and from one another?

• What means are in place to assess the appropriation of your mission statement by your trustees, faculty, staff, students, and alumni? What has that assessment indicated about the overall appropriation of your mission?

4. Focused Care for Students

At the heart of the Jesuit educational ideal is a communal care for the integral development of the men and women who have chosen to come for instruction, guidance, and friendship. Everyone involved in Jesuit higher education—faculty, staff, administration, and board members—plays a role in student development. The pursuit of wisdom and competence, the quest for psychological maturity and spiritual depth, the desire for ethical grounding, and the challenge of social solidarity and global awareness—these student concerns demand our attention and response. In their relationships with students, faculty and staff inevitably model what they value. In communicating those values, they act as mentors to their students. Today, students often seek to resolve the feeling of disconnect in their lives. We need to develop appropriate processes that will facilitate the kind of intellectual, ethical, social, and religious integration that Jesuit and Catholic education has long espoused.

Sample Focus Questions

• How are new faculty and staff both supported and challenged to fulfill their roles as mentors to the undergraduates and graduate students of your institution?

- How does your institution affirm the work that students do in areas of service and community building?
- How does your institution help students to confront problems that inhibit their academic, social, ethical, or spiritual growth?
- Practically, do you provide programs for substance abuse, sexual confusion, addictive behavior, and psychological upheaval?
- Do board members receive profiles of student needs, the institutional response to these needs, and, when appropriate, a timetable for remedial action?
- What opportunities do students have to care for and even to act as mentors to one another? Is there any explicit education in this and guidance in learning such skills, especially in the residence halls?

5. Well-Educated Justice and Solidarity

The call to justice and solidarity is complex. Justice looks first to the justice that is God's saving action for men and women. Catholic social justice centers on the establishment of the kingdom of God within the hearts of men and women and then within their societies. Solidarity with the rest of the human race means the practical awareness that only by working together can the human family meet effectively the challenges of worldwide hunger, ignorance, disease, and violence. But solidarity also means the extending of care to those close at hand who have been ignored or abandoned within our society. Solidarity also means a commitment to change the economic, political, and social structures that enslave, dehumanize, and destroy human life and dignity. Each Jesuit university must examine its own social environment, including its own commitment to justice and solidarity. Through community service, service-learning projects, immersion experiences, and faculty-student research projects, more and more Jesuit institutions have provided supervised opportunities for their students to meet and to learn from people from other economic and social groups. By confronting the poverty both in themselves as well as in others, students, faculty, staff, administrators, and board members have come to understand how precious is human dignity and how dependent it is on adequate food, water, housing, health care, and education.

Sample Focus Questions

- What courses or programs effectively raise social-justice questions in your institution? What research projects focus on issues of injustice and the need for global solidarity?
- Are there service-learning programs, immersion experiences, community-service opportunities in your institution? Do such programs include a process to select participants, to prepare them, to supervise their involvement, to help them to reflect on their experiences, and then to integrate these experiences into their lives?
- How are students of different economic, racial, ethnic, and social backgrounds incorporated into your school culture and how do they enrich that culture?
- Have faculty and student research projects assisted the neighboring community or the broader community?
- How does your institution work with its alumni to help them understand their solidarity with one another and their mission to work for a better world?
- Are there internal issues of injustice that your university needs to confront?

Conclusion

An institution of higher education has always provided its greatest service when it has promoted academic excellence on all levels. This practical esteem for the intellectual life has characterized Jesuit higher education from its beginnings. But the reshaping of the contemporary world according to the justice, peace, and love preached by Christ and cherished by the church characterizes its apostolic ambition. World realities and personal faith have prompted a new understanding of Jesuit humanism, one that integrates academic excellence with social responsibility.[5] These two goals must be in harmony in any Jesuit college or university. These characteristics can have practical meaning and implementation only if each institution adapts them to the realities of its own life and rhythm.

Within the shared Ignatian heritage abides a rich variety of histories, local traditions, pastoral needs, and educational opportunities. Every Jesuit university has its own resources and constituencies. Ignatian adaptation asks, "How does this principle or strategy fit your situation?" Therefore, these characteristics are neither commands nor commercials. Rather they are invitations to deepen a commitment already shared and to confirm a direction already undertaken.

NOTES

1. *Ex Corde Ecclesiae*, "On Catholic Universities," no. 13, in *Catholic Universities in Church and Society: A Dialogue on* Ex Corde Ecclesiae, ed. John P. Langan, SJ (Washington, DC: Georgetown University Press, 1993), 229–53.

2. "The Jesuit University in the Light of the Ignatian Charism," address by Father General Peter-Hans Kolvenbach to the International Meeting of Jesuit Higher Education, Rome, May 27, 2001, para. 57 (available at http://www.jesuits-europe.org/doc/univ2001e.htm).

3. "The Service of Faith and the Promotion of Justice in American Jesuit Higher Education," speech given by Father General Peter-Hans Kolvenbach at Santa Clara University, October 6, 2000, and "Jesuits and University Life," in Documents of the 34th General Congregation, Decree 17, no. 6 [both reprinted in their entireties in this volume—Editor].

4. Ibid., no. 7.

5. "By means of a kind of universal humanism a Catholic University is completely dedicated to the research of all aspects of truth in their essential connection with the supreme Truth, who is God. It does this without fear but rather with enthusiasm, dedicating itself to every path of knowledge, aware of

being preceded by him who is the Way, the Truth, and the Life (John 14:6), the Logos whose Spirit of intelligence and love enables the human person with his or her own intelligence to find the ultimate reality of which he is the source and end who alone is capable of giving fully that Wisdom without which the future of the world would be in danger," *Ex Corde Ecclesiae* "On Catholic Universities: Apostolic Constitution of August 15, 1990", no. 4 (Washington, DC: United States Catholic Conference, n.d.).

Higher Standards

Dean Brackley, SJ

From *America*, 2006

Five years ago last October, the superior general of the Jesuits, Peter-Hans Kolvenbach, delivered a historic address at Santa Clara University in California, urging that the promotion of justice should have a central place in Jesuit higher education. Father Kolvenbach was not simply innovating. Ten years earlier Pope John Paul II had written in his apostolic letter *Ex Corde Ecclesiae* that "the Christian spirit of service to others in promoting social justice is especially important for each Catholic university and should be shared by professors and fomented among students" (#34). The document called for research on "the promotion of justice for all, a more equitable distribution of world resources and a new economic and political order that will better serve the human community at the national and international level" (#32).

While promoting justice may not be the chief work of higher education, according to *Ex Corde Ecclesiae*, it is indispensable for Catholic colleges and universities. This emphasis, which responds to greater social awareness in the church and wider society, has far-reaching implications. The promotion of justice is one of those factors that distinguishes Catholic colleges and universities, calling them beyond the models, both liberal and conservative, commonly held up for imitation. Our schools cannot measure their educational excellence by the same yardstick as Harvard or Stanford. Neither can they afford to turn in on themselves as confessional enclaves.

Far from distorting the mission of the university, the promotion of justice should enhance it. But how? Let me suggest seven higher standards for Catholic higher education.

First, the university community should strive to *understand the real world*. Ignacio Ellacuría, SJ, the rector of the Jesuit university in El Salvador who was murdered in 1989, used to insist that reality is the primary object of study. That is less obvious than it sounds. Many students graduate from college with little understanding of homelessness, abortion, or their own country's military adventures. Last year during the U.S. electoral campaign, polls revealed a striking level of ignorance on vital political issues.

By all means, let us lose ourselves in great works of art. They teach us about life and shape us to live better. But let us resist the kind of obsession with narrow subspecialties that distracts us from the wider reality.

A second standard is related to this: *focus on the big questions*. Wisdom, not mere information, is the goal of education. Again, let us study obscure insects and obscure authors and master the periodic table of the elements. But let that study be part of a quest to understand what life means, how life and well-being are threatened, and how they can flourish. Let the most important questions structure learning—questions about the drama of life and death, about injustice and liberation, good and evil, grace and sin. In the language of faith, the cross is the center of reality—Jesus' cross and all the other crosses. At the foot of the cross, reality comes into focus. Lacking that perspective, wisdom turns to folly.

Third, our universities need to *free us from bias*. We know how debates in the classroom and the lounge about free trade and the war in Iraq can drone on and achieve little, because they are based on unexamined assumptions. Moreover, teachers frequently offer answers to questions students are not asking, because the problems lie beyond their experience. Sophistry and propaganda compound the problem. How are teachers to help students unmask deception today, when war is waged on false pretenses and Fox News claims to be impartial? Does impartiality mean giving equal time to the Swift-boat veterans? What does impartiality mean in practice?

Seeking truth includes uncovering hidden interests inside us and outside us. In the spirit of the Enlightenment, most modern thinkers prescribe reason and conscious awareness as the means to overcome bias. Yet although reality is reasonable, it is naive to suppose that reason alone will take us to it. Discovering truth requires reason integrally considered—that is, rooted in experience and practice and nourished by contemplation, affectivity, and imagination. Only such an "enriched reason" that engages the whole person—intellect, will, and emotions—produces wisdom.

Above all, the pure-reason paradigm overlooks the need for moral conversion. Cognitive liberation requires personal change. In the end, prejudice is embedded in my identity, so that to question my world is to question me. Naturally, I resist.

We need wholesome crises to help expand our horizons. Frequently, such experiences occur when students engage in activities, like service learning, that draw them into close contact with poverty and suffering. There they are mugged by reality. The humanity of the people they encounter, some of them victims of injustice, crashes through students' defenses, provoking a salutary disorientation, much like the experience of falling in love. When the anonymous masses take on three dimensions for students, their horizons open. Their world is reconfigured. Some things move from the margin to the center and others from the center to the edge.

Today, this kind of experience is a necessary part of education for the middle-class "tribe," to which most of the population of Catholic colleges and universities belongs. At Santa Clara, the Jesuit general argued that service among poor people should be a normal part of students' academic programs. This can happen close to home. At the same time, I am deeply impressed with the educational impact of semester-abroad programs for U.S. students, like the Casa de la Solidaridad in El Salvador. While semester-abroad programs abound in Europe for U.S. students, we need to open more such programs in poor countries.

Engaging suffering people and injustice frequently brings to the surface in students the crucial question, What am I doing with my life? This suggests a fourth standard. As formative of the whole person, Catholic education should *help students discover their vocation in life—above all, their vocation to love and serve.*

Students are assaulted by different worldviews and versions of the good life as never before. They wrestle with what is really true and right. For some the world seems to fall apart once a semester. Their search is intense, because more is at stake than ideas. Confronted by contradictory role models—a Mother Teresa on one hand, a Britney Spears on the other—they are searching for an identity and a mission. But while contemporary society might offer them jobs, the only vocation it seems to propose is getting and spending. Besides helping students with their careers, we need to help them discover their vocations. That might be to raise children, discover galaxies, drive a truck—or a combination of these. But whatever it is concretely, faith and reason point to a deeper human calling that we all share—namely, to spend ourselves in love.

Twenty-five years ago, a few months before she was killed in El Salvador, Ita Ford, a Maryknoll sister, wrote to her young niece, Jennifer, back in Brooklyn, "I hope you come to find that which gives life a deep meaning for you. Something worth living for—maybe even worth dying for—something that energizes you, enthuses you, enables you to keep moving ahead. I can't tell you what it might be. That's for you to find, to choose, to love." Ita invited Jennifer to discover her deepest calling, to find herself by losing herself. Higher education should awaken the dramatist or the chemist in us, but also that deepest vocation that is the call of Christ.

According to Peter-Hans Kolvenbach, "The real measure of our Jesuit universities lies in who our students become . . . and the adult Christian responsibility they will exercise in future towards their neighbor and their world." This holds for all Catholic universities.

Economic diversity is a fifth standard for our schools. Last May Amherst College awarded an honorary degree to Nelson Mandela. He used the occasion to appeal to the U.S. academic world: "In this world under threat, colleges and universities remain our best hope," Mandela said. "Your central mission, the pursuit of truth, must lead the way. . . . We depend on you to point us toward solutions to our problems."

Mandela then addressed the issue of who gets into college. "The challenges of ensuring full access, according to ability rather than wealth or privilege, have not been met," he said. "Until they are, we will forfeit some of the talent and genius that the world sorely needs. All institutions of higher education have the obligation to open the door more widely."

The diversity that people celebrate on campus these days must include economic diversity. This is easier said than done, as costs and tuition rise sharply each year and financial aid plummets. Administrators strive to provide facilities that will attract more affluent students, who can pay full freight and compensate for scholarship students who cannot. These facilities sometimes include first-rate food service, pools, fitness centers, and other amenities. Yet all of this can foster an upscale consumer culture on campus that risks undermining the promotion of justice and compounds the alienation of lower-income and minority students.

How can we cut this Gordian knot? Here are three suggestions: promote a culture of simplicity on campus; maximize scholarships based on need, rather than athletic or scholastic ability; include $50 million for scholarships in the next capital campaign.

A sixth higher standard is *truth in advertising*. Catholic universities should welcome people of other communions and faiths, and of no faith, as first-class citizens. At the same time, our schools must be places where the Catholic tradition is studied, critically debated, and handed on. Now that we take pluralism for granted, we can no longer treat our traditions, or faith, as we once did. We should fear for the future if students are graduating with first-class training in, say, economics and only a First Communion or a Newsweek understanding of the faith. Even more, keeping faith requires orthopraxis, including conspicuous respect for the rights of workers and all vulnerable members of the learning community.

Lastly, our universities should *speak to the wider world*. At the Central American University (UCA) in El Salvador, we speak of *proyección social*, "social projection"; in this term we include all those means by which the university communicates, or projects, social criticism and constructive proposals beyond the campus into the wider society. In practice, our *proyección social* at the UCA involves media appearances, publications, the work of the Human Rights Institute, the pastoral center, the university radio, and similar instruments.

Orthopraxis is costly. In 1989 six Jesuits and two women were murdered at the UCA because of the university's *proyección social*. Even so, nine months after the killings at the UCA, John Paul II's *Ex Corde Ecclesiae* called for *proyección social*. The document states that Catholic universities must "demonstrate the courage to express uncomfortable truths, truths that may clash with public opinion but that are also necessary to safeguard the authentic good of society" (# 32). Our Catholic colleges and universities in the United States already practice this when they take public stands on abortion and related issues.

This standard also raises important questions. Who speaks for the university? How is it possible to take into account its different stakeholders and constituencies? How can accountability and the right to dissent be ensured? And there are other issues. Should the university call for an end to the death penalty? Should it speak out against torture at Abu Ghraib, the violation of rights at Guantánamo, and the destruction of Fallujah; criticize inequitable tax policy and the lack of health care for the poor; point out how Hurricane Katrina revealed serious neglect of the common good; defend the rights of gay and lesbian persons? Perhaps universities can help the Catholic Church recover its voice and moral authority in the aftermath of the sexual abuse scandals.

A new emphasis on promoting justice builds on the rich heritage of Catholic higher education. It refocuses tired debates of liberal versus conservative, confessional versus secularist. It may provoke misunderstanding, persecution, and financial troubles—at the UCA we have known eighteen bombings and martyrdom. But it will also produce a stronger sense of identity and mission, along with more lasting and universal good.

Soul Education: An Ignatian Priority

Howard Gray, SJ

From *Spirit, Style, Story: Essays Honoring John W. Padberg, SJ*, 2002

Introduction

Rowan Williams, in his study of Teresa of Ávila, suggests that mysticism is perhaps less a state of prayer than a worldview, a way of interpreting life rather than an ecstatic removal into a higher life.[1] He is not denying that mysticism is an event, but he is calling attention to another way of looking at union with God. Recently, there has been a recovery of Ignatian spirituality as a hermeneutic, a way of interpreting life, rather than an inspiration for work, or a spur to dedication, or a discerning way to critique life.[2] I want to approach the topic of Ignatian spirituality and its relationship to higher education, a topic that John Padberg has spent his life exploring and communicating, by adapting Williams's worldview approach and aligning myself with those who see this spirituality as an interpretative prism. Therefore, I begin with the familiar expression of purpose that introduces the Ignatian *Constitutions* of the Society of Jesus:

> The end of this Society is to devote itself with God's grace to the salvation and perfection of the members' own souls, but also with great

diligence to labor strenuously in giving aid toward the salvation and perfection of the souls of their fellow men [and women].[3]

In his translation of the *Constitutions*, the late George Ganss, a man to whom the contemporary Society of Jesus owes a deep debt of gratitude, notes that *animas* in Ignatius's Spanish means "the person," first the men of the Society and their entire selves, and then the persons they serve—men and women in their total reality.[4] Ganss insists that this understanding of Ignatian vocabulary corrects the misunderstanding of those who read Ignatius as having "an exaggerated dualism or even Neoplatonism in his thought."[5]

Years ago when I first read Ganss's note, I found it a liberating insight. In time this fairly modest reflection opened up a way of viewing Ignatian spirituality and its enterprise that explained its reverence for the human. Simply put, the Ignatian instinct is to help people become fully alive. I would like to continue to explore this "soul education," this way of reading spirituality as exploring how people can become as fully present to their humanity as possible. In this view God is the ground and the goal of human life. This reflection has three parts: (1) Ignatian education is about appropriation, (2) Ignatian education is about the social ramifications of learning, and (3) Ignatian education reconciles a plurality of experiences within a Catholic commitment.

Ignatian Education and Appropriation

As a ten-part program detailing Jesuit formation, communal life, and work, the Jesuit *Constitutions* represent the last great work of Ignatius. Composition of the *Constitutions* engaged his energies from 1547 to his death in 1556. Consequently, this in-house document offers an important commentary on Ignatian spirituality in dialogue with its culture—ecclesiastical and secular. But to illustrate how to enter into this world, I want to use a reflection by a non-Jesuit, the novelist Larry Woiwode. In his memoir, *What I Think I Did,*

Woiwode recalls how when he was twelve he loved to walk around his town, "outside my habitation—in the gap of a railroad line along a dirt track that led through pastures or rows of clattering corn to a woods . . . halfway between my parents and the lake."[6] Woiwode recounts that on these walks,

> The chill of presence slithered over me as if I were shedding leaves myself and I looked up. It was the presence of God, I thought, as I watched the trees sway as if ascending the sky. . . . One presence was here, I knew, as I turned with my face raised, in the trees and sky, and in the earth that held me as I turned. The presence has put all this in place to instruct me about myself and the complications of the love I felt for Him. I had been told to love Him but the words of the language I knew couldn't reproduce the language pouring from everything here with a familiarity I couldn't define. I was given a glimpse of it when I read, "The heavens declare the glory of God . . . Day unto day utters speech . . . no speech or language where their voice is not heard . . . since the creation of the world His invisible attributes are clearly seen. . . . All things were created through Him and for Him . . . and in Him all things consist."[7]

Woiwode's youthful encounter stayed with him because it represented his appropriation of all he had been taught by his parents, pastors, nuns, and nature. This is what I mean by soul education: the personal appropriation of teaching, experience, and insight that mark what one business ethician calls "a defining moment" of one's life.[8]

It has gradually dawned on me that the reading of Ignatian texts as a way to enter into a tradition has severe limitations. The reason lies, I believe, in the hermeneutic used to explore and to explicate the text. If the Ignatian tradition is only an object of inquiry, it resists what it is supposed to do. Let me use an example to illustrate this point.

In the summer of 1997 a remarkable group of scholars assembled at Boston College to focus their expertise and energies on the topic "The Jesuits: Cultures, Sciences, and the Arts, 1540–1773." At the closing session of this conference Michael Buckley and Luce Giard offered an important addendum to the proceedings.[9]

While the scholars had illumined *what* the early Jesuits had accomplished, they had avoided or neglected the question of *why* Jesuits had engaged their cultures of Europe, Asia, Latin America, and Africa. Jesuits' presence in mathematics, science, music, and art of their day presumed an inspiring presence that initiated their search and sustained its progress. Like Larry Woiwode, the early Jesuits lived not only out of an intellectual curiosity to know or an artistic drive to create but out of a religious pilgrimage toward meeting the God in whom all things consist.[10]

Consequently, the goal of Ignatian tutelage, as it had been codified in the texts of the *Exercises* and the *Constitutions*, is not information but appropriation, an integration into the very activity of God within created reality. This goal has important ramifications for how one approaches the reading of Ignatian texts.

First, the textual tradition (that is, the way most people in higher education enter into the Ignatian tradition) is and must be open to literary, historical, and theological analysis and critique: what do these words mean in terms of their cultural matrix? This critical reading will not yield the meaning of the text but only a reading of the text, a way of controlling the data and integrating this data into an intellectual mind-set antecedent to the reading. For example, in part 7 of the *Constitutions*, there is a section that attempts to describe the internal dynamic that, ultimately, operates within the Jesuit community to sustain its union even as its membership is dispersed throughout the world in various ministries.

The chief bond that cements the union of the members among themselves and with their heads is on both sides—the love of God our Lord. For when the superior and the subjects are closely united to His Divine and Supreme Goodness, they will very easily be united among themselves "through that same love which will descend from the Divine Goodness and spread to all other people" and particularly to the body of the Society.[11]

What this important section from the *Constitutions* asserts is that in proportion as Jesuits link themselves to God, so will they be united to one another and to their General Superior. This union with God, in turn, generates love in the people for whom they work as well as for the members of the Jesuit community.

This text can be parsed, analyzed, and read within the context of a wider and older religious tradition that acknowledges the power of conviction and the socialization of an ideal. But that reading stays outside the experience of that union. When teaching this text to a group of Jesuits, for example, my presumption is not only that they will understand its terms but that they will want to incorporate its meaning into how they live and work. Their Jesuit hermeneutic, then, is not understanding but appropriation.

When we desire more participation in the distinguishing characteristics of Jesuit education, we must ask ourselves if we can really achieve this appropriation of a textual tradition. Do we have a right to ask this?

This is not an insignificant query. Can you invite non-Jesuits, non-Christians, nonbelievers, into a tradition that asks for appropriation, a reading of the textual tradition that presumes you want to enter into its experience? Can non-Jesuits understand truly the Ignatian purchase on how community works as a gift from God: to be united "through that same love which will descend from the Divine Goodness and spread to all other people"?[12]

I would say yes for three reasons. First, the Ignatian tradition presumes that prior to any person's assimilation into the tradition, God has been active in that man's or woman's life.[13] Second, the activity of God is within the specifics of a man's or woman's personal history, temperament, talents, graces.[14] Third, God works in all toward good, not evil; toward consolation, not desolation; toward building up justice, faith, hope, confidence, human freedom, and productivity.[15]

How, then, practically speaking, can people outside the tradition participate in that tradition? In the *Constitutions* there is an Ignatian strategy designed to help novices in the order assimilate a process by which they can find how God dwells in their lives and works. What is remarkable is that this process, as a process, does not demand that one be a Catholic, much less a Jesuit. It is soul education, a process that invites novices—people learning how to be Jesuits—to trust their experience as a source of revelation and direction. The process does call for a certain psychological focus that includes self-composure and openness.[16] It suggests three activities: be attentive to the reality about you, reverence what you encounter, and appreciate how this kind of presence leads to revelation, what Ignatius calls devotion and what Woiwode has described as "the presence of God."

Whether one is a teacher or a counselor, an administrator or a plant manager, this ability to focus so that "the other" is truly present to him or her, and then to reverence the reality that one has discovered, leads to another discovery, that of a presence, a reality that invites appropriation. Such appropriation represents an acceptance that can, finally, only be called love. The point is that whether the professional work is coaching, research, or academic planning, what the Ignatian tradition offers is not a time-consuming addition to an already heavy workload. Rather it is a way of proceeding within one's profession, a style of professional alertness and dedication. It is a process that enables a person to become "a soul," someone trying to live in mutuality with or openness to all other realities.

One can verify the presence of this activity by the threefold criteria I outlined earlier. First, what I have appropriated comes from who I am and the way God has worked within me. Second, what I have appropriated is in harmony with my personal history, psychological makeup, or grace. Third, what I have appropriated leads toward something good for me, for my work, for the community.

The Ignatian tradition does not indoctrinate nor does it enforce; it invites a willingness to appropriate reality into a person's life. It is an education of soul, of becoming more humanely alert and responsive to the world about you. What you accept accepts you too.

Ignatian Education and the Social Ramifications of Learning

While the recent emphasis of the Jesuit Superior General, Peter-Hans Kolvenbach, has been on the role of higher education in forming a social consciousness, this emphasis is not new.[17] From its inception the Society of Jesus has focused on "the care of those souls for whom either there is nobody to care or, if somebody ought to care, the care is negligent. This is the reason for the founding of the Society. This is its strength. This is its dignity in the Church."[18] This dictum was coined by one of the giants among the early Jesuits, Jerome Nadal, and developed from Ignatius's mystic experiences at Manresa, the small town where for almost a year he underwent an intense self-scrutiny and graced reorientation of his life. At Manresa, Ignatius composed most of the text of *The Spiritual Exercises* and there moved away from a life of solitude toward a life of pastoral service. His expression of this shift was direct and simple: he had been called by God "to help people."

In *The First Jesuits*, John O'Malley provides an overview of how many of these pastoral works—albeit inspired by a fundamental mission to preach and to teach the word of God—included prominently the implementation of the word of God, particularly in the care of the poor, the unlettered, those in prison and hospitals, and prostitutes.[19] The contemporary Jesuit emphasis on social justice as a constitutive element in the life of faith is, therefore, not an innovation. This emphasis on social justice and solidarity is in continuity with the foundation and original mission of the Society of Jesus. More important, this commitment is an expression of its apostolic integrity. By *apostolic integrity* I mean that the work of contemporary Jesuits finds its deepest religious instincts in the prophetic teaching of Jesus about the dignity of the poor, the widow, the orphan—the social and religious outcasts of his day. To preach and to teach the gospel of Christ, to translate its significance to our postmodern world, to confront some of the economic and social fallout from globalization—this has to be part of the professional awareness within every Jesuit work, but especially in higher education.

Father Kolvenbach's Santa Clara presentation sparked enthusiasm and, for many of us, suggested a most fruitful area for renewed cooperation within our institutions. But what I want to focus on is that this call to social action touches the soul (i.e., the animation of men and women) in the work of higher education.

My experience is that the significant core of faculty and staff who are proactive in developing the Ignatian tradition within their institutions can also hear this call to social justice and solidarity with some frustration. Their scholarship and research, their teaching and departmental responsibilities, their counseling and advising absorb time and energy. Their own family commitments demand—also in the name of justice and solidarity—energies and attention that leave scant time or energy to undertake works that directly help the poor, comfort the marginalized, and confront the oppressors. Consequently, guilt and fatigue rather than dedication and inspiration become the dominant reactions to the summons to social justice and solidarity. I do not think that it is Ignatian to make good people feel guilty about what they cannot do. This concern has led me to reconsider how to integrate social justice into the life of the university.

First, the service programs that our students undertake, the efforts to integrate academic courses with field experiences involving social justice (for example, Boston College's Pulse Program), and the volunteer work that students, staff, and faculty support—these are genuinely both education and social justice. Second, we influence social action among our students by offering them the opportunity to devote a year or more to postgraduate service in a program like the Jesuit Volunteer Corps (JVC) or in a Nativity-type inner-city school. Third, the teaching and scholarship that explore the ramifications of economic justice or the common good or the dignity of the human person are indispensable to the unique contribution that a university as a university makes toward the mission of social justice. Fourth, the ethical environment of a university community—the way we hire, promote, and pay; the way we deal with one another; the civility and care that we extend to our colleagues—is either an ethos of justice or one of neglect or even injustice. This litany of activities demonstrates the social-justice commitment of our universities. This commitment should give us all a deep sense of consolation. But what I want to suggest is that within the mainstream tasks of teaching and research, counseling and advising, there runs a current of spiritual energy—grace, if you will, or manifestations of soul—that we also need to acknowledge, cherish, and develop. The risk is that in looking for "the more" beyond us, we lose "the more" that lies deeply within what we already do.

In the introduction to that part of the Jesuit *Constitutions* that deals directly with education, Ignatius proposes three constitutive elements in the formation of an effective Jesuit: he must have solid learning, be able to communicate what he has learned, and live and work in such a way that he gives "good example."[20] These same three characteristics should also inform the kind of education that Jesuits offer.

In the first part of this essay I emphasized the mutuality of Ignatian spirituality. Whatever one gives, one also receives, or better, it is impossible to donate without becoming a beneficiary. In guiding someone through the Spiritual Exercises, in preaching or counseling or teaching, you discover what God wishes you to learn as well. The unspoken reality is relationship, and its recurring symbol is conversation, the dialogue that creates a climate of mutual donation.[21]

In our work in the classroom, in student services, in research, we are all laboring for sound learning, to make truth, wisdom, and competency come to life. The culture of a university is learning. In the Ignatian tradition this process is sacred. For in the act of learning mathematics, Shakespeare, economics, or chemistry, something about the way God works within knowledge touches the soul and enlivens our humanity. And in the act of communicating our knowledge, skills, or care, in our conversation and generosity, God reveals. And in the integrity to our various professions, we present ourselves as stewards of God's continuing care of the world.

As educators we need to exercise that attention, reverence, and devotion to ourselves. We need some moments to possess what we profess, to cherish its meaning for us, to recognize something greater than ourselves that makes learning happen.

In a university culture there are many traditions that form our common consciousness. But in the process of being true to sound learning, in the asceticism of effective communication, and in the integrity of professing our commitment to the young generations before us, we witness that a university, finally, carries its own justice within its own soul and creates its own solidarity.

Ignatian Education Reconciles a Plurality of Experiences within a Catholic Commitment

The papal document *Ex Corde Ecclesiae* and its application in the United States have occasioned a number of reflections. My intention is not to summarize these reactions but to present my own take on the focus these documents have invited. First, the decree and its application in the United States present a genuine issue. How does a university that claims a faith tradition as an essential component in its mission implement that faith component? Moreover, how does the university fulfill this mission in a secular and pluralistic academic and cultural climate? Finally, how does a university implement this mission with a concomitant fidelity to academic freedom and to ethical and professional priority within U.S. higher education? I am not arguing about how the church documents answer these concerns; I am saying that there is an issue of identity and integrity for universities that claim a Catholic tradition. Second, any implementation of the Catholic character of a university steers a prudent course between enforcement and neglect. Third, and to my mind most important, how does one read and communicate the term *Catholic*?

Similarly, there are issues surrounding the pluralism that characterizes higher education in the United States. First, pluralism cannot be reduced to a bland tolerance that stands for no real personal or professional convictions. Neither can pluralism mask a clever delaying tactic, such as waiting for the right political moment to suppress all opposition. Pluralism has to be an ethical relationship, some mutual commitment to the good that can be obtained precisely because there are different opinions. I do not claim that I can satisfactorily treat these issues here, but I think that they must be on the agenda of every university community. The Ignatian purchase of being "Catholic" is complex. On the one hand, for Ignatius Catholicism was the way to God. He could only have been a Roman Catholic; that was his birth identity, his culture, his context for contemplative reflection and for energetic action.[22] But what is remarkable is that he placed in the forefront of this faith the experience of God, unique to each individual, and yet a source of union among people.

In *The Spiritual Exercises* Ignatius repeatedly underscores both the individual's right to find God in his or her own way and the duty of the one who guides this experience to maintain a respectful distance to avoid interfering in this personal encounter with God.[23] For Ignatius every individual has the right to his or her soul and to discover God for her- or himself. The church was a privileged guide in this journey of finding God, but Ignatian spirituality is not "churchy."[24] For Ignatius God could be found in all things, but only if one first found "all things." This is my reason for insisting on that part of the Jesuit *Constitutions* that presents attention and reverence as prior to devotion; that is, the integrity of being present to the creature is the only way to honor the Creator. This Ignatian regard for individual experience has at times been misrepresented as isolation from the social. It is far from this distortion. The Ignatian regard for individual religious experience originates from an esteem for human freedom and liberality.[25] Freedom for Ignatius is the power to donate, not simply to act. And liberality is the ability to act generously for something greater than oneself. For Ignatius, one discovers one's soul only when one freely donates one's life to something greater than oneself. Ignatius called this an election, a choice to be a particular kind of self, to orient one's life with an abiding commitment to do something good and enduring.

Note how inherent in this Ignatian process is the assumption that there are many ways to God. Experience emerges out of individual histories; is contextualized by one's talents, culture, and graces; and is communicated by a personal set of symbols and rhetoric. It is for all these reasons that Ignatius insists on the principle of adaptation within the Spiritual Exercises, that is, fitting the movements, presentations, and strategies of this program to people.[26] In brief, Ignatius believed that people should be helped to encounter, not to perform.

This is the point where the Ignatian tradition and religious pluralism become tricky. Ignatius does not give us an adequate model for the kind of ecumenism and plurality we honor in today's university community. But Ignatian spirituality provides the tools to assemble a model that reflects our theological and academic values. And the principle that allows us to reassemble these Ignatian tools to construct this model is that of adaptation, fitting general principles or communal strategies to individual reality.[27]

My view is that Catholicism can been seen in two ways, much as law can be understood in two ways. *Law*, as *lex*, can mean the codes that govern conduct within a society.[28] But law can also mean *jus*, human rights, the fundamental human desires for a home, for personal security, for food and education, for human dignity. So, too, to be a Catholic can mean living within those social codes that define the publicly believing body: codes of formal belief, such as the divinity of Christ; codes of conduct, such as prohibitions against the taking of innocent life; and codes of worship, such as the rituals that guarantee legitimate Catholic celebration of the Eucharist. Living within these social codes is an important way to be an authentic Catholic. In his "Rules for Having the Right Attitude toward the Church," Ignatius promotes this understanding of being a Catholic. However, the main thrust of *The Spiritual Exercises* and even the *Constitutions* is to facilitate the context for the discovery of God. For Ignatius, to be a Catholic is to find how the human and the divine come together. The figure of Jesus is central to his prayer not only as the privileged object of devotion but also as the exemplar of action. It is this sense of Catholic tradition that most resonates with the pluralism of the university. The Ignatian tradition invites people to find their way to [bring] the divine and the human together.

Let me be very clear here. To be Catholic is to live an authentic union with the institutional church. But to be a Catholic is also to live an authentic union with God, the only final Absolute. Ignatius made that distinction and so must we. The end of belief, of ethical conduct, and of worship—of keeping the law—is to find the love that guides all law.

To dedicate oneself to an educational process like Ignatian/Jesuit higher education is to take risks. Martin Marty, a major contemporary academic figure, puts it this way:

> Those who favor one or another expression of religion have to take their risks with its exposure on the academic front. But they will have seen those who advocate study of it and who study it well to be servants

of a public scene in which educators and educated alike will deal more fairly with the reality around them than they did when too readily the academy reduced our society to the conception of being a secular one. Humans as individuals and in society are too full of passions, of intelligence, of mystery to be properly characterized as members of such a reduced society.[29]

Jesuit higher education, which has been so much a part of John Padberg's Jesuit career, possesses a proud and fruitful tradition of religious seriousness and academic pluralism. *And* is the operative word here. Ignatius loved doublets: "*both . . . and*" or "*yes . . . but.*" Living like this is risky business, but that is what every great university community strives to become—a community where risk is a way of life.[30]

NOTES

1. Rowan Williams, *Teresa of Ávila* (London: Continuum, 2000), 143–73.

2. This is significant in the work of John W. O'Malley, SJ, in *The First Jesuits* (Cambridge, MA: Harvard University Press, 1993), and in "The Historiography of the Society of Jesus: Where Does It Stand Today?" in *The Jesuits: Cultures, Sciences, and the Arts, 1540–1773*, ed. John W. O'Malley et al. (Toronto: University of Toronto Press, 1999), especially 27–29.

3. *The Constitutions of the Society of Jesus*, trans. George E. Ganss, SJ (St. Louis: Institute of Jesuit Sources, 1984), [3].

4. *Constitutions*, 77–78, [10].

5. *Constitutions*, [10].

6. Larry Woiwode, *What I Think I Did* (New York: Basic Books, 2000), 133.

7. Ibid., 135.

8. Joseph L. Badaracco Jr., "The Discipline of Building Character," in *Harvard Business Review on Leadership* (Boston: Harvard Business School Press, 1998), 89–113.

9. "Reflections," in O'Malley, *The Jesuits*, 707–12, 713–16.

10. Howard J. Gray, SJ, "What Kind of Document," in *The Way Supplement* 61 (Spring 1988), 24–25.

11. *Constitutions*, [671].

12. Ibid.

13. I take this both from the first twenty annotations from *The Spiritual Exercises*, trans. George E. Ganss, SJ (St. Louis: Institute of Jesuit Sources, 1992) and [22] from the General Examen in the *Constitutions*.

14. *Exercises*, no. 18.

15. *Exercises*, no. 332, no. 335.

16. *Constitutions*, [250].

17. Peter-Hans Kolvenbach, SJ, "Faith, Justice, and American Jesuit Higher Education," in *Studies in the Spirituality of Jesuits* 31, no. 1 (January 2001): 13–29. [This is one of the Kolvenbach addresses that appear earlier in this section of *A Jesuit Education Reader*. —Editor]

18. O'Malley, *The First Jesuits*, 33.

19. O'Malley, "Works of Mercy," in *The First Jesuits*, 165–99.

20. *Constitutions*, [307].

21. Howard J. Gray, SJ, "Contemporary Jesuits as Friends in the Lord," in *Review of Ignatian Spirituality* 29, no. 89 (1998): 41–56.

22. Jose Ignacio Tellechea Idigoras, *Ignatius of Loyola: The Pilgrim Saint*, trans. Cornelius M. Buckley, SJ (Chicago: Loyola University Press, 1994).

23. *Exercises*, no. 15.

24. O'Malley, *The First Jesuits*, 284–328.

25. Michael J, Buckley, SJ, "Freedom, Election, and Self-Transcendence: Some Reflections upon the Ignatian Development of a Life of Ministry," in *Ignatian Spirituality in a Secular Age*, ed. George P. Schner (Waterloo: Wilfrid Laurier Press, 1984), 65–90.

26. *Exercises*, no. 18.

27. Ibid.

28. Howard J. Gray, SJ, "Being Catholic in a Jesuit Context," in *America*, May 20, 2000, 23–26.

29. Martin Marty, *Education, Religion and the Common Good* (San Francisco: Jossey-Bass, 2000), 139–40.

30. This paper was first delivered as a talk at St. Louis University on February 26, 2001.

Further Reading

The complete text of the stunning 1973 address to alumni of Jesuit schools ("Men [and Women] for Others") by then Jesuit general superior Pedro Arrupe can be found in *Justice with Faith Today: Selected Letters and Addresses [of Pedro Arrupe]* (St. Louis: Institute of Jesuit Sources, 1980), II, 123–38.

A year and a half later, delegates from all over the Jesuit world gathered in Rome under Arrupe's leadership for the Thirty-second General Congregation of the order. The most famous document that the congregation produced was undoubtedly decree 4: "Our Mission Today: The Service of Faith and the Promotion of Justice" (*Documents of the Thirty-first and Thirty-second General Congregation of the Society of Jesus* [St. Louis: Institute of Jesuit Sources, 1977], 411–38, nos. 47–130). Shorter and more readable is decree 2: "Jesuits Today" (400–409, nos. 11–42), which was written last and recapitulates all the work of the congregation.

Brian Daley, SJ, scholar of early Christian writings and professor of theology at Notre Dame, raises the question of why Jesuits, members of a religious order, have been engaged in largely "secular" education almost from the beginning to this day ("'Splendor and Wonder': Ignatian Mysticism and the Ideals of Liberal Education," in *Splendor and Wonder: Jesuit Character, Georgetown Spirit, and Liberal Education*, ed. William J. O'Brien [Washington, DC: Georgetown University Press, 1988]). His answer is convincing.

Two major documents came from Assembly '89 at Georgetown: the keynote address by then Cornell University President Frank F. T. Rhodes (*America*, July 29–August 5, 1989) and the address by Jesuit head Peter-Hans Kolvenbach (Washington, DC: Jesuit Conference, n.d.).

From General Congregation 34 (1995), we have already presented in this reader "Our Mission and Culture" and "Jesuits and University Life." Also recommended are "Our Mission and Justice" (*Documents of the Thirty-Fourth General Congregation of the Society of Jesus* [St. Louis: Institute of Jesuit Sources, 1995], d. 3, 39–48, nos. 50–74); "Our Mission and Interreligious Dialogue" (d. 5, 67–81, nos. 128–57); "Jesuits and the Situation of Women in Church and Civil Society" (d. 14, 171–78, nos. 361–72); and "The Intellectual Dimension of Jesuit Ministries" (d. 16, 183–87, nos. 394–403).

Carrying the Thirty-fourth General Congregation documents on culture and on interreligious dialogue a step further, Scottish Jesuit theologian John McDade delivered a paper at "Jesuit Education 21" (1999) titled "The Jesuit Mission and Dialogue with Culture." McDade suggests that Christianity needs to be engaged both in proclaiming God's incarnate Word to secular human cultures (including that of critical post-modernity) and learning from dialogue with them a fuller sense of what it means to be human. Indeed Christianity needs them in order to understand itself and maintain its own identity (*Conference Proceedings on the Future of Jesuit Higher Education*, ed. Martin Tripole [Philadelphia: St. Joseph's University Press, 2000], 56–66).

Peter-Hans Kolvenbach's Xavier University address on the challenge of interreligious dialogue, while mostly treating fundamentals, does begin to indicate the complexity of issues involved. A more sophisticated sense of these issues comes out in "A Charism for Dialog: Advice from the Early Jesuit Missionaries in Our World of Religious Pluralism," by Francis X. Clooney, SJ (*Studies in the Spirituality of Jesuits*, March 2002) and in two recent essays in *Commonweal*, the lay Catholic biweekly: Clooney's "Learning to Listen: Benedict XVI and Inter-Religious Dialogue" and Peter C. Phan's "Speaking in Many Tongues: Why the Church Must Be More Catholic" (January 12, 2007). After a good number of years at Boston College, Clooney is now Parkman Professor of Divinity at Harvard Divinity School. Phan, a Vietnamese American who holds the Ignacio Ellacuría Chair of Catholic Social Thought at Georgetown University, has written or edited twenty books and three hundred essays.

Michael Buckley developed his ideas on justice and higher education beyond his address at Spring Hill in 1990; his mature word can
be found in "The Search for a New Humanism: The University and
the Concern for Justice," *The Catholic University as Promise and Project:
Reflections in a Jesuit Idiom* (Washington, DC: Georgetown University
Press, 1998), 105–28 and 201–204.

As a complement to the Kolvenbach address at Santa Clara (2000),
see his shorter one at Spring Hill (October 4, 2004), available at
http://www.shc.edu/kolvenbach/kolvenbachSHC/address.

The scholar of Ignatian spirituality and Jesuit education Joseph
Tetlow, SJ, has written a number of essays that can help us to understand what constitutes a Jesuit college or university. The most readily
accessible is "Intellectual Conversion: Jesuit Spirituality and the
American University" (*Spirit, Style, Story: Essays Honoring John W. Padberg*,
ed. Thomas Lucas, SJ [Chicago: Loyola Press, 2002], 93–115).

When I was a student at a Jesuit high school fifty-some years
ago, we were taught that the goal of Jesuit education was *eloquentia
perfecta*, "perfect eloquence," both in the spoken and written word.
What my Jesuit teachers and I were unaware of at the time was the
eminent place given to the fine arts—including music and theater
and dance—in the early centuries of Jesuit education. So my final
recommendation for further reading in this section is a tiny gem by
writer, actress, and teacher Judith Rock, "The Rhetoric of the Body"
(*Conversations on Jesuit Higher Education*, Fall 1998, 47–48).

The Issue of
Catholic Identity

Introduction

In 1967, just a few years after the close of the Second Vatican Council, twenty-some leaders in American Catholic higher education met on two different occasions and produced what is now commonly referred to as the "Land O'Lakes Statement," after the Wisconsin location of their meeting.[1] The statement was an important preparation for the worldwide conference "The Catholic University in the Modern World" held in Kinshasa, Congo, the following year. That conference issued a brief declaration, many of whose points were taken from the Land O'Lakes statement. The two statements together informed the dialogue that ensued between American Catholic universities on the one hand and American bishops and the Vatican Congregation for Catholic Education on the other. This dialogue led gradually into the composition of various drafts of Pope John Paul II's apostolic constitution on Catholic universities, which was published in final form in August 1990. It was titled after its first three words in Latin, *Ex Corde Ecclesiae* ("From the Heart of the Church").

The very mention of *Ex Corde* has been likely to arouse fear and anger among American Catholic university administrators and faculty. But it is important to distinguish between the body of the pope's document—especially the introduction and part 1—as issued in 1990 and the norms of application later dictated to the American church by the Vatican. The body of the document is really the place to begin a discussion today of the issue of Catholic identity. It resonates with the earlier statements and goes beyond them, as Paul Reinert has said, in being a "more authoritative, more nuanced, and richer and 'thicker' description of the Catholic university in the modern world." Sadly, as Reinert has also said, this richness has been too little mined.

The 2002 document from the Society of Jesus in the United States, "Communal Reflection on the Jesuit Mission in Higher

Education" (text included in the previous section of this reader) lists in its preface four essential characteristics of a Catholic university from *Ex Corde*. Important as these are, the bald characteristics do not give even a taste of the pope's wholesome vision. Unfortunately, the pope's treatise is too long to be included in this anthology.

What is offered here is nevertheless substantial. We begin with a questioning view of the Catholic character of Jesuit universities by distinguished historian of American Catholicism David O'Brien of the College of the Holy Cross, "Conversations on Jesuit (and Catholic?) Higher Education: Jesuit Sí, Catholic . . . Not So Sure." And in counterpoint to that, we have "The Truly Catholic University," offering the positive convictions of Rick Malloy, SJ, of the anthropology and sociology department at St. Joseph's University. Suzanne Matson of the Boston College English department, who calls herself an agnostic, tells in "Collegium, Catholic Identity, and the Non-Catholic," how her participation in the weeklong summer program "Collegium on Faith and Intellectual Life" made her look at herself and her work with a new appreciation and at her situation in her school with a new level of comfort.

The late Monika Hellwig, longtime professor of theology at Georgetown University and more recently executive director and then president of the Association of Catholic Colleges and Universities, presents "The Catholic Intellectual Tradition in the Catholic University." It is exciting to see in detail what the content of the tradition encompasses and the ways we pass that tradition on and contribute to its living and growing character.

We close this section with a sharp, brief statement by the president of the University of Notre Dame, John Jenkins, CSC. Entitled "Closing Statement on Academic Freedom and Catholic Character," it is the result of the president's intensive consultation with people inside and outside (alumni) the university. At issue was the university's allowing the sometimes acclaimed but controversial play *The Vagina Monologues* to be performed on campus for several years running. The local bishop, John D'Arcy, had objected. He charged that the play is offensive to women and "antithetical to Catholic teaching on the beautiful gift of human sexuality. [It] violates the truth about women, the truth about sexuality, the truth about male and female and the truth about the human body." The president's statement speaks for itself.

_____

NOTES

1. *Jesuit Education 21: Conference Proceedings on the Future of Jesuit Higher Education* (Philadelphia: St. Joseph's University Press, 2000), 386–87. Paul Reinert, SJ, was the longtime president of St. Louis University and a participant at the Land O'Lakes gathering.

Understanding the Terminology: Suggested Readings from *Do You Speak Ignatian?*

• Vatican Council II

Conversations on Jesuit (and Catholic?) Higher Education: Jesuit Sí, Catholic . . . Not So Sure

David J. O'Brien

Excerpted from *Conversations on Jesuit Higher Education*, 1994

Conversations about Jesuit higher education are usually a lot friendlier, certainly a lot more civil, than conversations about Catholic higher education. Even the most crusty "cultured despiser" of religion finds Jesuits interesting, although perhaps most interesting when rather far away, say in sixteenth-century China or twentieth-century El Salvador. Most faculty, of course, despite prevailing stereotypes, don't despise religion at all. On Jesuit campuses they probably know and like at least a few Jesuits, partly because Jesuits have been working hard at being better known and liked. And, as teachers and scholars, Jesuits enjoy enormous respect. After all, Jesuit academics are almost always extremely well educated. One professor said of a newly arrived Jesuit colleague: "he's studied everything, everywhere."

But Catholic, that's another matter. One woman theology professor remarked that "the word Catholic conjures up a whole set of images of the university ready to pounce on people" and "scholars are understandably not too keen on that" (*New York Times*, May 1, 1991). Perhaps partly as a result, at Jesuit colleges and universities the word *Jesuit* is much displayed, but *Catholic* is harder to find. When there is a discussion of Catholic identity, it is usually abstract, often boring, or when concrete (dealing with the Vatican and bishops and orthodoxy), threatening. Academically, Catholic character partakes of a museum, a heritage worth preserving to satisfy antiquarian curiosity or provide weapons against one or another modernist aberration. Theology in general, Catholic theology specifically, and campus ministry are available for those who are interested, but they occupy a role comparable to that of the local parish, voluntary options having more to do with private life and personal interests than with the serious work of research and teaching.

Marginalized as it may be, Catholic, as in "Catholic college or university," nevertheless remains a nagging problem. The Galileo case was settled recently (wasn't that a relief?) but the unfortunate— and altogether unjust—treatment of Charles Curran, the Catholic University of America theologian driven from Catholic higher education for views little different from those held by most American Catholics, disastrously resuscitated ancient suspicions about the church.[1]

There may reside in those suspicions some of that visceral anti-Catholicism common among intellectuals, but nervousness about Catholic connections leading to ecclesiastical pouncing also reminds one of the poster whose caption reads: "Just because you're paranoid doesn't mean they're not out to get you." After all, the Vatican in recent years has been disciplining prominent theologians, cracking down on dissent, and issuing doctrinaire pronouncements on all sorts of controversial matters, often without asking the advice of the church's own experts. And, as control of colleges and universities by religious orders has grown less reliable, the Vatican has taken ever-greater interest in their affairs.

Church law already requires theologians to secure a mandate from the bishops if they teach in Catholic universities. In 1989, after prolonged negotiation, the pope issued an apostolic constitution on higher education, *Ex Corde Ecclesiae*, which affirms academic freedom and recognizes the autonomy of the university's internal government but retains the requirement of a mandate and insists on some form of juridical accountability of Catholic universities to church authorities.[2]

An important committee of the American bishops has proposed a set of legal norms to implement that apostolic constitution, a move almost all college and university presidents regard as impractical and unnecessary. Until now, the bishops have depended on dialogue with university presidents—on conversation, if you will—to maintain a delicate balance between hierarchical and academic responsibilities, but there are many prelates who favor a more aggressive and legalistic approach. So, after a generation of wearying efforts to affirm the autonomy of colleges and universities from formal church control, and to guarantee academic freedom while remaining faithfully Catholic, church connectedness remains a chronic problem.

The Ambiguity of Catholicity

Of course these matters don't bother faculty and students very much. At Jesuit schools, the Jesuits are supposed to take care of such Catholic matters, to keep Rome, worried bishops, and restorationist sectarians at arm's length and worried Catholic parents and alumni more or less satisfied. But, quite apart from the shrinking number of Jesuits, the Catholic problem is not so easily dealt with. For one thing, while Rome and its backers demand tighter links between church and school, there are external factors working in the other direction. All Catholic colleges and universities depend heavily on public support, for example. The courts have been far more flexible in dealing with church-related higher education than with church-sponsored elementary and secondary schools, but there are significant pressures to avoid even the appearance of religious discrimination or proselytization, pressures intensified at schools that wish to operate in the respectable academic mainstream, as do all the Jesuit schools.[3]

In fact, the quest for academic respectability, fueled by the drive of Catholic minorities to enter the middle classes, has been the most dynamic force for change in Catholic higher education since 1945. It has brought to these schools high-quality teaching, increasingly impressive research, highly professional faculties, more diverse students, and an array of services comparable to the best private institutions. It led to the creation of independent boards of trustees, with lay persons in the majority, legal separation of the schools from their founding religious communities, faculty participation in academic governance, and academic policies heavily influenced by the discipline-centered bureaucracies that dominate contemporary university life. It also left huge question marks punctuating legitimate worries about Catholic identity,[4] questions that remain after skillful leaders have finished persuading Catholic constituencies that their schools remain faithfully Catholic while simultaneously convincing courts, funding agencies, and nervous faculty that it doesn't really matter all that much.

The result is a balancing act requiring great skill. Father Theodore M. Hesburgh, former president of Notre Dame, was for many years the premier spokesman for American Catholic higher education before both the hierarchy and the general public. . . .

American Catholic universities, under lay boards and recognizing academic freedom, "are not a direct arm of the church," Hesburgh argues, but they are "if anything, more professedly Catholic than ever. . . ." What is the most important thing to be done for the future of the enterprise? Hesburgh's answer: "Guard your Catholic character as you would your life."[5] . . .

For better or worse, the experience of Catholic higher education over the last generation exemplifies a new, more flexible, and ambiguous church practice in the United States, one that the Vatican has not yet understood but one whose challenges and responsibilities American Catholics, including those of us in higher education, have yet to face as well.

From Problem to Possibility

Let me offer several propositions as the basis for that difficult discussion of the Catholic element of Jesuit and Catholic education, in hopes of moving from the chronic contestation of the past to a more positive and constructive collaboration.

I. American Catholic colleges and universities have a responsibility to relate in some way to the hierarchy and to the Catholic community.

Vatican II did not change everything. Even bishops most friendly to higher education, like Bishop James Malone of Youngstown, Ohio, regularly point out that "Vatican II opened new perspectives on decentralizing authority" but it also "left in place patterns of leadership which guarantee strong centers of authority within Catholic polity." Malone and other bishops expect to be more than potted plants at graduation. As Bishop Malone puts it, "Bishops have a role to play in relation to these university institutions on behalf of the Catholic community and its faith tradition."[6]

There can be little question of the U.S. hierarchy's strong moral support for Catholic higher education. . . .[7] A standing committee of bishops and presidents played a major role in insuring open communication, building trust, and working to explain American practices to the Vatican.

Yet it is also clear that this informal and altogether American arrangement, now endangered by the Apostolic Constitution [*Ex Corde Ecclesiae*] and the growing power of a few less sympathetic bishops, depends not only on episcopal self-restraint but also on the willingness of boards of trustees to insure that there is what *Ex Corde Ecclesiae* calls an institutional commitment to Catholicism, that orthodox faith is taught and dissent is kept within acceptable, and unembarrassing, boundaries, and that the school in some way serves the church. . . . It is not clear that local communities (in some cases not even trustees) have wrestled with the problem of defining those responsibilities and translating them into institutional policies. . . .

That said, there are many reasons to take Catholic affiliation seriously. Some are practical: the historical tradition, or saga, of the school, which has given it a distinctive place in the local community and often sustains its unique spirit; the support of Catholic alumni, parents, and benefactors; the presence of significant numbers of students attracted by the Catholic professions of the school; the continuing, if reduced, support and presence of the sponsoring religious community. Then there is simple integrity: the need to be truthful by translating Catholic professions into concrete practice. And perhaps there is still a chance that these schools can draw upon the resources of the Catholic tradition and the contemporary church to make a real contribution to American culture—that they can serve, in some special way, the common good.

Most of all, taking Catholic responsibilities seriously depends on whether one thinks the Catholic Church is important and Catholic education worthwhile. At times even believers do not seem altogether convinced; in most places public discussion of the question has not even taken place. So the heart of the problem may be less "secularization," as some supposed friends of Catholic higher education argue, or the anti-intellectual attitudes of conservative Catholics and ecclesiastical bureaucrats, but the loss of nerve among Catholic academics themselves. In any event, the Catholic issue needs to be placed on the table.

2. Developing a positive expression of Catholic identity requires commitment and strategy: something must be done.

Most schools, including Jesuit schools, articulate their Catholicity in terms of the leadership role of religious orders; the presence of strong theology departments, usually containing an emphasis on self-consciously Catholic theology; the presence of campus ministry and a strong pastoral and liturgical life; opportunities for spiritual growth and Christian service; and many specific programs and projects serving the local and national church. It is these features of the schools that are highlighted when the question of Catholic identity is raised. They manifest a continuing commitment to remain Catholic in some sense.

It is less clear that these elements meet the responsibilities of Catholic colleges and universities. Pope John Paul II looks to the Catholic universities to promote the dialogue between Christian faith and human culture. Bishop Malone expects Catholic colleges and universities to serve the church by assisting Catholics to understand their new roles of leadership in American society and by participating in the public life of the Catholic community. The bishops, in widely heralded pastoral letters on war and peace and the American economy, appealed to the colleges and universities to engage in research and teaching aimed at peace and economic justice. Others suggest that colleges and universities should turn their attention to the newer Catholic groups, Hispanic and Asian, and assist them to make their way in the United States, as they assisted European immigrants in the past. And there are some who would lead the schools in a more confessional direction, modeled on the best of the evangelical Protestant schools. . . .

As Boston College President Donald Monan, SJ, has pointed out, even the definition of the situation—increasing excellence in teaching, research, and administration but declining Catholic identity—suggests that the real work of most of the faculty and professional staff—teaching, conducting research, and administering—has nothing to do with whatever it is that makes the university Catholic.[8] So the separation of faith from the problems of daily life, and especially from the problems of public life, is institutionalized on Catholic as on other campuses.

Effective strategies to overcome these divisions and develop programs to enrich the intellectual life of the church will thus require serious attention to some of the most perplexing problems of modern culture. Enforcing orthodoxy on the theology department and sexual orthopraxis on the student services office will not do, and more will be needed than simply recruiting new vocations to the sponsoring religious order or hiring more Catholic faculty.

As Bishop Malone says, "Catholic educators themselves must engage in a high-level examination of their collective purpose and develop an overall strategy." . . .

American Catholic academic leaders have organized effectively to defend their interests against Roman intervention, but most of the time they respond to the actions of ecclesiastical authorities with indifference or the same shrug of resigned helplessness characteristic of most American Catholics. This reflects a refusal to take a share of responsibility for the life and work of the institutional church, with which, for better or worse, the destiny of Catholic higher education is inextricably intertwined.

Other elements of an effective strategy would include:

(i) Expansion of cooperative programming with the local and national church, bringing academic resources into more direct contact with church ministries, as has been done in programs to train lay ministers and religious educators. Areas in need of immediate attention include the education and formation of clergy, deacons, and religious, . . . the fostering and support of independent lay movements, and the continuing effort to initiate national dialogue on the moral dimensions of public policy. . . . We will say no, as we should, to the restoration of ecclesiastical control; but we must find creative ways to say yes to the Catholic community, whose vitality and intellectual strength is a civic as well as a religious good.

(ii) Faculty development programs aimed at strengthening and motivating those already on campus to relate their teaching and research to the needs of the church and identifying and supporting Catholic graduate students and junior faculty. We need to develop Catholic studies programs to provide the institutional base and support for Catholic scholarship and teaching. Support for Catholic intellectual life in Catholic colleges and universities is an institutional responsibility, shared by everyone. . . . The institution shows its support by devoting financial and human resources to theology and campus ministry, but also to Catholic intellectual life. . . .[9]

(iii) Deliberate action to influence faculty hiring to insure a critical mass of faculty in all disciplines committed to the school and alert to the agenda of the American church, a step that will require courage and honesty from sponsoring religious communities and Catholic faculty and administrators.

Most important is the formation of leadership among trustees, administrators, faculty, and students. The number of religious and lay personnel on campus and nationally who are committed to a constructive ecclesial role for Catholic higher education and are willing to do something about it is limited. They must be willing to work together to influence the direction of particular institutions and Catholic higher education generally. Their effort should be open, honest, and constructive. . . .

3. Catholic identity carries with it some specific academic responsibilities.

The academic implementation of Catholic identity requires programs that support Catholic scholarship, reintroduce religion into the intellectual life and into general education, make knowledge of the Catholic tradition and of the life of the contemporary church accessible, and integrate considerations of civic and social responsibility—both public and private morality—into research and teaching not only for undergraduates but in graduate and professional schools as well.

Theology departments labor under multiple and often conflicting assignments. . . . When they attempt to meet the need of today's students for an honest examination of fundamental religious and moral questions, they are attacked by Catholic conservatives; when they try to provide opportunities for serious study of Catholic history, doctrine, and moral teaching, they get hit from the other side for "privileging" Catholicism.

Often, with campus ministry, the theology department is made to bear entire responsibility for the Catholic mission and identity of the institution. Yet it is clear that this responsibility rests on the institution as a whole, that it should involve efforts to bring Catholic faith to bear on all areas of learning, and that it aims at graduating persons who have made their religious and moral commitments intelligible. These objectives require systematic attention in every department and school by scholars and teachers for whom this work provides their central intellectual and educational commitment. One way to do this is to establish Catholic Studies programs, through which the schools could provide a home for Catholic scholarship, organize projects to serve the intellectual and educational needs of Catholic students and of the church, while providing a basis to make religious interests a factor in at least some personnel decisions.

4. Catholic higher education makes sense only in terms of Catholic intellectual life.

Despite its rich flowering in recent years, Catholic theology has had minimal impact on American academic culture. . . . Catholics have first of all [says Michael Lacey] to "take responsibility for [their] convictions and exercise and argue those convictions in the political, academic and ecclesial arenas," in public.[10] . . .

"I would recommend [Lacey continues] that rather than thinking simply in terms of gradually developing through marginal improvements a great, comprehensive Catholic university, we think instead about creating a more modest, more flexible, more specialized and altogether more modern institutional form . . . some kind of institute for advanced study to be devoted to the needs of Catholic scholars in all of the humanities and the social sciences." Such a center might awaken interest in Catholic ideas among American academics. It might catch the attention of Catholic scholars now not very interested in religion. After all, no university can honestly claim Catholic identity unless a critical mass of the faculty is intellectually committed to Catholicism. But intellectually committed Catholic scholars will not automatically emerge from secular graduate schools; they need to be identified, recruited, and supported. Most of all, they need to be invited to share in a sustained dialogue on issues that matter. Such a center, or some comparable project, might initiate that dialogue.

There are small signs of what may be a historic shift in understanding of religion's role in scholarship and teaching.[11] Catholic intellectuals and educators can help nudge that change along. In any event, Catholic higher education will not achieve any of its objectives without a faculty seriously engaged at once with Catholicism and with the issues of contemporary culture. Identifying and supporting such people must be the first priority of Catholic—and Jesuit—colleges and universities. . . .

5. One key to revitalizing Catholic higher education lies in its commitment to education for justice.

Catholic schools have a special responsibility to attempt to integrate religious questions into general education and to offer interested students, including those in professional and graduate programs, opportunities to engage the Catholic tradition and to learn of the life and work of the contemporary church. They also share with all other schools an obligation to assist faculty and students to think through their social and civic responsibilities, especially in the context of the specific forms of learning they pursue. Catholic teaching at all levels insists on the connection among faith, scholarship, and the search for justice and peace. The Jesuits in particular have made the service of faith and promotion of justice, in the context of a preferential option for the poor, central elements of their educational mission.

In colleges and universities, the justice imperative is usually connected with community service programs for students, and courses in ethics in departments and schools. . . . For one thing, the ethics involved are usually personal and professional. They highlight the moral problems people face when working in particular fields, and they locate the center of action in the person and his or her conscience. . . . Alert to the multiple temptations of modern society, we learn how to draw the line over which one cannot step without losing integrity.

Even when drawn further, to do good, the good is usually personal, involving legal or medical assistance or efforts to hire minorities and women. Less is learned about how to transform sinful social situations such as a class-biased justice and medical system, so that it might become easier to be good. Still less is heard about the organizational and political commitments that might be required to make justice a reality.

A second problem is that ethics is philosophical, not theological; it tends to separate value questions from meaning or faith questions.

In the process, decision makers (including professors and students) are abstracted from communities of meaning and value, churches, parties, movements. The person who makes ethical evaluations is not a Protestant, Catholic, or Jew; a fundamentalist or a liberal; a Republican or a Democrat. Detached from communities of meaning, dropped into structures that are simply given, the abstract person finds that justice is a matter of choosing the best available option. Goodness becomes just another art of the possible, in an age of shrinking possibilities.

The world-transforming goodness of a Gandhi, a John XXIII, or an Óscar Romero, in contrast, arises from faith, from powerful convictions about meaning; in the absence of serious reflection on such matters—that is, on religion—one tends to adapt to changing historical circumstances. Perhaps that worked humanely when everyone believed that somehow things were always getting better. In light of the Holocaust and other human-being-made tragedies, defeatist meanings (after all, what can I do?) easily fill the void left by the fragmentation of knowledge and the decline of public dialogue. The gap between the claims of education and the realities of culture enlarges, the chasm between sophisticated technical knowledge and helplessness in dealing with larger questions of life becomes all but impassable.

So, what can be done to reintroduce matters of faith into research and teaching, to make meaning part of the agenda of Catholic higher education? A start is to insist that ideas have consequences; this was the late Michael Harrington's summary of his Jesuit education. In his undergraduate years at Holy Cross, the presence of Jesuit priests, their distinctive garb, their unusual celibate and communal way of life, bore living witness to this conviction. They believed, and because they believed what they did, life was different. They seemed convinced that those beliefs were completely reasonable and, therefore, that they should shape the lives of people and nations, not just their own. One could, then, study and come to some conclusions; those conclusions should influence how one lived one's life as spouse and parent, as worker and citizen. Thus, if educators, and especially university presidents, speak of faith and justice, they have to show that these ideals make a difference for them and for their communities and institutions. If not, they make meaning (that is, religion) merely private, fit for chapel and voluntary discussion group, but not for classroom, laboratory, or the streets.

Secondly, Jesuit scholar Walter Ong suggests that we need to think differently about the question of "maintaining a genuine Catholic identity" amid a more diverse faculty and student body. "Jesus lived in a historical world and founded His church in a describable historical context," Ong writes. "He thereby necessarily designed it for some kind of continuing development through history in the various and developing cultures across the world." Why did the early Christians use the Greek word *katholikos*, with its meaning of "through the whole," to describe the church? Why did they not choose the Latin word *universalis*, closer to the word "universal" so often given as the definition of Catholic? The Latin word suggests something of territory and jurisdiction; perhaps it leads to the constant definition of Catholic identity in terms of relationships in the church's organizational chart. But the Greek suggests something different, something more like yeast, as in the passage in Matthew's Gospel: "The reign of God is like yeast which a woman took and kneaded into three measures of flour. Eventually the whole mass of the dough began to rise." Thus the kingdom is a limitless, growing reality, destined ultimately to be present everywhere and to affect everything, but not by converting everything into itself. "Yeast acts on the dough," Ong writes, "but it does not convert all the dough into yeast, nor is it able to do so or meant to do so." So, today, we can no longer say with Hilaire Belloc that "the Church is Europe and Europe is the Church," but we can say with Karl Rahner that the post–Vatican II church, with its awakening local churches across the globe, is authentically present almost everywhere. In each place it tries to build itself into the culture and incorporate the culture into itself. Ong takes this metaphor and speaks of how the faith engages each discipline, how it welcomes scholars and students of all cultures, how it opens itself to the ongoing revelations of a vast and dynamic universe. Thus the yeast "has a great deal to engage itself with" and to "penetrate all of God's creation we need the collaboration of knowledgeable people."[12] Everyone is needed. And in that image Catholicism for the academic community turns from nagging problem to generous invitation to probe the deepest meanings of our common endeavors. . . .

NOTES

1. Charles E. Curran, *Catholic Higher Education, Theology and Academic Freedom* (Notre Dame, IN: University of Notre Dame Press, 1990); William W. May, ed., *Vatican Authority and American Catholic Dissent: The Curran Case and Its Consequences* (New York: Crossroad, 1987).

2. Text in *Current Issues in Catholic Higher Education* 11 (Winter 1991), 31–42. A crucial passage reads: "Every Catholic university, as Catholic, must have the following essential characteristics: (1) a Christian inspiration not only of individuals but of the university community as such, (2) a continuing reflection in the light of Catholic faith upon the growing treasury of human knowledge, to which it seeks to contribute by its own research, (3) fidelity to the Christian message as it comes to us through the church, and (4) an institutional commitment to the service of the people of God and of the human family in their pilgrimage to the transcendent goal which gives meaning to life" (paragraph 13). It should be noted that this wording is taken directly from a document developed in 1972 by university leaders from around the world. See "The Catholic University in the Modern World" in Alice Gallin, OSU, ed., *American Catholic Higher Education: Essential Documents, 1967–1990* (Notre Dame, IN: University of Notre Dame Press, 1992), 37.

3. I have explored at greater length the questions raised in this section in "The Church and Catholic Higher Education," *Horizons* 17 (Spring 1990), 7–29, reprinted in *Current Issues in Catholic Higher Education* 13 (Winter 1993), 14–25.

4. There is a lively debate about this process, centered on the charge of "secularization," often with the suggestion that university leaders irresponsibly jettisoned essential elements of Catholicity in order to gain respect from secular academic leaders. See, for example, Philip Gleason, "American Catholic Higher Education, 1940–1990: The Ideological Context," in George M. Marsden and Bradley J. Longfield, eds., *The Secularization of the Academy* (New York: Oxford University Press, 1991), 234–58; James Tunstead Burtchaell, CSC, "The Decline and Fall of the Christian College," two parts, *First Things* 1 (April 1991), 16–29, and 2 (May 1991), 30–38.

5. "Catholic Education in America," *America*, October 4, 1986, 160–163.

6. Malone, "How Bishops and Theologians Relate," *Origins*, July 31, 1986, 171.

7. See the strong 1980 pastoral statement of the U.S. bishops, "Catholic Higher Education and the Pastoral Mission of the Church," in Gallin, *American Catholic Higher Education*, 129–34.

8. Donald Monan, SJ, "The University in the American Experience," address to the International Federation of Catholic Universities, Toulouse, France, 1991; manuscript in author's possession.

9. Thomas Landy, SJ, with the backing of the Lilly Endowment, has organized "Collegium," an excellent summer theological institute for junior faculty at Catholic institutions and for graduate students interested in the possibility of teaching at a Catholic university. Offices are at Fairfield University. The Society for Values in Higher Education, located at Georgetown University, and the Association for Religion and the Intellectual Life, with offices at the College of New Rochelle, offer programs and publications centered on the relationship between religion and higher education.

10. Michael Lacey, "The Backwardness of American Catholicism," paper presented to the 46th annual meeting of the Catholic Theological Society of America, June 12, 1991; Shea, "Is There a Borderline Between Church and Culture? The Place and Task of Catholic Higher Education," The Killeen Lecture, St. Norbert's College, September 27, 1990, and "Dual Loyalties in Catholic Theology," *Commonweal*, January 31, 1992.

11. See, e.g., Michael J. Lacey, ed., *Religion and Twentieth Century Intellectual Life* (Cambridge: Cambridge University Press, 1988) and Mark R. Schwehn, *Exiles from Eden: Religion and the Academic Vocation in America* (New York: Oxford University Press, 1993).

12. Walter J. Ong, SJ, "Yeast: A Parable for Catholic Higher Education," *America*, April 7, 1990, 347–49, 362–63.

The Truly Catholic University

Richard G. Malloy, SJ

From *America*, 2004

Catholic universities are not "really" Catholic. So, at least, charges Burton Bollag, writing in the *Chronicle of Higher Education* in April.

As one who is on the front lines in the classroom and in campus ministry and lives in a freshman dorm at St. Joseph's University in Philadelphia, I can attest that this Jesuit university is truly Catholic, not in a seminary style, but in the more important spirit of the apostolic constitution *Ex Corde Ecclesiae*, a papal document on Catholic higher education issued in 1990. We at St. Joseph's are mission-driven and engaged in the struggle to convert young people, many of whom have not yet fully incorporated the Catholic faith into their ways of thinking and being.

To those who want to start up seminaries for laypeople, where students attend daily Mass and pray the rosary every night, I say: "Great! But don't pretend you're reaching out to the majority of Catholic eighteen- to twenty-four-year-olds in the United States." Such seminary-style schools are tailoring their ministry and message to an already-converted crowd. Anyone can pretend to have a "really" Catholic university when all students and faculty admitted are already ardently practicing Catholics, albeit in distinctly pre–Vatican II ways. We in the more traditional Catholic universities are engaging today's young adult Catholics in the complicated, contentious, and controversial "media-ized" world within which our students (and many of our younger faculty members) have been formed and now live.

"If you were accused of being Catholic, would there be enough evidence to convict you?" With this question, I often challenge the students in my classes at St. Joseph's University or during the evening programs on "basic Catholicism" we run in the dorms. We want the young adults, many of them only nominally Catholic, to ponder and pursue the intrinsic power and promise of our Catholic way of being. Our desire is that they come to know the living God who offers us the opportunity to become partakers of the divine nature (2 Pet. 1:4). We want them to experience Catholicism as a viable pathway to ultimate union with God. We attest that Catholic social teaching has much to offer through its analysis of the contemporary condition of our world. Indeed, most intelligent young adults find that body of thought interesting, intriguing, and attractive. We hope our students begin to realize that the Catholic faith is a fascinating, lifegiving, sane alternative to the hedonistic, materialistic, and nihilistic ways of life offered them by other cultural currents amid which we all swim.

Students' Lives as Mission Territory

This is my mission territory, deep in the imaginations, the heads and hearts of today's millennial generation. We take what the Catholic parents and Catholic schools of today send to us: on the whole, rather ill informed, only partly converted, and often quite confused young adult Catholics, as Dean Hoge described them in *Young Adult Catholics* (2001).

College is the last stop for these students before the workaday world gets them for the next fifty years. Our mission is to present them with the Catholic faith while they are attending a university. Here what "Catholic" means has to take into account and engage the real students at hand, the young people who are the reason for any university's existence and mission. These young adults are moving through the slow and multidirectional processes of human development. Faith must be presented where these young people are, not where we think they ought to be.

As a Jesuit on a university campus today, I am immersed in the cultural world of young adults. (Come and spend a weekend in the dorms!) It is here that we strive to point our students toward the divine at the depths of human experience. To do so is not easy. I am trying to reach a generation formed in the turbulent waves of the postmodern world, a social order without foundations, lacking clear, unquestionable authorities, devoid of communally accepted, bedrock truths. For these young adults, there have always been one hundred channels and the immensity of the Internet. They know music lyrics much more intimately than Scripture passages, movie scenes (often word for word) more than church rituals, and are convinced that capitalism is real and operative while unable to give a cogent definition of grace. Capitalism makes demands on their lives. Students tremble at the thought of never getting a high-paying job, yet salvation in Christ is a vague notion at best. The gospel of the Donald too often trumps the call of the good news of Jesus.

Partly because of their intense focus on getting ahead and "making it," most Catholic students reveal a daunting ignorance of our tradition's beliefs and practices, though they exhibit an intimate and extensive knowledge of what was needed to get into a top-tier university. A Catholic student at an Ivy League university once phoned me, looking for help with an art history paper. The question: "Who denied Jesus, was it Peter or was it Paul, and if you don't know, can you tell me where I can look it up?" Even though many cannot name the four Gospels, college students can quote verbatim from episodes of "The Simpsons" that deal with religion.

Some charge that Catholic students "lose the faith" while in college. In fact, only a very small percentage of "Catholic" students coming to Catholic universities see the practice of the faith as central to their lives. Most students I have met hold some basic hope that there is a God. But a commitment to Jesus elicits subtle resistance. Somehow young people sense that a real relationship with Jesus entails certain radical challenges to the behaviors taken for granted by too many college students raised on endless showings of "Animal House." Cheating on tests, or on significant others, is too present a pain for some, too easy a way out for many. From experience they know the loneliness, emptiness, and dangers of the dynamics of "friends with benefits" and "hooking up." Obviously, seriously following Jesus contradicts the practice of consuming copious amounts of alcohol and drugs on campus. Most important, students sense that the radical call for social justice voiced by Jesus and the church contradicts their current life goals: money, affluence, and comfort.

The Catholic Church as an institution is not an easy sell to the majority of this millennial generation. A mall culture inculcates in them (and in their parents) an expectation that you can and ought to "have it your way," as at a McDonald's. An uncompromising, legal-istic, rules-bound Catholicism is not only incomprehensible to these young people, it is appallingly unattractive. Denying women access to real power in the organization makes church leaders seem out of touch with the real world in which women teach, preach, and lead in our society. Faculty members live in a professional world in which the right of women to be treated equally is a given. Bishops do not inhabit this sort of universe. Bishops, who have had such difficulty handling clergy scandals, do not impress such faculty members, or those in their twenties, who are looking for leadership in their lives. Even when our bishops take a prophetic stance, as they did in 2003 by opposing the war with Iraq, faculty and young people are not paying any more attention than their parents paid earlier to the church's teaching on birth control. Many faculty members think the church is simply not listening to their questions about power and the status of laypeople in the institution. Even worse, young adults are not greatly interested in these questions. Catholic universities in the twenty-first century present a challenging pastoral situation: how should we respond?

Our Response: Dialogue and Diversity

Too many conservative Catholics imagine we can dictate Catholicism to young adults. Monologues are safe. The speaker—that is to say, the authority—can control the discourse. What a monologue cannot provide is an arena within which a young adult can formulate, choose, and live out a free response.

The goal ought to be to engage young adults in dialogue. Dialogues are risky, especially in settings where diversity is valued. Jesuit leadership at the society's Thirty-fourth General Congregation (1995) called for "dialogue, a spiritual conversation of equal partners, that opens human beings to the core of their identity." John Paul II, in *Ex Corde Ecclesiae*, also champions dialogue: "A Catholic university must become more attentive to the cultures of the world of today, and to the various cultural traditions existing within the church in a way that will promote a continuous and profitable dialogue between the Gospel and modern society."

Dialogues lead to conversions. In the same way that churches should be hospitals for sinners and not showcases for saints, our universities should be developers of dialogue and schools for searchers, not "camps for conservative Catholics" or "oracles of orthodoxy." Young adults trying to ascertain what our faith means and how it is to be lived out are not accepting simple answers from the simpleminded. When the church deems premarital sex immoral, those who promulgate the teaching need cogent arguments to support this view. (There are many such arguments, but too many church officials fail to articulate them in a style comprehensible to the MTV generation). When the excesses of "unbridled capitalism" are decried, those who present the teaching must have answers to the questions posed by young adults raised in an era of right-wing talk radio. If the institutional church is going to refuse dialogue, and decrees that the issue of women priests cannot even be discussed, one should not be surprised when faculty and young people shake their bewildered heads and sadly walk away.

Lost in all the bombastic rhetoric and charges of "not being really Catholic" is a celebration of the pluralism that has always strengthened, not threatened, truly Catholic ways of life. Thomas Clarke, SJ, once articulated the argument that we need schools steeped in the practice of theological reflection to overcome the limitations of religious education done in strictly seminary styles or according to the canons of absolutely academic theology. Seminary-style colleges, where the Catholic tradition and answers are simply passed on unquestioned and unexamined, may be welcomed by a small number of Catholics, but only a miniscule percentage of today's Catholic students will opt for that kind of college experience. Theology departments can avoid the responsibility and challenge of catechesis, but the question arises: why do we require students to take three theology courses? To foster their ongoing conversion, the vast majority of Catholic students need creatively Catholic universities that lead and engage students and faculty in theological reflection in all areas of human learning.

Theological reflection is a dialogue about God and how God relates to all that we humans hope for and endeavor to achieve. It is also a dialogue about God in ways that lead to personal and social transformation. Theological reflection permeates all really Catholic classes, courses, service-learning opportunities, and service projects overtly, or more subtly, in ways the mysterious Holy Spirit uses. Visit a creatively Catholic university and you will see a vast array of programs, professors, and people doing theological reflection in a wide variety of ways. The fact that students recite the rosary every day is not proof that a place is "really" Catholic. Catholicism, as a tradition of thought, a faith vision, and a vibrant, justice-fostering way of life is best experienced through theological reflection in multiple arenas.

In previous eras, Jesuits and other Catholic educators could be like bass fishermen. When you're going for bass, and they are biting, you can throw out any old lure and the fish smack it. Today we have to be more subtle and precise, more like trout fishermen. You can float a fly right by a trout's nose, and if it is not what they are biting on that day, you'll fail to catch anything. In the same way, we cannot be anachronistic in our efforts to attract the majority of today's young Catholic adults. We must be as willing, ready, and able to discuss "Wall Street," "American Pie," and "Dogma" as to discuss "The Mission," "The Apostle," and "The Passion of the Christ." Young Catholic adults have questions about faith and the church, questions often rooted in their experience of twenty-first-century life and culture. To ignore those questions and attempt to impose poorly understood ritual practices on uncomprehending twenty-year-olds is not really Catholic. Such blind ritualism frustrates rather than fosters conversion.

A faith that does not stay close to perennial questions is no faith at all. Faith flourishes in the search for God, and in communion with others working for justice through love. A faith with all the answers is nothing more than an ideology; and, as we saw all too often in the bloody twentieth century, when ideologies roam the earth, men, women, and children are killed. Simplistic, unquestioned, unexamined faiths become ideologies. The sad truth of the matter is that ideologies imposed brutally on people destroy freedom, and true freedom is the essence of real Catholicism. "For freedom Christ has set us free" (Gal. 5:1).

Freedom means accepting people where they are on their life journey. Any school can accept only the already converted and claim to be "really" Catholic. The rest of us courageously take up the mission of reaching out to today's Catholic young adults, especially those who are not fully formed in our Catholic faith. We take the young-adult Catholics who actually live in the United States today and labor to continue the transformation in Christ begun in their family life, school experiences, and parish settings. For intelligent, searching, questioning young Catholics, we offer the promise of freedom, the revelation of service, and the challenge of Christ. Anyone who wants a really Catholic education is welcome to apply.

Collegium, Catholic Identity, and the Non-Catholic

Suzanne Matson

From *Conversations on Jesuit Higher Education,* 1994

As a non-Catholic teaching at a Jesuit university, it is hard to know what my place is or should be in the discussion about the nature of Catholic higher education. Though in my teaching and academic life I feel myself to be a fully participating member of my institution, calls to action in O'Brien's article [the first one in this section] such as his general urging for "deliberate action to influence faculty hiring to insure a critical mass of faculty in all disciplines committed to the mission of the school and alert to the agenda of the American church" make me, first of all, wonder what some of those phrases mean, exactly; and second, to feel suddenly not part of my university's "critical mass" if being so means being Catholic, or being even a professed Christian. That sentence alone in O'Brien's essay shifts me from feeling myself to be integral in my university community to being someone on the non-"critical" margins.

I first confronted this issue of my "university identity" when my dean invited me to be Boston College's faculty representative at an eight-day conference called "Collegium," the first of three planned summer institutes founded by Thomas Landy, SJ, on the topic of "Faith and Intellectual Life" (O'Brien mentions "Collegium" in a footnote to his essay). The invitation filled me with distress. Here

I was, a tenure-track assistant professor being asked not only to attend a conference on the "Christian academic vocation" but to reveal, by accepting or declining the invitation, something about my spiritual positioning—an aspect of self that to me felt profoundly personal. Never before had I needed to face so pointedly my position as an agnostic within a Catholic-university community. I found "Collegium's" stated goals to be appealing: discussions of and encounters with particular forms of Christian spirituality, as well as opportunities in the week for reflection and writing. Yet the word "faith" started me checking my mental pockets with alarm: I don't have it, I don't think I've ever had it. *Have I?* Such is the position of the agnostic: nothing is final, not even doubt.

I wrote the dean that perhaps I wouldn't be the best faculty member to "represent" Boston College. I explained why I didn't refuse the invitation, but I clarified who it was he had invited, and in writing that letter felt uncomfortably exposed. I also began questioning my relationship to the university in a way I never had, even upon being hired. What was I doing on a Jesuit campus, anyway? Was accepting the job at BC some monumental act of hypocrisy? At the time I thought not. The question of religion came up not at all during departmental interviews and only in the most diplomatic of ways in the academic vice president's office. I was asked, "How do you see yourself fitting in at a Jesuit university?" In its simplicity and openness, the question allowed the candidate wide scope. I said something about feeling myself to be in alignment with what I perceived to be the intellectual and humanitarian values of the Jesuits. It was a careful question, and a careful reply. Apparently it was enough.

But was it enough? Should it have been? When the dean got back to me about "Collegium," he said he had checked with its director, Tom Landy, to make sure that someone with more "questions than belief" would have a place at the conference. The answer from Tom Landy was yes, with the warning that I would be in the minority and the hope that I would come anyway.

I did go, with considerable angst and trepidation. On the train down from Boston to Fairfield I spied two or three others with the same distinctive notebook of readings we had been sent in advance, but I stayed buried behind my *New Yorker*, putting off the inevitable as long as possible. It was just as well that I conserved my energy, for the eight days that followed were all-consuming. Each day held a major presentation by a distinguished theologian, one or two small-group sessions for discussion, panel presentations by "mentors" (senior colleagues), spirituality sessions, and a liturgy.

Although I was certainly in a minority and a nonbeliever, I soon discovered in group and personal discussions that almost no one's faith was seamless, or unchanging, or without internal challenges. The small-group sessions fostered a sense of acceptance and exchange that left no one out on the sidelines, and began conversations that continued as people strolled outside after supper, pausing in twos and threes on the grass until the late June darkness pushed us inside—where the talk still continued sometimes until midnight. It was as if once the topic were broached—how one's spiritual and intellectual life intersected—no one could get enough of comparing experiences, sharing ideas, articulating why and how they had come to an academic vocation and what that had to do with fundamental questions of meaning for them.

By the end of the week I was exhausted, stimulated, and felt mentally more energized for a summer of my own writing than I had been before I came. The theologians who addressed us offered ideas on sacramentality, community, and social justice that seemed important, generous, and hospitable, ideas that in one way or another have become part of the texture of my own thinking. I didn't leave "Collegium" vowing to convert to Catholicism or ready to reclaim my Protestant heritage. I did leave with some defenses evaporated, a new feeling of identification with my home university, and a lot of things to keep thinking about.

In retrospect, it was risky to give up the privacy of silence on the subject of religion, especially in a professional context. It was possible to lose the compartmentalization that allowed me to think that matters of religious doubt could be kept quite separate from everything else in my life. I still have more questions than belief, but I no longer fear the conversation that talks about and probes the shape of faith.

The Catholic Intellectual Tradition in the Catholic University

Monika K. Hellwig

From *Examining the Catholic Intellectual Tradition,* 2000

We are in an age of increasing ecumenical activity in scholarship and in university circles. For example, Scripture scholarship has become almost totally interdenominational. Traditions in sacred music have continuously borrowed from one another, as have conventional representations in the visual arts. Catholic programs in philosophy now have on their required reading lists books that were formerly listed in the Index of Forbidden Books and therefore inaccessible to Catholic students through normal channels. Recent trends in the study of literature have tended to abandon any claim to a canon of required classics. The study of history and of religion now addresses many cultures and languages.

In the midst of this, several questions arise. First of all, is depth of knowledge being sacrificed for the sake of breadth? In university studies, especially at the undergraduate level, this is no idle question. Secondly, are we abandoning efforts towards the integration of knowledge? Thirdly, are we in danger of losing our distinctive identity? Catholic universities and colleges, responsible more than any other body for the care and continuity of the Catholic intellectual tradition, are particularly challenged by these three questions.

The first of these questions, about the risk of losing depth, has exercised educators in the broader higher education field for some time. The extension of postsecondary education to a much larger proportion of the population has meant in many cases lowered expectations and less personal intellectual exchange between professors and students. While this may be quite efficient in technical fields, it impoverishes study in the humanities. It may be reducing higher education simply to longer schooling. Because religiously motivated schools of all traditions are concerned with assimilation of culture and critical discernment about values, this trend to the less personal in favor of the more technically efficient is damaging to the essential fabric of religious higher education.

The question about sacrificing depth for breadth is closely related to the second question, namely, whether we are achieving any integration in higher education. It has been fashionable, even in Catholic circles, to say that integration of studies is no longer possible in a pluralistic society, that each student must find some sort of personal balance or integration, but that it cannot be found in the planning of programs and curricula. Clearly, this is not a problem if education is seen as a matter of acquiring certain specialized skills and the means of access to information. If education is seen as preparation for life and for societal responsibilities, the lack of integration is disastrous because there is no foundation for making serious decisions about lifestyle, social participation, career goals, and so forth. Religiously sponsored institutions cannot surrender the task of integration.

The third question is whether we are in danger of forgetting and losing our identity. This risk is built into the pattern of contemporary developments in communication technology. It is caused in part by rapid sequences of change in the economy, upsetting employment patterns, calling for quick retraining of large numbers of the newly unemployable. It is a function of the political restlessness and reshaping of the world's alliances and balance of power with consequent shifting of what needs to be known for practical purposes. It is part of the culture, with its unquestioning favoring of the new over the already tested and the consequent changing relationships between the generations. All these are but a few of the external factors that tend to erode both the integration of higher education and the identity of religiously sponsored institutions. Erosion of identity is not a matter of any conscious decision to abandon the particular religious identity of an institution, but rather a combination of many new demands and the subtle influence of the secular expectations of the wider academy.

All these forces contribute to a situation in which a Catholic university or college cannot take its Catholic identity for granted in the way we might have done in the earlier decades of the twentieth century. It is not by anyone's failure or fault that U.S. Catholic colleges and universities had in many cases moved unnoticed toward secularization in the seventies and early eighties, to discover with a jolt in the late eighties that without taking thought and action they would not retain their distinctive identities. Such action had to address hiring policies, public statements of the institutions about their identity, leadership of the central administration, departments of theology and philosophy, the focus of university-sponsored research, structure and formation of boards, continuing bonds with the sponsoring religious community or diocese, student recruitment, campus ministry, and much else. But most basic to the whole enterprise is the institution's respect and care for the Catholic intellectual heritage.

This paper discusses two topics: what defines the Catholic intellectual tradition; and how we can expect it to be present in the life of a university or college.

The Catholic Intellectual Tradition: Content

Our tradition is alive and growing in the present while greatly enriched and supported by many texts, objects, architectural structures, customs and rituals, modes of thought, expression and action, and relationships and organizations from the past. Because it is alive, it cannot be reduced to a treasury of deposits from the past, though it certainly contains such a treasury. Perhaps the most fruitful way of thinking about the Catholic intellectual tradition is in terms of two aspects: the classic treasures to be cherished, studied, and handed on; and the way of doing things that is the outcome of centuries of experience, prayer, action, and critical reflection.

The classic treasures are like crystallized deposits precipitated out of the living stream. If we reach far back into our history, they include the Scriptures, some primitive formulations of Christian faith and prayer, the rudiments of the rituals of Eucharist and baptism, the most basic elements of church and Christian calendar, and so forth. But based on Scripture, and growing with the centuries, are commentaries on Scripture and elaboration of biblical themes in further expressions, both those that are explicitly religious and those that are more generally exercises of the Christian imagination in art and literature. Based on the primitive formulations of faith, we see through the centuries the elaboration of catechesis, theology, religious drama, fiction, and poetry, and vast systems of Christian philosophy. Based on the primitive formulations of Christian prayer, we can trace whole systems of spirituality with their texts and commentaries, their rules for living, and their exhortations, their hagiography, devotions, pilgrimages, shrines, and much else. Based on the rudimentary forms of Eucharist and baptism, we see the elaboration through the centuries of a complex sacramental system, whole traditions of liturgy and of sacred music, of church and monastic architecture, of the symbolism of incense, gestures, processions, bells, and vestments.

In the course of time, certain formulations became classic, not to prevent later developments but to form a touchstone against which later developments were to be seen and judged. These certainly include the pronouncements and explanatory texts handed down to us from the great church councils of antiquity, and in a broader sense the whole body of patristic writings, followed by the medieval and modern councils and the writings of the medieval doctors and certain modern theologians. These become classic by being habitually affirmed in retrospect by the discerning Christian community.

Certain figures in history became classic elements of the Christian story and heritage: Helena and Constantine, Macrina and Basil, Monica and Augustine, Benedict and Scholastica, Francis and Clare, Albertus Magnus and Thomas Aquinas, Catherine of Siena and Teresa of Ávila, to mention but a few whose personal stories are closely interwoven with the history of the Christian people. These are stories not to be forgotten or neglected. They come out of the memory and understanding of generations of believers who resonated with their lives, actions, or teachings.

Likewise, certain texts in literature became classics, throwing light on the Christian journey through history, on Christian faith and life and understanding of the big issues. Immediately coming to mind are *Piers Plowman*, *The Divine Comedy*, *The Canterbury Tales*, and such modern classics as *Murder in the Cathedral*, *A Man for All Seasons*, and *Four Quartets*. Nor should we exclude from the treasury great Protestant and Orthodox classics like *Paradise Lost*, *The Pilgrim's Progress*, and *The Brothers Karamazov*. The treasures of Christian lyric poetry and hymnody are too many to list.

Much can be said, and more is yet to be discovered, about the treasures of Christian art and architecture, both the explicitly religious and the wider expression in decorative and representative art, in the building of hospitals, pilgrim shelters, schools, and universities; in the structuring of cities, towns, and villages among believers, expressing their hierarchy of values and their vision of reality. There is much to be studied and treasured in music, both sacred and profane, that expresses the Christian consciousness, whether in orchestral, operatic, choral, or chamber music; whether medieval plainchant, Baroque polyphony, or modern classical and folk styles. Of course much of this is studied in art history or musicology, but by contemporary academic conventions it tends to be stripped of its religious relevance and studied only from a technical perspective. When these things are appreciated as part of the Christian intellectual heritage, they are studied in a way that tends to integrate the disciplines by relating everything to the meaning of human life in its relationship to the transcendent.

Something similar can be said of the development of experimental science and of technology. We have a heritage in which the development of the printing press, for instance, and the earliest discoveries in genetics were seen in their relationship to the meaning of human life and its ultimate destiny. The very notoriety and conflict generated by

Galileo's demonstration of the Copernican hypothesis or Darwin's demonstration of the tenability of the evolutionary thesis testify to the relevance that the natural sciences have had to the integration of human life and knowledge with a spiritual focus.

We have, then, a treasury of many components in the Catholic intellectual tradition that should not be left hidden or unexplored because of the pressure of contemporary busyness. It should not be left unexplored. It is enriching, supportive, inspirational, and full of insight and wisdom for present and future generations of Catholic people. There is a further reason for keeping this treasury available and engaged with contemporary reality: it is wealth that the Catholic community holds in trust for the whole human community, whom it may profit in many ways.

Catholic Intellectual Tradition: Our Approach to Knowledge

All of the foregoing, however, is only one aspect of the Catholic intellectual tradition. The other aspect is the way we have learned to deal with experience and knowledge in order to acquire true wisdom, live well, and build good societies, laws, and customs. Central to this are values and assumptions that we share with all religious traditions. These include the conviction that human life has meaning and that the meaning can be known. Further, they include the understanding that the basic principles of moral right and wrong are given and not humanly invented. Beyond this we hold in common with all religious traditions the deliberately fostered yearning for communion with the ultimately transcendent, and the understanding that in some way this is connected with the way we relate to one another.

These are foundational principles that we usually treat as presuppositions and therefore do not even examine. They are seldom called into question by ordinary people. Yet the drift of modern philosophies, especially since the end of the Second World War, suggests that it is urgent that some of us in scholarly circles reflect seriously on these underlying principles and their consequences at the levels at which contemporary science and technology, contemporary analysis in the humanities, and contemporary philosophy and social sciences influence the shaping of our society.

Beyond the common base that we share with all religious traditions there is, of course, a Christian core that we share with our fellow Christians. At its simplest, this is the conviction that in the person of Jesus of Nazareth we have an utterly trustworthy interpretation of the meaning and destiny of human life, of human relationship with God, and of what constitutes a good life. From this simple beginning, the Christian community over the centuries has elaborated ways of worship, structures of society, beliefs, and expectations, all of which go to make up a way of proceeding. Among Christian communities, however, some characteristic emphases and understandings are more particularly Catholic. In this essay, I would like to point to some that have direct implications for Catholic higher education and scholarship. These are: commitment to the continuity between faith and reason, respect for the cumulative wisdom of the past, an anti-elitist bent, attention to the community dimension of all human behavior, concern for integration of goals and objectives, and keen awareness of the sacramental principle.

The first of these, the continuity of faith and reason, leads Catholic universities and colleges to include philosophy and theology as essential components of the liberal arts core of undergraduate education, and to offer public lectures on current issues in public, professional, and private life, to address these issues from a faith perspective. In contrast to some strands of Christian tradition, the Catholic tradition has strongly emphasized the need to think through the coherence of the faith and to face challenges to it from secular events and knowledge. We see this as a practice of faith, not a rejection of it. And this has led Catholic universities to develop philosophical traditions that train the mind to think clearly about the implications of the faith. The fact that the Scholastic tradition as it was passed on earlier in the twentieth century no longer serves this need adequately does not mean that we should abandon the project, but rather that we must find new philosophical vehicles to pursue it.

The second characteristic emphasis that I have singled out is that of respect for the cumulative wisdom of the past. In contrast to the position of some Christian communities that look for Christian wisdom only in Scripture or only in the legacy of the pre-Constantinian era, the Catholic community has set great store by knowledge of the cumulative wisdom of all the Christian centuries. Indeed, we have inherited and preserved the attitude of the second-century Greek apologists for Christianity in appreciating even the wisdom of pagan traditions as seen and adapted in the light of the faith. Catholic universities, therefore, have typically had strong programs in the humanities and often outstanding programs in classics at a time when others have tended to abandon the classical languages and deal with classical literature and mythology only very lightly.

The third characteristic mentioned above is the anti-elitist bent. This is another way of expressing that mark of the church that we used to call universality. Salvation and all other human goods are intended by the creator for all. All human beings and all peoples and nations are precious to God, who is at all times self-revealing to them. There is, therefore, a certain intellectual humility required in Catholic scholars and Catholic institutions, as well as a certain sense of responsibility for the conduct and use of scholarship, time, and resources. Non-elitism means responsibility to the whole community for what we choose to research and write, for the resources we use up in doing it, and for the way we use time when the labor of others indirectly makes possible our leisure for study and scholarly work. But non-elitism also means writing in a style that is accessible to non-specialists and teaching in a way that is helpful to all students. It means making strenuous efforts to include the underprivileged or excluded from society. It also means treating respectfully cultures and customs alien from our own.

The fourth characteristic is closely related to this. Attention to the community dimension of all human actions means that there cannot be a pursuit of any and all kinds of research or teaching simply out of the intrinsic interest of the subject, as though it were all a game without consequences. Critical discernment must be exercised as to the impact of releasing certain kinds of information into the society, as with increasingly powerful weaponry, or the effect of using resources for one kind of research that are badly needed for another kind that addresses urgent human need. Similarly, to say that there is a community dimension to all human actions also implies that teaching can never be without reference to the impact on the students and, through them, on their society. This applies, for instance, to the kinds of questions that are unfolded in relation to the maturity of the students to deal with such questions. And it applies to the kind of literature that is read in relation to the ability of the students to be discerning about the values expressed or implied, and about the behavior described. Moreover, the community dimension means that everything that is taught is placed in the context of what the students will do with their knowledge and the impact on their community.

This relates in turn to a fifth characteristic, namely, the concern to integrate knowledge as a basis for true wisdom in the living of one's life. Perhaps one of the most troubling aspects of rapid change and technical development in our times is that people of all ages have to learn so much so fast. They have to master so much instrumental knowledge and skill at such speed of assimilation that the more significant questions of meaning and purpose are often crowded out. The integration of learning in a coherent worldview or philosophy of life is a necessary basis for living a good, productive, well-directed life. It is necessary, though not sufficient, for setting proper priorities, for attaining a proper hierarchy of values, and even for attaining an appropriate intellectual humility in work and career, and in relations with other people.

A sixth characteristic, the final one mentioned here, is the experience and understanding that modern Catholics have come to name the sacramental principle. This refers not only to the seven sacraments that are central to Catholic worship, but to a broader experience that has to do with the way human beings use their memory and imagination. Our perception of reality is never in terms of raw experience, but is always arranged, interpreted, focused by the active mind of the perceiver. How we do this depends in large part on what we have experienced in the past, how those about us interpreted the experiences in which we shared, the representational art about us, the stories we heard, the way space and society had already been organized for us, and so forth.

Two faculties play a role in this: memory, which records what has been, and imagination, which arranges the elements of experience in a meaningful pattern. An insight that Catholics particularly inherited from their Jewish or Hebrew past is that this is the way a people shapes its culture, and likewise the way the culture shapes the people. It can happen almost by default, a real risk in a pluralistic, rapidly changing society like ours, or it can be the outcome of focused contemplation and critical reflection.

It has been a continuing practice of the Catholic community to build on religious memories by story and image, in literature and art, in music and architecture, in the liturgy and in extra-liturgical devotions, and in the elaboration of symbols of all kinds. The purpose of this is to shape the memories and the imagination of succeeding generations of believers so that they will interpret all their experiences in terms of the pervasive presence of the sacred and in terms of a history of salvation. The value that this gives to the education of the imagination is a precious heritage with implications for all education and in a special way for higher education. It demands a foundation in the liberal arts, a style of education that fosters contemplation, and a respect for works of scholarship that take a long time. This is all rather countercultural in our times.

The Role of the Catholic University

Some of the most significant contributions to Catholic culture, and to culture in any tradition, have been made by individuals working in relative isolation. Some important Catholic scholarship of our times comes from professors in large secular institutions and from independent scholars not employed by universities. But the Catholic universities are the normal trustees of Catholic learning; and the whole intellectual heritage would be greatly impoverished in their absence. In light of all that has been said above, some desirable components and aspects of a Catholic university emerge.

As we all know, at the minimum a Catholic university should be a true university in the accepted sense, and it should maintain a lively familiarity with the treasures of the tradition and the way of proceeding in the tradition. But this still leaves many questions: who, where, when, and how? It may be well to begin in the library. It is not only a question of library holdings, but also of the welcoming atmosphere, style of architecture and interior decoration, works of art displayed, and most of all the placing of the collection. The significance of this last point is that what is most central to the character and purpose of the university should be most accessible, most attractively arranged, and offer the best possibilities for browsing and for sitting comfortably to read.

What has been said about the library could be said about the entire campus. Once a campus exists, its basic architectural pattern is established. However, at any opportunity to reshape the campus, the principle might be kept in mind that the very layout of the buildings ought to express the priorities and the relationship among the various activities of the campus, and that utility or efficiency need not mean ugliness. That may seem to some a trivial consideration in relation to the construction of curricula, the choice of programs, and so forth, but in the context of the sacramental principle, the visual-kinesthetic impact of the campus sets an important tone even before any activity is engaged. Of particular interest, of course, is the placing and design of the university's main chapel, whether it is the focus to which the eye and the steps are naturally drawn as to the center, or whether it is hidden away to be discovered only by devotees. Again in terms of the sacramental principle, the quality, character, and placement of statuary and other art about the campus is significant.

What can be said about space can also be said about time. In these days of external and financial pressures for maximum efficiency and maximal use of buildings, there are great temptations for weekend programs to spill into Sunday, even Sunday morning, for spring break to replace Holy Week and Easter, and for weekday feasts and holy days to disappear. Much is conveyed by the cessation of routine activities on special occasions that would never be communicated in the reading of books about it. The regular tolling of a bell for a daily celebration of Eucharist becomes part of consciousness even for those who do not darken the chapel door. The solemn celebrations of Eucharist at the beginning of the academic year, at graduation, on the occasion of faculty or student deaths, and at other special occasions, similarly help to constitute the character of the school even for those who do not participate. In aid of efficiency and conformity to more general academic expectations, there is pressure to eliminate all the particular Catholic markers in space and time that constitute the particularity of the environment. It is important that we resist this pressure in order to maintain our own particular identity.

The role of campus ministry, which has developed in the universities and colleges of the United States as the presence of the sponsoring communities has dwindled in numbers, could be defined as something more than individual care of souls. Given appropriate appointments, it could be the focal point of scholarly interdisciplinary conversations in which the encounter of faith and culture could take place in some depth and with some continuity. With an investment in occasional significant outside speakers, the participation of top administrators, and perhaps an occasional formal reception, this could become the intellectual focus of the school.

The seriousness and focus of the curriculum, especially for undergraduates, begin with the manner and style of recruitment of students. A university or college that states its identity and character clearly in its literature, and takes care that admission personnel understand and support this statement, will certainly attract both faculty and students who are attuned to the institution's expectations. That being so, it will be easier to maintain in the structure of the curriculum the components of the Catholic intellectual tradition. It may be important to note in passing that the Catholic colleges and universities of the United States are almost alone among the Catholic universities of the world in offering all students a liberal arts foundation including an introduction to philosophy and theology. Elsewhere, students entering the university begin immediately to concentrate in their specialized field, though they may have had a more extensive and intensive secondary education before they come.

The foundation in the liberal arts is important in developing both a more effective use of the imagination in creative approaches to personal, technical, professional, and societal challenges, and better honed skills in critical thinking and evaluation. In our society, it is rapidly becoming countercultural to spend time in the undergraduate years on laying this foundation rather than going directly into professional preparation. Moreover, even where liberal arts programs remain, they are often so dissipated into unrelated elective offerings, each focusing rather narrowly in its own field, that the benefits of a truly liberal education are lost. Those benefits ought to include the integration of learning, the realization of the community dimension, increasing experience of the continuity of faith and reason, a deepening respect for and appreciation of the cumulative wisdom of the past, progressive transcending of facile and unexamined prejudices and, of course, the integration of life and learning.

Both philosophy and theology play a central role in such a liberal education. It is a role that is little appreciated in our culture. It is thrown in question by the prevailing interpretation of the constitutional separation of church and state, an interpretation followed even by some of the large private foundations on whose financial assistance private higher education has become steadily more dependent for its very survival. For Catholics this role of philosophy and theology is central to our intellectual tradition. It follows from the need to integrate one's life and activities with a focus on ultimate ends. This clearly requires the development of analytical and critical skills, and is immensely helped by acquaintance with the great thinkers of the past, the questions they raised, the ways in which they worked toward answers, the kinds of answers they found satisfactory or unsatisfactory. That is the function of philosophy, and it involves the foundational questions for the natural and social sciences, for the appreciation of art, music, and literature, for an approach to history, a grasp of languages and mathematical reasoning, and much else.

It has been the custom in Catholic higher education in the past to teach an introduction to the branches of philosophy according to later presentations of Thomistic thought. In our time, when so much has changed and is constantly changing, it may be more consistent with the Catholic intellectual tradition to teach an introduction to philosophy through a tracing of the history of philosophy. Our tradition cherishes the cumulative wisdom of the past. In philosophy this retracing of the past is a particularly apt introduction to the main lines of thought of the great thinkers, each developing further what had been handed on through the centuries of Western thought. If there were unlimited time, one might look at the traditions of India and China. Given the time constraints of the undergraduate years, it seems more relevant to the project of Catholic higher education to furnish our students with a common memory of the development of the great questions in their own tradition. On the whole, that is what is sadly lacking for most educated people of our culture and society. In providing a certain breadth, their education has often failed to give them either solid cultural roots of their own or a common memory shared with others in their milieu. This last is so important for meaningful conversation because it offers a common vocabulary understood in a common sense, as well as providing reference points, assumptions, accepted modes of argumentation, and such like.

As mentioned above, the teaching of theology to all students in Catholic higher education is a very important contribution to the passing on of the Catholic intellectual tradition. This much is clear. What is less clear, even now more than four decades after the Second Vatican Council, is just what should be the content of theology for an educated laity. It is clear that to go back to a popularization of traditional seminary formation misses the mark. It is equally clear that the trend of recent decades does not fulfill the need. The recent tendency has been to offer some introduction to critical Scripture scholarship, some discussion of foundational questions concerning the nature of faith and religious language, concerning traditional efforts to demonstrate the existence of God, what is meant by claims of revelation, and other questions common to all traditions. Sometimes even these are not required, and each student can make a personal selection of courses from a slate of electives. This seems to fall far short of the role that theology should play in the education of students in Catholic undergraduate programs.

If theology is really to play an integrating and focusing role, our programs probably need to declare themselves boldly and devote more time to the theological sequence. To achieve the essential purpose, we need minimally to offer students an introduction both to the understanding of Scripture in their own culture and intellectual environment, and to a coherent, well-informed, and intelligent grasp of their own faith tradition with its creedal content. Moreover, we need to engage faculty and graduate students in the difficult questions about their own tradition.

At the same time, it is evident that the whole burden of a Catholic focus and integration of the curriculum cannot simply be carried by the theology and philosophy departments. That burden must be shared by all departments in ways appropriate to their disciplines, but in a special way by literature, history, fine arts, and some components of psychology, sociology, and political theory. It is a question of relating everything to the greater whole, to human destiny, responsibility for society and culture, stewardship of the resources of creation, and so forth. It is also a question of knowing, taking seriously, and engaging the wisdom of our tradition in the questions that arise. And it is a question of treating the material learned in the student's major field not only as a matter of technical competence but as a matter of wisdom for life.

The character and identity of a Catholic university need to be evident not only in undergraduate education but also in the graduate and professional programs and in the original scholarly work and research of the faculty. This is even more difficult to achieve in the present climate of higher education and scholarship worldwide. The university world is still firmly rooted in the Enlightenment with its secularizing tendencies and its disregard for the particular in favor of the universal and whatever can be broadly standardized. The claim that a particular tradition such as the Catholic has something of value to contribute to research in politics, economics, psychology, and so forth is still suspect in most circles. The idea that a religiously based ethics should be part of the curriculum of professional schools seems quite absurd to many of our colleagues. But a countercultural stance on these issues belongs to the very core of the Catholic university's task in the world. It is there that the wisdom of our tradition meets those who make the decisions for society, and it is there that the engagement of the Catholic intellectual tradition with the culture can effectively happen.

The requirements for realizing this are exacting. We need competent scientists, social scientists, and scholars in all fields who are sufficiently formed in the Catholic intellectual tradition themselves to bring their graduate students and already qualified practitioners to an understanding, appreciation, and critique of the issues that arise. Almost all of the professors in various fields in our universities and colleges have themselves been educated at the doctoral level in the large state university graduate schools under the post-Enlightenment secularizing and specializing influences. If they have had a formation in the Catholic intellectual tradition, this will at best have been at the undergraduate level, but for many will have ended at the secondary level or with parish instruction for the sacrament of confirmation. That is a very fragile foundation on which to provide their graduate students with serious faith-based analysis of issues in their fields. It is clear that in order to realize the potential of a Catholic university in some fullness, continuing education or self-education of the faculty is an indispensable prerequisite. This can be done with reading circles guided by competent people, with public lectures, faculty-run seminars and colloquia, summer institutes attended by invitation, and other such initiatives. It can engage good theology and philosophy faculties with their colleagues as well as with their students.

The other side of this is the selection, focus, and conduct of research. It has become customary on the university campuses for research of some kind to be required for promotion and tenure, but for the nature of that research to be entirely at the discretion of each individual professor. The endeavor of the International Federation of Catholic Universities, on the other hand, is to build connections among Catholic universities so that joint major research projects can be undertaken that relate to such problems as world hunger, development of Third World cities and economies, the international illegal drug trade and the agricultural economies integrated into it, development of legal systems in emergent nations, conflict resolution over major land claims, armaments control mechanisms, world literacy, and other peace, justice, and development issues. Clearly, the ideal Catholic university would have a focus in research and scholarship that would further the Catholic intellectual tradition in bringing both the classic treasures and the way of proceeding into play in relation to contemporary culture and society. This requires rather a bold stand on the part of the institution to assert its research priorities and to hire and give grants by the criteria of those priorities.

There is, of course, nothing in the inner logic of our intellectual tradition that would require that we hire only Catholic professors or admit only Catholic students. The requirement is rather the contrary, namely, that it is important for a Catholic university to have both faculty and student participants of other traditions. Being open to the cumulative wisdom not only of our own but of other traditions happens more readily when we meet them in their living representatives. Moreover, an authentic dialogue of faith and culture is more likely to happen where other perspectives are represented. And again, while it is good that students get a firm grounding in their own tradition, being segregated from others in their intellectually formative years does not prepare them to live in a pluralistic society and in an ecumenical age. Complementarity and ecumenical exchanges are an important aspect of scholarship for the faculty and of education for the students.

At the same time, it is becoming increasingly clear that a critical mass of faculty, administrators, and staff really committed to the Catholic mission of the institution is essential if the character of the institution is to survive. It is a matter requiring careful attention in our time. Much could be taken for granted in the past when the sponsoring religious congregations were a strong presence on each campus and guaranteed continuity in the spirit of the foundation. These were men and women with a solid formation in Catholic experience, worship, and thought, as it was mediated through a particular congregational spirituality and apostolate. Moreover, it was accepted without dispute that the founding congregation's vision and philosophy was the criterion by which all things were judged in the conduct of the institution. Such is no longer the case on most campuses, where the faculty at large is the arbiter in many matters. If that faculty does not share the ideals of the founders, those ideals will not remain the philosophy and spirit of the institution.

There is, of course, a further consideration: the character of the board of directors. Boards have largely assumed the guiding function of the sponsoring congregations. They select the president and make major decisions concerning property, financing, and priorities. It is critical that trustees be selected not only for their contacts and skills but also for their commitment to the Catholic identity, character, and ideals of the institution. In the long run, it is the board that sets the direction in which the institution will grow. Board members are likely to be in the same position as the faculty in relation to the Catholic intellectual tradition. They are likely to have had their last education in the tradition in the undergraduate years at most, but perhaps only at the secondary level, or only in parish preparation for confirmation. If the Catholic universities are to realize their potential as participants in the shaping and the handing on of the intellectual tradition, there also need to be ongoing programs of board formation in order to support the spirit and focus of the institution.

Conclusion

We are the heirs and trustees of a great intellectual and cultural tradition founded on Christian faith and enhanced by grace and by many centuries of testing for fidelity and authenticity. It is a trust not only for the benefit of the church but also for the benefit of the world. The Catholic universities play a key role in bearing this trust with its treasury of classic deposits and its long-developed approach to life and learning. The conditions for fidelity to our trust have changed a good deal in the twentieth century. If we are still moving experimentally and are not always clear and successful in what we are doing, that is not from ill will or unconcern, but due to the uncharted nature of our situation. On the other hand, we cannot afford to let the future of our universities take their course without careful attention, reflection, and planning. In this planning the characteristic contribution that the Catholic universities can make must be not one criterion among others but the guiding principle of the whole project. And in this the Catholic universities and colleges of the United States have a particular role to play because of the unique character of their undergraduate programs, because of their sheer numbers among the Catholic universities of the world, and because of their excellent academic standing among the universities of the continent.

Closing Statement on Academic Freedom and Catholic Character

John I. Jenkins, CSC

University of Notre Dame, April 5, 2006

Last January, I raised a challenge for Notre Dame: to consider how we can affirm the highest principles and practices of a university—ensuring the academic freedom to explore the full range of ideas and expressions produced by human thought and creativity—and, at the same time, to affirm our Catholic character and engage the Catholic intellectual tradition in a way that shapes and enriches the educational experience of our students.

The challenge is not to do just one of these—or even to do both of them in parallel—but to promote academic freedom and affirm our Catholic character in a way that integrates the two and elevates both. This university was founded on the conviction that these goals are not just compatible, but essential, beneficial, and mutually reinforcing.

We have had this discussion of lofty ideals largely in the context of a single play. But we have to make sure that this event, or any single event, does not take on any undue stature. It is not more important than the principles we are discussing; it is a test of how we apply them.

Over the past ten weeks, I have met, talked to, and heard from hundreds of men and women—faculty, students, and administrators;

alumni and friends. I have met individually with department chairs and faculty; attended a forum put on by the College of Arts and Letters; and participated in meetings of the Faculty Senate, the Student Senate, and the Graduate Student Council. I have read the e-mails sent to me, and I have carefully and faithfully read the news coverage and opinions in *The Observer*. I thank everyone who took the time to share their thoughts; I have been impressed by the passion, intelligence, and civility of this debate.

Some of the individuals I've talked with are adamantly opposed to the performance or expression on campus of a work, play, book, or speech that contradicts Catholic teaching. To them, we must say, with all respect: "This is a Catholic *university*." We are committed to a wide-open, unconstrained search for truth, and we are convinced that Catholic teaching has nothing to fear from engaging the wider culture.

Others I talked to were appalled that we would raise any question about the content, message, or implications of a work of art, drama, or literature here on campus. To them, we have to say, with the same respect: "This is a *Catholic* university." It is founded upon our belief that love of God and neighbor are eternal teachings that give context and meaning to our search for truth. As I said, Catholic teaching has nothing to fear from engaging the wider culture, but we all have something to fear if the wider culture never engages Catholic teaching. That is why the Catholic tradition must not only inspire our worship and our service on campus; it should help shape the intellectual life of the university. Our goal is not to limit discussion or inquiry, but to enrich it; it is not to insulate that faith tradition from criticism, but to foster constructive engagement with critics.

Like any university, we have a responsibility to foster intellectual engagement with various perspectives and forms of knowledge, but as a Catholic university, we have the added responsibility of fostering engagement among these perspectives and forms of knowledge with the Catholic intellectual tradition. As Pope John Paul II wrote, the Catholic university is "a primary and privileged place for a fruitful dialogue between the Gospel and culture" (*Ex Corde Ecclesiae*, 334).

Grounded in the gospel of Jesus Christ, the Catholic intellectual tradition develops through this dialogue with culture, as it encounters new questions and discoveries; as it speaks on emerging social questions; as it applies the truths of the gospel to complex situations wrought by advances in science. How our ancient but evolving Catholic tradition expresses itself in the future depends to a large extent on the work of this and other Catholic universities. After all, a Catholic university is where the church does its thinking, and that thinking, to be beneficial, must come from an intellectually rigorous engagement with the world.

For these reasons, I am very determined that we not suppress speech on this campus. I am also determined that we never suppress or neglect the gospel that inspired this university. As long as the gospel message and the Catholic intellectual tradition are appropriately represented, we can welcome any serious debate on any thoughtful position here at Notre Dame.

The only exception I can imagine would come in the case of expression that is overt and insistent in its contempt for the values and sensibilities of this university, or of any of the diverse groups that form part of our community. This sort of expression is not at issue in the current debate, nor do I expect it to be an issue in the future.

These are the general principles that have emerged from the many discussions I have had with members of the Notre Dame family. I believe they are principles that a large majority of this community can embrace. It is now time to apply these principles to the matter at hand, and to make decisions regarding the performance of The Vagina Monologues on campus and other matters related to academic freedom and our Catholic character.

In the ten weeks since my faculty address, I have seen The Vagina Monologues performed by our students, and I have discussed the play with its performers and supporters. I still believe—as I said in my address to the faculty—that its portrayals of sexuality stand apart from, and indeed in opposition to, Catholic teaching on human sexuality. Of course, as I have described, there must be room in a university for expressions that do not accord with Catholic teaching, and that is true in the case of this play.

My concern with The Vagina Monologues was not simply with some of its content, but with the prominence given to it by annual performances over five years, accompanied by publicity and fundraising activities. It is essential that we hear a full range of views on campus, including views contrary to Catholic teaching. But because we are a Catholic university, we must strive to bring these various views into dialogue with the Catholic intellectual tradition. This demands balance among diverse views and the inclusion of the Catholic perspective. There are no sharp, easily drawn lines here, and achieving this balance requires discretion and judgment.

Thanks to the efforts of some faculty members, this year's performance of *The Vagina Monologues* was brought into dialogue with Catholic tradition through panels that followed each performance. Panelists presented the Catholic teaching on human sexuality, and students and faculty engaged one another and these issues in serious and informed discussion. These panels taught me and perhaps taught others that the creative contextualization of a play like *The Vagina Monologues* can bring certain perspectives on important issues into a constructive and fruitful dialogue with the Catholic tradition. This is a good model for the future. Accordingly, I see no reason to prohibit performances of *The Vagina Monologues* on campus, and do not intend to do so.

Now, let me address the important issues and causes that animated the performers. In my faculty address, I made it clear that I saw many laudable goals in the play: to help women develop a positive, accepting attitude toward their own bodies; to encourage them to see their sexuality as a gift to be cherished; to urge them to take pride in their identity as women; and—the most urgent goal—to inspire us to work with greater determination to eliminate violence against women.

Notre Dame must do more to advance these goals. The student leaders of *The Vagina Monologues* have proposed producing a play written in their own voices and describing their own experiences, entitled *Loyal Daughters*. This production will be put on entirely by Notre Dame students in consultation with the faculty advisers they have chosen. I will do all I can to support this effort.

In addition, I have formed an ad hoc committee composed of faculty, administrators, and students, charged with fostering a wide-ranging discussion of gender relations, roles, and ways to prevent violence against women. This committee, which I will chair, will help enrich our discussion of issues critical to the lives of women here at Notre Dame and beyond. . . .

Finally, in my earlier address I raised general questions about decisions to sponsor events on controversial subjects, particularly events that may promote opinions that the university plainly does not endorse. I have been having extensive discussions with departmental chairs about this issue.

We have reached a written understanding, which is available online at http://president.nd.edu/closingstatement/common proposal/.

The key points of our agreement are these: Sponsoring speakers and events is an indispensable means for promoting debate on controversial subjects—an important mission of any university. Academic departments are best situated to decide what events should or should not be sponsored. Sponsors have a role in communicating the academic rationale for controversial events. They also have a responsibility to make clear—on campus and off—that sponsorship does not imply endorsement of the views expressed by a speaker or of an event as a whole. Finally, we agreed to work together to promote a vibrant intellectual environment in which multiple viewpoints and voices on controversial topics are heard; an appropriate balance among viewpoints is maintained; and, when a significant issue in Catholic teaching is touched upon, the Catholic tradition is presented.

This agreement will be presented to the Academic Council for consideration. If accepted, it will provide guidelines for sponsoring academic events at Notre Dame.

These three initiatives—the conception and performance of *Loyal Daughters*, the formation of the ad hoc committee, and the guidelines for sponsoring academic events—form the substantive results of our two-month discussion.

In addition, and just as important, we can say that here at Notre Dame, over the past ten weeks, strong differences in opinion were revealed, and views that were passionately held were passionately expressed. Yet whatever the differences, members of this community conducted a serious, thoughtful, reasoned exchange about matters that affect our future. The role of a university is to conduct such vigorous exchanges about the values and principles of the wider society. It can be far more difficult and contentious to engage in *self-reflection* and to debate the values and principles that will shape our own smaller society here at the university. We had that debate and, together, we held it to a very high standard.

The deep reflection on our ideals and actions inspired by this discussion should not end here. We must channel the energy awakened by this debate to serve the causes that animate the debate—the need for open, unrestricted academic inquiry; the need to foster a constructive engagement with the Catholic intellectual tradition; and the pressing need for the University of Our Lady to be a rising force for defending and advancing the rights and dignity of all women, everywhere. May God bless our efforts.

Further Reading

The English translation of *Ex Corde Ecclesiae*, Pope John Paul II's 1990 "Apostolic Constitution . . . On Catholic Universities" is available as a forty-three-page booklet in many a Catholic university library or from the Office for Publishing and Promotion Services of the U.S. Catholic Conference, in Washington, DC; publication no. 399-X.

The Monika Hellwig essay comes from a two-volume collection of essays edited by Anthony Cernera and Oliver Morgan: *Examining the Catholic Intellectual Tradition* (Fairfield, CT: Sacred Heart University Press, 2000).

Cathleen Kaveny, professor of law and professor of theology at Notre Dame University, illuminates further what John Jenkins, the Notre Dame president, treated in his statement: "The Perfect Storm: 'The Vagina Monologues' and Catholic Higher Education" (*America*, May 8, 2006, 14–19).

A steady stream of works dealing with Catholic—or Christian—higher education and its struggles—some rather pessimistic, some more optimistic—have appeared over the past twenty years. I list a number of quality ones here, by date of publication:

Eric O. Springsted, *Who Will Make Us Wise? How the Churches Are Failing Higher Education* (Cambridge, MA: Cowley Publications, 1988).

Charles E. Curran, *Catholic Higher Education, Theology, and Academic Freedom* (Notre Dame, IN: University of Notre Dame Press, 1990).

John Paul II, *Ex Corde Ecclesiae* (1990).

John Coleman, SJ, "A Company of Critics: Jesuits and the Intellectual Life," *Studies in the Spirituality of Jesuits* (November 1990).

William P. Leahy, SJ, *Adapting to America: Catholics, Jesuits, and Higher Education in the Twentieth Century* (Washington, DC: Georgetown University Press, 1991).

Alice Gallin, OSU, ed., *American Catholic Higher Education: Essential Documents, 1967–1990* (Notre Dame, IN: University of Notre Dame Press, 1992).

George Marsden and Bradley Longfield, eds., *The Secularization of the Academy* (New York: Oxford University Press, 1992).

John P. Langan, SJ, ed., *Catholic Universities in Church and Society: A Dialogue on* Ex Corde Ecclesiae (Washington, DC: Georgetown University Press, 1993).

Mark Schwehn, *Exiles from Eden: Religion and the Academic Vocation in America* (New York: Oxford University Press, 1993).

David O'Brien, *From the Heart of the American Church: Catholic Higher Education and American Culture* (Maryknoll, NY: Orbis, 1994).

Theodore M. Hesburgh, CSC, ed., *The Challenge and Promise of a Catholic University* (Notre Dame, IN: University of Notre Dame Press, 1994).

Philip Gleason, *Contending with Modernity: Catholic Higher Education in the Twentieth Century* (New York: Oxford University Press, 1995).

Denise Lardner Carmody, *Organizing a Christian Mind: A Theology of Higher Education* (Valley Forge, PA: Trinity Press International, 1996).

Michael J. Buckley, SJ, *The Catholic University as Promise and Project: Reflections in a Jesuit Idiom* (Washington, DC: Georgetown University Press, 1998).

James T. Burtchaell, *The Dying of the Light: The Disengagement of Colleges and Universities from Their Christian Churches* (Grand Rapids, MI: Eerdmans, 1998).

Monika K. Hellwig, as president of ACCU, contributed several articles to the journal *Current Issues in Catholic Higher Education* between 1998 and 2000.

Examining the Catholic Intellectual Tradition, eds. Cernera and Morgan (Fairfield, CT: Sacred Heart University Press, 2000).

Alice Gallin, OSU, *Negotiating Identity: Catholic Higher Education since 1960* (Notre Dame, IN: University of Notre Dame Press, 2000).

John R. Wilcox and Irene King, eds., *Enhancing Religious Identity: Best Practices from Catholic Campuses* (Washington, DC: Georgetown University Press, 2000).

Robert Benne, *Quality with Soul: How Six Premier Colleges and Universities Keep Faith with Their Religious Traditions* (Grand Rapids, MI: Eerdmans, 2001).

Timothy R. Lannon, SJ, "The Role of Presidents Promoting Catholic Identity at Jesuit Universities," *Conversations on Jesuit Higher Education* (Fall 2001): 32–38.

Dennis O'Brien, *The Idea of a Catholic University* (Chicago: University of Chicago Press, 2002).

Peter Steinfels, *A People Adrift: The Crisis of the Roman Catholic Church in America* (New York: Simon & Schuster, 2003), 131–61.

James L. Heft, SM, ed., *Believing Scholars: Ten Catholic Intellectuals* (New York: Fordham University Press, 2005). (Heft, University Professor of Faith and Culture and Chancellor at the University of Dayton, is at work on a book-length study of Catholic higher education.)

Francis X. Clooney, SJ, ed., *Jesuit Postmodern: Scholarship, Vocation, and Identity in the 21st Century* (Lanham, MD: Lexington Books [Rowman & Littlefield], 2006).

Melanie M. Morey and John J. Piderit, SJ, *Catholic Higher Education: A Culture in Crisis* (New York: Oxford University Press, 2006).

Ignatian/Jesuit
Pedagogy

Introduction

What makes Jesuit education Jesuit is not just the content of what is taught and learned but also the manner or style or method of the teaching and learning. Thus, we have had a section on "Principles," and now we also have one on "Pedagogy." Considering the Ignatian *Spiritual Exercises* as a treatise on process and method, Robert Newton, then headmaster of Regis High School in New York City (1977), developed his *Reflections on the Educational Principles of the Spiritual Exercises*. His "Summary Conclusion" appears here along with a series of telling self-examination "Questions for Teachers." Complementary to Newton's booklet is the much larger corporate work of the International Center for Jesuit Education in Rome: *Ignatian Pedagogy: A Practical Approach* (1993). We have here the précis of this work by Xavier's Sharon Korth. Both of these approaches were developed in the context of secondary education, but could be adapted for higher education.

Ignatian Pedagogy makes much of the *context* of learning—the student's context—and the teacher needs to understand this context as fully as possible. The next selection, "Postmodern Spirituality and the Ignatian *Fundamentum*," by Tim Muldoon of Boston College, provides important insight into the world of today's college student and that student's readiness for Ignatian spirituality. On the other hand, Rick Malloy, SJ, of the anthropology department at St. Joseph's University (who also lives in a student residence hall), identifies some negative aspects of contemporary culture as they disrupt the learning of college students in "Liberating Students—From Paris Hilton, Howard Stern, and Jim Beam." In his essay, he also offers some ways to help students free themselves from these impediments.

Finally, without any explicit connection to Ignatian pedagogy, but certainly in resonance with it, Parker Palmer, a writer, teacher, and activist working independently of any (educational) institution, shares his conviction that "we teach who we are." Our knowledge of self and the health of our relationship with self are just as important for good teaching as our knowledge of our students and of our subject ("The Heart of a Teacher: Identity and Integrity in Teaching").

Understanding the Terminology: Suggested Readings from *Do You Speak Ignatian?*

* Pedagogy, Ignatian/Jesuit
* *Ratio Studiorum*

Reflections on the Educational Principles of the *Spiritual Exercises*: Summary Conclusion and Questions for Teachers

Robert R. Newton

From *Reflections on the Educational Principles of the Spiritual Exercises*, 1977

Summary Conclusion

The purpose of this analysis was to explore the educational principles that underlie the learning experience of the *Spiritual Exercises*. An assumption was made that, since the *Spiritual Exercises* provided the experience that formed the Jesuit spirit and gave it method and direction, an analysis of the *Spiritual Exercises* as an educational treatise would shed light on the fundamental principles of Jesuit education.

This exploration is given added impetus by the realization that the contemporary rediscovery of the original method of the *Spiritual Exercises* has led to a renewal and rearticulation of the authentic Jesuit charism and vocation. A return to the *Spiritual Exercises* as the original source of the Jesuit educational tradition could be expected to generate analogous benefits.

Jesuit education is instrumental. Education is not an end in itself but a means to the service of God. This is an insight that must have its explicit expression in the motivation of the faculty and the planning of programs.

Jesuit education is student-centered. Its goal is to produce an independent learner who internalizes the skills of learning and eventually is able to act without the support of the formal educational environment. The educational process is adapted to the individual and, to the extent possible, responds to his abilities, needs, and interests. Jesuit education emphasizes the self-activity of the student and attempts to make him the primary agent in the learning situation. The goal of the teacher is to decrease while the student increases in direction of his own learning.

Jesuit education is characterized by structure and flexibility. The organization of the educational process is systematic and sequential and aimed toward a definite overall purpose. However, within the general framework, significant freedom and adaptation is both expected and encouraged. Flexibility within structure also marks individual units, which both follow a definite pattern and procedure and promote personal response and self-direction within the prescribed framework. The structure always includes a definite statement of objectives and systematic procedures for evaluation and accountability, for constant reflection on how to improve performance.

Jesuit education is eclectic. It draws on the best methods and techniques available and incorporates into its method whatever helps toward its goals.

Jesuit education is personal. Rather than a superficial grasp of a multiplicity of ideas, it emphasizes profound penetration of essential truths.

Jesuit education, like the *Spiritual Exercises*, is a curious blend—structure and flexibility, prescription and adaptation. It is a living tradition which, like any other form of life, carries with it an internal structure that gives it definition and identity. At the same time, it has the capacity, without violating those fundamental principles that define it, to adjust itself to new situations and times. The experience of the *Spiritual Exercises* was intended to produce persons who, though single-minded in their pursuit of the greater glory and service of God, are flexible rather than brittle. The spirit of Jesuit education is the same. Though supported and sustained by permanent ideals and principles that give it identity, it is able to adapt itself to new challenges and situations. Jesuit education is at the same time both a clearly defined and a flexible ideal; it is this combination of apparently opposed characteristics that is the source of its strength.

Perhaps the simplest way to view the *Spiritual Exercises* is as a treatise on process and method. It is founded, to be sure, on the assumption that, given careful attention and a generous openness, an individual can hear in himself the voice of God speaking to him in a personal way. But the power of the *Spiritual Exercises* also lies in the carefully devised method by which the person can dispose himself to achieve this understanding and awareness; and further, in the subtle but masterful way in which the method itself is internalized by the retreatant and taken from the retreat as one of its primary outcomes. Ignatius has so devised the experience that not only has the person experienced God but he has also emerged from the retreat having absorbed and practiced the means by which he can renew and deepen this experience.

The goal of Jesuit education might be stated in a similar manner. It is a practicum in method. It is based on the assumption that the person can discover and personalize the truth. But its power lies in the method that brings about the confrontation of the person with what is true; and further, in the way in which the method of discovering the truth is itself internalized and taken from the formal learning experience as one of its primary benefits. Ideally the student has emerged from his Jesuit education having practiced and absorbed the means by which he can enlarge and deepen his grasp of the truth.

The *Spiritual Exercises* produce in the retreatant an enriching experience of God and a method to encourage and enable further growth; Jesuit education produces in a student a satisfying experience of the truth and a method to promote and enable continued learning.

Questions for Teachers

To help readers focus attention on the principles of Jesuit education described in this booklet, Robert Newton prepared a supplement. "Questions for Teachers" may be used by faculty members to evaluate whether their efforts in teaching reflect the educational principles flowing from the *Spiritual Exercises*.

Education as an Instrument

Do you have an active awareness of your day-to-day efforts as aimed explicitly at an ultimate goal that is religious?

Do you sense that you as an individual and your faculty as a group are consciously aware of this ultimate goal in both everyday and major decisions?

Is the instrumental character of your personal work and that of the school in general evident to the students and their families—both in what is said to them and in what they can observe?

Developing Independence and Responsibility

Is more of the initiative in your course transferred to your students as the course develops? Do students become less dependent on you and visibly more self-directed? Is this goal built into your course objectives and reflected in your teaching methodology?

Do you regard as equally important or more important than content the development of method by which students can continue to learn in your subject?

Systematic Organization of Successive Objectives

Is the structure and sequence of the educational program in your school based on a coherent, explicitly articulated rationale that is known and accepted by the faculty? Is there an awareness of how the different disciplines and courses fit into an overall rationale?

Are proposals for adaptation of the overall structure or innovations (for example, new programs) judged in the light of their consistency with the accepted rationale and plan?

Structured Flexibility

Wherever possible and reasonable, do you adjust your course to the needs and capacities of your students—so that within the overall plan and educational experience, there is adaptation to individuals or subgroupings of students? Are there alternative objectives for different students, provision of different ways to accomplish objectives, and adjustment of the rate of learning to students of varying abilities?

Patterned Activity

Do you promote in your classes patterned activity which allows the student to develop systematically the most efficient and effective way to approach learning in your subject?

Do your students take this "patterned approach" from the course as one of its primary outcomes?

Self-Activity

Are you consciously seeking ways to minimize your activity as teacher while simultaneously expecting students to increase their level of initiative and activity in classes and the course?

Are students expected to "think for themselves" or is the level of activity predominately recall and comprehension?

Reflection and Accountability

Do you have built into your interaction with students regular patterns of evaluation and accountability?

Does your method of making students accountable go beyond externally imposed norms to promote in the students patterns of self-reflection, self-analysis, and self-criticism?

Are students in your courses developing the habit of analyzing and improving their own performance?

Teacher Role

Are you continually searching for ways in which you can reduce your students' dependence on you for learning in your course?

At the end of the course are your students capable of continuing to learn without your constant help, or perhaps with only occasional assistance from you?

Variety of Techniques

Are you in general alert to current developments in educational methodologies and flexible in incorporating those that will help your course?

Would you regard yourself or your school as a model for other schools of an up-to-date awareness and creative organization and application of contemporary methods?

Personal Appropriation

Do you teach in a way that challenges students to achieve a personal rather than a purely academic grasp of your subject?

Do your students see the importance of your subject and emerge from the course with more than a thorough but uninvolved grasp of the matter?

Summary

Do you consider your course a practicum in method through which the student emerges as an efficient learner who has internalized the principles of how to learn in your discipline?

Precis of *Ignatian Pedagogy: A Practical Approach*

Sharon J. Korth

A previously unpublished summary of the document developed by the International Center for Jesuit Education, Rome, 1993

What Is the Goal?

Ignatian education strives to develop men and women of competence, conscience, and compassion. It is a collaborative process between and among faculty and students that fosters personal and cooperative study, discovery, creativity, and reflection to promote lifelong learning and action in service to others.

The Ignatian pedagogical paradigm is a practical teaching framework that is consistent with and effective in communicating the Ignatian values and worldview. Faculty, regardless of discipline, can utilize this approach so that their teaching is academically sound and at the same time formative of persons for others.

What Is the Process?

Ignatian pedagogy is a model that promotes the goal of Jesuit education, speaks to the teaching-learning process, addresses the faculty-student relationship, and has practical meaning and application for the classroom. Similar to the process of guiding others in the Spiritual Exercises, faculty accompany students in their intellectual, spiritual, and emotional development. They do this by creating the conditions, laying the foundations, and providing the opportunities for the continual interplay of the student's experience, reflection, and action to occur. Throughout the process it is important that faculty be sensitive to their own experience, attitudes, and opinions, lest they impose their own agenda on their students.

The Ignatian pedagogical process includes the following elements: context, experience, reflection, action, and evaluation. Through consideration of the factors and context of students' lives, faculty create an environment where students recollect their past experience and assimilate information from newly provided experiences. Faculty help students learn the skills and techniques of reflection, which shapes their consciousness, and they then challenge students to action in service to others. The evaluation process includes academic mastery as well as ongoing assessments of students' well-rounded growth as persons for others.

Context

Since human experience, always the starting point in Ignatian pedagogy, never occurs in a vacuum, we must know as much as we can about the actual context within which teaching and learning take place. We as faculty need to understand the world of our students, including ways in which family, friends, social pressures, politics, economics, media, and other realities impact them. For a relationship of authenticity and truth to flourish between faculty and student, there has to be built a mutual trust and respect that grows out of a continuing experience of the other as genuine companion in learning. We need to know how to create an atmosphere for learning where we help one another and work together with enthusiasm and generosity, attempting to model concretely in word and action the ideals we uphold for our students and ourselves.

Experience

Experience for Ignatius meant to "taste something internally," which involves the whole person—mind, heart, and will—because without internal feeling joined to intellectual grasp, learning will not move a person to action. To enhance learning, we faculty should first create the conditions whereby students gather and recollect the material of their own experience in order to distill what they already understand in terms of facts, feelings, values, insights, and intuitions related to the subject matter at hand. Later we guide students in assimilating new information and further experience so that their knowledge will gain in completeness and truth. We select activities that take students beyond rote knowledge to the development of the more complex learning skills of understanding, application, analysis, synthesis, and evaluation. Through an eclectic mix of direct activities (such as conversations and discussions, simulations, role plays, laboratory investigations, field trips, service projects, etc.) and vicarious activities (reading, listening to a lecture, etc.), we strive to create learning experiences that involve the cognitive as well as affective responses, having students consider the questions, "What is this?" and, "How do I react to it?" We also help students integrate learning experiences in the classroom with those of home, work, peer culture, etc.

Reflection

Reflection and discernment were integral parts of Ignatius's learning process. Reflection is a thoughtful reconsideration of some subject matter, experience, idea, purpose, or spontaneous reaction, in order to grasp its significance more fully. Thus, reflection is the process by which meaning surfaces in human experience by understanding the truth being studied more clearly; understanding the sources of one's sensations or reactions in the consideration; deepening one's understanding of the implications for oneself and others; achieving personal insights into events, ideas, truths, or the distortion of truth; coming to an understanding of who I am . . . and who I might be in relation to others. Reflection is a formative and a liberating process that forms the conscience of learners in such a manner that they are led to move beyond knowing to undertake action. Faculty lay the foundations for "learning how to learn" by engaging students in the skills and techniques of reflection. A major challenge to faculty is to formulate questions that will broaden students' awareness and impel them to consider viewpoints of others.

Action

For Ignatius, love is shown in deeds, not words. Faculty hope that students are impelled to move beyond knowing to action—action that is for the welfare of society. It is our role as faculty to see that opportunities are provided that will challenge the imagination and exercise the will of the students to choose the best possible course of action to flow from and follow up on what they have learned. Through experiences that have been reflected upon, students make the truth their own and serve others. Faculty help students to consider their experience from a personal, human point of view, while remaining open to where the truth might lead.

Evaluation

Ignatian pedagogy aims at formation, which includes but goes beyond academic mastery. Here we are concerned about students' well-rounded growth as persons for others. Traditional ongoing academic evaluation can alert faculty to possible needs for use of alternative methods of teaching; it also offers special opportunities to individualize encouragement and advice for academic improvement for each student. On the other hand, periodic evaluation of the student's growth in attitudes, priorities, and actions consistent with being a person for others is essential. Faculty should foster relationships of mutual trust and respect that set a climate for discussion and growth. Useful evaluative processes include mentoring and reviews of student journals, as well as student self-evaluation in light of personal growth profiles, leisure time activity, and voluntary service to others. Internal or external feedback may serve to launch the learner once again into the cycle of the Ignatian learning paradigm.

What Is the Challenge?

Consistent use of the Ignatian paradigm can help the growth of a student

- who will gradually learn to discriminate and be selective in choosing experiences;
- who is able to draw fullness and richness from the reflection on those experiences;
- who becomes self-motivated by his or her own integrity and humanity to make conscious, responsible choices.

In addition, and perhaps most importantly, consistent use of the Ignatian paradigm can result in the acquisition of life-long habits of learning that foster attention to experience, reflective understanding beyond self-interest, and criteria for effective action. Such formative effects were characteristics of Jesuit alumni in the early Society of Jesus. They are perhaps even more necessary for responsible citizens of the third millennium.

The Ignatian pedagogical paradigm applies to all curricula and students of all ages and backgrounds, is fundamental to the teaching-learning process in and out of the classroom, helps faculty be better teachers, personalizes learning, and stresses the social dimension of both teaching and learning. The challenge for faculty, therefore, is to find ways to bring the Ignatian pedagogical paradigm to the subjects we teach and the programs we run, knowing that it needs to be adapted and applied to our own specific situations. Through this process we will find ways to accompany our students on their journeys of becoming fully human persons.

Postmodern Spirituality and the Ignatian *Fundamentum*

Tim Muldoon

From *The Way*, 2005

Shortly after the Second Vatican Council, the Jesuit theologian Karl Rahner suggested that the church was entering a third major phase in its history. It had begun as a sect within Judaism, but Paul's mission to the Gentiles had inaugurated a process that led to Christianity becoming a shaping force for European culture, and later for its colonial offshoots. But now, with Vatican II, it was becoming for the first time a truly global reality.[1]

We can set this idea against Samuel P. Huntington's account of how democracy has grown in the world in three waves. The first wave followed the American and French Revolutions; the second followed World War II; and the third involves mainly Catholic countries in Central and South America, East Asia, and Central and Eastern Europe.[2] In short, both ecclesial Christianity and political democracy are becoming global realities.

What do these movements have to do with Christian spirituality? A great deal. For if spirituality is the lived practice of faith in the concrete, everyday experiences of our lives, then culture has an important impact on spirituality. For example, we who live according to a belief in a church that is "one, holy, catholic, and apostolic" must exercise a certain measure of imagination in cultures that are immersed in postmodernity. Unlike those whose worldviews were limited to the towns or villages near their places of birth, we today look out at a world that is amazingly diverse. Our awareness of "otherness" has multiplied because of our immediate access to knowledge of people and places very different from home. In such a world, the church can scarcely be described as "one," and the claim to catholicity is, at best, ambiguous.

In the postmodern, global context, the practice of Christian faith is a deliberative choice of a kind quite different from anything faced by earlier generations. The phenomenon of globalization confronts us with the realities that Christian faith is certainly not the only religious option available to us, and that Christians constitute only a minority of the world's population. These realities, moreover, raise deep questions about Christology, soteriology, worship, morality, ecclesiology, and a host of other issues. The ways in which we answer these questions will certainly have an impact on our spirituality.

Another decisive influence on how Christian faith is practiced in the postmodern era comes from the global spread of democracy. At the root of the democratic ideal is a kind of faith that all human beings, being created equal, ought to have a share in the structures of power that govern the community.[3] As early as the 1820s, the Frenchman Alexis de Tocqueville observed that what was unique in the sensibility of the United States was the manner in which democracy persuaded the people of their individual worth. Unlike their forebears in different parts of Europe, these U.S. Americans rejected hierarchical social systems, preferring to see themselves as equals and thus equally capable of judging what constituted a good society.[4] The spread of democracy in the nineteenth and twentieth centuries represented a kind of gospel in itself, a way of rendering claims about the means to salvation. Democracy persuades people that they are capable of judging for themselves what is ultimately true or false. Democracy exalts individuals by persuading them that they can discern the nature of reality through the intelligent application of the faculty of conscience.

The dual movements of globalization and democratization have had profound effects on our perception of truth. Awareness of global diversity leads many to question the very possibility of universal truth. Cultural relativism is the belief that the very existence of a plurality of worldviews means that there are no criteria by which to judge one against another. Minimally, awareness of pluralism should make us conscious of the fragility of human understanding. According to a Nigerian proverb, where one thing stands, another thing stands beside it. My way of thinking cannot be considered the only way of thinking, and so responsible intelligence demands that we discern together which way of thinking is most authentic.

Democratization also exalts the individual conscience. There are both positive and negative dimensions to this privileging of the individual. Positively, it demands that individuals appropriate for themselves the means by which to make reasoned judgments. In the area of religion, this means that the individual can no longer rely on the community or the cleric for faith: the individual must come to the act of faith through personal initiative, personal response to the invitation of God. Postmodernity, in this perspective, presents Christians with an opportunity for growth, an opportunity to look into the meanings of accepted doctrines in order to discover anew the ways in which God invites people to intimacy. The negative dimension, however, is that democratization can persuade the individual that faith is a private enterprise. And where faith becomes privatized, it becomes a consumer commodity, governed by economics. A democratized faith can, in the extreme case, become an attempt to answer the question, "what's in it for me?"

The church is witnessing the effects of globalization and democratization on its youngest members. Young adults in the West have grown up in a world where these two forces have been formative. To cite one example, studies in the United States demonstrate that young adults are more influenced by popular culture—ruled by a consumerism that is in many ways the result of democratization—than by Christian tradition. They are more likely than older people to regard different world religions as equally valid; they are unlikely to consider the influence of religious leaders as the most meaningful in their lives; they are less likely than older generations to attend formal worship regularly; they are likely to see religious affiliation as an option rather than as a duty.[5]

Those formed at the end of the Cold War understand democracy as salvation from communism, economics as the primary hermeneutical lens with which to understand the world, pluralism as the post-modern equivalent of religious tolerance, and religion as a personal choice to help people get in touch with themselves. Choosing to be a Christian is not unlike choosing a political party. It arises out of the democratic ideal of self-development; it has something to say about the good community; and it is fine as long as one does not violate the only moral absolute in a pluralist world: do not judge others. Young people in the Western world have been raised in a culture that sees religion as another product to consume.[6] Further, they have been led to believe that the customer is always right.

The market for spirituality over the last decade has boomed, driven by the generation born after the Second World War who are now reaching late-middle age. A cursory glance at those authors, both Christian and non-Christian, who have written on spirituality in recent years reveals that the majority grew up during the turbulent decades following the war. The culture that formed their world-views was rapidly changing; structures of authority were collapsing in ways that made many question whether anything in society was constant. For Roman Catholics, especially, the Second Vatican Council represented the changing of the unchangeable. The church, which had remained the same for as long as anyone could remember (for some four hundred years since the Council of Trent, for those who knew their church history), was undergoing massive, visible changes: masses were said in the vernacular; scores of clergy and religious were moving into lay life; and an emphasis on the church as the people of God was replacing the notion of a privileged, clerical elite. This generation began to see Christian faith as a personal commitment more than as a cultural inevitability; and they were perhaps the first to speak their minds on a grand scale about what constituted the authentic practice of faith. The theological and moral debates that followed the council, especially those in response to the watershed encyclical *Humanae vitae* (continuing the ban on artificial contraception), were the result of a community coming into critical awareness of its own responsibility for appropriating the meaning of Christianity on a personal level. In this respect, Catholics were beginning to catch up with their Protestant brothers and sisters in understanding faith as a personal commitment to following Jesus. Matters religious were profoundly political; having been given the responsibility of discerning what the demands of faith were, Christians across the ideological spectrum accepted the corresponding responsibility of contributing to public debate about authentic Christian spirituality.

Over the last decades, many laypeople have developed greater ownership of their faith and their church. They have developed the kind of understanding of spiritual growth once reserved for clerics—an understanding that God calls all Christians to spiritual maturity through the process of lived reflection on the implications and demands of faith. This development contrasts with the facile image of the layperson as someone who is to be passively obedient to church authorities, an understanding that prevailed in Catholic magisterial documents in the period between Vatican I (1870) and Vatican II (1962–65).[7]

There is, however, a more negative side to this growth. An important element in the maturation of many adults in the church today has involved critical reflection on the expressions of faith—liturgy, morality, spirituality—such that many see the practice of critical reflection as itself constitutive of faith. What is overlooked, however, is that authentic criticism can take place only when there is something to criticize: one can come to critical awareness of one's faith only if one has a faith in the first place. The younger generations of the church have grown up in an ecclesial context where criticism is the rule. Their parents (in many cases) are adults who have come to think critically about their own faith, and who wanted their children also to develop critical thinking in matters religious. Very often, their teaching took the form of a negative understanding of religious faith: "I don't force my children to go to church, because I want them to decide for themselves." Criticism—an intellectual exercise undertaken by free people in a democratic society as they expressed their ability to think for themselves—often preceded or even replaced faith formation. Young people were taught to be critical consumers of information and thoughtful purveyors of religious truth, not merely passive *tabulae rasae* ("blank slates") upon which religious authorities could impress sectarian doctrine. What they were not taught, however, was the joy in (I do not use the expression "reason for") making the act of faith in God revealed in Jesus Christ.

The effect of this formative period on many young people has been to give them the ability to think critically about religious truth-claims in a postmodern world. My students are comfortable judging certain doctrines acceptable and others not so—regardless of whether the doctrines arise out of Christian or other traditions. They are consumers of religious truth—fascinated by it, in many cases, and content to determine the pragmatic value of various truth-claims. They can navigate ambiguity. Though they are sometimes naive, they know that religious commitment should be balanced against the more fundamental ethic of respect for all religions. To many, spiritual growth is the unfolding of the self; it is a kind of discipline by which one grows into an ethical person. Their soteriology (theory or theology of salvation) is thoroughly pluralistic: my faith saves me; your faith saves you. It all depends on which God you believe in.

Yet what these students often lack is a true understanding of why faith matters. They may be persuaded of its worth in civil society as a code of ethics—which they value, since they are schooled in the historical examples of those, such as Nazi doctors or Stalinist government workers, who were rational but not ethical. They may recognize its importance in the ordering of society. They may be drawn to its language of mystery, particularly around liminal (threshold) issues such as love, death, and suffering. They may appreciate how human history testifies to the archetypal drive for religious meaning, and how Christianity highlights the fundamental cycles of life, death, and rebirth. They can see religious faith as a kind of commitment to live deeply the search for meaning in a fractured world. All these perspectives are valuable, and may be what Justin Martyr referred to as the "seeds of faith," inasmuch as they suggest to young people that faith is important. But what is so utterly foreign to many is the experience of falling in love with God. Religion, for them, is an intellectual exercise rooted in the individual conscience, rather than a response to a God who holds out a hand to say, "let's have an adventure!"

At the same time, though, young adults immersed in the postmodern, postrational, posthegemonic, postcolonial world have begun to recognize an element in their personal lives that challenges socially defined conceptual categories. They feel a hunger for spirituality, a hunger that leaks out of their art, their casual conversations, their experiences of love and suffering. They have recognized that something in their experience leads them to seek transcendence, even as they frequently criticize the church for being an organization that seems actively to hide it. Their turn to find spiritual meaning in places other than the church ought not to dissuade us from asking what resources in our tradition address their fundamental hunger. In my experience, one of the most provocative comes from the tradition of Ignatian spirituality.

The Ignatian *Fundamentum*

Saint Ignatius of Loyola's sixteenth-century *Spiritual Exercises* begins with what he calls the "First Principle and Foundation." This is a deceptively simple statement of what one must embrace in order to progress spiritually, and it offers us a provocative point of departure for considering what authentic Christian spirituality might look like in the postmodern era. Ignatius suggests that we are created to praise, reverence, and serve God our Lord, and by these means to achieve our eternal well-being. This observation rests upon an understanding of what constitutes the spiritual life, namely, the pervasive practice of responding to an ever-present God. In referring to this understanding, I follow the usage of Joseph A. Tetlow of the Latin term *fundamentum* rather than the English "foundation."[8] This Latin term, which is found in all the Latin sixteenth-century directories of Ignatius's *Spiritual Exercises*, connotes God's intimate involvement in the whole of a person's life. Too often, the "Principle and Foundation" is thought of as just one element in Ignatius's program, as step one in Ignatian prayer. The truth is that the *fundamentum* more properly refers to the very objective of the entire spiritual life.

Ignatius's text then develops his basic thesis: everything on earth is to help people in working toward the end for which they were created; we should use things only in so far as they help us to achieve that end; we must be indifferent to everything as long as we are fixed on that end; we ought to desire only that end. What emerges from a cursory reading of the "Principle and Foundation" is a blueprint for moral and spiritual growth—an almost instrumental understanding of a human being as a creature "for" some greater purpose that God determines. I am reminded of Thérèse of Lisieux, who likened herself to a plaything in the hands of the child Jesus, or of Teresa of Calcutta, who spoke of herself as "God's pencil." Ignatius proposes that we exercise our faculty of imagination in order to envision what it might be like to be an instrument of God, designed for something beautiful.

My interest here is in how Ignatius gets us thinking about ourselves in an entirely fresh way. While the language he uses is certainly familiar to traditional Catholics, its disarming simplicity also invites today's postmoderns to explore issues about humanity and God within a Christian frame of reference. My thesis is this: Ignatian spirituality speaks to postmoderns because it is based on a personal, thus imaginative, exploration of the gospel, and it invites people to choose freely to deepen their intimacy with God through a deepened understanding of who they themselves are. The invitation to come to know God in this way is radically different from the approach that has become familiar to so many: that of learning the doctrines and moral teachings of the church in religious education, and developing the critical thinking that sometimes leads us to question whether any doctrine can be judged true. Ignatian spirituality is not primarily doctrinal, because it is not primarily an exercise of reason. It is instead a practice of imagination, with all the affective dimensions that unfold in imagination, often without the explicit consent of the intellect. I wish to focus on three themes that comprise the Ignatian *fundamentum*—three themes that, when appropriated by the seeking person, lead one to spiritual growth through intimate encounter with God. These themes are imaginative play, fundamental receptivity, and self-transcending love.

Imaginative Play

For those immersed in a thoroughly pluralist world, any spiritual practice that is predicated on obedience to doctrinal claims is unlikely to be persuasive. To put it a different way, traditional devotions such as the rosary, Eucharistic adoration, Mass attendance on first Fridays, and even Bible study may be perceived as exclusive. The conventional wisdom for many religious educators over the years has been that a community must share its practices and beliefs with the young, in order that they might come to assume adult roles in the community. But in a thoroughly pluralist world, young adults achieve a measure of critical consciousness that very often leads them to question the relevance of the beliefs and practices of their faith community. Many wonder why they should spend the time and energy going to church when they are not certain that what it offers is right.

Ignatian spirituality offers a "user-friendly" way into the life of prayer which appeals to the uncertain. The basic counsel is simple: imagine what it would be like if God were creating you every moment of your life. Ignatius's First Principle and Foundation has been read (mistakenly) as a doctrinal claim that one must accept in order to undertake the Spiritual Exercises. What I propose, instead, is that the Principle and Foundation is an invitation to imaginative play. What, it asks, might it be like if God took the time and care to create my entire life, moment by moment, in order that my acceptance of this creation—and my participation in it—might reflect beauty, as a work of art reflects the creativity of an artist? What might it be like if God were a person who invests in my very being, and places me in a world where I can use everything to achieve perfection?[8a]

The postmodern person who is wary of arrogant claims to authority and truth can, in good conscience, accept an invitation to exercise imagination. Whereas the more traditional models of mission often assumed the superiority of Christian doctrine, the invitation to imaginative play makes no such claims. Instead, it proposes that the language and conceptual apparatus of Christian tradition can provide a story through which to explore the relationship between God and a person on an individual level. It might be objected that such a dynamic falls prey to the individualism that ignores the corporate dimensions of Christian spirituality. But this imaginative play is merely a method, not the goal of the Spiritual Exercises. The method is merely the medium through which one eventually comes to consider the meaning of the relationship between God and humanity.

Fundamental Receptivity

Moral theologians in the latter half of the twentieth century began speaking of a "fundamental option," of a person's basic decision to choose God's will. They contrasted the fundamental option with specific moral choices—some of which were sinful—in order to argue that individual sins need not represent a decision to end one's relationship with God.[9]

I prefer to speak of "fundamental receptivity" as a goal of Ignatian spirituality. Whereas the term "option" suggests a kind of primordial act of conscience, the term "receptivity" more adequately renders what a person constantly practices in the process of living the spiritual life. The Ignatian *fundamentum* is not a once-and-for-all decision, but rather a formative process that knits God and the human person in an ever-deepening relationship. A person who practices imaginative play around the theme of God's creation of the self has already assented, on some level, to the invitation to know God. As that person continues to imagine related themes, using biblical stories and religious symbols, the person continues to explore the ways in which the imagination proposes matters for thought or feeling.

Imagining the stories of saints led Ignatius himself to discern more and more clearly how attracted he was to the idea of doing something great for God. Imagination allowed him to explore the meaning of saints' lives, and thus to become aware of feelings and thoughts that he had not previously considered. Further, he came to enjoy those feelings and thoughts, so that eventually he was able to name what he was experiencing: a desire to serve God in the context of the Church. Ignatian spirituality gently proposes that a person explore the feelings and thoughts that arise spontaneously while imagining God's relationship to the self. What is especially attractive about this proposal is the fact that it is the individual who generates the feelings and thoughts. Over time, the practice can lead a person to greater and greater receptivity to knowing and serving God.

Self-Transcending Love

The goal of Ignatian spirituality is a self-transcending love of God and of the other. If a person is given the freedom to explore God's relationship to the self—in the Examen[9a] especially—the response is gratitude. Authentic receptivity to God involves receiving love that enables one in turn to love others. For many the attraction to the practice of spirituality will originate in a desire for self-development. But over time they will discover a truth that Jesus taught: one must lose one's life in order to find it. There is something intuitive about love, justice, service to others—something that cannot be denied by people of good will, whether religious or not. Ignatian spirituality leads a person to deeper appreciation of God's love, and by extension to the expression of love in acts of solidarity, justice, and mercy. Its necessarily social orientation represents a conscientious response to the evils of the world which avoids any temptation to use power. Ignatian spirituality is not a "revolution" in the sense of a social movement; such movements have often eventually used power unjustly in seeking to overturn unjust uses of power. Rather, it is an invitation to change society by becoming a changed person within society. For the postmodern person, wary of the frequently murky ways in which power has been exercised, authentic spirituality involves a critical social awareness.

If the practice of Ignatian spirituality leads a person to a deeper knowledge of God, then it is about enabling a person to develop a firm *fundamentum*—the rock upon which Jesus proposes that the wise person build a house. In an era when the very notion of certain knowledge is suspect, this tradition offers a challenge: do not think of knowing about God as an exercise of reason, with all the difficulties that that entails. Think instead of coming to know God through greater knowledge of oneself. In doing so, one comes to recognize that at the very *fundamentum* of one's lived existence is a loving creator, working with each person to co-create their daily life.

Postmodernity and the *Fundamentum*

In the postmodern age, the objective of those who undertake the Spiritual Exercises—and indeed, of those who wish to practice authentic Christian spirituality—is an ownership of the *fundamentum*. Far from being an introductory exercise or a passing comment, the *fundamentum* represents what St. Paul calls "the mind of Christ," and is thus what every Christian ought to strive for.[10] It is interesting to note that Paul's instruction to the Corinthians—who were themselves in the midst of debates over authority in the first century—addressed how those who were "infants in Christ" might progress to spiritual maturity. Their situation, and Paul's counsel, have a message for us in the twenty-first century.

If postmodernity involves questions about the possibility of religious authority, it is no surprise that there has arisen in recent decades an interest in religious "experience." For, in the absence of trust, people must rely on their own faculties. In response to the Corinthians' squabbles over whom to believe, Paul underscores that it is ultimately God alone who is the author of spiritual growth (1 Cor. 3:7). The *fundamentum* can be seen as an attentiveness to the God who is constantly working with us to co-create our lives—a kind of *lectio divina* [literally "divine reading," a way of praying with scripture] in which the text is our own experience but that we read through the lens of sacred scripture. For young people who trust only their own experience, it is important that we suggest to them that Ignatian spirituality offers a new way to discover the God who has been present with them throughout their lives.

NOTES

1. Karl Rahner, "Basic Theological Interpretation of Vatican II" (1979), in *Theological Investigations*, vol. 20, trans. Edward Quinn (London: Darton, Longman and Todd, 1981), 77–89, especially 83. Rahner's focus was on the Catholic Church gathered at the Council; for the purposes of this article, however, I will refer to the term "Church" in the more abstract sense of those who profess faith in Jesus Christ.

2. Samuel Huntington, *The Third Wave: Democratization in the Twentieth Century* (Norman, OK: University of Oklahoma Press, 1991).

3. Compare the language of the 1948 United Nations Universal Declaration of Human Rights: "the peoples of the United Nations have in the Charter reaffirmed their faith in fundamental human rights, in the dignity and worth of the human person and in the equal rights of men and women. . . ." While the document does not explicitly endorse democracy per se, it is clearly influenced by Western models of government (Online at http://www.un.org/Overview/rights.html).

4. Alexis de Tocqueville, *Democracy in America* (1831), online at the University of Virginia's Web site, http://xmads.virginia.edu/~HYPER/DETOC/toc_indx.html.

5. Two recent studies include Dean R. Hoge and others, *Young Adult Catholics: Religion in the Culture of Choice* (Notre Dame, IN: University of Notre Dame Press, 2001), and James D. Davidson and others, *The Search for Common Ground: What Unites and Divides Catholic Americans* (Huntington, IN: Our Sunday Visitor Books, 1997).

6. Vincent J. Miller explores the impact of consumer culture on religion in *Consuming Religion: Christian Faith and Practice in Consumer Culture* (New York: Continuum, 2003).

7. Paul Lakeland explores the development of the understanding of the layperson in this period in his book *The Liberation of the Laity: In Search of an Accountable Church* (New York: Continuum, 2003).

8. Joseph A. Tetlow, "The *Fundamentum*: Creation in the Principle and Foundation," *Studies in the Spirituality of Jesuits* 21, no. 4 (September 1989), 1–53. Compare Gilles Cusson, *Biblical Theology and the Spiritual Exercises*, trans. Mary Angela Roduit and George E. Ganss, ed. George E. Ganss (St. Louis: Institute of Jesuit Sources, 1987 [1968]).

[8a. Compare Muldoon's reading of the First Principle and Foundation as an invitation to "imaginative play" with Patrick Heelan's sense of "aesthetic play" as a way to reconnect with our sacred stories (see the first reading in the section on the "Current Problematic" in this reader).—Editor]

9. See, for example, Karl Rahner's theory of fundamental option in "Some Thoughts on a Good Intention" (1955), *Theological Investigations*, vol. 3, trans. Karl-H. Kruger (Baltimore: Helicon Press, 1966). Compare Pope John Paul II's more critical account in the encyclical *Veritatis Splendor*, nn. 65 and 66.

[9a. See the clear brief treatment of the Examen by Dennis Hamm in the "Prayer" section of the companion volume, *An Ignatian Spirituality Reader*.—Editor]

10. In 1 Corinthians 2–3, Paul is instructing Christians about what distinguishes the spiritual person from the unspiritual person, indicating that the former has "the mind of Christ."

Liberating Students—From Paris Hilton, Howard Stern, and Jim Beam

Richard G. Malloy, SJ

An expanded version of the one that appeared in *Conversations on Jesuit Higher Education*, 2007

Challenging and Transforming College Culture

A self-described, disgruntled conservative Catholic challenges me: "Father, why do all these Catholic kids go to Catholic colleges and lose their faith?" My response is to challenge the questioner's underlying premise. Frankly, the majority of Catholic eighteen-year-olds do not come to college with a deep and vibrant faith. They come to college more with the hope of "meeting and mating" than with the desire to develop discipleship with Jesus. The faithful practice of Catholicism is not a central component of their lives. Students desire more to "facebook.com" than to meet God and others face to face (see 1 Cor. 13:12). Students do not realize that the way to understand themselves, others, and our world is intimately connected to the ways we love, and that the ways we live and love are rooted in the manners in which we imagine our relationship to God, that is, faith. Why don't they know the power and freedom of faith, and what can we do about it?

We need to examine what blinds and oppresses college students to the liberating action of God in their lives, and develop strategies that will help them work toward their own, and our, liberation. Liberation theology's method examines what oppresses and impoverishes people, and then calls us to bring the liberating power of the gospel into dialogue with the situation. College students today, although usually economically fairly well off, often lack the spiritual resources and cultural capital necessary to live satisfying and enriching faith lives. A vibrant, living practice of faith in the loving, challenging God of Jesus Christ, can free students from oppressive cultural currents. Students free from slavery to the idols of Budweiser and Jim Beam are ready for the intellectually joyous adventure college can be, and for many, is. Students free for the adventure of becoming their deepest, truest selves, and not Paris Hilton and Howard Stern "wannabes," will relate to themselves, others, and God in ways that make for a world of peace and justice for all.

For a sizable minority, faith is a constitutive dimension of the fabric of their lives, and rare is the college student who will opine that spirituality (but not necessarily religion) is unimportant. Yet most college students pay tuition because they think a college degree will open the door to a high-paying job, not put them on the path to salvation. If told they won't get to heaven, most students will respond, "Whatever." If told they will never get a decent-paying job, students will tremble. In order to develop in students' lives the practices of Catholicism, we must do what God has always done for people: name and address that which is oppressing them and work toward liberation.

Let's prophetically oppose the idols, the false gods demanding student sacrifice and death. Let's offer the practice of a full and flexible Catholic faith that will help college students establish an adult relationship with the Lord of love and life. We can ignite in young adult hearts and minds transformative energies now lying dormant on the beer-soaked floors of *Animal House* and *Old School* modes of being. But Web sites like "collegehumor.com" and "drunkuniversity. com" graphically display the destructive cultural dynamics coursing through collegians' daily lives. Books like Ariel Levy's study of raunch culture (*Female Chauvinist Pigs: Is Raunch Culture the New Women's Liberation?*)[1] and Pamela Paul's investigation of pornography's pervasive influence (*Pornified: How Pornography Is Transforming Our Lives, Our Relationships, and Our Families*)[2] reveal what we are up against.

As teachers and administrators in Jesuit, Catholic institutions of higher education, we are called to challenge and change the ways in which students unthinkingly respond to the cultural currents within which too many of our students swim, and in which too many drown. Fostering the liberation of our students will provide them with the character building, soul satisfying practices and expertise in relational dynamics they now lack. Such practices they will desperately need to build happy, healthy, holy, and free lives in the future. What may appear to be a young adult's loss of "faith" may be a shedding of childhood conditioning and practices. During college years, they are invited to open their minds and hearts to a God who may not be the God of one's parents or the idols of one's culture.

"It's so hard to be me." Teresa, a stunningly beautiful high school senior, bemoans the fact that she has to wear certain name-brand clothes and apply makeup so perfectly each day. Asked why she feels the need to live in such a manner, she replies, "People expect it of me." She is looking forward to the chance to start new at college. There she imagines she will be free from all those expectations that have oppressed her in high school. College administrators and faculty should rush in and seize the opportunity to create campus experiences that will help students like Teresa confront culturally oppressive practices (e.g., Pimp N' Ho parties, the twenty-first birthday "hour of power," "friends with benefits," lower-back "tramp stamp" tattoos, oral sex on demand).

Students like Teresa deeply desire to free themselves and form communities in the light of Jesus' call to serve and love others. They just aren't being shown how. Corrupt seniors can show "fresh meat frosh," that is, females, to the keg parties the first nights of the semester, but we can't get first-year students to attend freshmen retreats. They think they want beer, when what they deeply desire is what we all want: God.

Consciously Constructing College Culture

Ignatian spirituality is rooted in the practice of discerning desires. God's grace in our lives functions to transform our desires, leading us to want and choose what God wants and chooses. In discovering our deepest, truest desires, we most immediately and passionately find God. What do we desire for and from our students? What do we want our college students to look and sound like? What kind of campus culture must we construct in order to see our desires realized? Actually, the top twenty percent of today's students are better than they have ever been: smarter, more intellectually curious, harder working, more likely to engage in significant service, more aware of and open to religious formation. But the bottom forty percent really make me worry about who will be running my nursing home!

Teachers' desires and students' desires differ dramatically. A kid wants to sit in the back row, hat on, bleary eyed, sipping Starbucks. I want a young adult sitting in the front row, hat off, bright eyed and prepared for class, enthused about engaging the course material. While we want students to do significant amounts of service, many of our undergrads want to hit the bars five, six, even seven nights a week.

What I want is a school full of students like St. Joseph's University's orientation leaders, the "Redshirts." These upperclassmen and women return to school several weekends during the summer, selflessly, happily working sixteen-hour days introducing incoming freshmen to the spirit of Hawk Hill. The first-year students begin to learn the meaning of our motto "The Hawk Will Never Die," as they see these upperclassmen and women at 2:00 A.M. on a Sunday morning, one hundred strong and sober, leading some two hundred freshmen singing "American Pie," "Breakfast at Tiffany's," "Plastic Jesus" (that seventies classic played and led by this husky Jesuit), and a whole bunch of songs I never heard of by groups like Guster, the Red Hot Chile Peppers, and Bare Naked Ladies. The kids were amused when they found out I had no idea that the last group was composed of three guys.

The "Redshirts" haven't lost their faith while at St. Joseph's; they have found or developed their faith. They have come to believe that service with and for others is more enriching and more fun than endless games of beer pong. They are at 10:00 P.M. Mass on Sunday nights and in class on Monday mornings and on Project Appalachia over spring break. These students get everything out of a Jesuit education one can get because they generously give and share so much of the grace and goodness of their hearts. "Redshirts" who betray the values of their office are excoriated by their peers. Students want students in whom they can believe, in whom they can place their trust.

Addressing Oppressions

Why are many students so unlike the Redshirts? Students fail to receive all that a Jesuit education has to offer because they choose to succumb to cultural currents oppressing them. They uncritically accept that college ought to be a drinking experience, rooted in the pursuit of sexual and other pleasures, while putting the questions of life's purpose and meaning on hold for four years. Watching freshmen pour out of the dorm in which I live on a Tuesday or Friday or Sunday night, I realize they are interested in anything but Jesuit education. The guys are slovenly and unkempt, baseball caps on backward, while the young women are tube topped, short skirted, and high heeled, all perfumed and "hoochied up" ("hoochy" meaning, "too short, too tight, too much"). These "novice adults" wander the surrounding neighborhoods searching for alcohol. At 3:00 A.M. one night, I observe a young woman drunkenly stumble back into the dorm. As she stares blearily about, she proceeds to vomit.

   Suggesting that radical rules be enforced that address and abolish such behaviors is met with, "Well, young people have to learn to be responsible. That entails their making mistakes." Still, conditions that facilitate students' chances of living up to expectations that college be an alcohol-soaked bacchanal have to be radically transformed. Students spending much more on booze than they do on books is insane. Worse, students are losing more than their money while worshiping at the dark altars of Bud Light. Each year 1,400 deaths and

70,000 sexual assaults and date rapes result from campus drinking across the nation.[3]

Eradicate the Drinking Culture

Challenge and discipline students who want college to be primarily a drunken binge. The three martini lunch is a relic of the past in business circles, and anyone "wasted" or "retarded" (student lingo for "intoxication") at the office Christmas party will not be getting a promotion. Clear any alcoholic haze coloring students' thinking by enacting strong institutional responses to unacceptable behaviors. Hire a few "alcohol cops." Send them to the off-campus bars and apartments, and sanction and fine students engaged in the destructive partying. Suspend students who insist on drinking irresponsibly until they are ready to assume the responsibility of being adult learners. Don't let students stay in college if they will not act like adults. Really, demanding that students live in ways that make peace rather than war with campus neighbors is simple justice. We rattle on about being "men and women for and with others" and service learning. Service starts with stopping sophomores from urinating on people's front yards.

Ignite Intellectual Curiosity and Invite the Uninterested to Leave

The saddest students are the ones who just aren't interested. Professors aren't boring; students are bored. Tell the boozed and bored, and those *Bright College Years* author Anne Matthews calls the "aggressively apathetic," to get interested, or leave.[4] Put us out of their misery. Here's a radical solution: allow professors to drop students from class. Ryan Maher, SJ, once noted that high school kids at St. Joe's Prep in Philadelphia gave rapt attention to coaches. Why? If they didn't, the coach would throw them off the team. Why must a teacher of theology or Western civilization put up with recalcitrant loafers who simply don't want to learn the material? Kick out sullen, back row seated malcontents, who can poison a whole class with their sour, negative attitude. Don't wait until the end of the semester to flunk them. Bounce the bozos and throw the knuckleheads out of the course in the first weeks of the semester so that others will feel free to participate and energetically engage the material without being labeled "nerds" by the hungover cohort.

A sophomore in my Anthropology of Love course flunked the first test. I asked him what was going on. He informed me that he didn't like the books in the course. One book was on cross-cultural sexual practices. He couldn't claim that was boring! He told me he was an English major and he'd rather be reading novels. I said if that's how he felt, he should drop the course. "No," he replied, "I'm gonna stay and get my three credits." I said, "No, you are going to drop the course." Since I could not drop him from the course, I wrote him a letter informing him that he had failed the course. I had not taught him anything in five weeks, nor had he learned anything. He had done virtually no work for the first third of the semester. Therefore, in good conscience, I could not certify that he had earned, or would be able to earn, three credits for the course. He could withdraw now, or take the "F." He squawked to deans and chairperson, but then, a few weeks later, slept through the second test and wanted to drop the course after the deadline for doing so had passed. He still got the "W."

Grant teachers the power to remove the lazy, idle, classroom-space occupiers (I refuse to call them students), and undergraduates will get the message that they must be active learners. No more sleeping in class and getting a "C" from adjunct professors terrified of receiving poor student evaluations. If teachers drop too many kids, give administrators the power to overrule the decision. But, I guarantee, placing more power and responsibility back in teachers' hands will transform the classroom atmosphere. Once students realize they must be active learners, a profound liberation can occur. They will be unable to keep up if they insist on partying four, five, six nights a week. They will start actually doing the assigned reading. They will be awake and alive in class. Soon, students will experience the utter joy of learning. Recently, I studied Brian Greene's *The Elegant Universe* and *The Fabric of the Cosmos.*[5] There is a fascination and joy in learning about string theory's conjectures on the possibility of multiple universes and time travel. I tell students, "Truly become lifelong learners and you will never be bored again. There is nothing as soul satisfying as really learning." Every teacher has sat up all night, reading until five in the morning, unable to put the book down. It's a disgrace if students get through four years of Jesuit education and never feel that thrill of being entranced by a book.

We sit on the crest of the wave of the greatest increase in knowledge in the history of the human family. Our students are given four years to tackle the endlessly energizing task of mastering a bit of that vast array of human wisdom. Four years to master critical thinking. Develop excellent communication skills. Gain a more than passing familiarity with perennial theological and philosophical issues. Explore history. Understand the scientific method and science's effects on human existence. Such learning is crucial, for the continuation of civilization rests on our being able to live as intelligent and ethically responsible persons. Lifelong learners are better able to love and live. That we be learners and lovers is what God desires for us all, and requires of those whose parents are spending over $40,000 a year so their son or daughter can attend a university.

Explore Ultimate Meanings

Once students are weaned away from the bars and booze, and turned on to learning, we can help them seriously engage in the development and deepening of their faith lives. We need to structure the turning off of 24/7 computers, iPods, the omnipresent cell phones, and all the other flickering lights and noise. Challenge students to stop, be still and alone for a while. Encourage them to notice their souls. How concretely and specifically to do that is the subject of a final part of this essay. . . . [L]et's realize that college is not job training. A university exists to challenge students to think, learn, and grow; to allow faculty to teach students, and also explore and expand the boundaries of their academic discipline; to serve the community by graduating young adults who are intellectually equipped to meet the challenges of constructing and continuing the complex civilization on which our lives depend. We need to be asking serious questions about ultimate matters. What is a human person and how ought men and women live? What are the social, economic, and political dynamics that affect our world, and how have we, and how will we, channel these forces in the future? Who is God and how does God relate to us? What are we to do with the incredible opportunities of this twenty-first century? How will we fashion our fragile world and make of it an ecologically sustainable world of peace and justice for all?

The wisdom of our Catholic faith, especially Catholic social teaching, has much to contribute to such discussions. Out of respect for, and fear of offending, non-Catholics in the student body or on the faculty, we sometimes hesitate to articulate the faith freely and forcefully. But we can teach a vibrant and challenging Catholicism. The Hindu, Muslim, Jewish, and Protestant members of our Jesuit university communities are not offended by a full, fair, and flexible exposition of our faith. They are intrigued and energized by being invited to participate in the mission of Jesuit higher education. In so doing, they share with the community the strengths of their traditions. Liberation emerges from our being a community of communities, responsible to, and respectful of, one another. In union with others, and as disciples of Jesus, we can help free oppressed students by lovingly cooperating with the mysterious ways grace glides in their hearts and lives. Teach students to pay less at the bars and pay more attention to grace, and they will be free to discover faith and hope and love.

Soulwork: Four Practices to Begin Helping Students Discover the Joy of Liberation

To begin creating campus cultures wherein liberation is more probable, we need to change, at the very least, what students do with their

time. Forty hours a week partying does not add up to a Jesuit education. Yet forty hours a week only studying does not necessarily ensure
a Jesuit education either. Jesuit education, at the core, is about what
kind of person one is becoming through freely chosen and discerned
pathways. Someone who has been educated in a Jesuit school should
have an answer for the ancient question *Quo vadis?* ["Where are you
going?"] After four years at a Jesuit university, students should know
where they are heading, and, most importantly, why they are going
in that direction. To help our students develop life-giving habits that
will last a lifetime, we should look to values and practices proven
transformative through the centuries. Four simple practices in education have disappeared in our 24/7, iPod drenched, video game
infiltrated, facebook frenzied college campuses. Students literally fear
silence, are terrified of solitude, have never heard of Sabbath, and
are in desperate need of sleep. Addressing these matters will prepare
students to deal with questions of faith, God, and religion.

Silence

Listen and *silent* are spelled with the same letters. To listen one has to
be silent. One has to shut off all the noise in all its insidious guises,
from the ubiquitous clangs of the cell phone, to the bodies attached
to blaring iPods, to the basketballs and lacrosse balls bouncing off
the dorm walls at 2:00 A.M. There is so much noise impinging on
students' consciousness, they have a hard time listening, not only in
class, but to that still small voice of their deepest truest self. To structure in times of silence would signal to students that the full-time job
of becoming an adult necessitates extended periods when a person
steps back, stops, reflects, thinks, ruminates, wonders, and ponders.
To be an educated person means one has been taught and disciplined
to examine where one is going and how one is getting there.

Solitude

Students have never been introduced to the joys of being with their
own selves and thus cannot imagine communing with their souls.

Connection and community emerge where real individuals exist and can freely choose to relate. We should require that our students spend some time with themselves before they uncritically and unconsciously hook up with someone else in sexual liaisons dangerously devoid of meaning, spirit, or purpose, and before they contract to spend years of their lives in service to faceless corporations. In solitude one discovers one's character, who and what one actually is. Character is who a person is when no one else is looking. Character and integrity are in too short supply in our society, and to challenge our students to spend time alone and develop their character and deepest truest selves while at a Jesuit university will serve well both them, and our society.

Sabbath

Since the dawn of recorded time, religions have structured in times of rest, repose, relaxation, and recreation because, over the centuries, humans have learned what happens when Hobbesian ideologies reign and society becomes a "war of all against all"—leading to lives that are "solitary, nasty, brutish, and short."[6] Structuring Sabbath practices into culture restrains those who want to compete longer and longer hours, thus leveling the playing field by holding all to the same rules of production. In a world devolving into insane levels of competition and commerce, Jesuit universities can stand as sentries of sanity and Sabbath rest. Out of the freely chosen structuring of work rhythms and recreation times, a better life can emerge for all on campus.

Sleep

This is the simplest and sanest solution to student problems: require that students sleep. The rise in psychological and physical illness on campus cannot ignore the fact that by week ten of the semester the vast majority of the students are literally sleep deprived. Turn off the electricity in the dorms between the hours of two and eight and make the students go to bed, alone. An old, wise spiritual director once noted that most spiritual problems can be helped by a bowl of soup and a good night's sleep. Much of the anxiety, fear, worry, discouragement, and sadness so many students routinely exhibit is most likely related to the lack of structure in their lives and their complete unwillingness to account for how they use their time. Chronically tired students can rarely strive to be their best.

Addressing such seemingly simple matters as silence and sleep, solitude and Sabbath, will go far in fashioning a college experience in which students can begin to explore the deeper meanings of life: God, religion, and spirituality. As the book of Exodus so powerfully teaches, liberation follows our confronting conditions of slavery. Our students are enslaved. It is time to set them free.

NOTES

1. Ariel Levy, *Female Chauvinist Pigs: Is Raunch Culture the New Women's Liberation?* (New York: Free Press, 2005).

2. Pamela Paul, *Pornified: How Pornography Is Transforming Our Lives, Our Relationships, and Our Families* (New York: Times Books, 2005).

3. *Time* magazine, April 22, 2002.

4. Anne Matthews, *Bright College Years: Inside the American Campus Today* (New York: Simon and Schuster, 1997).

5. Brian Greene, *The Elegant Universe: Superstrings, Hidden Dimensions, and the Quest for Ultimate Theory* (New York: Vintage Books, 2003), and *The Fabric of the Cosmos: Space, Time, and the Texture of Reality* (New York: Vintage Books, 2004).

6. Samuale Enoch Stumph, *Socrates to Sartre: A History of Philosophy*, 6th ed. (Boston: McGraw-Hill, 1999), 216–217.

The Heart of a Teacher: Identity and Integrity in Teaching

Parker J. Palmer

From *Change*, 1997

We Teach Who We Are

I am a teacher at heart, and there are moments in the classroom when I can hardly hold the joy. When my students and I discover uncharted territory to explore, when the pathway out of a thicket opens up before us, when our experience is illumined by the lightning-life of the mind—then teaching is the finest work I know.

But at other moments, the classroom is so lifeless or painful or confused—and I am so powerless to do anything about it—that my claim to be a teacher seems a transparent sham. Then the enemy is everywhere: in those students from some alien planet, in that subject I thought I knew, and in the personal pathology that keeps me earning my living this way. What a fool I was to imagine that I had mastered this occult art—harder to divine than tea leaves and impossible for mortals to do even passably well!

The tangles of teaching have three important sources. The first two are commonplace, but the third, and most fundamental, is rarely given its due. First, the subjects we teach are as large and complex as life, so our knowledge of them is always flawed and partial. No matter how we devote ourselves to reading and research, teaching requires a command of content that always eludes our grasp. Second, the students we teach are larger than life and even more complex. To see them clearly and see them whole, and respond to them wisely in the moment, requires a fusion of Freud and Solomon that few of us achieve.

If students and subjects accounted for all the complexities of teaching, our standard ways of coping would do—keep up with our fields as best we can, and learn enough techniques to stay ahead of the student psyche. But there is another reason for these complexities: we teach who we are.

Teaching, like any truly human activity, emerges from one's inwardness, for better or worse. As I teach, I project the condition of my soul onto my students, my subject, and our way of being together. The entanglements I experience in the classroom are often no more or less than the convolutions of my inner life. Viewed from this angle, teaching holds a mirror to the soul. If I am willing to look in that mirror, and not run from what I see, I have a chance to gain self-knowledge—and knowing myself is as crucial to good teaching as knowing my students and my subject.

In fact, knowing my students and my subject depends heavily on self-knowledge. When I do not know myself, I cannot know who my students are. I will see them through a glass darkly, in the shadows of my unexamined life—and when I cannot see them clearly I cannot teach them well. When I do not know myself, I cannot know my subject—not at the deepest levels of embodied, personal meaning. I will know it only abstractly, from a distance, a congeries of concepts as far removed from the world as I am from personal truth.

We need to open a new frontier in our exploration of good teaching: the inner landscape of a teacher's life. To chart that landscape fully, three important paths must be taken—intellectual, emotional, and spiritual—and none can be ignored. Reduce teaching to intellect and it becomes a cold abstraction; reduce it to emotions and it becomes narcissistic; reduce it to the spiritual and it loses its anchor to the world. Intellect, emotion, and spirit depend on each other for wholeness. They are interwoven in the human self and in education at its best, and we need to interweave them in our pedagogical discourse as well.

By *intellectual* I mean the way we think about teaching and learning—the form and content of our concepts of how people know and learn, of the nature of our students and our subjects. By *emotional* I mean the way we and our students feel as we teach and learn—feelings that can either enlarge or diminish the exchange between us. By *spiritual* I mean the diverse ways we answer the heart's longing to be connected with the largeness of life—a longing that animates love and work, especially the work called teaching.

Teaching Beyond Technique

After three decades of trying to learn my craft, every class comes down to this: my students and I, face-to-face, engaged in an ancient and exacting exchange called education. The techniques I have mastered do not disappear, but neither do they suffice. Face-to-face with my students, only one resource is at my immediate command: my identity, my selfhood, my sense of this "I" who teaches—without which I have no sense of the "Thou" who learns.

Here is a secret hidden in plain sight: good teaching cannot be reduced to technique; good teaching comes from the identity and integrity of the teacher. In every class I teach, my ability to connect with my students, and to connect them with the subject, depends less on the methods I use than on the degree to which I know and trust my selfhood—and am willing to make it available and vulnerable in the service of learning.

My evidence for this claim comes, in part, from years of asking students to tell me about their good teachers. As I listen to those stories, it becomes impossible to claim that all good teachers use similar techniques: some lecture nonstop and others speak very little, some stay close to their material and others loose the imagination, some teach with the carrot and others with the stick.

But in every story I have heard, good teachers share one trait: a strong sense of personal identity infuses their work. "Dr. A is really *there* when she teaches," a student tells me, or "Mr. B has such enthusiasm for his subject," or "You can tell that this is really Prof. C's life."

One student I heard about said she could not describe her good teachers because they were so different from each other. But she could describe her bad teachers because they were all the same: "Their words float somewhere in front of their faces, like the balloon speech in cartoons." With one remarkable image she said it all. Bad teachers distance themselves from the subject they are teaching—and, in the process, from their students. Good teachers join self, subject, and students in the fabric of life because they teach from an integral and undivided self; they manifest in their own lives, and evoke in their students, a "capacity for connectedness." They are able to weave a complex web of connections between themselves, their subjects, and their students, so that students can learn to weave a world for themselves. The methods used by these weavers vary widely: lectures, Socratic dialogues, laboratory experiments, collaborative problem-solving, creative chaos. The connections made by good teachers are held not in their methods but in their hearts—meaning heart in its ancient sense, the place where intellect and emotion and spirit and will converge in the human self.

If good teaching cannot be reduced to technique, I no longer need suffer the pain of having my peculiar gift as a teacher crammed into the Procrustean bed of someone else's method and the standards prescribed by it. That pain is felt throughout education today as we insist upon the method *du jour*—leaving people who teach differently feeling devalued, forcing them to measure up to norms not their own.

I will never forget one professor who, moments before I was to start a workshop on teaching, unloaded years of pent-up workshop animus on me: "I am an organic chemist. Are you going to spend the next two days telling me that I am supposed to teach organic chemistry through role-playing?" His wry question was not only related to his distinctive discipline but also to his distinctive self: we must find an approach to teaching that respects the diversity of teachers as well as disciplines, which methodological reductionism fails to do.

The capacity for connectedness manifests itself in diverse and wondrous ways—as many ways as there are forms of personal identity. Two great teachers stand out from my own undergraduate experience. They differed radically from each other in technique, but both were gifted at connecting students, teacher, and subject in a community of learning.

One of those teachers assigned a lot of reading in her course on methods of social research and, when we gathered around the seminar table on the first day, said, "Any comments or questions?" She had the courage to wait out our stupefied (and stupefying) silence, minute after minute after minute, gazing around the table with a benign look on her face—and then, after the passage of a small eternity, to rise, pick up her books, and say, as she walked toward the door, "Class dismissed."

This scenario more or less repeated itself a second time, but by the third time we met, our high SAT scores had kicked in, and we realized that the big dollars we were paying for this education would be wasted if we did not get with the program. So we started doing the reading, making comments, asking questions—and our teacher proved herself to be a brilliant interlocutor, co-researcher, and guide in the midst of confusions, a "weaver" of connectedness in her own interactive and inimitable way.

My other great mentor taught the history of social thought. He did not know the meaning of silence and he was awkward at interaction; he lectured incessantly while we sat in rows and took notes. Indeed, he became so engaged with his material that he was often impatient with our questions. But his classes were nonetheless permeated with a sense of connectedness and community.

How did he manage this alchemy? Partly by giving lectures that went far beyond presenting the data of social theory into staging the drama of social thought. He told stories from the lives of great thinkers as well as explaining their ideas; we could almost see Karl Marx, sitting alone in the British Museum Library, writing *Das Kapital*. Through active imagination we were brought into community with the thinker himself, and with the personal and social conditions that stimulated his thought.

But the drama of my mentor's lectures went farther still. He would make a strong Marxist statement, and we would transcribe it in our notebooks as if it were holy writ. Then a puzzled look would pass over his face. He would pause, step to one side, turn, and look back at the space he had just exited—and argue with his own statement from an Hegelian point of view! This was not an artificial device but a genuine expression of the intellectual drama that continually occupied this teacher's mind and heart.

"Drama" does not mean histrionics, of course, and remembering that fact can help us name a form of connectedness that is palpable and powerful without being overtly interactive, or even face-to-face. When I go to the theater, I sometimes feel strongly connected to the action, as if my own life were being portrayed on stage. But I have no desire to raise my hand and respond to the line just spoken, or run up the aisle, jump onto the stage, and join in the action. Sitting in the audience, I am already on stage "in person," connected in an inward and invisible way that we rarely credit as the powerful form of community that it is. With a good drama, I do not need overt interaction to be "in community" with those characters and their lives.

I used to wonder how my mentor, who was so awkward in his face-to-face relations with students, managed to simulate community so well. Now I understand: he was in community without us! Who needs twenty-year-olds from the suburbs when you are hanging out constantly with the likes of Marx and Hegel, Durkheim, Weber, and Troeltsch? This is "community" of the highest sort—this capacity for connectedness that allows one to converse with the dead, to speak and listen in an invisible network of relationships that enlarges one's world and enriches one's life. (We should praise, not deride, First Ladies who "talk" with Eleanor Roosevelt; the ability to learn from wise but long-gone souls is nothing less than a classic mark of a liberal education!)

Yet my great professor, though he communed more intimately with the great figures of social thought than with the people close at hand, cared deeply about his students. The passion with which he lectured was not only for his subject, but for us to know his subject. He wanted us to meet and learn from the constant companions of his intellect and imagination, and he made those introductions in a way that was deeply integral to his own nature. He brought us into a form of community that did not require small numbers of students sitting in a circle and learning through dialogue.

These two great teachers were polar opposites in substance and in style. But both created the connectedness, the community, that is essential to teaching and learning. They did so by trusting and teaching from true self, from the identity and integrity that is the source of all good work—and by employing quite different techniques that allowed them to reveal rather than conceal who they were.

Their genius as teachers, and their profound gifts to me, would have been diminished and destroyed had their practice been forced into the Procrustean bed of the method of the moment. The proper place for technique is not to subdue subjectivity, not to mask and distance the self from the work, but—as one grows in self-knowledge—to help bring forth and amplify the gifts of self on which good work depends.

Teaching and True Self

The claim that good teaching comes from the identity and integrity of the teacher might sound like a truism, and a pious one at that: good teaching comes from good people. But by "identity" and "integrity" I do not mean only our noble features, or the good deeds we do, or the brave faces we wear to conceal our confusions and complexities. Identity and integrity have as much to do with our shadows and limits, our wounds and fears, as with our strengths and potentials.

By *identity* I mean an evolving nexus where all the forces that constitute my life converge in the mystery of self: my genetic makeup, the nature of the man and woman who gave me life, the culture in which I was raised, people who have sustained me and people who have done me harm, the good and ill I have done to others, and to myself, the experience of love and suffering—and much, much more. In the midst of that complex field, identity is a moving intersection of the inner and outer forces that make me who I am, converging in the irreducible mystery of being human.

By *integrity* I mean whatever wholeness I am able to find within that nexus as its vectors form and re-form the pattern of my life. Integrity requires that I discern what is integral to my selfhood, what fits and what does not—and that I choose life-giving ways of relating to the forces that converge within me: do I welcome them or fear them, embrace them or reject them, move with them or against them? By choosing integrity, I become more whole, but wholeness does not mean perfection. It means becoming more real by acknowledging the whole of who I am. Identity and integrity are not the granite from which fictional heroes are hewn. They are subtle dimensions of the complex, demanding, and life-long process of self-discovery. *Identity* lies in the intersection of the diverse forces that make up my life, and *integrity* lies in relating to those forces in ways that bring me wholeness and life rather than fragmentation and death.

Those are my definitions—but try as I may to refine them, they always come out too pat. Identity and integrity can never be fully named or known by anyone, including the person who bears them. They constitute that familiar strangeness we take with us to the grave, elusive realities that can be caught only occasionally out of the corner of the eye.

Stories are the best way to portray realities of this sort, so here is a tale of two teachers—a tale based on people I have known whose lives tell me more about the subtleties of identity and integrity than any theory could.

Alan and Eric were born into two different families of skilled craftspeople, rural folk with little formal schooling but gifted in the manual arts. Both boys evinced this gift from childhood onward, and as each grew in the skill at working with his hands, each developed a sense of self in which the pride of craft was key.

The two shared another gift as well: both excelled in school and became the first in their working-class families to go to college. Both did well as undergraduates, both were admitted to graduate school, both earned doctorates, and both chose academic careers.

But here their paths diverged. Though the gift of craft was central in both men's sense of self, Alan was able to weave that gift into his academic vocation, while the fabric of Eric's life unraveled early on.

Catapulted from his rural community into an elite private college at age eighteen, Eric suffered severe culture shock and never overcame it. He was insecure with fellow students and, later, with academic colleagues who came from backgrounds he saw as more "cultured" than his own. He learned to speak and act like an intellectual, but he always felt fraudulent among people who were, in his eyes, to the manor born.

But insecurity neither altered Eric's course nor drew him into self-reflection. Instead, he bullied his way into professional life on the theory that the best defense is a good offense. He made pronouncements rather than probes. He listened for weaknesses rather than strengths in what other people said. He argued with anyone about anything—and responded with veiled contempt to whatever was said in return.

In the classroom, Eric was critical and judgmental, quick to put down the "stupid question," adept at trapping students with trick questions of his own, then merciless in mocking wrong answers. He seemed driven by a need to inflict upon his students the same wound that academic life had inflicted upon him—the wound of being embarrassed by some essential part of one's self.

But when Eric went home to his workbench and lost himself in craft, he found himself as well. He became warm and welcoming, at home in the world and glad to extend hospitality to others. Reconnected with his roots, centered in his true self, he was able to reclaim a quiet and confident core—which he quickly lost as soon as he returned to campus.

Alan's is a different story. His leap from countryside to campus did not induce culture shock, in part because he attended a land-grant university where many students had backgrounds much like his own. He was not driven to hide his gift but was able to honor and transform it by turning it toward things academic: he brought to his study, and later to his teaching and research, the same sense of craft that his ancestors had brought to their work with metal and wood.

Watching Alan teach, you felt that you were watching a craftsman at work—and if you knew his history, you understood that this feeling was more than metaphor. In his lectures, every move Alan made was informed by attention to detail and respect for the materials at hand; he connected ideas with the precision of dovetail joinery and finished the job with a polished summary.

But the power of Alan's teaching went well beyond crafted performance. His students knew Alan would extend himself with great generosity to any of them who wanted to become an apprentice in his field, just as the elders in his own family had extended themselves to help young Alan grow in his original craft.

Alan taught from an undivided self—the integral state of being that is central to good teaching. In the undivided self, every major thread of one's life experience is honored, creating a weave of such coherence and strength that it can hold students and subject as well as self. Such a self, inwardly integrated, is able to make the outward connections on which good teaching depends.

But Eric failed to weave the central strand of his identity into his academic vocation. His was self divided, engaged in a civil war. He projected that inner warfare onto the outer world, and his teaching devolved into combat instead of craft. The divided self will always distance itself from others, and may even try to destroy them, to defend its fragile identity.

If Eric had not been alienated as an undergraduate—or if his alienation had led to self-reflection instead of self-defense—it is possible that he, like Alan, could have found integrity in his academic vocation, could have woven the major strands of his identity into his work. But part of the mystery of selfhood is the fact that one size does not fit all: what is integral to one person lacks integrity for another. Throughout his life, there were persistent clues that academia was not a life-giving choice for Eric, not a context in which his true self could emerge healthy and whole, not a vocation integral to his unique nature.

The self is not infinitely elastic—it has potentials and it has limits. If the work we do lacks integrity for us, then we, the work, and the people we do it with will suffer. Alan's self was enlarged by his academic vocation, and the work he did was a joy to behold. Eric's self was diminished by his encounter with academia, and choosing a different vocation might have been his only way to recover integrity lost.

When Teachers Lose Heart

As good teachers weave the fabric that joins them with students and subjects, the heart is the loom on which the threads are tied: the tension is held, the shuttle flies, and the fabric is stretched tight. Small wonder, then, that teaching tugs at the heart, opens the heart, even breaks the heart—and the more one loves teaching, the more heartbreaking it can be.

We became teachers for reasons of the heart, animated by a passion for some subject and for helping people to learn. But many of us lose heart as the years of teaching go by. How can we take heart in teaching once more, so we can do what good teachers always do—give heart to our students? The courage to teach is the courage to keep one's heart open in those very moments when the heart is asked to hold more than it is able, so that teacher and students and subject can be woven into the fabric of community that learning and living require.

There are no techniques for reclaiming our hearts, for keeping our hearts open. Indeed, the heart does not seek "fixes" but insight and understanding. When we lose heart, we need an understanding of our condition that will liberate us from that condition, a diagnosis that will lead us toward new ways of being in the classroom simply by telling the truth about who, and how, we are. Truth, not technique, is what heals and empowers the heart.

We lose heart in part because teaching is a daily exercise in vulnerability. I need not reveal personal secrets to feel naked in front of a class. I need only parse a sentence or work a proof on the board while my students doze off or pass notes. No matter how technical or abstract my subject may be, the things I teach are things I care about—and what I care about helps define my selfhood.

Unlike many professions, teaching is always done at the danger-ous intersection of personal and public life. A good therapist must work in a personal way, but never publicly: the therapist who reveals as much as a client's name is derelict. A good trial lawyer must work in a public forum but unswayed by personal opinion: the lawyer who allows his or her feelings about a client's guilt to weaken the client's defense is guilty of malpractice.

But a good teacher must stand where personal and public meet, dealing with the thundering flow of traffic at an intersection where "weaving a web of connectedness" feels more like crossing a freeway on foot. As we try to connect ourselves and our subjects with our students, we make ourselves, as well as our subjects, vulnerable to indifference, judgment, ridicule.

To reduce our vulnerability, we disconnect from students, from subjects, and even from ourselves. We build a wall between inner truth and outer performance, and we play-act the teacher's part. Our words, spoken at remove from our hearts, become "the bal-loon speech in cartoons," and we become caricatures of ourselves. We distance ourselves from students and subject to minimize the danger—forgetting that distance makes life more dangerous still by isolating the self.

This self-protective split of personhood from practice is encour-aged by an academic culture that distrusts personal truth. Though the academy claims to value multiple modes of knowing, it honors only one—an "objective" way of knowing that takes us into the "real" world by taking us "out of ourselves."

In this culture, objective facts are regarded as pure while subjec-tive feelings are suspect and sullied. In this culture, the self is not a source to be tapped but a danger to be suppressed, not a poten-tial to be fulfilled but an obstacle to be overcome. In this culture, the pathology of speech disconnected from self is regarded, and rewarded, as a virtue.

If my sketch of the academic bias against selfhood seems over-done, here is a story from my own teaching experience. I assigned my students a series of brief analytical essays involving themes in the texts we were going to be reading. Then I assigned a parallel series of autobiographical sketches, related to those themes, so my students could see connections between the textbook concepts and their own lives.

After the first class, a student spoke to me: "In those autobiographical essays you asked us to write, is it OK to use the word 'I'?"

I did not know whether to laugh or cry—but I knew that my response would have considerable impact on a young man who had just opened himself to ridicule. I told him that not only could he use the word "I", but I hoped he would use it freely and often. Then I asked what had led to his question.

"I'm a history major," he said, "and each time I use 'I' in a paper, they knock off half a grade."

The academic bias against subjectivity not only forces our students to write poorly ("It is believed" instead of "I believe"), it deforms their thinking about themselves and their world. In a single stroke, we delude our students into believing that bad prose turns opinions into facts and we alienate them from their own inner lives.

Faculty often complain that students have no regard for the gifts of insight and understanding that are the true payoff of education—they care only about short-term outcomes in the "real" world: "Will this major get me a job?" "How will this assignment be useful in 'real' life?"

But those are not the questions deep in our students' hearts. They are merely the questions they have been taught to ask, not only by tuition-paying parents who want their children to be employable but also by an academic culture that distrusts and devalues inner reality. Of course our students are cynical about the inner outcomes of education: we teach them that the subjective self is irrelevant and even unreal.

The foundation of any culture lies in the way it answers the question, "Where do reality and power reside?" For some cultures the answer is the gods; for some it is nature; for some it is tradition. In our culture, the answer is clear: reality and power reside in the external world of objects and events, and in the sciences that study that world, while the inner realm of "heart" is a romantic fantasy—an escape from harsh realities perhaps but surely not a source of leverage over "the real world."

We are obsessed with manipulating externals because we believe that they will give us some power over reality and win us some freedom from its constraints. Mesmerized by a technology that seems to do just that, we dismiss the inward world. We turn every question we face into an objective problem to be solved—and we believe that for every objective problem there is some sort of technical fix.

That is why we train doctors to repair the body but not to honor the spirit; clergy to be CEOs but not spiritual guides; teachers to master techniques but not to engage their students' hearts—or their own. That is why our students are cynical about the efficacy of an education that transforms the inner landscape of their lives: when academic culture dismisses inner truth and pays homage only to the objective world, students as well as teachers lose heart.

Listening to the Teacher Within

Recovering the heart to teach requires us to reclaim our relationship with the teacher within. This teacher is one whom we knew when we were children but lost touch with as we grew into adulthood, a teacher who continually invites me to honor my true self—not my ego or expectations or image or role, but the self I am when all the externals are stripped away.

By inner teacher, I do not mean "conscience" or "superego," moral arbiter or internalized judge. In fact, conscience, as it is commonly understood, can get us into deep vocational trouble. When we listen primarily for what we "ought" to be doing with our lives, we may find ourselves hounded by external expectations that can distort our identity and integrity. There is much that I "ought" to be doing by some abstract moral calculus. But is it my vocation? Am I gifted and called to do it? Is this particular "ought" a place of intersection between my inner self and the outer world, or is it someone else's image of how my life should look?

When I follow only the ought, I may find myself doing work that is ethically laudable but that is not mine to do. A vocation that is not mine, no matter how externally valued, does violence to the self—in the precise sense that it violates my identity and integrity on behalf of some abstract norm. When I violate myself, I invariably end up violating the people I work with. How many teachers inflict their own pain on their students—the pain that comes from doing a work that never was, or no longer is, their true work?

The teacher within is not the voice of conscience but of identity and integrity. It speaks not of what ought to be, but of what is real for us, of what is true. It says things like, "This is what fits you and this is what doesn't." "This is who you are and this is who you are not." "This is what gives you life and this is what kills your spirit—or makes you wish you were dead." The teacher within stands guard at the gate of selfhood, warding off whatever insults our integrity and welcoming whatever affirms it. The voice of the inward teacher reminds me of my potentials and limits as I negotiate the force field of my life.

I realize that the idea of a "teacher within" strikes some academics as a romantic fantasy, but I cannot fathom why. If there is no such reality in our lives, centuries of Western discourse about the aims of education become so much lip-flapping. In classical understanding, education is the attempt to "lead out" from within the self a core of wisdom that has the power to resist falsehood and live in the light of truth, not by external norms but by reasoned and reflective self-determination. The inward teacher is the living core of our lives that is addressed and evoked by any education worthy of the name.

Perhaps the idea is unpopular because it compels us to look at two of the most difficult truths about teaching. The first is that what we teach will never "take" unless it connects with the inward, living core of our students' lives, with our students' inward teachers.

We can, and do, make education an exclusively outward enterprise, forcing students to memorize and repeat facts without ever appealing to their inner truth—and we get predictable results: many students never want to read a challenging book or think a creative thought once they get out of school. The kind of teaching that transforms people does not happen if the student's inward teacher is ignored.

The second truth is even more daunting: we can speak to the teacher within our students only when we are on speaking terms with the teacher within ourselves.

The student who said that her bad teachers spoke like cartoon characters was describing teachers who have grown deaf to their inner guide, who have so thoroughly separated inner truth from outer actions that they have lost touch with a sense of self. Deep speaks to deep, and when we have not sounded our own depths, we cannot sound the depths of our students' lives.

How does one attend to the voice of the teacher within? I have no particular methods to suggest, other than the familiar ones: solitude and silence, meditative reading and walking in the woods, keeping a journal, finding a friend who will simply listen. I merely propose that we need to learn as many ways as we can of "talking to ourselves."

That phrase, of course, is one we normally use to name a symptom of mental imbalance—a clear sign of how our culture regards the idea of an inner voice! But people who learn to talk to themselves may soon delight in the discovery that the teacher within is the sanest conversation partner they have ever had.

We need to find every possible way to listen to that voice and take its counsel seriously, not only for the sake of our work but also for the sake of our own health. If someone in the outer world is trying to tell us something important and we ignore his or her presence, that person either gives up and stops speaking or becomes more and more violent in attempting to get our attention.

Similarly, if we do not respond to the voice of the inward teacher, it will either stop speaking or become violent: I am convinced that some forms of depression, of which I have personal experience, are induced by a long-ignored inner teacher trying desperately to get us to listen by threatening to destroy us. When we honor that voice with simple attention, it responds by speaking more gently and engaging us in a life-giving conversation of the soul.

That conversation does not have to reach conclusions in order to be of value: we do not need to emerge from "talking to ourselves" with clear goals, objectives, and plans. Measuring the value of inner dialogue by its practical outcomes is like measuring the value of a friendship by the number of problems that are solved when friends get together.

Conversation among friends has its own rewards: in the presence of our friends we have the simple joy of feeling at ease, at home, trusted, and able to trust. We attend to the inner teacher not to get fixed but to befriend the deeper self, to cultivate a sense of identity and integrity that allows us to feel at home wherever we are.

Listening to the inner teacher also offers an answer to one of the most basic questions teachers face: how can I develop the authority to teach, the capacity to stand my ground in the midst of the complex forces of both the classroom and my own life?

In a culture of objectification and technique we often confuse authority with power, but the two are not the same. Power works from the outside in, but authority works from the inside out. We are mistaken when we seek "authority" outside ourselves, in sources ranging from the subtle skills of group process to that less-than-subtle method of social control called grading. This view of teaching turns the teacher into the cop on the corner, trying to keep things moving amicably and by consent, but always having recourse to the coercive power of the law.

External tools of power have occasional utility in teaching, but they are no substitute for authority, the authority that comes from the teacher's inner life. The clue is in the word itself, which has "author" at its core. Authority is granted to people who are perceived as "authoring" their own words, their own actions, their own lives, rather than playing a scripted role at great remove from their own hearts. When teachers depend on the coercive powers of law or technique, they have no authority at all.

I am painfully aware of the times in my own teaching when I lose touch with my inner teacher, and therefore with my own authority. In those times I try to gain power by barricading myself behind the podium and my status while wielding the threat of grades. But when my teaching is authorized by the teacher within me, I need neither weapons nor armor to teach.

Authority comes as I reclaim my identity and integrity, remembering my selfhood and my sense of vocation. Then teaching can come from the depths of my own truth—and the truth that is within my students has a chance to respond in kind.

Institutions and the Human Heart

My concern for the "inner landscape" of teaching may seem indulgent, even irrelevant, at a time when many teachers are struggling simply to survive. Wouldn't it be more practical, I am sometimes asked, to offer tips, tricks, and techniques for staying alive in the classroom, things that ordinary teachers can use in everyday life?

I have worked with countless teachers, and many of them have confirmed my own experience: as important as methods may be, the most practical thing we can achieve, in any kind of work, is insight into what is happening inside us as we do it. The more familiar we are with our inner terrain, the more sure-footed our teaching—and living—becomes.

I have heard that in the training of therapists, which involves much practical technique, there is a saying: "Technique is what you use until the therapist arrives." Good methods can help a therapist find a way into the client's dilemma, but good therapy does not begin until the real-life therapist joins with the real life of the client.

Technique is what teachers use until the real teacher arrives, and we need to find as many ways as possible to help that teacher show up. But if we want to develop the identity and integrity that good teaching requires, we must do something alien to academic culture: we must talk to each other about our inner lives—risky stuff in a profession that fears the personal and seeks safety in the technical, the distant, the abstract.

I was reminded of that fear recently as I listened to a group of faculty argue about what to do when students share personal experiences in class—experiences that are related to the themes of the course, but that some professors regard as "more suited to a therapy session than to a college classroom."

The house soon divided along predictable lines. On one side were the scholars, insisting that the subject is primary and must never be compromised for the sake of the students' lives. On the other side were the student-centered folks, insisting that the lives of students must always come first even if it means that the subject gets short-changed. The more vigorously these camps promoted their polarized ideas, the more antagonistic they became—and the less they learned about pedagogy or about themselves.

The gap between these views seems unbridgeable—until we understand what creates it. At bottom, these professors were not debating teaching techniques. They were revealing the diversity of identity and integrity among themselves, saying, in various ways, "Here are my own limits and potentials when it comes to dealing with the relation between the subject and my students' lives."

If we stopped lobbing pedagogical points at each other and spoke about who we are as teachers, a remarkable thing might happen: identity and integrity might grow within us and among us, instead of hardening as they do when we defend our fixed positions from the foxholes of the pedagogy wars.

But telling the truth about ourselves with colleagues in the workplace is an enterprise fraught with danger against which we have erected formidable taboos. We fear making ourselves vulnerable in the midst of competitive people and politics that could easily turn against us, and we claim the inalienable right to separate the "personal" and the "professional" into airtight compartments (even though everyone knows the two are inseparably intertwined). So we keep the workplace conversation objective and external, finding it safer to talk about technique than about selfhood.

Indeed, the story I most often hear from faculty (and other professionals) is that the institutions in which they work are the heart's worst enemy. In this story, institutions continually try to diminish the human heart in order to consolidate their own power, and the individual is left with a discouraging choice: to distance one's self from the institution and its mission and sink into deepening cynicism (an occupational hazard of academic life) or to maintain eternal vigilance against institutional invasion and fight for one's life when it comes.

Taking the conversation of colleagues into the deep places where we might grow in self-knowledge for the sake of our professional practice will not be an easy, or popular, task. But it is a task that leaders of every educational institution must take up if they wish to strengthen their institution's capacity to pursue the educational mission. How can schools educate students if they fail to support the teacher's inner life? To educate is to guide students on an inner journey toward more truthful ways of seeing and being in the world. How can schools perform their mission without encouraging the guides to scout out that inner terrain?

As this century of objectification and manipulation by technique draws to a close, we are experiencing an exhaustion of institutional resourcefulness at the very time when the problems that our institutions must address grow deeper and more demanding. Just as twentieth-century medicine, famous for its externalized fixes for disease, has found itself required to reach deeper for the psychological and spiritual dimensions of healing, so twentieth-century education must open up a new frontier in teaching and learning—the frontier of the teacher's inner life

How this might be done is a subject I have explored in earlier essays in *Change*, so I will not repeat myself here. In "Good Talk about Good Teaching," I examined some of the key elements necessary for an institution to host noncompulsory, noninvasive opportunities for faculty to help themselves and each other grow inwardly as teachers. In "Divided No More: A Movement Approach to Educational Reform," I explored things we can do on our own when institutions are resistant or hostile to the inner agenda.

Our task is to create enough safe spaces and trusting relationships within the academic workplace—hedged about by appropriate structural protections—that more of us will be able to tell the truth about our own struggles and joys as teachers in ways that befriend the soul and give it room to grow. Not all spaces can be safe, not all relationships trustworthy, but we can surely develop more of them than we now have so that an increase of honesty and healing can happen within us and among us—for our own sake, the sake of our teaching, and the sake of our students.

Honesty and healing sometimes happen quite simply, thanks to the alchemical powers of the human soul. When I, with thirty years of teaching experience, speak openly about the fact that I still approach each new class with trepidation, younger faculty tell me that this makes their own fears seem more natural—and thus easier to transcend—and a rich dialogue about the teacher's selfhood often ensues. We do not discuss techniques for "fear management," if such exist. Instead, we meet as fellow travelers and offer encouragement to each other in this demanding but deeply rewarding journey across the inner landscape of education—calling each other back to the identity and integrity that animate all good work, not least the work called teaching.

Further Reading

The essay by Parker Palmer consists of edited excerpts from the introduction, chapter 1, and chapter 5 of *The Courage to Teach: Exploring the Inner Landscape of a Teacher's Life* (San Francisco: Jossey-Bass Publishers, 1997). The essays he mentions in the third-to-last paragraph appear as chapters 6 and 7. Earlier and later works by Palmer relevant to education and learning are:

To Know as We Are Known: A Spirituality of Education (San Francisco: HarperSanFrancisco, 1993).

Teaching from the Heart: Seasons of Renewal in a Teacher's Life (Hoboken, NJ: Jossey-Bass, 1998).

"Spiritual Formation and Social Change," in *Fugitive Faith: Conversations on Spiritual, Environmental, and Community Renewal*, ed. Benjamin Webb (Maryknoll, NY: Orbis Books, 1998), 56–67.

Let Your Life Speak: Listening for the Voice of Vocation (Hoboken, NJ: Jossey-Bass, 2000).

A Hidden Wholeness: The Journey toward an Undivided Life (Hoboken, NJ: Jossey-Bass, 2004).

Nicely congruent with Palmer's philosophy is the testimony of Lillie Albert, professor of education at Boston College, about her own growth as a scholar-teacher whose work is now informed by her spirituality ("The Call to Teach: Spirituality and Intellectual Life," *Conversations on Jesuit Higher Education*, Fall 2000, 338–42).

Putting Students First: How Colleges Develop Students Purposefully, by Larry A. Braskamp, Lois Calian Trautvetter, and Kelly Ward (Bolton, MA: Anker Publishing Co., 2006) shows us how giving a clear priority to students can focus all the work of a school.

Following up on the essay by Tim Muldoon, you may want to familiarize yourself with the online magazine for "spiritual seekers in their twenties and thirties," Bustedhalo.com and read Michael Hayes and Brett Hoover's "Virtual Church for Young Adults: BustedHalo.com" (*The Way*, April 2006, 69–82). In addition to Rick Malloy's "Liberating Students," you can profitably consult the other fine pieces in the spring 2007 issue of *Conversations* ("Jesuit Education and Today's Student: A 'Disconnect'?").

Xavier University's Ignatian Mentoring Program places new tenure-track faculty who choose together with senior faculty mentors experienced in Ignatian spirituality and Jesuit education. Both faculty mentors and the new faculty have found two books helpful: *Mentoring for Mission: Nurturing New Faculty at Church-Related Colleges*, by Caroline Simon and others (Grand Rapids, MI: Eerdmans, 2003) and Edward Sellner's *Mentoring: The Ministry of Spiritual Kinship* (Cambridge, MA: Cowley Publications, 2002).

Thomas Landy, the founder of "Collegium," a weeklong summer program on faith and the intellectual life (referred to by Suzanne Matson in the section on Catholic identity and by Joanna Ziegler in the section on practical applications), has collected a series of essays that illuminate the vocation of the teacher-scholar in Catholic higher education: *As Leaven in the World: Catholic Perspectives on Faith, Vocation, and the Intellectual Life* (Lanham, MD: Sheed & Ward [Rowman & Littlefield], 2001).

Finally, Fordham University's Graduate School of Education sponsored a symposium on the four-hundredth anniversary of the Jesuit *Ratio Studiorum*. Papers from that symposium (two of which are included here in the "History" section) and important recent documents on Jesuit education—including the full text of *Ignatian Pedagogy: A Practical Approach*—edited by Vincent J. Duminuco, SJ, have been published by Fordham University Press (*The Jesuit Ratio Studiorum of 1599: 400th Anniversary Perspectives*, 2000).

Practical
Applications:
Walking the
Ignatian/Jesuit Walk

Introduction

The final major section of this reader deals with "Practical Applications." We might say that the essay by Joanna Ziegler of the College of the Holy Cross—"Wonders to Behold and Skillful Seeing: Art History and the Mission Statement"—represents the humanities and that the essay by Seattle University's Trileigh Tucker—"Just Science: Reflections on Teaching Science at Jesuit Universities"—represents science. From her social science and legal perspective, Susan Behuniak of LeMoyne College explores "where and with whom is my heart," declaring a teacher's "feigned neutrality" an obstacle to what we hope our students will become. Finance professor and now Spring Hill College administrator Suzanne Erickson, in "It's Noble But Is It Possible?" sees two reasons why a college-wide mission focus is not possible, in professional schools like business. Without trying to "convert" the entire business school faculty, Xavier marketing professor Roshan "Bob" Ahuja shows what he could do and did do in "Marketing to the Poor." And Kathleen Kane, management professor at the University of San Francisco, brings some clarity to the thorny question of "Value-Oriented Hiring and Promotion," in part by telling how she organized her tenure application according to the Jesuit educational mission as articulated by the late Robert Mitchell, SJ (see the "Principles" section).

Wonders to Behold and Skillful Seeing: Art History and the Mission Statement

Joanna Ziegler

From *Conversations on Jesuit Higher Education*, 2000

When the current mission statement of the College of the Holy Cross was being drafted about a decade ago, I had only a vague idea of what the academic life at a Jesuit Catholic college involved. Nearly everywhere on campus, from assembly hall to lunchroom, conversation had to do with mission. Admittedly, I was one of a number of faculty who heard these discussions from afar. Matters of faith and social justice, emerging as key tenets of the mission and thus prevalent in the discussions, seemed, from the distant vantage point of my discipline, quite removed from the affairs of art and architectural history. I admired the mission statement as one might admire the sights of a foreign land—as a sympathetic, even enthusiastic, spectator, yet a stranger to most of what dwells there. What could an art historian possibly bring to, of all things, a dialogue on poverty and social justice? If anything, the talk about Catholic and Jesuit mission only emphasized that my beloved Western art—with its elitist, aristocratic, and male-centered history—was far removed from social justice and gender equality. This apparent disjunction endured until three years ago when my estrangement from the mission ended dramatically.

In 1997, the College invited me to apply to Collegium: A Colloquy on Faith and the Intellectual Life. According to the online description, Collegium was, and is, a summer seminar for

> faculty from its member institutions and for advanced graduate students from universities throughout the United States and Canada. The seminars provide a collegial environment in which participants from diverse backgrounds, faiths, and disciplines can discuss the sources and implications of a Christian academic vocation. . . . Collegium seminars invite scholars to explore some of the most compelling aspects of the Catholic intellectual tradition and to develop their own sense of vocation as intellectuals in a contemporary context.[1]

In that summer of '97 I joined the gathering of Collegium scholars at St. John's College, St. John's Abbey, in Collegeville, Minnesota.

Looming above our activities was Marcel Breuer's mighty Abbey Church. We worshipped there daily, singing side by side with the "black monks" in the stark serenity of the vast, vaulted choir. The bells calling the monks to chant the divine praises of the Liturgical Hours marked the passing of time. The bell tower, perfect symbol of Benedictine life, stood solidly before the church like some serene colossus. Monks moved about us in their regular duties of teaching, counseling, writing, and other monastic chores. As I walked from my room to the refectory, housed at the monastery, I passed the buildings and people that symbolized and shaped the life of this profoundly religious community.

Our business, however, was not to experience life in a Benedictine monastery. It was to share experiences of teaching and research at Catholic institutions of higher learning: "to discover how [we] can make a particular contribution to [our] institution's identity that respects and explores Catholicism's traditions and goals, while also respecting and taking advantage of [our] own religious perspectives and talents." This we did intensely, meeting throughout the day in small groups, assisted by an assigned "mentor," and coming together in plenary sessions, in which guest speakers presented topics of general concern and encouraged collective discussion and debate.

There was time for private as well as communal reflection, and time for casual talk at meals and in the later hours of the evening. We could participate, or not, in a daylong retreat of a particular form of spirituality—Ignatian, Franciscan, Benedictine, Dominican, Christian Feminist. I learned a lot from the stories of other faculty and graduate students—that they, too, were trying to find their professional bearings with what seemed to be the indefinite compass of our respective missions.

The space we occupied to do all this—the monastic buildings crowned by the powerful stark presence of the Abbey Church—communicated as directly and effectively as did the sessions that faith and spirituality can be immediate and relevant to ordinary daily life, when embedded in routine and given the architectural environment to shape and symbolize it.

Together, the conversation among fellows, the inescapable presence of the monastic architecture, and the living Benedictine community permanently altered my relationship to Holy Cross's mission. The mission became a place where henceforth I would draw strength and tackle questions of authority and freedom. It invited me to search for ideas that can lead to spiritual and ethical questions, and for ways in which spirituality can show that ideas have equally important ethical consequences.

For me, that experience epitomized the nature of what this essay is about—"Living the Mission"—especially as it continues to reshape my pedagogy and my professional identity. I wish the story I am about to unfold were seamless and easy, and that the wonderful insights gained at Collegium had been brought home to Holy Cross, yielding the bounty and sustaining the fervor they promised. The reality, however, is that for all my enthusiasm and commitment to "live the mission," it remains, three years later, hard and sometimes confusing work. Confidence and optimism mingle with doubt, as the project of linking art to contemporary issues of living spiritually is alternately embraced and marginalized by the academic community.

I have developed several new courses (two of which are co-taught with Philosophy faculty), which we will explore presently.[2] Reaction to them, however—where there has been recognition—has been largely mixed. Does this have to do with the traditional discipline of art history, I wonder, so often seen as irrelevant (even antithetical) to social justice and Catholic activism? Is it that Philosophy, sadly disengaged from practice and remarkable now for its hermetic feats of analytical language, has lost its allure—not to mention its relevance in the face of market-driven education? Or is it that art historians exemplify the ivory-tower scholar, toiling in the antiseptic vaulted silence of archive and museum—a perfect study in contrast to the mission-oriented activist-educator, serving up soup and otherwise volunteering in support of the poor and marginalized in the "real world" of inner-city slums?

"Living the Mission" affects professional practices and identity as well, beyond the college's gates and in the field of disciplinary inquiry. Art history is currently defined as a project to locate history—to locate subjectivity in the past—in quantifiable evidence and hard data, whose footings lie deep in sociology. Thus, any sort of personal, contemporary experience of historical form—the very thrust of my courses regarding art and contemplation—is looked upon skeptically, even censoriously as something better left to personal rather than professional journals.[3]

Part of this story, then, is about the taxing demands of persevering in a relationship of art conjoined to spirituality as a serious academic pursuit, that is, as a matter of genuine and significant intellectual content such as befits an academic discipline. For now, art history (as serious "scientific" study) and spirituality (as religious nonacademic experience—as a matter of faith) compete for ultimate authority in their absolutely separate domains. My attempt to live the mission is, in a very real sense, an effort to bridge that separation.

Central to this quest for the unity of art and spirituality are the courses I've developed, both alone and in conjunction with colleagues from Philosophy, Christopher Dustin and Joseph Lawrence. I am interested in ways that art—the practice of really looking at it—joins spiritual experience with rigorous intellectual content. Art history can do this, I believe, if viewed and taught as a practice—one that, like other practices, is governed by discipline and daily routine. In the courses mentioned above, practice is the continual and repeated engagement with a single work of art.[4]

The cornerstone of these courses is the integration of practice with theory. Students are required to visit the local Worcester Art Museum on a weekly basis. I would prefer daily, but this is impractical for our students. In the introductory art history course, for example, students are asked to choose one painting by one of three artists: Thomas Gainsborough, Claude Monet, or Robert Motherwell. They must write one paper a week on the same painting for the entire semester—thirteen weeks, thirteen papers in all. I implore them— for this is all but impossible to require—not to consult outside reading, even to avoid reading the museum label, if possible. Their charge is to describe what they see in the picture as precisely and faithfully as they can in approximately five typed pages. With this paper and related notes handed in, they then return to the museum the following week to take up the process all over again.

The results have been surprising and enlightening. Although space prevents a full accounting here, some highlights of what occurs help to reveal the genuine intellectual content of the relationship between art and spirituality and its ultimate link to the mission. Generally speaking, the only repetitive activity most Holy Cross students experience (short of "mashing" buttons on a television remote) is in playing a sport or in building their bodies—actually valuable starting points for us, by the way. My assignment, far from soccer fields and wellness rooms, therefore fills students with dread—of boredom and monotonous papers. Yet, wondrously, transformation does take place. Writing does evolve, from opinionated, narcissistic proclamations—including, of course, willful reactions of "I know what I like and I know what I don't"—to skillful and nuanced descriptions of brushstroke, color, and surface texture. Through this practice, students become disciplined beholders, able to communicate precise knowledge of what is affectionately and invariably identified, somewhere along the thirteen weeks, as "my work of art." The true makeup and content of the painting become accessible to them, with time—and, curiously, it is often deeply personal. This experience of familiarity and objectivity can forever alter a young person's views on talent and learning—demonstrating that accomplishment, indeed the joy of creative knowing, requires discipline and practice, and requires it again and again.

I am most concerned in this context, however, with the contemplative process that underlies this assignment, and especially with what it shares with other forms of contemplation. First, looking becomes habit. It is a dependable, weekly occurrence, with a repeated pattern, which I prescribe: traveling to the museum at the same time each week, entering the same door of the museum, sitting in the same place—in other words, repeating the same procedures each time, week after week. In fact, this aspect of the assignment came to me during the daylong exposure to Ignatian spirituality at Collegium. Father Brian Linanne, SJ, encouraged us to return to one spot, throughout the day of reflection, so that despite the randomness of our mood or temper, just being in a single place would foster reliability, or "readiness." By this process, we are open to communication with God, regardless of where our emotions or senses might wander. Moreover, repetition, grounded in physical discipline, promotes concentration.

As a participant in repetitive practice, the student is now a whole person, awakened to emotional and sensory stimuli, and ready, indeed fully able, to look and—this is the important point—to be open to the painting on its terms rather than his or her own. This teaches students how to cultivate "awareness" and "mindfulness" by repetition and physical ritual. As all great contemplative practices teach us, we must learn to leave our will behind so the air of spiritual enlightenment might flow freely about us. The habit and disciplined practice of looking at art teaches us, through example, how to accomplish this.

Conceived as something akin to a skill, the art of looking (or spectatorship) can occasion contemplation and mindfulness—inner states that are recognized nearly universally as the true paths toward spiritual awareness. Eastern meditation practices, Zen Buddhism, Benedictine spirituality, Western mysticism, Emersonian pragmatism, and stress-reduction exercises, to name but a few, all seek to attain "wisdom" through attention and awareness. Concentration is the cornerstone. As I envision it, then, the study of art—outside the studio—might appropriately take its place alongside other contemplative practices. It shapes contemplative consciousness by insisting on routine physical discipline, which enables readiness, and, in so doing, shows students the spiritual and intellectual depth of artistic creativity—for them as beholders, no less than for the creators.

Faith and creativity share a paradox, as I see it. Fidelity and stability, gained through practice, prepare the way to true freedom. Only with readiness can one hope to transcend the constraints of practice (therein lies the paradox) and enter that place that is mysterious and immeasurable. The experience is so unlike the routine activity that gave rise to it that all the names given that experience through time—transcendence, divinity, creativity, performance, ecstasy—cannot begin to capture its true nature.

For me, to pursue the *mysterium tremendum* of creativity in history springs from and reflects the mission of Holy Cross, which in clear language calls upon "diverse academic disciplines" to engage in "dialogue about basic human questions concerning moral character, meaning in life and history, obligations to one another, and social justice." Although the approach outlined here falls outside the current boundaries of my discipline, I am encouraged in this pursuit by the mission's call for "diverse interpretations of the human experience . . . [and] that sense of the whole which calls us to transcend ourselves and challenges us to seek that which might constitute our common humanity."

In some ways, my approach seems to return to what is known as Formalism, a method that works from the form of a created image or object, without taking into account its historical, economic, or social context. Now largely viewed by art history as mere "empty" analysis, Formalism today has a negative, to some scholars even unconscionable, ring to it, as art historians increasingly apply sociological frameworks—Marxist, feminist, or postmodernist, for example—in order to understand and to give meaning to works of art. Gods and saints and heroes, even the flowers of a Monet garden, are rather harshly showcased as economic and political products of power and oppressive consciousness. Even the word "art" itself has become suspect.

Perhaps more disconcerting than its supposed similarity with Formalism is the emphasis I place on the training or practice involved in looking. I emphasize the word *training*, for what happens in my classroom—and by extension the museum—seems more in line with studio or fine art, rather than art history per se. Colleagues who paint, sing, or dance embrace the sort of training I require of my students. Yet for art historians, it can smack of art appreciation and, worse, appear to offer an insufficient amount of quantifiable, documentable, "hard" evidence—the currently favored material for serious intellectual content. Too much emphasis on sensory and practical information, too much prominence given to the present, and too little time spent on word and theory, is how my approach is seen to fall short of current standards in teaching art history.

The joining of faith and spirituality with art—an important element in my approach—is a legitimate and long-standing aspect of art history, to be sure, but only when firmly lodged in period styles, such as Gothic or Renaissance. Professional groups have priorities, and, at the moment, for works of art to have religious or spiritual significance, they must be of explicitly religious subject matter or have clearly devotional applications. In this view, the emphasis I place on developing a personal, present-day relationship with a work of art belongs, somehow, in the realm of New Age therapy rather than hewing to the "exacting" professional standards of contemporary art history, which tend to see and confine works of art firmly within the time frame of their production.

For me, therefore, the message of the mission poses a dilemma. It asks me to heed its call, when to do so I must step beyond the boundary—to put it bluntly, to write myself out of the norms of publishable scholarship—of the very discipline that brought me to the College in the first place. True, the mission statement has inspired and enriched my thinking on creativity immeasurably, but I have had to leave the collegial setting of my discipline to pursue that thinking and to nurture thought into action.

On sabbatical this year, for example, I reflected upon the contemplative lessons of great art and on the future of making scholarly use of those lessons. I read a broad range of contemplative literature, which led, in part, to this essay and others like it. Meanwhile, my colleagues in art history were off to the archives and conferences in Europe, or reading vast amounts of poststructuralist and deconstructionist theory. It may seem to them, therefore, that in my current activities I am abandoning the rigors of on-site research and voluminous bibliography-hunting for an apparently more relaxed, home-based form of intellectual pursuit. Such is by no means the case; reflection and contemplation are time-honored pillars of academic inquiry and pursuit. Nor do I want for challenges.

Where are the signposts of the mission, so visible in campus conversation, as I thrash my way in isolation through the underbrush of this dilemma? The mission statement is a demanding document, more so than might appear on the surface. It presents a test of commitment to a purpose that diverges from the one that led me to Fenwick Hall and the Art department some years ago. When I took my place among the other faculty of my department, I vowed to be a loyal member of the field by bringing the best and most recent of its scholarly developments to our students. The evolution of the mission statement threw this vow into question, asking in a very tangible sense that I reassess and perhaps reorient my understanding of what I do and how that relates to the mission. This I have done—but now, where am I "current" as an art historian? What is my bibliographic base? Who, really, are my peers? And to what field do I or will I belong? "Living the Mission" has been, in a word, costly.

Nonetheless, I am convinced that the path I have chosen serves both my discipline and the mission of my college. The study of art history, I believe, is strengthened and advanced by the very innovation, freedom of inquiry, and transcendence of ourselves—called for in the mission statement—that are involved in seeking "that which might constitute our common humanity." Spirituality and religion are served by bringing students, through training and discipline in the contemplative art of seeing, to a state of openness, revelation, and understanding. I believe this approach—developed in the context of a Jesuit Mission, conjoining intellect and spirituality—could and should have much broader implications for the field of art history. Moreover, in the face of the horrific, coarsening, and desensitizing effect of much of today's popular media culture—I offer television's *The Sopranos* as *prima facie* evidence—I firmly believe that a renewed quest for the humanizing value of appreciative, creative seeing provides a viable, teachable pathway to an awareness of compassion and social justice.

"Living the Mission" most assuredly will require that all of us involved by choice or desire, rather than by definition, in mission-oriented vision and endeavors will need to work hard to position spirituality and faith so as to be accepted as genuine matters of intellectual—yes, of scholarly—life. Toward that end, I would invoke a note of hope: that academia, and especially art history, will harken to Philosophy when it says, with Homer, that a divinely, beautifully crafted piece of work is indeed a "wonder to behold" and that through making and learning to see such works, as art history promises, the "order of the heavens can be made to appear."

NOTES

1. Our group had the gift of John Thompson as mentor. His openness, intelligence, grace, and wisdom will stay always fixed in my memory. He was hugely important to the meaningful experience I had at Collegium, as well as its endurance in my life. All quotations about Collegium have been taken from the Web site http://www.fairfield.edu/collegium.

2. For an additional perspective on Jesuit tradition in the arts, see *Conversations* 14 (Fall 1998).

3. One great exception to the general trends of current art history is Marcia Brennan, whose work on abstract expressionist aesthetics and gender will radically revise the discipline. She promises to breathe optimism, joy, and affirmative values back into ideas that lately seem imprinted with a sort of negativity and antagonism.

4. Some of this material is taken from my article, "Practice Makes Reception: The Role of Contemplative Ritual in Approaching Art," forthcoming in Tom Landy, ed. *As Leaven in the World: Catholic Perspectives on Faith, Vocation, and the Intellectual Life* (Franklin, WI: Sheed & Ward, 2001).

Just Science: Reflections on Teaching Science at Jesuit Universities

Trileigh Tucker

From *Conversations in Jesuit Higher Education,* 2001

Introduction

Several years ago, my university began a search for a new dean of the School of Science and Engineering, and as part of the process, the search committee developed a set of questions to ask all candidates. Having gotten increasingly interested in justice issues in recent years, I suggested in an e-mail to all science and engineering faculty (about fifty-five) that one of the questions should ask about candidates' interest in justice issues. Two faculty members sent public e-mails in response, both disagreeing with my suggestion. One stated, "I would suspect that science and justice would overlap only rarely, if ever." The other said that "politics," as a matter of individual conscience, should be left out of the dean candidate selection process. No faculty member responded publicly in favor of explicitly discussing justice in the dean search, although several told me privately that they agreed with this suggestion.

Fortunately, our new dean turned out to be a person with a strong commitment to justice, whom we were very excited to welcome as part of our campus community. But the resistance from thoughtful, intelligent faculty both surprised me and motivated me to think more carefully about whether, why, and how justice and college science should be interconnected, particularly at Jesuit universities. (I am considering only natural science in this essay, not the social sciences nor the technological developments that stem from natural science.)

Interactions Between Science and Justice

Science's Role in Society

Perhaps the most straightforward role of science in promoting justice in human society is the generation of information that can be used to help remedy injustice. The most basic form of human dependence on nature concerns our absolute physical reliance on it: breathable air, drinkable water, fertile soil. What constitutes a healthy natural environment, and whether all humans have equal access to these essential natural supplies, are justice-related questions on which scientists—biologists, physicists, chemists, earth scientists—can help to shed light.

It has become clear in recent years that there are profound injustices generated by the ways humans interact with the natural environment. One set of injustices is created by intense, localized activities that present significant short-term health threats to less-powerful individuals and groups. For example, scientific and statistical work generated the 1987 landmark study by the Commission for Racial Justice of the United Church of Christ, which documented a clear correlation between siting of toxic waste facilities and locations of marginalized populations across the United States, independent of community socioeconomic status.[1] Another set of injustices arises from long-term, global changes that may present threats not only to individual human lives but also to complex living systems that support humans—not only in the present but also in future generations of humans and other creatures who have no say about the damage being done to them. Climate change, almost certainly caused by tremendous fossil-fuel burning and chemical emissions by the industrialized countries, is already causing problems for people in less-developed countries. These problems took a long time to create, and their solutions will also require a long time to take effect, even if implemented today. Future generations will pay much of the cost of consumption by today's developed countries.

Example after example shows that the world's poor suffer the most from environmental degradation, and that it is the world's wealthy who contribute most to environmental damage, in large part through their highly disproportionate consumption of the world's resources.[2] Scientists' work is essential to understand and remedy this situation. Having the ability to generate such useful information, are we scientists morally bound to see that our research is used to help heal injustice, as we understand it? I don't see how we can avoid this imperative: withholding life-giving information is akin to withholding food that it is within our power to give to starving people.

A more complex relationship between science and society lies in the infrastructure of the scientific enterprise. Scientific research is a major U.S. industry, funded both by private enterprise and by tax dollars. Although scientific research itself is supposed to be morally neutral, how this scientific research interacts with the rest of society raises profound justice questions:

- In what geographic areas is scientific research conducted, and how does this research affect people living in these areas?
- Who ultimately benefits from the research, and who pays the various short- and long-term costs of the research?
- Who funds the research, and why?
- How are decisions made about which of a set of competing proposals will receive funds?
- To what uses will resulting information be put?

A third form of justice-related interaction between science and society lies in the proposal that scientific theories are not always neutral but can reflect and promote cultural biases. Examples are rampant throughout the history of science; for instance, the "scientific finding" that "women's low brain weights and deficient brain structures were analogous to those of the lower races, and their inferior intellectualities [were] explained on this basis."[3] Science's reputation as a "fact-based," "neutral" enterprise can blind both nonscientists and scientists to its potential biases, which can then perpetuate injustices.

Justice Issues within the Scientific Community

Scientists sometimes unconsciously extend their conviction that science is morally neutral to mean that the scientific community is outside of justice-related evaluation: "those questions don't apply to our work." A professional whose career is based on her or his demonstrated ability to make objective, unbiased evaluations of scientific observations and theories does not necessarily apply this well-honed skill to applications of junior faculty toward tenure or toward annual reviews of another's performance. And science faculty at universities around the country, like most faculties, are still disproportionately white and male, and hold higher ranks than women and nonwhites, even when comparing within age groups.[4] There is little question that racism and sexism are still creating situations of injustice within the scientific community.

Scientists' Concerns about Justice and Science

Personal, Not Professional

A number of scientists would probably contend that it is fine for a scientist to care about justice and injustice—on her or his own time, but not in her or his professional life. As a professional, a scientist is supposed to be objectively interested in facts, processes, and theories about the natural world (which are communal in nature, agreed upon or argued over by the scientific community), not questions of fairness or moral rectitude (which are considered private assessments and therefore not appropriate for communal interactions in the workplace; or which do not relate to the nonhuman realm of interest of the professional natural scientist).

These convictions are often derived ultimately from a healthy respect for the impartiality of science. One of the gifts initially brought by modern science to the seventeenth-century world was respect for the individual as a source of true observations. Ideally, anyone who carefully observed or measured a phenomenon would find the same data, independent of who she or he was, and independent of external authorities such as the church or government. In part because of this history, modern scientists tend to be strongly suspicious of "external" ethical or moral frameworks, which they see as potentially constraining their scientific research.

Diminishment of Scientific Truth

A concern of many thoughtful scientists about bringing justice into the realm of scientific inquiry is that allowing a moral attachment to outcomes may inhibit free investigation and diminish instead of expand the truth of science. Scientists are aware that many opposing conclusions can be promoted from a single data set, by emphasizing particular subsets of those data and by using loaded language in communicating about the data.[5] The observations and statistics are the same for each scientist, but the implications of these numbers may vary according to the conviction of the individual. If a scientist hopes that her or his investigations will help heal injustice, is it not possible or even likely, the argument goes, that the scientist will unconsciously bias her or his investigations in favor of a particular set of data that seem to support a justice-promoting conclusion?

Because of the long history of scientific conclusions reflecting societal prejudices (not only prejudices we abhor but those with which we are in alignment), we must admit the reality of this possibility. I believe that reconciliation of this concern lies in a deep conviction about the compatibility of truth and justice; that it is a scientist's—

and any human being's—duty to rigorously seek truth, to be continually skeptical about and retest any of one's conclusions, to seek contrasting views from one's colleagues, and to trust that justice need not fear truth but actually depends fully on it. To seek this truth, we must work hard to understand our own biases so that we can try to release them in the cause of justice.

Inhibition of Scientific Research

Another authentic concern of scientists has to do with the relationship between scientific research and its potential technological uses. Many scientists fear that others' concern for justice—by others' definitions of justice—will require them to stop their research for fear of its potential technological applications: for instance, developing deadly missiles or cloning "perfect" human beings. Scientists point out that technological outcomes of their research are unknown, and that if research were halted from a fear of negative applications, just as many positive, life-giving ones might be lost as well. It can be easy for even a highly ethical scientist to conclude that she or he is not morally responsible for the unpredictable outcomes of her or his work. How much responsibility a scientist has for either immediate or potential long-term applications of her research is a matter for the individual scientist—but in our current scientific culture, even asking the question is discouraged.

The above objections, and others, are often raised out of a healthy respect for the importance of keeping science distant from the biases of society. But ironically, this distance also allows perpetuation of those biases as scientists stay uninvolved with the societal context of our profession. Even without complete knowledge about how our research might be used, we as scientists can begin to ask challenging ethical questions about our work. We can also hold ourselves open to nonscientists' questioning the values, assumptions, and ethical bases of our research. Engaging in such reflection and dialogue is squarely in the Jesuit tradition, as we try to help guide our profession toward a greater call for justice in all realms.

Interactions between Justice and College Science

Why Bring Justice Issues into College Science at All?

As a long-time teacher of science courses for non-science majors, I can aver that most of these students initially come into a required science course with trepidation or even resentment. Teaching science through consideration of its relationship to justice issues can open science to these students in a way that they find meaningful and inviting. More importantly, at liberal-arts universities, non-science majors often constitute a much larger proportion of all graduates than science majors—and therefore the majority of college-educated citizens. Their required college science course(s) may be their first, or even only, acquaintance, as adults, with science as a human endeavor and a way of interacting with the natural world. Such a course may therefore be a particularly powerful communicator of values embedded in the practice of science. All ways of practicing science express values, whether implicit or explicit— including values about whether science should concern itself with questions of justice.

For science majors, there are additional considerations. All students should be educated not only about their profession's intellectual content and ways of proceeding, but also about its interactions with society, including its implications for justice work. These aspects of professional education are occasionally made explicit in graduate school, rarely in college, even though many students will go directly into the scientific workforce after graduation. Scientists who have not deeply considered their profession's societal responsibilities are unlikely to be open to non-scientists' judgments on this topic—so who then is to assess whether science is in an appropriate relationship to justice? At Seattle University, approximately twenty percent of our undergraduates major in science. Do we want one-fifth of our graduates to go out into the broader world believing that their profession need not be concerned with justice?

Ways to Raise Justice Questions in Science Courses

Science through case studies. I have found that studying concrete situations in which scientific principles are critical to evaluating and resolving an unjust situation is a highly effective way to reach two goals: to get students immediately engaged in trying to understand the science behind the situation and to help them see connections between science and justice. For example, in my introductory geology class (typically taken by non-majors to satisfy their science requirement), I have used the Green Belt Movement of Kenya, founded by Wangari Maathai in 1977, as a case study. This situation raises justice-related issues such as the role of local versus colonial jurisdiction, empowerment of the poor, and the importance of sustainable development that takes into account the needs of future generations. To fully understand the role of the Green Belt movement, students must understand how soil develops, how deforestation affects soil erosion, plate tectonics (to explain why Kenya has no fossil-fuel deposits of its own), and climatology (to understand what constitutes sustainable agriculture for this region). Role-plays, with students taking different viewpoints on a justice question, can promote the valuable understanding that scientific information can be used to support either side of a debate.

In choosing justice-related case studies, I think it is important to bring in local situations as well as distant ones. Studying stories from across the world helps students understand their roles as global citizens but can also lead students to believe that injustice happens somewhere else, to "others." Studying stories from our own "backyards" helps science students see that the requirement to work for justice applies everywhere.

Scientists as examples. Using scientists' biographies to help students understand a particular branch of science is valuable because it reminds students of a fact that science courses often neglect: the existence of science requires scientists, human beings who inevitably bring not only our intellects but also our personalities, backgrounds, and biases to our work. Students should learn that science is a human endeavor with the strengths and limitations of all human endeavors: strokes of genius and exquisite beauty, and unconscious biases and value assumptions.

Students also respond strongly to guest speakers, local scientists who work actively to promote justice through their work. I've also found that their talking with my class can be an affirming experience for the scientists as well, since they often feel they may not discuss their justice-related work with their professional colleagues.

Student research, service learning, and internships. Another highly effective way to help students connect justice and college science is for them to conduct their own research and fieldwork in this area. Their work may involve only library research, but more effective is hands-on learning in which students also interview people who have been involved with situations of injustice, or in which they perform scientific research themselves to make a real contribution to remedying injustice.

Many of our Environmental Studies majors have worked in the South Park area of Seattle. Most of the area is zoned for heavy industry and is characterized by a largely nonwhite residential population and a median household income below Seattle's average. Along with numerous sites hosting toxic chemicals, the South Park area contains two Superfund sites. Several Seattle University students have completed internships with people working to clean up toxics in the neighborhood. Some have collaborated with the Community Coalition for Environmental Justice, analyzing land-use and population data for South Park. Others have used phytore-mediation techniques to help clean a creek feeding the nearby Duwamish River. In these projects, students come to understand stream dynamics, toxicology, groundwater chemistry, fish biology, and soil development. They also become passionate about their work and consider their project supervisors to be "eco-heroes" who are true role models for authentic living.

Modeling justice in the classroom. One of the most dangerous ideas about college education, in my opinion, is that it is not "the real world." The idea that the way we interact in college "doesn't really count" means that students can leave our universities without experiencing a mutually accountable community. We talk in the classroom about working for justice—but the classroom community itself is often an absolutely centralized power structure. In the classroom as well as every other venue of societal life, an authority's hidden (or sometimes explicit) biases and prejudices can thwart the call to live in right relationship. Because students who have been accepted to a college typically performed well in similar pre-college educational systems, they tend to accept and promote this power structure, along with many of an authority's biases.

Many of the authority relationships manifested in the classroom are appropriate and effective ways to promote true learning. But I am continually astounded at how easy it is to fall into other authority patterns that are less healthy, in which I fail to respect or learn from my students' insights and wisdom. Even with attentiveness, any of us can unintentionally promote prejudices that inhibit the creation of a just community in our classes. For example, a few years ago I was preparing to give a talk at a national science conference, and I chose some slides of students doing geology class exercises. In one of my preliminary run-throughs, I (fortunately) noticed that in every slide, a male student was performing the action, and female students were looking on. Was this a matter of which slides I chose? Which classroom scenes I decided to capture on film? Or did this gender imbalance characterize my class as a whole, and had I simply captured an accurate picture of what happens on a regular basis? If so, was there something I was unknowingly doing to perpetuate or even increase that imbalance? If I had happened not to notice the pattern in my slides, I could have perpetuated through my presentation the bias that men are most actively engaged in science, and that women are more passive, less interested. Of course, the same violation of justice is manifested in the often-reported tendency of teachers to call preferentially on male students or white students for active class participation.[6] We must be always vigilant for our own prejudiced thoughts and actions. As teachers interested in justice, we can share our authority by explicitly inviting class discussions on topics such as power structures in the classroom; gender and science; race and science. We can also model a concern for justice by expanding our realm of care beyond the micro-community of our classroom; we can consider together with our students what information or education we as a class could offer to help remedy a specific situation in which justice has been violated.

Some Proposals for College Science

1. No student should graduate from college with a science degree without having taken at least one course that deals with issues of justice and science. This is not to say that all science courses must raise these issues. But we are not preparing our students to be contributing world citizens unless they reflect on the role of their profession in society and in promoting a more just world.
2. In a college's offerings of science courses for non-majors, at least a few courses should raise questions about the relationships between science and justice.
3. Science faculty should take professional time to reflect on questions of how their work interfaces with justice. Such reflection could be part of an annual faculty retreat, informal lunches hosted by the dean, a lecture or discussion series, or other forms appropriate to the university.

Summary

One of the charisms of Ignatian spirituality is that it is world affirming, believing that "God can be discovered, through faith, in all natural and human events." If our Jesuit education is to be world affirming, we must be attentive to the discoveries of natural science. If our Jesuit education is to be communal and companionate, we must engage in a dialogue with scientific culture. And if our Jesuit education is to flow from the "faith that does justice," we must reflect deeply, and then act, on the profound interrelationships between science and justice in human societies.

_____

NOTES

1. Commission for Racial Justice, United Church of Christ (Charles Lee, director, Special Report on Toxic Injustice), *Toxic Wastes and Race in the United States: A National Report on the Racial and Socio-economic Characteristic of Communities with Hazardous Waste Sites* (New York: United Church of Christ, 1987).

2. Aaron Sachs, "Eco-Justice: Linking Human Rights and the Environment," Worldwatch Paper 127 (Worldwatch Institute, 1995).

3. John S. Haller and Robin S. Haller, *The Physician and Sexuality in Victorian America* (Urbana: University of Illinois Press, 1974), quoted in Sandra Harding, ed., *The "Radar" Economy of Science* (Bloomington: Indiana University Press, 1993).

4. National Science Foundation, *Women, Minorities, and Persons with Disabilities in Science and Engineering: 1998* (Arlington, VA: National Science Foundation, 1999), 99-338.

5. An example used by theoretical physicist Brian Martin compares two studies published in the prestigious journals *Science* and *Nature*, concerning how exhaust from supersonic jets affects stratospheric ozone. One scientist refers to the "shield" of ozone, the "burden" of NO_2, and the "threat" to ozone. The other refers simply to the "ozone layer," "amounts" of NO_2, and how chemicals "interact with, and thus attenuate" ozone. Each scientist quoted by Martin "emphatically denied they had engaged in 'pushing'" a viewpoint (Brian Martin, *The Bias of Science* [Canberra, Australia: Society for Social Responsibility in Science, 1979], quoted by Linda Jean Shepherd in *Lifting the Veil: The Feminine Face of Science* [Boston: Shambhala, 1993], 111). Even if neutral language is used in contrasting studies, one scientist might emphasize (perhaps by consciously or unconsciously allocating more text to) the statistical probabilities of a phenomenon and another to the statistical uncertainties.

6. David J. Hess, *Science and Technology in a Multicultural World: The Cultural Politics of Facts and Artifacts* (New York: Columbia University Press, 1995), 257.

On "Where and with Whom Is My Heart?"

Susan M. Behuniak

From *Conversations on Jesuit Higher Education*, 2003

It is revealing that those who align themselves with the marginalized, the hated, the oppressed, the suffering, the poor, or the powerless are roundly criticized for identifying with whom their hearts lie, when those who speak for the mainstream and adopt the voice of the powerful, the privileged, the idealized, or the norm do so under the cloak of neutrality, objectivity, and universality. I think that Paulo Freire got it right when he said, "Washing one's hands of the conflict between the powerful and the powerless means to side with the powerful, not to be neutral." For those of us who name both where we stand and with whom, the academic norm that we have broken is not that of having a point of view but of daring to reveal it.

Admittedly, asking where and with whom is my heart is a political, even a radical question, but it is also a thoroughly academic one. It is radical because it goes to the very root of the purpose of education, that of humanizing us, and it is academic because it questions knowledge itself—how it is constructed, by whom, for what purposes, and indeed, what counts as knowledge at all. It is a question that critics sometimes blast as the product of "political correctness" but one that has always seemed to me to be inspired by "intellectual correctness," because it pursues the whole truth, the whole story, by including voices usually ignored. Perhaps the best example of its effectiveness has been within feminism, where it has been employed to challenge "truths" through personal accounts that document a contrary, a different, or at minimum a parallel universe. In this, it asks the mainstream to cast its gaze out to the margins and to be so moved by what it sees that the truth, and perhaps even the world, is changed.

For example, when we study the issue of poverty in my American national politics course, I am often startled by the number of students whose objections to social welfare programs are dismissive of human suffering and impervious to data that show the millions of children who are poor and the mere sliver of the budgetary pie allotted to social welfare as compared to defense or to corporate aid. The numbers, pie charts, and diagrams don't budge them. But I find that a personal story does. I recount standing in a checkout line in a grocery store as an adolescent with my mother, who paid for part of our bill in food stamps. Some people viewed these stamps as licenses to question our food choices, disparage us with stereotypes, and humiliate us with glares. "Assistance" comes with a cost, I tell my students. Then I emphasize that my brief experience with hard times barely skims the surface of what poverty is, how it feels, and what it means, so I ask them to list the things that poverty denies a child, and then we discuss what role, if any, the government should have. Now the analysis—the struggle with the data, with the people, with values, with political ideologies, with rights and responsibilities—can take place. It is by standing with the poor and encouraging my students to at least hear their stories that I challenge them to consider whether their stances reflect the whole story or just a privileged version.

Since I research and teach in the field of constitutional law, I am well acquainted with the objections to abandoning neutrality. For it is in the field of law, if anywhere, that there is a consciously articulated effort to suppress the heart in favor of the head, to employ legal reasoning over the pull of personal stories, and to focus on the process while disregarding the result. But just as educating "the mind" can neglect to address the needs of what the Jesuit tradition calls "the whole person," so can legalism fail to speak to the realities of the human condition.

Support for supplementing sterile legalism with personal knowledge came recently from an unexpected source, Justice Clarence Thomas, a conservative jurist who usually sits silent during oral arguments before the U.S. Supreme Court. But in December 2002 while hearing arguments in *Virginia v. Black*, a case that uses free speech rights to challenge the constitutionality of the state's law against cross-burning, Thomas interrupted Michael R. Dreeben, the attorney representing the Justice Department (who was defending the law), to question whether he was in fact "understating" the effects of a burning cross. Referring to one hundred years of lynchings in the South as a "reign of terror" of which the cross was a symbol, Thomas spoke not so much as a judge but as a black man. He chided Dreeben: "I think that what you're attempting to do is to fit this into our jurisprudence rather than stating more clearly what the cross was intended to accomplish, and indeed, that it is unlike any symbol in our society." Here was a moment when abstract legal analysis was asked to come to terms with concrete experience—of how a burning cross is interpreted not as free expression but as a physical threat when you are black. Thomas was arguing that for justice to be done, particularized knowledge must be heard.

This holds true not only for the courtroom, but also for the classroom. Articulating where we stand as teachers is sound pedagogy. How can we insist that students develop "a voice," reveal their values, and make courageous decisions when we hide our own behind a curtain of feigned neutrality? Indeed, to teach effectively, we must role model what we implore them to become. Yet, let me emphasize that in revealing where we stand it must be distinguishable, not just in our minds but most especially in the minds of our students, from demanding that they stand where we do. Our revelation must be an invitation to engage in earnest discussion and open reflection, and never a threat nor a requirement to conform. We must remember that academic freedom is not ours alone, just as the obligation of intellectual honesty is not theirs alone.

It's Noble but Is It Possible?

Suzanne M. Erickson

From *Conversations on Jesuit Higher Education*, 2003

Father Peter-Hans Kolvenbach's challenge to the Jesuit colleges and universities assembled in Santa Clara in 2000 was inspiring and challenging, perhaps more than we knew at the time. I greeted Father Kolvenbach's plea to return to our roots, to explore what being Jesuit means in a university setting, with enthusiasm and excitement. I feel strongly that the Jesuit universities need to stand for something unique and distinctive and to provide that "something" along with educational excellence to all of our students. A preference for the poor, a worldview, a focus on career as a way to improve society, seems to me to be a distinctive competence indeed.

I am a tenured finance professor within a Jesuit business school. As such, I cannot speak for other professional schools and probably do not even speak for all of my colleagues in business. Caveat stated, to me personally, the challenge to think about business as a means to an end broader than shareholder wealth maximization, is exciting and energizing. In my biased view of the world, the business school is the school in all of our universities where the "Jesuit stamp" should be most pronounced. We are preparing tomorrow's business leaders. We are educating people who will have to choose between breaking rules for personal gain and making the right choice for the greatest number. To make a priority of molding ethical business leaders that will make a difference in people's lives through their compassionate leadership seems to me a noble calling indeed.

As much as I support Father Kolvenbach's challenge in theory, I am doubtful whether it can ever come to pass in reality. The impediments to change in professional schools stem from two sources. First, we faculty in professional schools are wholly unprepared, by our training, to deal with issues of social justice and a preferential option for the poor. Second, even if we were to make up our educational deficiencies, the reward structures within our schools and within our professions work against our pursuing these issues in any meaningful way.

Preparation

My colleagues and I all received our doctoral training in the theories of our chosen fields. We were never encouraged to look beyond the very narrow perspective of a subdiscipline within a discipline. Indeed, we would have been viewed as non-academic had we brought up the impact of business on the poor. Anything we now know about what it means to be Jesuit we have learned since being at our respective universities, by seeking out answers to our questions. While there are opportunities to educate ourselves, and my university provides many, there is certainly no obligation or reward for doing so. The burden for learning what it means to be Jesuit, and how to act upon that knowledge professionally, falls squarely on the faculty member after arriving at his or her Jesuit institution, if the faculty member should be so inclined. This leads to the second impediment.

Rewards

An untenured faculty member must rationally operate under the assumption that he or she may not get tenure. This means that the faculty member's research must be conventional enough that it would pass the grade at any business school. This effectively precludes any research with a Jesuit slant to it in my field. To be published in the accepted journals of our field, research must follow a certain format, tackle generally accepted issues, and fit into the established view of what acceptable business research is. For a faculty member to investigate issues of social justice as they relate to business would be career suicide. If for any reason the faculty member were denied tenure, the research would not pass the rigor test of most other universities.

But let's assume for the moment that the junior faculty member is indeed a good candidate for tenure at his/her Jesuit institution. How would a body of research focusing on issues of social justice stack up in a tenure file at a Jesuit institution? Many universities "grade" research by the journal it is published in. Certainly in my field I cannot think of a single finance journal that would find questions of social justice as appropriate material for their readers. The faculty member could publish in business ethics, but journals outside our subspecialty are typically viewed with suspicion. Is the faculty member publishing in business ethics because she can't hack it in finance? If the school ranks journals to grade research and the faculty member does not publish in the ranked journals, then clearly the research is not adequate.

This leads to the problem facing all faculty in our institutions. If faculty are evaluated on their research, journal rankings are inevitable. Accepting journals outside of our fields opens Pandora's box. If business ethics is OK for finance, is sociology OK? Clearly this is a path down which we do not want to venture.

The Solution

There may be a solution, but it requires a unity of purpose and a degree of enlightenment that I do not currently see in most universities. For our teaching and research to reflect the fundamental values of Jesuit education, the reward system in our universities must reflect the importance of this work. For the reward systems to be changed, the top administration of the university, the deans, and indeed the faculty themselves must view issues of social justice as a priority. Unfortunately, I believe we are a long way from this consensus. I fear that reaching consensus on the importance of mission in our daily lives will be a Herculean task. Until the deans, administration, and faculty agree on a vision for our mission, however, reward systems cannot change.

Even if consensus on the mission is achieved, restructuring of the reward system will require an implementation based on a holistic view of research. Simple rankings of journals will no longer suffice. Research will have to be read and evaluated for its contribution. Contribution to the mission of the university would be viewed as valuable and appropriate. This would undoubtedly take a lot of time. Are we that committed to living the mission?

What I am proposing is truly not radical. I am not arguing that research on social justice is all we do in professional schools; I am arguing that we make space for it in what we do. Not every faculty member will find these issues interesting and that is fine. But surely in a Jesuit university there must be space for the researcher who wants to investigate the effect of business actions on the greater good.

Imagine just for a moment what a truly Jesuit university could look like. Faculty would pursue high levels of all kinds of research, traditional theoretical, applied, pedagogical, as well as research that relates our professions to the mission of the university. Our research informs our teaching and helps students think beyond themselves to living as "men and women for others." A Jesuit degree would guarantee an employer that the student was technically proficient, ethically grounded, and able to take a global perspective on issues of importance. Jesuit graduates would be widely perceived as being different, as offering more.

One thing we in business know for sure is that you get what you measure. If the reward structure and compensation system are not changed, it is certain that behaviors will not change and Father Kolvenbach's vision will remain just that.

Marketing to the Poor

Roshan "Bob" Ahuja

From *Xavier* Magazine, 1993

When I came to Xavier University, it took a while to get accustomed to people talking about the "service of faith and the promotion of justice." The idea seemed quite different from the successful corporate tactics I had been taught.

I learned a great deal about Xavier's Ignatian vision from the publication "Assembly 1989: Jesuit Ministry in Higher Education," by Peter-Hans Kolvenbach, the superior general of the Society of Jesus. One passage particularly jumped out at me. Father Kolvenbach said: "Concern for social problems should never be absent; we should challenge all of our students to use the option for the poor as a criterion, making no significant decision without first thinking of how it would impact the least in society."

I began to see how the Ignatian vision invited faculty and students to discover, on their own, the feelings of the heart. At this time, I began to seek ways to integrate Ignatius Loyola's vision of education into my daily teaching activities.

For instance, I asked myself if marketing managers consider "the least in society" when they make strategic marketing decisions. I also sought to discover ways I could consider the least in my teaching. I had always taught students how to use contemporary theories to sell more products, to gain more market share in a competitive world, to improve advertising, to persuade the consumer to buy more. Now, I asked myself: Had I taught the students how to manipulate consumers? Had I concentrated too much on teaching them how to discover consumers' perceptions in order to manipulate them in the direction the company wanted? Had I spent too little time talking to students about discerning the effect marketing strategies had on the least in society? My answer was a resounding "yes."

I fully realized that the theories I taught could easily be used to manipulate consumers into buying. Instead of influencing consumers through persuasion based on a reasoned logic, appeals are often made to manipulate them by repeatedly attempting to alter their perceptions of what is really valuable. Many times marketers aim these new "values" at those least able to detect what the researcher is doing—the poor, children, teenagers, single parents, the elderly, etc. I began to question the tactics marketers are willing to use to sell a product.

I began to realize I was teaching my students to take advantage of consumers considered least.

If I came to this realization, I hoped some students would also. However, I knew this type of insight and learning does not result from the typical lecture and note-taking teaching model. Rather, I would need a teaching model that helped the student discern whether unfair attempts to influence people were present in the marketplace. I did not want to tell them. I knew my job was to get them to ask questions regarding the fairness and justice in the marketplace. If they searched and found the answer on their own, then they bought into the learning experience, and I was only the guide.

I began by assigning a paper that would cover the least in society. The assignment, one of three papers due in the course, asked the students to choose a group they considered "Least in Society," a group in need of or deserving special attention. The group could be a current target market for a company (for example, children) or a group not usually targeted by companies (for example, the least, single mothers).

Two things were important in the assignment. First, that the students identify a group they (not me) considered least, and second, that they interact with these people. I instructed the students to go into the field to study the least, to talk with members considered least, and to perform in-depth interviews with four or five of these group members. I also asked them to talk to marketers targeting this least group. Finally, I asked them to write a paper detailing their research and their feelings about the marketers' actions.

The students used market research techniques to answer several questions. For example, are consumer behavior theories used by marketers to manipulate those least in society? What obligations and responsibilities do marketers of goods and services (both profit and nonprofit) have to people considered least? What are organizations presently doing to meet the needs of the least? And, finally, what can I (the student) do about it?

I asked the students to suspend judgment until their research was complete. In other words, I wanted them to think critically about what they observed and felt.

Let me give some examples of what several undergraduate students did to fulfill this assignment and their opinions of its value to them.

Brian studied cigarette ads and thought the least paper was relevant because he learned how some cigarette companies applied consumer behavior theories in the marketing of cigarettes to women. For example, he found that the women he interviewed began smoking when they were in their teens in an attempt to feel older and more sophisticated. He found that many cigarette advertisements play on these facts and display women smoking in sophisticated settings or display the female smoker as someone who is independent of others.

Crystal studied the effect advertisements had on children growing up in single-parent families. She felt marketers thrive on the least and that they are easy targets. She believed there was no hope in the immediate future for changing the way things are done (in marketing and advertising). The least will stay the least for quite some time.

Walter studied liquor ads in minority neighborhoods. He gained insight into how marketers use certain theories to manipulate the consumer into believing their product is the best. He also felt marketers stimulate a need for their products in an immoral way. Walter believed this manipulation would continue to go on as long as it works.

Jill studied firms that sell Mastercards to college students. She felt most students do not understand how high interest rates charged by most credit card companies can affect them financially. She believed most students want the immediate gratification of using a credit card and that companies take advantage of these desires.

Finally, I'd like to share some recent MBA student reactions to this assignment and its relevance to the themes discussed in the course and its application to real-world marketing problems.

- "I thought it was a good way to teach theories in class because we actually got a chance to talk to people being manipulated and the companies doing the manipulation."
- "Good topic. A perspective very easily overlooked. Excellent to perceive the other side of poverty often ignored."
- "The least paper is a good learning experience. It gives the student another perspective on marketing—one other than profit (marketer's perspective), and it addressed ethics in business."
- "It is a good way to touch on ethics, especially the degrees of manipulation."

And one student remarked that she had heard of the Ignatian vision in her theology and philosophy classes but never in her business courses.

I replied, "Well, you have now."

Value-Oriented Hiring and Promotion and the University of San Francisco's *Vision 2005*

Kathleen Kane

From *Conversations on Jesuit Higher Education*, 1997

During the past two years, the University of San Francisco (USF) has engaged in the creation of a document entitled *Vision 2005*, which sets forth the collective vision of the community for the immediate future. Representatives of every constituency of the university have been involved. The first draft of *Vision 2005* was distributed in April 1997 and instantly provoked a great deal of conversation and debate. Some of the most heated of the discussions have centered on the section of the report dealing with our Catholic and Jesuit identity.

The draft called for promoting USF's Catholic and Jesuit identity in a number of ways, but by far the most controversial was its recommendation that questions of institutional identity and mission be brought into play in hiring and promotion processes. Specifically, this section of the document recommended that support of the mission of USF either be a fourth area in consideration for tenure or that it be given weight within each of the other three areas: teaching, research, and service. Further, it recommended that attention to mission and identity be integrated formally into the hiring process. The specifics were to be agreed upon after a university-wide dialogue and discussion of the entire *Vision 2005* document.

As a member of the task force that drafted the controversial section of the document, I was surprised and dismayed by a strong, negative reaction to the proposal. Almost as soon as the first draft of the document was made available on the Internet, we began to hear such comments as, "Now we will all have to go to Mass and confession," and, "Next they will want quotas of Catholics on the campus." As yet, we have not had a campus-wide open dialogue to begin to resolve the controversy, perhaps because emotions are so strong and so polarized. As a proponent of a strong Catholic and Jesuit identity, my desire is to see USF become what it says it is without alienating or disregarding the diversity of viewpoints we have always honored and respected in our community. The fear seems to be that by promoting a strong Catholic and Jesuit identity, USF would be in danger of becoming an institution "for Catholics only."

Is this fear justified? I think not. Granted, as someone only six years into her academic career, I may still have much to learn about the politics of the university. Moreover, as a non-Catholic with no previous experience of Jesuit or Catholic education, I may not have a great deal of historical perspective to draw upon. On the other hand, as a relatively recently hired non-Catholic, for whom USF has been an introduction to Jesuit higher education, my background is similar to that of increasing numbers of my colleagues. And as a professor of organizational behavior and management, my academic training should be of some help. In the comments that follow, then, I shall try to offer what I hope will be a useful—and perhaps fresh—perspective on a complex set of problems.

Some Models

People attach a variety of meanings to the phrase, "hiring and promoting for the mission." To some it means hiring quotas for Catholics and giving special weight to Catholics in the promotion process. To others it means hiring and promoting people who think in similar ways, a kind of "old-boy network" made up of those who have a specific view of what it means to be Catholic and Jesuit. At the other end of the spectrum, it may mean nothing more nor less than attracting and retaining individuals who treat others with respect and who embody in their lives and work values consistent with the religious tradition in which USF stands.

For some, an approach to hiring and promotion similar to the one in place at Pepperdine University would be desirable at USF. The Pepperdine strategy seeks to insure that a very large percentage of faculty and administrators will be members of the Church of Christ. According to a member of the Pepperdine faculty, the university has recently asked each department to ascertain the number of faculty who are Church of Christ members, and has given each department a target number to attain. Some at USF believe that such a practice could begin to rectify past practices that have, they say, rendered us "no more Catholic than a secular institution." Others at USF consider this practice to be diametrically opposed to Jesuit ideals of tolerance for multiple voices and perspectives, and therefore completely unacceptable as a way to promote our identity. Still others fear that this practice would create a "right-wing" atmosphere in the university, in which discussions and critical thought that were judged "religiously incorrect" would be banned or severely discouraged, with disastrous results for the intellectual life of the university.

Another approach to the promotion of the mission encourages the creation and support of a critical mass of thinkers (whether Catholic or not) who are versed in the teachings and history of the Catholic Church. At the moment, USF has a Center for Judaic Studies and is in the process of starting a Center for Islamic Studies, but has no center dedicated to Catholic studies. The chief virtue of this approach, and the reason why I regard it as superior to the Pepperdine model, is that it puts intellectual activity and accomplishment, and not the individual's religious belief, at the center of the issue. It would seem to me that it is entirely appropriate for an institution calling itself Catholic to be a center for research into such subjects as the Catholic intellectual tradition, Catholic social teaching, and the like. Its presence, alongside the Judaic Center and the Islamic Center, would be a concrete expression of the ability of Catholicism to coexist with the university's catholic commitment to pluralism.

Hiring and promoting for mission can also mean attracting and retaining people of good character, specifically religious questions aside. When UCLA recently invited Michael Milken, the Wall Street "junk bond king," to become a lecturer at its business school, I immediately felt grateful that I worked at a Jesuit business school. I knew that we at the McLaren School would never give institutional support—and the sanction that such support implies—to a man convicted of a variety of illegal financial dealings. Offering a coincidental but telling contrast was the recent visit to USF of Ben Cohen of Ben and Jerry's Ice Cream, who spoke to a large, enthusiastic crowd. Ben and Jerry's is known worldwide for its creative and consistent commitment to ethical and socially responsible business practices. I am proud to say that Ben Cohen—not Michael Milken—represents the values we promote in the business school and campus wide. When a colleague recently challenged my view that Milken should be unwelcome at USF, arguing that Jesuit education is also committed to the proposition that all sides of a question must be heard, I realized that it wasn't the mere fact of his presence, but the context in which UCLA presented him, that so offended me. UCLA's invitation appeared to be value neutral, even approving and supportive. It was as if Milken had never broken laws or violated ethical standards. In fact, a UCLA dean commented that Milken's conviction on securities fraud should not preclude him from teaching and that, "We have very mature adult students who can hear different views and decide for themselves." In a Jesuit university, I would hope that if he had been invited, the visit would have been framed in such a way that there would be no doubt that the institution did not condone his crimes or regard them as "business-as-usual."

Applying the "Ben and Michael" issue to the hiring process, one would hope that a Ben Cohen, because he exemplifies the ethical and moral behavior we associate with our mission, would be viewed as a much more desirable colleague than a Michael Milken. I have heard comments at USF to the effect that acting ethically is "nice, but not enough," as if good acts are "enough" only if grounded explicitly in Catholic theology. But treating others with respect, I submit, must be at the heart of whatever we define Jesuit mission to be. And loving one's neighbor is not an exclusive franchise of any denomination.

Value-Oriented Hiring and Promotion

USF's mission statement is an inspirational document explicating values that are noble and easy to accept at face value. During the last two years, as a member of the President's Council for the Mission of the University, I have become increasingly concerned with the question of how to put those values into practice. Is there consensus in the community about our values and about how those values should shape our relationships with each other and the San Francisco community? Is the USF culture one that supports the everyday living of those values? Should we institute a kind of value-oriented hiring and promotion process in order to strengthen our culture in support of our mission?

In companies such as Hewlett-Packard, Toyota, Disney, and Microsoft, specific personnel and hiring practices have been instituted that insure that the organization hire only those who accept and practice the values and principles promoted by the company and its existing organizational culture. This has been an effective way to insure a good fit between employees and the company vision. In addition, it has created strong organizational cultures with dedicated and committed employees. The troubling aspect of this practice is that it can serve to perpetuate a kind of "old-boy network." It has the potential to create an insulated and isolated organization that could easily lose touch with the customers it was created to serve.

The question then is this: can USF institute a value-oriented approach without compromising the diversity and pluralism to which we are committed? I believe that our first task is to think and talk about those values and what they mean in how we actually do our work. Ideally, each member of the community would attempt to discover the meaning of the mission in his or her own professional life. This year, while writing a personal statement for my tenure file, I described the ways in which my teaching, research, and service supported USF's mission and how the mission supported my personal values and goals for my academic career. It was a valuable exercise in many ways, but the important outcome was the validation of my sense that USF was the right place for me to continue and ultimately complete my academic career, particularly as USF continues to move closer to its mission as a Catholic and Jesuit institution.

An essay by Father Robert Mitchell, SJ [former president of the University of Detroit and of Le Moyne College] delineates these five traits of Jesuit education: a passion for quality and excellence; the study of the humanities and sciences, no matter the specialization; a preoccupation with questions of ethics and values for both the professional and personal lives of students; the importance of the religious experience, for both Catholic and non-Catholic students; and the importance of and attendance to the individual needs of each student. With explicit, but nonrestrictive, value-oriented criteria such as these, we have a clear framework for integrating our values into our personnel processes.

Just as I completed a value-oriented assessment of myself as an applicant for tenure, I strongly advocate some manner of value-oriented assessment in the hiring and promotion processes. Administration and faculty need to work out the specifics, but I believe that it is essential to the well-being of the community as well as of each faculty member. Of all the jobs I have held in my life, including starting a business, being a junior faculty member was by far the most difficult to feel comfortable with. The first few years were fraught with uncertainty: How much of my time do students need? How much can I afford to give them? How much service time should be devoted to my department? to the business school? to the university? Where does research fit into the mix? A value-oriented approach can help ensure that applicants understand clearly what USF stands for, and how they can contribute. It can reduce at least some of that initial uncertainty, enabling new faculty members to be assimilated more quickly and effectively into university life. It can also allow the university to be more selective in its choice of faculty, as it gives prospective faculty members the opportunity to assess their own fit with the institution.

To the proposal that we explicitly screen candidates for values and beliefs congruent with the mission, I often hear the response, "People will say anything to get the job." Perhaps this is true of some, but I prefer to assume the goodwill and honest intentions of job applicants and trust that, if presented with clear options, most will make a choice congruent with their own values. It is possible that hiring errors in the past may be attributed more to a lack of clarity about mission than to the dishonesty of the candidates.

Can a hiring process detect candidates of good character? I believe it can, if the institution is clear about how that character can be revealed in various aspects of institutional life. Can a tenure and promotion process include criteria directly related to the mission? In my own case, I was able to link my entire tenure package to the mission of the university. It certainly did not hurt my case, and I believe that it helped, especially with certain constituencies. Most importantly, it helped give a focus and coherence to my personal statement and file by grounding them in a strong set of values and ideals. Again, the details and relative weights of mission-related criteria need to be discussed and in the USF case made part of the collective bargaining process. I hope that we may soon engage in this discussion with an openness to the possibilities inherent in this approach.

Questions remain: Are we a recognizably unique institution with something special to offer our students and society in general? What is that "something special"? What will we do in the future to demonstrate and live this unique character? Who will be willing and able to carry forward this unique character and vision for the future? I believe that I have begun to answer these questions for myself, but I also believe that the community must commit itself to open dialogue and conversation. This will take courage. These conversations will require mutual respect, the ability to negotiate and compromise, and a spirit of inclusion. They will require, that is, that we love our neighbors.

Further Reading

To complement the pieces included in this section of the reader, consult *Teaching as an Act of Faith: Theory and Practice in Church-related Higher Education* (New York: Fordham University Press, 2002), a collection of fourteen essays edited by Arlin C. Migliazzo, professor of history at Whitworth College in Spokane, Washington. The individual essays are organized under four headings: social sciences, natural sciences, fine arts, and humanities. Participants in Xavier University's Ignatian Mentoring Program have found some essays better than others, and at times one or another essay outside their own discipline the most valuable. The editor has also provided a very helpful eighteen-page bibliography on Christianity and higher education, divided into three sections: the formative period (1940–1980), the contemporary period (1980–2002), and a third section dealing with works on five different Christian traditions.

My partner in Ignatian Programs at Xavier, psychologist Debra Mooney, has come out with a third edition of her *Do You Walk Ignatian? A Compilation of Jesuit Values Expressed in the Work Day* (Cincinnati, OH: Xavier University, 2007). This thirty-page booklet explicates six key terms from *Do You Speak Ignatian?*. It includes questions for self-assessment, relevant quotations from a great variety of sources (sometimes unlikely ones), and personal testimony from a faculty member and a staff member.

Another Xavier resource—*Teaching to the Mission: A Compendium of the Ignatian Mentoring Program* (Cincinnati: Xavier University, Ignatian Programs, 2007)—shows some of the results of the first three years of the Ignatian Mentoring Program.

We may need to remind ourselves that learning and human spiritual growth happen outside of academics—and that student life and campus ministry professionals, among others, can play an important role in this growth. For an example of the possibilities, see David Nantais, "Houses of Formation: The Role of Residence Life in Promoting the Ideals of Jesuit Education," *Conversations on Jesuit Higher Education* (Fall 2001), 23–30.

Developing a sense of community among faculty, staff, and administrators is another area of growth and development for the university. I can attest to the advantage of taking small groups away from home and the workplace. People experience a sense of freedom from the ordinary pressures of life and work, and in an atmosphere of respect and appreciation they can talk about and listen to what really matters in their lives and work. Joseph Appleyard, SJ, of Boston College, has given theoretical foundation and practical, how-to details for this in his essay "The Languages We Use: Talking about Religious Experience," *Studies in the Spirituality of Jesuits* (March 1987). As a case in point, Boston College's Cohasset Weekends and Xavier's Grailville Weekends—which we adapted from Cohasset—have helped create on our campuses an atmosphere of friendship, care, and appreciation rather than the usual one of competition and criticism. They have also legitimated and promoted, in a way we never expected, "mission" talk on campus.

Epilogue

Introduction

As a parting challenge, I offer a recent essay by Timothy Hanchin of Boston College High School: "Messianic or Bourgeois? Communicating the Jesuit Mission." "Bourgeois" religion waters down or even eliminates the prophetic and countercultural edge of the genuine gospel— which theologian J. B. Metz terms "Messianic" religion. "Because of its humanist origins," writes Hanchin, "Jesuit education must vigilantly guard against the misuse of its language. . . . '[F]inding God in all things' [for instance], communicated apart from Ignatius's intense asceticism and the period of prayer during the Spiritual Exercises that is devoted to considering the suffering of Christ, can end up baptizing every human endeavor at the expense of self-critical awareness." The original context for Hanchin's essay was Jesuit secondary education. I believe, however, that his challenge is just as applicable to higher education. (I have edited the essay slightly to facilitate such an application.)

Messianic or Bourgeois? Communicating the Jesuit Mission

Timothy Hanchin

From *America*, 2006

Following a junior varsity lacrosse game one slushy spring afternoon in suburban Boston, I overheard a player ask another, "Can you be an MFO and take the water jug back to the bus for me, so I can catch a ride with my dad?" I wondered, "What is an MFO?" As a teacher in a Jesuit high school, I take modest pride in my ability to decode teen vernacular. But I was stupefied. I inquired and learned that MFO is shorthand for "man for others." Oh no, I thought, what have we done?

Those familiar with Jesuit education know the shared language often employed to describe its animating mission and distinct identity. The "Grad at Grad" ("Graduate at Graduation") urges our graduates to be intellectually competent, open to growth, religious, loving, and committed to doing justice. Catchphrases like *magis* ("the more"), *cura personalis* ("care for the person"), "finding God in all things," and "women and men for others" help make accessible the Jesuit tradition. Undoubtedly, this language galvanizes students and faculty to embody this identity and illuminate its mission to the world. It looks sharp on a Web site and tugs at the heartstrings of anxious and caring parents. . . .

But its ready-made, packaged presentation can also undermine its prophetic character. When this common language is invoked apart from its context within the life story of Ignatius Loyola, a great miseducation can occur. In that case, the countercultural character of our Ignatian education is supplanted by an affirmation of the status quo plus academic excellence, and a Jesuit . . . school becomes indistinguishable from other elite . . . schools. Our unique language becomes a marketing device for glossy admission pamphlets that contribute to the name-branding of Jesuit . . . education.

The catechetical task of communicating the memory of St. Ignatius to students is a dangerous one. It is dangerous because the marketability and accessibility of Ignatian-speak makes it vulnerable to an uncritical appropriation that baptizes the privileges of an American middle-class lifestyle. Yet the catechetical task is dangerous in a positive way as well. When the language communicates the Jesuit identity of the school through the narrative of St. Ignatius, it teaches students to see the world in a radically new way. In this way, Jesuit education fulfills its fundamental mission of teaching students to discern by seeing with new eyes.

Metz's Notion of the Bourgeois and Messianic

Johann Baptist Metz, a prize pupil of Karl Rahner, defines theology as interruption and introduces the categories of "bourgeois" and "messianic" religion. Bourgeois religion endorses the haves, the propertied, those whose seemingly guaranteed future allows them to take life for granted. Metz characterizes bourgeois religion as the adaptation of the gospel to society so that any tensions between discipleship and living in the world, particularly in the first world, are eliminated. In place of a messianic future animated by the virtues of repentance, unconditional love for the "least brethren,"

and compassion, bourgeois religion affirms autonomy, competitive struggle, property, stability, and success. A messianic religion
takes sides, without hatred, by asserting a universality of love that
reflects the partisan stance that Jesus took in privileging those on
the margins of society. In *Faith and the Future* Metz asks, "Is there
not a concept of universal Christian love in 'bourgeois' religion that
is just sloppy, and one that hardly needs any longer to prove itself as
love of enemies because the feeble and unpartisan way it bridges all
the agonizing contradictions means that it has no opponents left at
all?" Jesus was not nailed to a cross because he equated loving the
world with getting along with everyone or being nice. Jesus interrupted the world by challenging people to see the world in a new
way. Most profoundly, God interrupts the imagination of the world
by revealing God's self most completely in the stripped, insulted,
beaten-down, and spat-upon Christ.

Metz's theology of interruption resonates with the life story of
Ignatius Loyola. Ignatius's unceasing desire to "help souls" resulted
in continuing conversations with others about their relationship
with God, and these conversations often disrupted the expectations of his contemporaries. Ignatius's commitment to making faith
a public matter inevitably created adversaries. Of course suspicion
was heightened during the Spanish Inquisition, when an unschooled
drifter dressed in sackcloth while engaging others in spiritual conversations would be certain to raise an eyebrow. At Alcalá he was
arrested in connection with the disappearance of two noblewomen.
It was later learned that they had merely responded to his conversations by traveling and serving the poor in one hospital and then
another. Ignatius was released from prison on the condition that he
refrain from speaking publicly about faith until he had studied for
four more years. At the University of Salamanca he found himself
in prison following a dinner conversation with the local Dominican
friars. While his judges found no error in his message, he was
ordered once again to stop talking to people about God until he
completed further studies. Since Ignatius could not agree to these
restrictions, he took his studies to the University of Paris. The

resulting history of the Society of Jesus is characterized by an inextinguishable desire to continue these conversations in the farthest corners of the globe.

Ignatius inextricably linked love of God with love of neighbor. This is expressed in the common Jesuit expression "contemplative in action." When Ignatius lays down his arms before a statue of Our Lady in the Benedictine abbey at Montserrat, he exchanges his fine Spanish attire for the uniform of a beggar. During a visit home to Azpeitia, he refused to enjoy the comforts of his family's estate, and he slept with the poor, the orphaned, and the sick. During the famine winter of 1538 in Rome, Ignatius and his companions transformed their poor apartments into makeshift shelters. When begging was banned in Rome, Ignatius obtained a decree from the pope to alleviate the effects of the prohibition and founded the Society of Orphans. While other institutions were offering aid to prostitutes, with the stipulation that they spend the rest of their lives as religious penitents, Ignatius established the House of St. Martha, which offered hospitality without condition. Ignatius's devotion to Christ necessarily resulted in imaginative transformation of the world.

Jerome Nadal, a close associate of Ignatius, remarked that "the world is our home." In his book *Ignatian Humanism*, Ronald Madras identifies the unity and universality of truth as a defining characteristic of the Renaissance origins of Ignatian humanism. "Finding God in all things" is manifest in Matteo Ricci's recognition of natural law in Confucius, Pierre Teilhard de Chardin's embrace of Darwinism as pointing to all matter as having a heart, and Karl Rahner's ability to see Martin Heidegger as a conversation partner. Yet with this humanistic openness comes the danger of understanding "God in all things" as baptizing every human endeavor. The Ignatian worldview, because of its daring optimism, is naturally more susceptible to bourgeois hijacking. But Ignatian spirituality, when faithful to its origins in the life experience of Ignatius, makes visible suffering in the world and resists the temptation to avoid the fundamental contradictions that produce suffering. This is the punch behind the question posed by Pedro Arrupe, the former superior general of the Jesuits, "Have we educated you for justice?"

Watered-Down Language

Because of its humanist origins, Jesuit education must vigilantly guard against the misuse of its language. For example *magis* is rightly understood as the fruit of a discernment of spirits in search of that which "more" brings about union with God. Instead, it often becomes, at best, an unreflective motivation affirming that the more school activities I am involved in, the more I am of value to it. At worst, it means the busier I am, the more I find value in myself. After teaching at two Jesuit . . . schools, I can attest that the latter two translations are a real temptation among students and faculty alike. In this case, *magis* becomes a principle of bourgeois religion as it dangerously stamps an Ignatian seal of approval on a culture that equates constant busyness, mass productivity, and maximum efficiency with worth. Similarly, finding God in all things, communicated apart from Ignatius's intense asceticism and the period of prayer during the Spiritual Exercises that is devoted to considering the suffering of Christ, can end up baptizing every human endeavor at the expense of a self-critical awareness. In this way it risks becoming an Ignatian form of American exceptionalism. And to be "women and men for others" means much more than performing random acts of kindness or simply being nice. Pedro Arrupe articulated an education for justice that moves its graduates to confront unjust structures that produce poverty with imaginative transformation. Similar to what Metz calls class treason, this stance against the world in service of love for the world carries a great cost. The memory of the martyred Jesuits of the University of Central America in San Salvador [1989] keeps us mindful of the danger inherent in his discipleship.

Obvious questions of cognitive and moral development arise when applying the interruptive nature of Ignatian education to . . . students. Yet unless we connect the catchphrases used to communicate our Jesuit mission and identity with the story of Ignatius, our students may miss the imaginatively prophetic dimension of our spirituality. I believe that graduating seniors are capable of understanding that *magis* is not the same as overloading . . . resumes with activities and that being "women and men for others" means more than opening the door for a fellow student or carrying a bottle of water back to the bus for a teammate. Certainly this will not happen unless students and faculty are conversant with the narrative of Ignatius and the seminal . . . documents that further articulate this language. As the number of Jesuits at Jesuit schools continues to dwindle, the need for such formation becomes ever more pressing. I wonder how many graduating seniors from Jesuit . . . schools, or faculty members for that matter, have really understood the demanding rhetoric of Pedro Arrupe's landmark address, "Men for Others."

As Ignatian educators, we need to communicate both to our students and to the world. Our schools should look and be different from [other educational] institutions. Jesuit education must ultimately "interrupt" its students' worldviews so that they can begin to see the world as it is. Seeing the world with new eyes is at the heart of the Spiritual Exercises of St. Ignatius. It defines that most profound mystical experience of Ignatius at the Cardoner River early in his conversion. Jesuit education must do more than produce "nice" philanthropists. Herein lies the difference between a messianic and a bourgeois education.

Further Reading

As a summary and repetition of themes we have considered in *A Jesuit Education Reader*, you may want to consult Boston College's *Pocket Guide to Jesuit Education*. Here, in six short pages, is a chance to touch again "Ignatius the Pilgrim"; the founding of the Jesuits; how the Jesuits got involved in schools and why they were successful; a slightly different version of the paradigm for education/formation in the Jesuit spirit: "Be attentive, Be reflective, Be loving"; the crucial habit of discernment and its daily practice through the Examen of Consciousness; and the U.S. and worldwide character of Jesuit education, always open to adaptation and to drawing in people from a great variety of backgrounds and cultures. (For a copy of the guide, contact the Office of the Vice President for University Mission and Ministry, Boston College, Chestnut Hill, MA 02467-3802.)

A good number of resources are available on AJCU (Association of Jesuit Colleges and Universities) school Web sites. For example:

Boston College, Office of University Mission and Ministry: http://www.bc.edu/mission/exploring

Creighton University, Omaha, Collaborative Ministry Office: http://www.creighton.edu/CollaborativeMinistry/online.html

Loyola Marymount University, Los Angeles, Center for Ignatian Spirituality: http://www.lmu.edu/Page838.aspx

Loyola University Chicago, Office of Mission and Ministry: http://www.luc.edu/missionandministry

St. Louis University, "Jesuit Mission" (includes *Shared Vision* videos):
http://www.slu.edu/x844.xml

Xavier University (at the service of all U.S. Jesuit educational institutions):
http://www.jesuitresource.org

Appendices

Do You Speak Ignatian?
A Glossary of Terms Used in
Ignatian and Jesuit Circles

George W. Traub, SJ

Reprinted with permission from the 10th edition, published by Xavier University's Ignatian Programs (http://www.jesuit resource.org/ignatian-resources/do-you-speak-ignatian.cfm). Copyright © 2008, George W. Traub, SJ.

A.M.D.G.—*Ad Majorem Dei Gloriam* (Latin)—"For the greater glory of God." Motto of the Society of Jesus. [See MAGIS.]

Apostle/apostolate/apostolic—Apostle is the role given to the inner circle of twelve whom Jesus "sent out" (on mission) and to a few others like Saint Paul. Hence apostolate means a "mission endeavor or activity" and apostolic means "mission-like."

Arrupe, Pedro (1907–1991)—As superior general of the Society of Jesus for nearly twenty years, he was the central figure in the renewal of the Society after Vatican Council II, paying attention both to the spirit of Ignatius the founder and to the signs of our times. From the Basque country of northern Spain, he left medical school to join the Jesuits, was expelled from Spain in 1932 with all the other Jesuits, studied theology in Holland, and received further training in spirituality and psychology in the U.S. Arrupe spent twenty-seven years in Japan (where among many other things he cared for victims of the atomic bomb in Hiroshima) until his election in 1965 as superior general. He is considered the founder of the modern, post-Vatican II Society of Jesus.

Cura personalis (Latin meaning "care for the [individual] person")— A hallmark of IGNATIAN SPIRITUALITY (where in one-on-one spiritual guidance, the guide adapts the SPIRITUAL EXERCISES to the unique individual making them) and therefore of Jesuit education (where the teacher establishes a personal relationship with students, listens to them in the process of teaching, and draws them toward personal initiative and responsibility for learning [see "Pedagogy, Ignatian/Jesuit"]).

This attitude of respect for the dignity of each individual derives from the JUDAEO-CHRISTIAN VISION of human beings as unique creations of God, of God's embracing of humanity in the person of JESUS, and of human destiny as ultimate communion with God and all the saints in everlasting life.

Discernment (also "Discernment of spirits")—A process for making choices, in a context of (Christian) faith, when the option is not between good and evil, but between several possible courses of action all of which are potentially good. For IGNATIUS the process involves prayer, reflection, and consultation with others—all with honest attention not only to the rational (reasons pro and con) but also to the realm of one's feelings, emotions, and desires (what Ignatius called "movements" of soul). A fundamental question in discernment becomes "Where is this impulse from—the good spirit (of God) or the evil spirit (leading one away from God)?" A key to answering this question, says Ignatius in his SPIRITUAL EXERCISES, is that, in the case of a person leading a basically good life, the good spirit gives "consolation"—acts quietly, gently, and leads one to peace, joy, and deeds of loving service—while the bad spirit brings "desolation"—agitates, disturbs the peace, and injects fears and discouragement to keep one from doing good.

Education, Jesuit—IGNATIUS OF LOYOLA and his first companions, who founded the SOCIETY OF JESUS in 1540, did not originally intend to establish schools. But before long they were led to start colleges for the education of the young men who flocked to join their RELIGIOUS ORDER. And in 1547 Ignatius was asked to open a school for young LAY men.

By the time of his death (1556), there were thirty-five such colleges (comprising today's secondary school and the first year or two of college). By the time the order was suppressed in 1773, the number had grown to more than 800—all part of a system of integrated humanistic education that was international and brought together in a common enterprise men from various languages and cultures. These JESUITS were distinguished mathematicians, astronomers, and physicists; linguists and dramatists; painters and architects; philosophers and theologians; even what today would be called cultural anthropologists.

These developments are not surprising; the order's founders were all University of Paris graduates, and Ignatius's SPIRITUALITY taught Jesuits to search for God "in all things." After the order was restored (1814), however, Jesuit schools and scholars in Europe never regained the prominence they had had. Besides, they were largely involved in the resistance to modern thought and culture that characterized Catholic intellectual life through the nineteenth century and beyond.

In other parts of the world, especially in the United States, the nineteenth century saw a new birth of Jesuit education. Twenty-one of today's twenty-eight U.S. Jesuit colleges and universities were founded during that century. These schools served the needs of an immigrant people, enabling them to move up in the world while maintaining their Catholic belief and practice in a frequently hostile Protestant environment.

After World War II, U.S. Jesuit higher education (as American higher education generally) experienced enormous growth and democratization under the G.I. Bill. Significantly, this growth entailed a shift from a largely Jesuit faculty to one made up increasingly of lay men (and more recently women). Further, VATICAN COUNCIL II (1962–1965) released a great burst of energy in the

Catholic church and Jesuit order for engagement with the modern world, including its intellectual life. Finally, Jesuit schools in the 1970s and 1980s moved to professionalize through the hiring of new faculty with highly specialized training and terminal degrees from the best graduate schools.

These sweeping changes of the last fifty years have brought U.S. Jesuit schools to the present situation where they face crucial questions. Will so-called Jesuit institutions of higher education simply merge with mainstream American academe and thereby lose any distinctiveness and reason for existing—or will they have the creativity to become more distinctive? While taking the best from American education and culture, will they still offer an alternative in the spirit of their Jesuit heritage? Will they foster the integration of knowledge—or will specialization reign alone and the fragmentation of knowledge continue? Will they relate learning to the Transcendent, to God—or will SPIRITUAL experience be allowed to disappear from consideration except in isolated departments of theology? While developing the mind, surely, will they also develop a global, cross-cultural imagination and a compassionate heart to recognize and work for the common good, especially for bettering the lot of the poor and voiceless [see MEN AND WOMEN FOR OTHERS/ WHOLE PERSONS OF SOLIDARITY and THE SERVICE OF FAITH AND THE PROMOTION OF JUSTICE]—or will the dominant values present in them be self-interest and the "bottom line"?

Faber, Peter (1506–1546)—Latin and English version of Pierre Favre, University of Paris student from the south of France who roomed with IGNATIUS OF LOYOLA and FRANCIS XAVIER and together with them and several others founded the SOCIETY OF JESUS. In the course of seven years, he traveled some 7,000 miles and served in seven different western European countries. The largest part of his ministry was in Germany. There he drew up guidelines for ecumenical dialogue with Lutherans, but these were, sad to say, hardly put into practice. Among the early companions, he was known to be the finest guide for those making the SPIRITUAL EXERCISES.

Finding God in All Things—IGNATIAN SPIRITUALITY is summed up in this phrase. It invites a person to search for and find God in every circumstance of life, not just in explicitly religious situations or activities such as prayer in church (e.g., the Mass) or in private. It implies that God is present everywhere and, though invisible, can be "found" in any and all of the creatures which God has made. They reveal at least a little of what their Maker is like—often by arousing wonder in those who are able to look with the "eyes of faith." After a long day of work, IGNATIUS used to open the French windows in his room, step out onto a little balcony, look up at the stars, and be carried out of himself into the greatness of God.

How does one grow in this ability to find God everywhere? Howard Gray draws the following paradigm from what IGNATIUS wrote about spiritual development in the JESUIT *Constitutions*: (1) **practice attentiveness** to what is really there. "Let that person or that poem or that social injustice or that scientific experiment become (for you) as genuinely itself as it can be." (2) Then **reverence** what you see and hear and feel; appreciate it in its uniqueness. "Before you judge or assess or respond, give yourself time to esteem and accept what is there in the other." (3) If you learn to be attentive and reverent, "then you will **find devotion**, the singularly moving way in which God works in that situation, revealing goodness and fragility, beauty and truth, pain and anguish, wisdom and ingenuity."

God—Various titles or names are given to the Mystery underlying all that exists—e.g., the Divine, Supreme Being, the Absolute, the Transcendent, the All-Holy—but all of these are only "pointers" to a Reality beyond human naming and beyond our limited human comprehension. Still, some conceptions are taken to be less inadequate than others within a given tradition founded in revelation. Thus, Jews reverence "the Lord" (the name of God, *YHWH*, is holy and its vocalization unknown); and Muslims worship "Allah" (the [only] God).

Christians conceive of the one God as "Trinity," as having three "ways of being"—(1) Creator and covenant partner (from Hebrew tradition) or "Father" (the "Abba" of Jesus' experience), (2) incarnate (enfleshed) in JESUS—the "Son," and (3) present everywhere in the world through the "Spirit." IGNATIUS OF LOYOLA had a strong Trinitarian sense of God, but he was especially fond of the expression "the Divine Majesty" stressing the greatness or "godness" of God; and the twentieth-century Jesuit theologian Karl Rahner could talk of "the incomprehensible Mystery of self-giving Love."

The reluctance of some of our contemporaries to use the word God may be seen as a potential corrective to the tendency of some believers to speak of God all too easily, as if they fully understood God and God's ways.

Gospel (literally "good news")—The good news or glad tidings about JESUS.

Plural. The first four works of the Christian scriptures (Matthew, Mark, Luke, and John) that tell the story of JESUS—each with its own particular theological emphasis—and thus invite a response of faith and hope in him.

Ignatian—Adjective, from the noun IGNATIUS (OF LOYOLA). Sometimes used in distinction to JESUIT, indicating aspects of SPIRITUALITY that derive from Ignatius the LAY PERSON rather than from the later Ignatius and his RELIGIOUS ORDER, the SOCIETY OF JESUS.

Ignatian/Jesuit Vision, Characteristics of the—Drawing on a variety of contemporary sources which tend to confirm one another, one can construct a list of rather commonly accepted characteristics of the Ignatian/Jesuit vision. It . . .

- sees life and the whole universe as a gift calling forth wonder and gratefulness;
- gives ample scope to imagination and emotion as well as intellect;
- seeks to find the divine in all things—in all peoples and cultures, in all areas of study and learning, in every human experience, and (for the Christian) especially in the person of JESUS;
- cultivates critical awareness of personal and social evil, but points to God's love as more powerful than any evil;
- stresses freedom, need for DISCERNMENT, and responsible action;
- empowers people to become leaders in service, MEN AND WOMEN FOR OTHERS, WHOLE PERSONS OF SOLIDARITY, building a more just and humane world.

The relative consensus about these six characteristics should not be taken to indicate that they exhaust the meaning of the living IGNATIAN tradition. Like the living tradition of Christian faith, of which it is a part, no number of thematic statements can adequately articulate it. At the heart of both traditions stands the living person of JESUS, who cannot be reduced to a series of ideas.

No one claims that any of these characteristics are uniquely Ignatian/Jesuit. It is rather the combination of them all and the way they fit together that make the vision distinctive and so appropriate for an age in transition—whether from the medieval to the modern in Ignatius's time, or from the modern to the postmodern in ours.

Ignatius of Loyola (1491–1556)—Youngest child of a noble Basque family fiercely loyal to the Spanish crown (Ferdinand and Isabella), he was named Inigo after a local saint. Raised to be a courtier, he was trying valiantly to defend the fortress town of Pamplona in 1521 when a French cannonball shattered his leg. During a long convalescence, he found himself drawn away from the romances of chivalry that had filled his imagination from an early age to more spiritual reading—an illustrated life of JESUS and a collection of saints' lives.

After his recovery, he set out for the Holy Land to realize a dream of "converting the infidel." On the way he stopped in the little town of MANRESA and wound up spending nearly a year there during which he experienced both the depths of despair and great times of enlightenment.

Ordered to leave Palestine after being there little more than a month, Ignatius decided that he needed an education in order to be able to "help souls." In Barcelona, he went to school with boys a quarter his age to learn the rudiments of Latin grammar, then moved on to several Spanish university cities. In each he was imprisoned and interrogated by the Inquisition, because he kept speaking to people about "SPIRITUAL things," having neither a theology degree nor priestly ordination.

Finally, turning his back on his homeland, he went to the foremost university of the time, the University of Paris, where he began his education all over again and with diligence, after five years, was finally awarded the degree "Master of Arts." It was here at Paris that he changed his Basque name to the Latin *Ignatius* and its Spanish equivalent *Ignacio*.

While at the university, he had roomed with and become good friends with a fellow Basque named FRANCIS XAVIER and a Savoyard named PETER FABER. After graduation, these three, together with several other Paris graduates, undertook a process of communal DISCERNMENT and decided to bind themselves together in an APOSTOLIC community that became the SOCIETY OF JESUS. Unanimously elected superior by his companions, Ignatius spent the last sixteen years of his life in Rome directing the fledgling order, while the others went all over Europe, to the Far East, and eventually to the New World. And wherever they went they founded schools as a means of helping people to "FIND GOD IN ALL THINGS."

IHS—The first three letters, in Greek, of the name JESUS. These letters appear as a symbol on the official seal of the SOCIETY OF JESUS or JESUITS.

Inculturation—A modern theological concept that expresses a principle of Christian mission implicit in IGNATIAN SPIRITUALITY— namely, that the GOSPEL needs to be presented to any given culture in terms intelligible to that culture and allowed to grow up in the "soil" of that culture; God is already present and active there ("God's action is antecedent to ours"—Jesuit General Congregation 34 [1995], "Our Mission and Culture").

Thus in the first century Saint Paul fought against the imposition of Jewish practices on non-Jewish Christians. And in the sixteenth and seventeenth centuries, Jesuits like Matteo Ricci (1552–1610) and Roberto de Nobili (1577–1656) fought to retain elements of Chinese and Indian culture in presenting a de-Europeanized Christianity to those peoples, only to have their approach condemned by the Church in the eighteenth.

Ideally, the GOSPEL and a culture mutually interact, and in the process the gospel embraces some elements of the culture while offering a critique of others.

Jesuit—Noun. A member of the SOCIETY OF JESUS. The term was originally coined as a putdown by people who felt there was something terribly arrogant about a group calling itself the Company or SOCIETY OF JESUS, whereas previous RELIGIOUS ORDERS had been content to name themselves after their founder (e.g., "Benedictines," "Franciscans," "Dominicans"). Later the title was adopted as a short-hand name by members of the Society themselves, as well as by others favorable to them.

Adjective. Pertaining to the SOCIETY OF JESUS. The negative term, now that *Jesuit* has been rehabilitated, is *Jesuitical* meaning "sly" or "devious."

Jesus (also "Jesus [the] Christ," meaning Jesus "[God's] anointed one")—The historical person Jesus of Nazareth whom Christians acknowledge to be, by his life (what he taught and did) and his death and resurrection, the true revelation of God and at the same time the exemplar of what it means to be fully human. In other words, for Christians, Jesus shows what God is like and how they can live in response to this revelation: God is the compassionate giver of life who invites and empowers human beings, in freedom, together with one another, to work toward overcoming the forces of evil—meaninglessness, guilt, oppression, suffering, and death—that diminish people and keep them from growing toward ever fuller life.

In his SPIRITUAL EXERCISES, IGNATIUS has the retreatant devote most of the time to "contemplating" (i.e., imaginatively entering into) the life, death, and resurrection of Jesus, so as to become more and more a companion of Jesus. And when Ignatius and his companions from the University of Paris decided to establish a RELIGIOUS ORDER, he insisted that it be called the Company or SOCIETY OF JESUS [see JESUIT—Noun].

Judaeo-Christian Vision or Story, The—Here is a version of the Judaeo-Christian vision or story, told with certain emphases from IGNATIUS OF LOYOLA.

The great and mysterious Reality of personal love and self-giving that many call God is the origin and destiny of all creation, the whole universe. God is present and at work in everything, leading it to ful-filment. All things are originally good and potentially means for those creatures called human beings to find the God who made and works in them. Still, none of these things are God, and therefore they are all radically limited.

Indeed, in the case of human beings (who somehow image God in a special way), their relative freedom results in a new dimension of being whereby not just good but also evil exists in the world: selfishness, war, domination—racial, sexual, economic, environmental—of some over others. Human history, then, is marked by a struggle between the forces of good, or "life," and evil, or "death."

God has freely chosen to side with struggling, flawed humanity by participating more definitively in human life and living it "from the inside" in the historical person of JESUS of Nazareth. This irrevocable commitment of God to the human enterprise grounds and invites people's response of working with God toward building a community of justice, love, and peace—the "kingdom" or "reign" of God that Jesus preached and lived.

As with Jesus, so for his followers, it takes DISCERNMENT—a finely tuned reading of oneself and one's culture in the Spirit of God—to recognize in any given situation what helps the coming of God's reign and what hinders it. In the face of human selfishness and evil, the way ultimately entails self-giving, going through suffering and death in order to gain life—indeed, life everlasting. And along the way, because the followers of Jesus are wary of idolizing anyone or anything (that is, making a god of them), they are less likely to become disillusioned with themselves or others or human history for all its weight of personal and social evil. Rather do they continue to care about people and the human enterprise, for their hope is in God, the supreme Reality of personal love and self-giving.

Kolvenbach, Peter-Hans (1928–)—Dutch-born superior general of the SOCIETY OF JESUS from 1983, when the JESUITS were allowed to return to their own governance after a time of papal "intervention," until 2008, when he resigned at the age of eighty.

He entered the Jesuits in 1948, went to Lebanon in the mid-1950s, earned a doctorate from the famous Saint Joseph's University in Beirut, and spent much of his life there, first as a professor of linguistics and then as superior of the JESUIT vice-province of the Middle East.

By his own admission, he was relatively "ignorant of matters pertaining to justice and injustice," when he went from Beirut to Rome for Jesuit General Congregation 32 and witnessed the faith-justice emphasis emerge from the Congregation under the leadership of PEDRO ARRUPE [see THE SERVICE FAITH AND THE PROMOTION OF JUSTICE]. Still, as superior general, he worked tirelessly in collaboration with his advisors to implement and extend the direction in which his predecessor had been leading the Society [see MEN AND WOMEN FOR OTHERS/WHOLE PERSONS OF SOLIDARITY FOR THE REAL WORLD].

Laity (lay person/lay people)—The people of a religious faith as distinguished from its clergy; within Catholic circles, however, members of religious communities who are not ordained (i.e. "sisters" and "brothers") are often popularly associated with priests and bishops and not with lay people. (It would be more accurate to see them as neither, as having their own unique role and style of life; see RELIGIOUS ORDER/RELIGIOUS LIFE.)

Magis (Latin for "more")—The "Continuous Quality Improvement" term traditionally used by IGNATIUS OF LOYOLA and the JESUITS, suggesting the spirit of generous excellence in which ministry should be carried on. (See A.M.D.G.—AD MAJOREM DEI GLORIAM)

Manresa—Town in northeastern Spain where in 1522–1523 a middle-aged layman named IGNATIUS OF LOYOLA had the powerful spiritual experiences that led to his famous SPIRITUAL EXERCISES and later guided the founding and the PEDAGOGY of JESUIT schools.

Men and Women for Others/Whole Persons of Solidarity for the Real World—In a now famous address to alumni of JESUIT schools in Europe (July 31, 1973), PEDRO ARRUPE painted a profile of what a graduate should be. Admitting that JESUIT schools had not always been on target here, Arrupe called for a re-education to justice:

> Today our prime educational objective must be to form men-and-women-for-others . . . people who cannot even conceive of love of God which does not include love for the least of their neighbors; people

convinced that love of God which does not issue in justice for human beings is a farce. . . . All of us would like to be good to others, and most of us would be relatively good in a good world. What is difficult is to be good in an evil world, where the egoism of others and the egoism built into the institutions of society attack us. . . . Evil is overcome only by good, egoism by generosity. It is thus that we must sow justice in our world, substituting love for self-interest as the driving force of society.

Following up on what Arrupe had said, the current Jesuit head, PETER-HANS KOLVENBACH, challenged the 900 JESUIT and LAY delegates from the 28 U.S. Jesuit colleges and universities gathered for "Assembly '89" to teach our students to make "no significant decision without first thinking of how it would impact the least in society" (i.e., the poor, the marginal who have no voice). And eleven years later, speaking on "the faith that does justice" to a similar national gathering at Santa Clara University (October 6, 2000), Kolvenbach was even more pointed and eloquent in laying out the goals for the twenty-first-century American Jesuit university:

Here in Silicon Valley, some of the world's premier research universities flourish alongside struggling public schools where Afro-American and immigrant students drop out in droves. Nationwide, one child in every six is condemned to ignorance and poverty. . . . Thanks to science and technology, human society is able to solve problems such as feeding the hungry, sheltering the homeless, or developing more just conditions of life, but stubbornly fails to accomplish this.

The real measure of our Jesuit universities, [then,] lies in who our students become. Tomorrow's "whole person" cannot be whole without a *well-educated solidarity*. We must therefore raise our Jesuit educational standard to "educate the whole person of solidarity for the real world."

Solidarity is learned through "contact" rather than through "concepts." When the heart is touched by direct experience, the mind may be challenged to change. Our universities boast a splendid variety of in-service programs, outreach programs, insertion programs, off-campus contacts, and hands-on courses. These should not be too optional or peripheral, but at the core of every Jesuit university's program of studies.

Faculty are at the heart of our universities. Professors, in spite of the cliché of the ivory tower, are in contact with the world. But no point of view is ever neutral or value-free. A legitimate question, even if it does not sound academic, is for each professor to ask, "When researching and teaching, where and with whom is my heart?" To make sure that the real concerns of the poor find their place, faculty members need an organic collaboration with those in the Church and in society who work among and for the poor and actively seek justice.

What is at stake is a sustained interdisciplinary dialogue of research and reflection, a continuous pooling of expertise. The purpose is to assimilate experiences and insights in "a vision of knowledge which, well aware of its limitations, is not satisfied with fragments but tries to integrate them into a true and wise synthesis" about the real world. Unfortunately, many faculty still feel academically, humanly, and, I would say, spiritually unprepared for such an exchange.

If the measure of our universities is who the students become, and if the faculty are the heart of it all, then what is there left to say? It is perhaps the third topic, the character of our universities—how they proceed internally and how they impact on society—that is the most difficult.

In the words of [Jesuit] General Congregation 34, a Jesuit university must be faithful to both the noun "university" and to the adjective "Jesuit." To be a university requires dedication "to research, teaching, and the various forms of service that correspond to its cultural mission." To be Jesuit "requires that the university act in harmony with the demands of the service of faith and the promotion of justice."

[A] telling expression of the Jesuit university's nature is found in policies concerning hiring and tenure. As a university it must respect the established academic, professional, and labor norms, but as Jesuit it is essential to go beyond them and find ways of attracting, hiring, and promoting those who actively share the mission.

Every Jesuit academy of higher learning is called to live *in* a social reality and to live *for* that social reality, to shed university intelligence upon it and to use university influence to transform it. Thus Jesuit universities have stronger and different reasons than do many other academic institutions for addressing the actual world as it unjustly exists and for helping to reshape it in the light of the Gospel.

Order—see Religious Order/Religious Life.

Pedagogy, Ignatian/Jesuit—Having to do with Ignatian/Jesuit teaching style or methods.

In one formulation (Robert Newton's *Reflections on the Educational Principles of the Spiritual Exercises* [1977]), **Jesuit education is instrumental** (not an end in itself, but a means to the service of God and others); **student centered** (adapted to the individual as much as possible so as to develop an independent and responsible learner); **characterized by structure** (with systematic organization of successive objectives and systematic procedures for evaluation and accountability) **and flexibility** (freedom encouraged and personal response and self-direction expected, with the teacher an experienced guide, not primarily a deliverer of ready-made knowledge); **eclectic** (drawing on a variety of the best methods and techniques available); and **personal** (whole person affected, with goal of personal appropriation, attitudinal and behavioral change).

In another formulation (*Ignatian Pedagogy: A Practical Approach* from the International Center for Jesuit Education [Rome, 1993]), Ignatian pedagogy is a model that seeks to develop men and women of competence, conscience, and compassion. Similar to the process of guiding others in the Spiritual Exercises, faculty accompany students in their intellectual, spiritual, and emotional development. They do this by following the Ignatian pedagogical paradigm. Through consideration of the **context** of students' lives, faculty create an environment where students recollect their past **experience** and assimilate information from newly-provided **experiences**. Faculty help students learn the skills and techniques of **reflection**, which shapes their consciousness, and they then challenge students to **action** in service to others. The **evaluation** process includes academic mastery as well as ongoing assessments of students' well-rounded growth as persons for others.

Both these approaches were developed in the context of secondary education, but could be adapted for higher education. [See also EDUCATION, JESUIT and RATIO STUDIORUM.]

Ratio Studiorum **(Latin for "Plan of Studies")**—A document, the definitive form of which was published in 1599 after several earlier drafts and extensive consultation among Jesuits working in schools. It was a handbook of practical directives for teachers and administrators, a collection of the most effective educational methods of the time, tested and adapted to fit the Jesuit mission of education. Since it was addressed to Jesuits, the principles behind its directives could be assumed. They came, of course, from the vision and spirit of IGNATIUS. The process that led to the *Ratio* and continued after its publication gave birth to the first real system of schools the world had ever known.

Much of what the 1599 *Ratio* contained would not be relevant to Jesuit schools today. Still, the process out of which it grew and thrived suggests that we have only just begun to tap the possibilities within the international Jesuit network for collaboration and interchange. [See also EDUCATION, JESUIT and PEDAGOGY, IGNATIAN/JESUIT.]

Religious Order/Religious Life—In Eastern Orthodox and Roman Catholic Christianity (less frequently in Anglican/Episcopal Christianity), a community of men or women bound together by the common profession, through "religious" vows, of "chastity" (better called voluntary "consecrated celibacy" [and thus not to be confused with the imposed celibacy of Roman Catholic clergy]), "poverty," and "obedience." As a way of trying to follow JESUS' example, the vows involve voluntary renunciation of things potentially good: marriage and sexual relations in the case of "consecrated celibacy," personal ownership and possessions in the case of "poverty," and one's own will and plans in the case of "obedience."

This renunciation is made, not for its own sake, but "for the sake of [God's] kingdom" (Matthew 19:12), as a prophetic witness against a culture's abuse of sex, wealth (greed), and power (domination) and toward a more available and universal love beyond family ties, personal possessions, and self-determination. As a concrete form of Christian faith and life, it emphasizes the relativity of all the goods of this earth in the face of the only absolute, God, and a life lived definitively with God beyond this world.

This way of life first appeared in the second half of the first century in the person of "virgins" (mostly women but also some men) who lived at home and, by refusing to marry and produce offspring (they claimed to be "spouses of Christ"), countered the absolutist claims of the state (Rome) and hence many of them became martyrs. After Constantine's conversion to Christianity (313) and Christianity's establishment as the state religion, "religious life" developed further as a major movement away from the "world" and the worldliness of the church. The monastic life of monks and nuns is a variation on this tradition. At the beginning of the modern Western world, various new religious orders sprang up (the largest being the JESUITS) that saw themselves not as fleeing from the world but APOSTLES sent out into the world in service. In more recent centuries, many communities of religious women were founded with a similar goal of APOSTOLIC service, often with Jesuit-inspired constitutions.

The Service of Faith and the Promotion of Justice—In 1975, Jesuits from around the world met in solemn assembly to assess their present state and to sketch plans for the future. Following the lead of a recent international assembly ("synod") of Catholic bishops, they came to see that the hallmark of any ministry deserving of the name Jesuit would be its "service of faith" of which the "promotion of justice" is an absolute requirement. In other words, Jesuit education should be noteworthy for the way it helps students—and for that matter, faculty, staff, and administrators—to move, in freedom, toward a mature and intellectually adult faith. This includes enabling them to develop a disciplined sensitivity toward the suffering of our world and a will to act for the transformation of unjust social structures that cause that suffering. The enormous challenge, to which none of us are entirely equal, nevertheless falls on all of us, not just on campus ministry and members of theology and philosophy departments.

The Society of Jesus—Catholic RELIGIOUS ORDER of men founded in 1540 by IGNATIUS OF LOYOLA and a small group of his multinational "friends in the Lord," fellow students from the University of Paris. They saw their mission as one of being available to go anywhere and do anything to "help souls," especially where the need was greatest (e.g., where a certain people or a certain kind of work were neglected).

Today, numbering about 20,000 priests and brothers, they are spread out in almost every country of the world ("more branch offices," said PEDRO ARRUPE, "than Coca-Cola")—declining in numbers markedly in Europe and North America, but growing in India, Africa, Latin America, and the Far East.

The abbreviation "SJ" after a person's name means that he is a member of the Society of Jesus.

Spiritual/spirituality—The spiritual is often defined as that which is "non-material," but this definition runs into problems when applied to human beings, who are traditionally considered "body-spirits," both bodily and spiritual. In some modern philosophies and psychologies, however, the spiritual dimension of the human is denied or disregarded. And many aspects of our contemporary American culture (e.g., the hurried sense of time and need to produce, produce) make it difficult to pay attention to this dimension.

Fundamentally, the spiritual dimension of human beings can be recognized in the orientation of our minds and hearts toward ever more than we have already reached (the never-satisfied human mind and the never-satisfied human heart). We are drawn inevitably toward the "Absolute" or the "Fullness of Being" [see GOD]. Consequently, there are depths to our being that we can only just begin to fathom.

If every human being has this spiritual dimension and hunger, then even in a culture like ours, everyone will have—at least at times— some awareness of it, even if that awareness is not explicit and not put into words. When people talk of a "spirituality," however, they usually mean, not the spirituality that human beings have by nature, but rather a set of attitudes and practices (SPIRITUAL EXERCISES) that are designed to foster a greater consciousness of this spiritual dimension and (in the case of those who can affirm belief in God) a more explicit seeking of its object—the Divine or God.

IGNATIAN spirituality with its SPIRITUAL EXERCISES is one such path among many within Christianity, to say nothing of the spiritualities within other religious traditions, or those more or less outside a religious tradition. ("Peoples' spiritual lives [today] have not died; they are simply taking place outside the church" [Jesuit General Congregation 34, "Our Mission and Culture"].)

spiritual exercises (small *s* and *e*)—Any of a variety of methods or activities for opening oneself to God's spirit and allowing one's whole being, not just the mind, to be affected. The methods—some of them more "active" and others more "passive"—might include vocal prayer (e.g., the Lord's Prayer), meditation or contemplation, journaling or other kind of writing, reading of scripture or other great works of verbal art, drawing, painting or molding with clay, looking at works of visual art, playing or listening to music, working or walking in the midst of nature. All of these activities have the same goal in mind—discontinuing one's usual productive activities and thus allowing God to "speak," listening to what God may be "saying" through the medium employed.

The Spiritual Exercises (capital *S* and *E*)—An organized series of SPIRITUAL EXERCISES put together by IGNATIUS OF LOYOLA out of his own personal spiritual experience and that of others to whom he listened. They invite the "retreatant" or "exercitant" to "meditate" on central aspects of Christian faith (e.g., creation, sin and forgiveness, calling and ministry) and especially to "contemplate" (i.e., imaginatively enter into) the life, death, and resurrection of JESUS.

Ignatius set all of this down in the book of the *Spiritual Exercises* as a handbook to help the guide who coaches a person engaged in "making the Exercises." After listening to that person and getting a sense for where he/she is, the guide selects from material and methods in the book of the *Exercises* and offers them in a way adapted to that unique individual. The goal of all this is the attainment of a kind of spiritual freedom, the power to act—not out of social pressure or personal compulsion and fear—but out of the promptings of God's spirit in the deepest, truest core of one's being—to act ultimately out of love.

As originally designed, the "full" Spiritual Exercises would occupy a person for four weeks full-time, but Ignatius realized that some people could not (today most people cannot) disengage from work and home obligations for that long a time, and so it is possible to make the "full" Exercises part-time over a period of six to nine or ten months—the "Spiritual Exercises in Daily Life." In that case, the "exercitant," without withdrawing from home or work, devotes about an hour a day to prayer (but this, like nearly everything in the Exercises, is adaptable) and sees a guide every week or two to process what has been happening in prayer and in the rest of his/her life.

Most of the time people make not the "full" Spiritual Exercises but a retreat in the Ignatian spirit that might last anywhere from a week-end to a week. Such a retreat usually includes either a daily individual conversation with a guide or several daily presentations to a group, as preparation for prayer/SPIRITUAL EXERCISES.

Ignatius had composed and revised his little book over a period of twenty-five or more years before it was finally published in 1548. Subsequent editions and translations—according to a plausible estimate—numbered some 4,500 in 1948 or about one a month over four centuries, the total number of copies printed being around 4.5 million. It is largely on his Exercises—with their implications for teaching and learning in a holistic way—that Ignatius's reputation as a major figure in the history of Western education rests.

Spiritual Guidance/Direction—People are often helped to integrate their faith and their life by talking on a regular basis (e.g., monthly) with someone they can trust. This person acts as a guide (sometimes also called a spiritual friend, companion, or director) for the journey, helping them to find the presence and call of God in the people and circumstances of their everyday lives.

The assumption is that God is already present there, and that another person, a guide, can help them to notice God's presence and also to find words for talking about that presence, because they are not used to doing so. The guide is often a specially trained listener skilled in DISCERNMENT and therefore able to help them sort out the various voices within and around them. While he/she may suggest various kinds of SPIRITUAL EXERCISES/ways of praying, the focus is much broader than that; it is upon the whole of a person's life experience as the place to meet God.

Vatican Council II (Vatican II for short)—Convoked in 1962 by Pope John XXIII to bring the Catholic Church "up to date," this twenty-first Ecumenical (i.e. worldwide) Council signaled the Catholic Church's growth from a church of cultural confinement (largely European) to a genuine world church. The Council set its seal on the work of twentieth century theologians that earlier had often been officially considered dangerous or erroneous. Thus, the biblical movement, the liturgical renewal and the LAY movement were incorporated into official Catholic doctrine and practice.

Here are several significant new perspectives coming from the Council: celebration of liturgy (worship) in various vernacular languages rather than Latin, to facilitate understanding and LAY participation; viewing the Church as "the whole people of God" rather than just as clergy and viewing other Christian bodies (Protestant, Orthodox) as belonging to it; recognizing non-Christian religions as containing truth; honoring freedom of conscience as a basic human right; and finally including in its mission a reaching out to people in all their human hopes, needs, sufferings as an essential part of preaching the GOSPEL.

Today, Catholics are seriously divided on the question of Vatican II, some ("conservatives") considering it to have failed by giving away essentials of tradition and others ("liberals") feeling it has been too little and too imperfectly realized.

Whole Persons of Solidarity for the Real World—See MEN AND WOMEN FOR OTHERS.

Xavier, Francis (1506–1552)—Native like IGNATIUS of the Basque territory of northern Spain, Francis became a close friend of Ignatius at the University of Paris, came to share Ignatius's vision through making the SPIRITUAL EXERCISES, and realized that vision through missionary labors in India, the Indonesian archipelago, and Japan. He was the first JESUIT to go out to people of non-European culture. And as he moved from his early missionary endeavors in India to his later ones in Japan, it seems that the implications of what we call INCULTURATION started to dawn on him.

Contents of the
Companion Volume,
An Ignatian Spirituality Reader

Because the work of Jesuit education grows out of the unique spirituality that informs all ministries begun by the Jesuits, an understanding and appropriation of the Jesuit mission in education cannot be separated from that of Ignatian spirituality. Thus, I have edited a companion volume, *An Ignatian Spirituality Reader* (Loyola Press, 2008), which explains this spirituality and informs this present *Reader*. Here is the contents of that companion volume:

Ignatian Spirituality

Finding God In All Things

Prayer

The Spiritual Exercises

Acknowledgments

The Principle Underlying Early Jesuit Mission—and the Schools
Jesuit Mission Today
John W. O'Malley, conclusion to *The First Jesuits*. Reprinted by permission
of the publisher from *The First Jesuits* by John W. O'Malley, pp. 372–376
(Cambridge, MA: Harvard University Press). Copyright © 1993 by the
President and Fellows of Harvard College.

Jesuit General Congregation 34, "Our Mission and Culture," from *Documents
of the Thirty-Fourth General Congregation of the Society of Jesus* (St. Louis:
Institute of Jesuit Sources, 1995), pp. 49–65. Copyright © 1995 by the Institute
of Jesuit Sources. Used with permission.

Howard Gray, "The Ignatian Mission," from *In All Things: A Jesuit Journal of the
Social Apostolate* <http://www.inallthings.org> (Summer 2003), pp. 1–2. Used
with permission of the author and the U.S. Jesuit Conference.

History
The Boston College Jesuit Community, "Jesuits and Jesuit Education: A
Primer," from *Jesuits and Boston College: A Working Paper for Discussion* (The
Jesuit Community at Boston College, 1994), pp. 8–9. Used with permission.

John W. O'Malley, "How the First Jesuits Became Involved in Education,"
from *The Jesuit Ratio Studiorum: 400th Anniversary Perspectives*, ed. Vincent
Duminuco (New York: Fordham University Press, 2000), pp. 56–74.
Copyright © 2000 by Fordham University Press. Used with permission.

Howard Gray, "The Experience of Ignatius Loyola: Background to Jesuit
Education," from *The Jesuit Ratio Studiorum: 400th Anniversary Perspectives*,
pp. 1–21. Copyright © 2000 by Fordham University Press. Used with
permission.

The Current Problematic
Selective Summary of Patrick A. Heelan, "Ignatian Discernment, Aesthetic
Play, and Scientific Inquiry," from *Minding the Time, 1492–1992: Jesuit*

Education and Issues in American Culture, ed. Wm. J. O'Brien (Georgetown University Press, 1992), pp. 1–17. Used with permission of the author.

Dominic J. Balestra, "Where Loyalties Lie?" from *Conversations on Jesuit Higher Education* (Fall 2003), pp. 4–10. Used with blanket permission of *Conversations*.

Principles

Robert A. Mitchell, "Five Traits of Jesuit Education," excerpted from *Boston College Magazine* (1988). Used with permission of the author.

John B. Bennett and Elizabeth A. Dreyer, "Spiritualities of—Not at—the University," from *Theoform* (St. Paul University, Ottawa, Canada), 33 (2002), 123–129. Copyright © 2002 by L'Université Saint-Paul, Ottawa. Used with permission.

Jesuit General Congregation 34, "Jesuits and University Life," from *Documents of the Thirty-fourth General Congregation of the Society of Jesus* (St. Louis: Institute of Jesuit Sources, 1995), pp. 189–194. Copyright © 1995 by the Institute of Jesuit Sources. Used with permission.

Michael J. Buckley, "Education Marked with the Sign of the Cross" from *America* [1-800-627-9533; <www.americamagazine.org>] (September 1, 1990), pp. 100–103. Copyright © 1990 by *America*. Used with permission.

Peter-Hans Kolvenbach, "The Service of Faith and the Promotion of Justice in American Jesuit Higher Education," address delivered at Santa Clara University, October 6, 2000; printed by the University and used by their permission. Reprinted from *Faith, Justice, and American Jesuit Higher Education (Studies in the Spirituality of Jesuits* (January 2001), pp. 13–29.

Peter-Hans Kolvenbach, "The Service of Faith in a Religiously Pluralistic World: The Challenge for Jesuit Higher Education," *Conversations on Jesuit Higher Education* (Fall 2007), pp. 44–52. Used with blanket permission of *Conversations*.

The Society of Jesus in the U.S., "Communal Reflection on the Jesuit Mission in Higher Education: A Way of Proceeding (Washington, DC: Jesuit Conference [1616 P Street, NW, Suite 300, Washington, DC 20036], 2002). Copyright © 2002 by the Jesuit Conference. Used with permission.

Dean Brackley, "Higher Standards" from *America* [1-800-627-9533; <www.americamagazine.org>] (February 6, 2006), pp. 9–13. Copyright © 2006 by *America*. Used with permission.

Howard J. Gray, "Soul Education: An Ignatian Priority" from *Spirit, Style, Story*, ed. Thomas M. Lucas (Loyola Press, 2002), pp. 117–31. Copyright © 2002 by Thomas M. Lucas. Used with the permission of Loyola Press.

The Issue of Catholic Identity
David J. O'Brien, "Conversations on Jesuit (and Catholic?) Higher Education: Jesuit, Sí, Catholic . . . Not So Sure," excerpted from *Conversations on Jesuit Higher Education* (Fall 1994), pp. 4–12. Used with blanket permission of *Conversations*.

Richard G. Malloy, "The Truly Catholic University" from *America* [1-800-627-9533; <www.americamagazine.org>] (October 11, 2004), pp. 8–13. Copyright © 2004 by *America*. Used with permission.

Suzanne Matson, "Collegium, Catholic Identity, and the Non-Catholic," from *Conversations on Jesuit Higher Education* (Fall 1994), pp. 16–17. Used with blanket permission of *Conversations*.

Monika K. Hellwig, "The Catholic Intellectual Tradition in the Catholic University," from *Examining the Catholic Intellectual Tradition*, ed. Anthony J. Cernera and Oliver J. Morgan (Fairfield, CT: Sacred Heart University Press, 2000), pp.1–18. Copyright © 2000 by Sacred Heart University Press. Used with permission.

John I. Jenkins, "Closing Statement on Academic Freedom and Catholic Character," from the University of Notre Dame Alumni Association Web site [http://alumni.nd.edu/closingstatement.html]. Copyright © 2006 by the University of Notre Dame. Used with permission of the author.

Ignatian/Jesuit Pedagogy
Robert R. Newton, "Summary Conclusion" to *Reflections on the Educational Principles of the* Spiritual Exercises and "Questions for Teachers" (Washington, DC: Jesuit Secondary Education Association, 1977), pp. 26–33. Used with permission of the JSEA.

Sharon J. Korth, Précis of *Ignatian Pedagogy: A Practical Approach*. First published here with permission of the author.

Timothy P. Muldoon, "Postmodern Spirituality and the Ignatian *Fundamentum*," from *The Way* [theway@campion.ox.ac.uk 44] (January 2005), pp. 88–100. Copyright © 2005 by *The Way*. Used with permission.

Richard G. Malloy, "Liberating Students—From Paris Hilton, Howard Stern, and Jim Beam," an expanded version of the essay that appeared in *Conversations on Jesuit Higher Education* (Spring 2007), pp. 8–12. Used with permission of the author and with blanket permission of *Conversations*.

Parker J. Palmer, "The Heart of a Teacher: Identity and Integrity in Teaching," from *Change* (November/December 1997), pp. 15–21. Copyright © 1997 by Parker J. Palmer. Used with permission.

Practical Applications: Walking the Ignatian/Jesuit Walk

Joanna Ziegler, "Wonders to Behold and Skillful Seeing: Art History and the Mission Statement," from *Conversations on Jesuit Higher Education* (Fall 2000), pp. 43–48. Used with blanket permission of *Conversations*.

Trileigh Tucker, "Just Science: Reflections on Teaching Science at Jesuit Universities," from *Conversations on Jesuit Higher Education* (Spring 2001), pp. 42–47. Used with blanket permission of *Conversations*.

Susan M. Behuniak, "On 'Where and with Whom Is My Heart?'" from *Conversations on Jesuit Higher Education* (Fall 2003), pp. 39–40. Used with blanket permission of *Conversations*.

Suzanne M. Erickson, "It's Noble but Is It Possible?" from *Conversations on Jesuit Higher Education* (Fall 2003), pp. 41–43. Used with blanket permission of *Conversations*.

Roshan "Bob" Ahuja, "Marketing to the Poor" from *Xavier* magazine (Fall 1993), pp. 44–45. Used with permission of the author.

Kathleen Kane, "Value-Oriented Hiring and Promotion and the University of San Francisco's Vision 2005," from *Conversations on Jesuit Higher Education* (Fall 1997), pp. 30–33. Used with blanket permission of *Conversations*.

Epilogue

Timothy Hanchin, "Messianic or Bourgeois? Communicating the Jesuit Mission," from *America* [1-800-627-9533; <www.americamagazine.org>] (May 8, 2006), pp. 11–13. Copyright © 2006 by *America*. Used with permission.

Appendices

George W. Traub, *Do You Speak Ignatian: A Glossary of Terms Used in Ignatian and Jesuit Circles*, 10th edition (http://www.jesuitresource.org/ignatian-resources/do-you-speak-ignatian.cfm) (Xavier University, 2008), reprinted in entirety. Copyright © 2008 by George W. Traub, SJ. Used with the permission of Xavier University's Ignatian Programs.

Contributors

Roshan "Bob" D. Ahuja is professor of marketing at Xavier University in Cincinnati, where he has worked since 1987. His research has focused on children's influence in single-parent and two-parent households and on the ethics of viral or buzz marketing campaigns using children as buzz agents and under conditions of non-disclosure. He has published in *Journal of Business Ethics, Journal of Marketing Theory and Practice, Journal of Consumer Marketing*, and others.

Dominic J. Balestra is professor of philosophy at Fordham University and recently served as dean of its Arts and Sciences Faculty. He holds a BS in mathematics and a PhD in the philosophy of science from St. Louis University. His teaching, publications, and research interests are in early modern philosophy, history, and rationality of science, with its bearing on the relation between science and religion. He has served as president of Fordham's Faculty Senate, chair of the philosophy department, and member of the National Seminar on Jesuit Higher Education, which publishes *Conversations*.

Susan M. Behuniak is professor of political science and Francis J. Fallen, SJ, Chair at Le Moyne College, where she teaches courses on American politics and constitutional law. She is the author of *A Caring Jurisprudence: Listening to Patients at the Supreme Court* (1999), and co-author of *Physician-Assisted Suicide: The Anatomy of a Constitutional Law Issue* (2003). As a volunteer with Hospice of Central New York, she serves as a family caregiver and as an instructor.

John B. Bennett is provost emeritus at Quinnipiac University in Hamden, Connecticut. Having worked at four different academic institutions and at the American Council on Education—a higher education association based in Washington, DC—he enjoys a wide perspective on the academy. He has been both a tenured full professor and chief academic officer. He has written and spoken extensively on issues of academic administration, including the roles of department chairs and deans. He has also written widely on ethics and spirituality in the academy, metaphysics and process philosophy, and the philosophy of education. His most recent book is *Academic Life: Hospitality, Ethics, and Spirituality.*

Dean Brackley, SJ, was born in upstate New York in 1946. He entered the Jesuits in 1964, was ordained in 1976, and received his doctorate in theological ethics in 1980. In the 1970s and 1980s, he worked in social ministry and education on Manhattan's Lower East Side and in the Bronx and taught briefly at Fordham University (1989–90). Since 1990 he has taught theology and ethics at the Universidad Centroamericana (UCA) in El Salvador, Central America. His published works include *Divine Revolution: Salvation and Liberation in Catholic Thought* (1996; reissued, 2004) and *The Call to Discernment in Troubled Times* (2004).

Michael J. Buckley, SJ, is Bea Professor of Theology at Santa Clara University. Prior to this appointment, he was for fourteen years a member of the theological faculty at Boston College, during which time he served as the director of the Jesuit Institute and as Canisius Professor of Theology. Previously he was a member of the Pontifical Faculty of Theology at the Jesuit School of Theology at Berkeley, and has held various university positions, including visiting fellow at Cambridge University's Clare Hall, of which he is also a life member. Buckley is the author of numerous articles in systematic theology, philosophy, spirituality, science and theology, and the history of ideas. Among his books are: *The Catholic University as Promise and Project: Reflections in a Jesuit Idiom* (1998) and most recently *Denying and Disclosing God: The Ambiguous Progress of Modern Atheism* (2004). He has served as the president of the Catholic Theological Society of America, a trustee for a number of universities and for *Theological Studies,* and has participated on various boards and commissions. He presently serves on the Theological Consultants Board for Herder/Crossroad. Buckley received his BA and MA from Gonzaga University, his STM from Santa Clara University, and his PhD from the University of Chicago. He has received two doctorates *honoris causa.*

Elizabeth A. Dreyer is professor of religious studies at Fairfield University in Fairfield, Connecticut. She lectures and publishes widely on medieval women mystics, lay spirituality, and the theology of grace. She holds a doctorate from Marquette University and has served on the faculties of several institutions. Her most recent publications are *Minding the Spirit: The Study of Christian Spirituality* (edited with Mark S. Burrows), *Passionate Spirituality: Hildegard of Bingen and Hadewijch of Brabant, The Cross in Christian Tradition: Paul to Bonaventure* (editor), and *Holy Power, Holy Presence: An Exploration of Medieval Metaphors for the Holy Spirit*. She is also the general editor of the forthcoming series of books "Catholic Women Alive in the Spirit: Spirituality for the Twenty-first Century."

Suzanne M. Erickson is currently the executive director of Spring Hill College in Atlanta, an expansion campus of the Mobile, Alabama, college focused on accelerated adult programs. Previously she was an associate professor of finance at Seattle University, where she taught corporate and entrepreneurial finance for seventeen years. She has published *Raising Entrepreneurial Capital*, and several articles.

Howard Gray, SJ, presently serves as special assistant to the president of Georgetown University. Previously, he was founding director of the Center for Ignatian Spirituality at Boston College and rector of the Jesuit Community at John Carroll University, where he was also assistant to the president for mission and identity. Within the Jesuit order, Father Gray has filled a number of leadership positions including that of provincial superior of the Detroit Province, rector of the Jesuit community at the Weston Jesuit School of Theology (Cambridge, MA), and tertianship director.

Timothy Hanchin received a BA in religious studies from John Carroll University and an MDiv from Harvard University. He has taught theology at Regis High School in New York City, and he currently teaches at Boston College High School. He was a Jesuit volunteer in Seattle, and he has lived with Catholic Worker communities in West Virginia and Cleveland.

Monika Hellwig (1929–2006) was born in Breslau, Silesia, which was then part of Germany. Her Catholic father was an economist;

her mother, of Dutch Jewish background and an adult convert to Catholicism, was an accomplished sculptress. The family moved to Berlin in 1935, and then, to flee Hitler, to Limburg in the southern Netherlands. In 1939, Monika and her two sisters were sent to a boarding school in Edinburgh, Scotland.

After the war, Hellwig earned a law degree from the University of Liverpool and, at twenty-two, joined the Medical Mission sisters. After her novitiate, she was sent to the United States to study theology at the Catholic University of America. Later she was sent to Rome to be a ghostwriter for a Vatican official during Vatican II.

She returned to the States, left her congregation, and completed a doctorate in theology at Catholic University in 1968. She began to teach at Georgetown in 1967, and remained there for the next twenty-eight years, becoming the Landegger Distinguished Professor of Theology in 1990. Early in her years at Georgetown, she adopted three children.

Writing and lecturing extensively, nationally and internationally, she received thirty-two honorary degrees and fifteen named awards, and served as president of the Catholic Theological Society of America. Her published works include: *Understanding Catholicism, Jesus the Compassion of God, The Eucharist and the Hunger of the World, A Case for Peace in Reason and Faith,* and *Guests of God: Stewards of Divine Creation.*

In 1996 she left Georgetown to become executive director, and then president of the Association of Catholic Colleges and Universities, which she led until 2005. Just a month before her death, she had become a senior fellow of the Woodstock Theological Center at Georgetown University.

Patrick A. Heelan, SJ, studied geophysics, quantum field theory, and philosophy of science. He published many papers on how deeply interpretation is involved in perception and in the natural sciences through the human bodily engagement with things and measuring instruments. He taught at University College (Dublin), Fordham University, State University of New York at Stony Brook, and presently teaches courses on the philosophy of science, and science and religion at Georgetown University. A Festschrift in his honor was edited by Babette Babich-Strong: *Hermeneutics of Natural Science, Van Gogh's Eyes, and God: Essays in Honor of Patrick A. Heelan, SJ* (Dordrecht/Boston: Kluwer, 2002).

John I. Jenkins, CSC, was elected president-elect of the University of Notre Dame by the board of trustees on April 30, 2004, and became the university's seventeenth president on July 1, 2005. He served the previous four years as vice president and associate provost. An associate professor of philosophy at the university, Father Jenkins was religious superior of the Holy Cross priests and brothers at Notre Dame from 1997 to 2000. As religious superior, he was a fellow and trustee of the university, but he relinquished those posts to assume his new duties in the provost's office. A member of the Notre Dame faculty since 1990 and the recipient of a Lilly Teaching Fellowship in 1991–92, Father Jenkins teaches in the areas of ancient philosophy, medieval philosophy, and the philosophy of religion. He is the author of *Knowledge and Faith in Thomas Aquinas* (Cambridge University Press, 1997), and has published in *The Journal of Philosophy, Medieval Philosophy and Theology* and *The Journal of Religious Ethics.* He delivered the annual Aquinas Lecture at the University of Dallas in January 2000. Father Jenkins holds two degrees in philosophy from Oxford University, BPhil in 1987 and DPhil in 1989.

Kathleen Kane is professor at the business school of the University of San Francisco (USF). She was educated at Mills College and the Claremont Graduate University. She teaches, writes, and consults in the areas of trust in leadership, organizational culture, and vision and values. She has actively promoted the Jesuit mission by serving as codirector of mission and identity and as the USF delegate to the Jesuit Convocation Planning Team 2003. She has been awarded best paper at conferences and in journals and was honored with the USF Ignatian Faculty Award. She also earned the Distinguished Teaching, Research, and Service Awards from the USF School of Business.

Peter-Hans Kolvenbach, SJ, Dutch-born superior general of the Society of Jesus from 1983 until 2008, when he resigned at the age of eighty.

He entered the Jesuits in 1948, went to Lebanon in the mid-1950s, earned a doctorate from St. Joseph's University in Beirut, and spent much of his life there, first as a professor of linguistics and then as superior of the vice-province of the Middle East.

He attended Jesuit General Congregation 32 and witnessed the faith-justice emphasis emerge from the congregation under the leadership of Pedro Arrupe. As superior general, he worked tirelessly in collaboration with his advisors to implement and extend the direction in which his predecessor had been leading the Society.

He leaves a legacy to Jesuit higher education in a series of major addresses, most notably at Georgetown University (Assembly '89) and at Santa Clara University (2000).

Sharon J. Korth, is associate professor of human resource development at Xavier University in Cincinnati. She received her EdD from the University of Cincinnati and her MEd and BS from Miami University (Ohio). Her research and teaching interests include learning styles, instructional design, needs assessment, and evaluation processes in organizations. She has published in *Performance Improvement Quarterly, Innovative Higher Education, Journal on Education for Business, Psychological Reports, Performance Improvement,* and *Journal on Excellence in College Teaching.*

Richard G. Malloy, SJ, was born at Temple University Hospital in Philadelphia and later earned a doctorate in cultural anthropology from Temple. He hasn't gone very far in life!

After graduating from St. Joseph's Prep, he attended Lafayette College in Easton, Pennsylvania, and then entered the Jesuit novitiate in Wernersville, Pennsylvania. While in Jesuit formation, he spent two years teaching high school in Osorno, Chile, and one year in pastoral work in Santiago. From 1998 to 2003, Father Malloy lived and worked at Holy Name Church in Camden, NJ, as a member of the Jesuit Urban Service Team. During those years he earned the doctorate and began teaching at St. Joseph's University. From 2003 to 2005, he served as interim director of campus ministry at St. Joseph's. He lives in Sourin, a freshman dorm at St. Joseph's, where he is an assistant professor in the sociology department. He recently published *A Faith That Frees: Catholic Matters for the 21st Century* (Orbis).

Suzanne Matson is professor of English at Boston College. She has written three novels, *The Tree-Sitter, A Trick of Nature,* and *The Hunger Moon,* and two volumes of poetry, *Durable Goods* and *Sea Level.* Originally from Portland, Oregon, she lives in Newton, Massachusetts, with her husband and three sons.

Robert A. Mitchell, SJ (1926–2006), was the first president of the Jesuit Conference (the conference of the ten U.S. Jesuit provincials with their leader-president). After serving as provincial of the New York Province and Jesuit Conference president, he was president of two Jesuit schools—the University of Detroit, which merged with Mercy College to form University of Detroit–Mercy during the last part of his tenure (1979–1990) and Le Moyne College in Syracuse (1993–2000). Over the years he served on the boards of Georgetown, Boston College, Le Moyne, Loyola Marymount, and Detroit Mercy.

Tim Muldoon is a theologian, a husband, and a father of two young girls. He is the author of two books for young adults on spirituality, most recently *The Ignatian Workout: Daily Spiritual Exercises for a Healthy Faith* (Loyola Press, 2004). His third book, *Seeds of Hope for U.S. Catholicism*, is forthcoming in spring 2008. He currently serves as assistant to the vice president for university mission and ministry at Boston College.

Robert R. Newton is special assistant to the president of Boston College. A graduate of Scranton Preparatory School and the University of Scranton, he holds an STL from Woodstock College, an STM from Yale University, and an EdM and EdD from Harvard University. He served as headmaster of Regis High School in New York City, and taught at the University of San Francisco before coming to Boston College in 1980 as associate academic vice president. He is the author of numerous articles on curriculum and academic organization issues. As special assistant to the president of Boston College, he is responsible for various university-wide projects and initiatives.

David J. O'Brien is a historian and Loyola Professor of Roman Catholic Studies at the College of the Holy Cross. He has served on the National Seminar of Jesuit Higher Education and as president of the American Catholic Historical Association. He has been awarded honorary degrees by Loyola University of Chicago and the Jesuit School of Theology at Berkeley, and has been honored with the Pedro Arrupe, SJ, Award by the University of Scranton. Among his books is *From the Heart of the American Church: Catholic Higher Education and American Culture* (Orbis Books, 1994).

John W. O'Malley, SJ, is currently university professor in the theology department at Georgetown University. His specialty is the religious culture of early modern Europe, with specialization in Renaissance humanism and the Society of Jesus. His best known work is *The First Jesuits*, winner of several best-book awards and now translated into ten languages, and his latest is *Four Cultures of the West*. He is at present working on a book on the Second Vatican Council.

Parker J. Palmer is a writer, speaker, and activist. Author of seven books (including *A Hidden Wholeness, Let Your Life Speak,* and *The Courage to Teach*), he holds a PhD in sociology from the University of California, Berkeley, and nine honorary doctorates. In 1998, the Leadership Project, a national survey of ten thousand educators, named him one of the thirty "most influential senior leaders" in higher education and one of the ten key "agenda setters" of the past decade. In 2005, Jossey-Bass published *Living the Questions: Essays Inspired by the Work and Life of Parker J. Palmer.*

Trileigh Tucker is associate professor and director of the environmental studies program at Seattle University. She holds a PhD in geology from the University of North Carolina–Chapel Hill. Her research interests include intersections between science and religion, natural history, and contemplative dimensions of science, including ecology and the Spiritual Exercises. In addition, she teaches courses related to sustainability and to environmental justice and is involved with bioregional education.

Joanna E. Ziegler is professor of art history in the Department of Visual Arts at the College of the Holy Cross. Among her recent books is *Practicing Mortality: Art, Philosophy, and Contemplative Seeing* (Palgrave, 2005), coauthored with Christopher Dustin. Ziegler is a fellow with the Center for Contemplative Mind in Society and a board member of "Collegium: A Colloquy on Faith and the Intellectual Life."

Index

About the Editor

George W. Traub, SJ, has spent more than two decades fostering a greater understanding of the Jesuit mission and nurturing Ignatian identity in higher education. A Jesuit for more than fifty years, his passion has always been Ignatian spirituality—studying it, teaching it, writing about it, practicing it, and guiding others in this spiritual pathway. He has also spent more than thirty years in Jesuit education. In the early nineties, he was one of the founders of the Association of Jesuit Colleges and Universities' national network Coordinators for Mission and Identity. He received his graduate degree in theology and spirituality from Loyola University Chicago and his PhD in English literature from Cornell University. Currently he is Jesuit professor of theology and executive director of Ignatian Programs/Mission and Identity at Xavier University.

Traub is the author of *Do You Speak Ignatian? A Glossary of Terms Used in Ignatian and Jesuit Circles* (Xavier University, 1997), now in its tenth edition; is coauthor of *The Desert and the City: An Interpretation of the History of Christian Spirituality* (Macmillan, 1969; Loyola University Press, 1984); and has edited the forthcoming *An Ignatian Spirituality Reader* (Loyola Press, 2008), which is a companion volume to his reader on Jesuit education.